D0918209

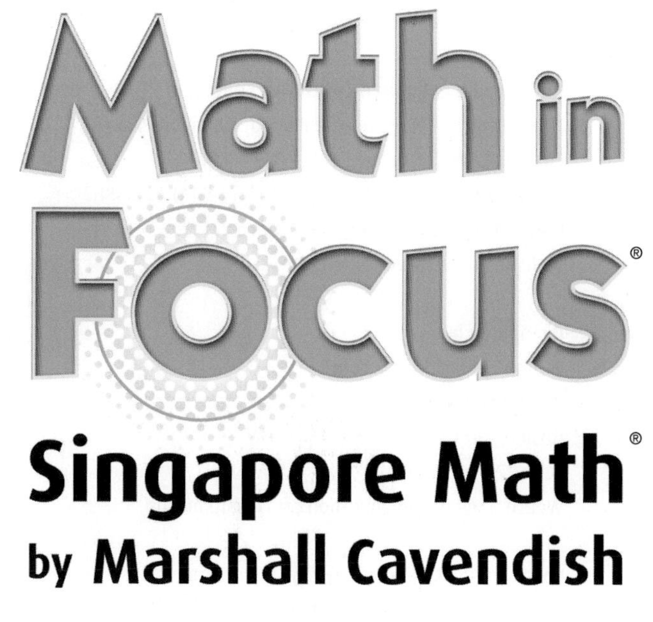

Student Book

Consultant and Author
Dr. Fong Ho Kheong

Authors
Chelvi Ramakrishnan and Michelle Choo

U.S. Consultants
Dr. Richard Bisk
Andy Clark
Patsy F. Kanter

U.S. Distributor

Houghton
Mifflin
Harcourt

Published by Marshall Cavendish Education
Times Centre, 1 New Industrial Road, Singapore 536196
Customer Service Hotline: (65) 6213 9444
US Office Tel: (1-914) 332 8888 | Fax: (1-914) 332 8882
E-mail: tmesales@mceducation.com
Website: www.mceducation.com

Distributed by
Houghton Mifflin Harcourt
222 Berkeley Street
Boston, MA 02116
Tel: 617-351-5000
Website: www.hmheducation.com/mathinfocus

Cover: © Don Hammond/Design Pics/Corbis,
© Dave Thompson/Life File/Photodisc/Getty Images.
Images provided by Houghton Mifflin Harcourt.

First published 2018

ISBN 978-1-328-88074-1

Printed in the United States of America

3 4 5 6 7 8 1401 23 22 21 20 19 18
4500690547 A B C D E

Contents

Look for **Practice and Problem Solving**

Student Book A and Student Book B	Workbook A and Workbook B
• **Let's Practice** in every lesson	• **Independent Practice** for every lesson
• **Put On Your Thinking Cap!** in every chapter	• **Put On Your Thinking Cap!** in every chapter

Look for **Assessment Opportunities**

Student Book A and Student Book B	Workbook A and Workbook B
• **Quick Check** at the beginning of every chapter to assess chapter readiness • **Guided Learning** after every example or two to assess readiness to continue lesson • **Chapter Review/Test** in every chapter to review or test chapter material	• **Cumulative Reviews** seven times during the year • **Mid-Year and End-of-Year Reviews** to assess test readiness

Metric Length, Mass, and Volume

12 Real-World Problems: Measurement

Bar Graphs and Line Plots

Fractions

S
Good Morning
1
A
I
U
S
I
CARE
C

Customary Length, Weight, and Capacity

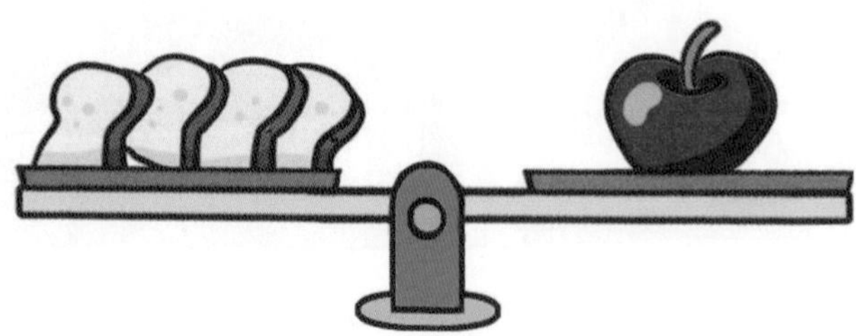

1 pt
1 pt
1 qt
1 qt
1 qt
1 qt

16 Time and Temperature

Angles and Lines

Two-Dimensional Shapes

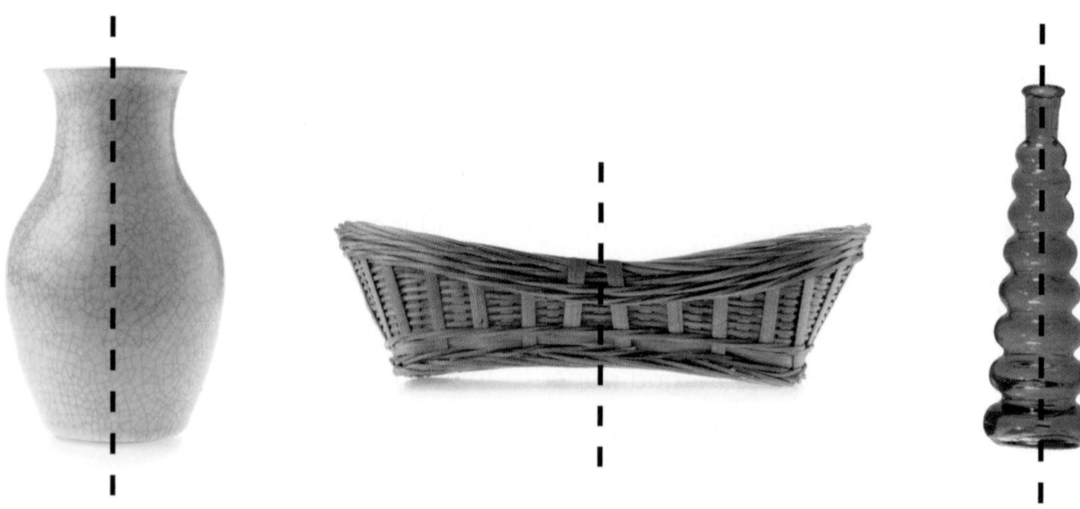

Area and Perimeter

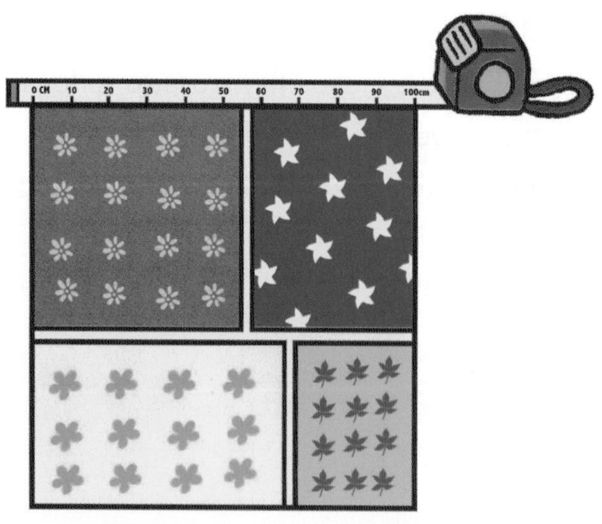

Welcome to

Math in Focus®

This exciting math program comes to you all the way from the country of Singapore. We are sure you will enjoy learning math with the interesting lessons you'll find in these books.

What makes *Math in Focus*® different?

- **Two books** You don't write in the in this textbook. This book has a matching **Workbook**. When you see the pencil icon ON YOUR OWN, you will write in the **Workbook**.
- **Longer lessons** Some lessons may last more than a day, so you can really understand the math.
- **Math will make sense** Learn to use bar models to solve word problems with ease.

In this book, look for

Learn
This means you will learn something new.

Guided Learning
Your teacher will help you try some sample problems.

Let's Practice
You practice what you've learned to solve more problems. You can make sure you really understand.

Now you get to practice with lots of different problems in your own **Workbook**.

Also look forward to *Games, Hands-On Activities, Math Journals, Let's Explore,* and *Put On Your Thinking Cap!*
You will combine logical thinking with math skills and concepts to meet new problem-solving challenges. You will be talking math, thinking math, doing math, and even writing about doing math.

What's in the Workbook?

Math in Focus® will give you time to learn important new concepts and skills and check your understanding. Then you will use the practice pages in the **Workbook** to try:

- Solving different problems to practice the new math concept you are learning. In the textbook, keep an eye open for this symbol ON YOUR OWN. That will tell you which pages to use for practice.
- *Put On Your Thinking Cap!*

  Challenging Practice problems invite you to think in new ways to solve harder problems.

  Problem Solving challenges you to use different strategies to solve problems.
- *Math Journal* activities ask you to think about thinking, and then write about that!

Students in Singapore have been using this kind of math program for many years.
Now you can too — are you ready?

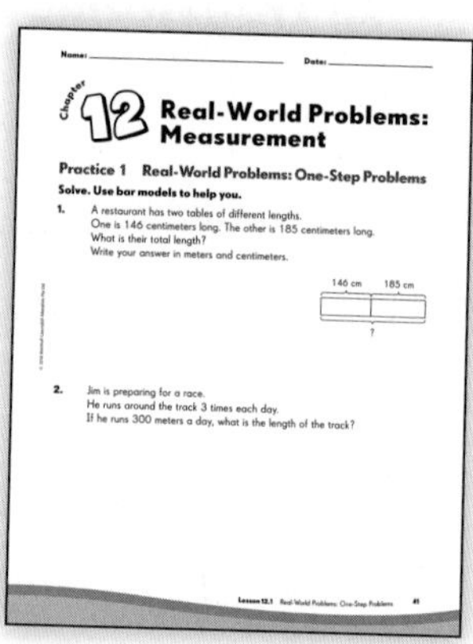

Name: ________ Date: ________

Chapter 12 **Real-World Problems: Measurement**

Practice 1 Real-World Problems: One-Step Problems

Solve. Use bar models to help you.

1. A restaurant has two tables of different lengths.
   One is 146 centimeters long. The other is 185 centimeters long.
   What is their total length?
   Write your answer in meters and centimeters.

   146 cm 185 cm
   ?

2. Jim is preparing for a race.
   He runs around the track 3 times each day.
   If he runs 300 meters a day, what is the length of the track?

Lesson 12.1 Real-World Problems: One-Step Problems 41

Money

Lessons

▶ You can add and subtract money the same way you add and subtract whole numbers.

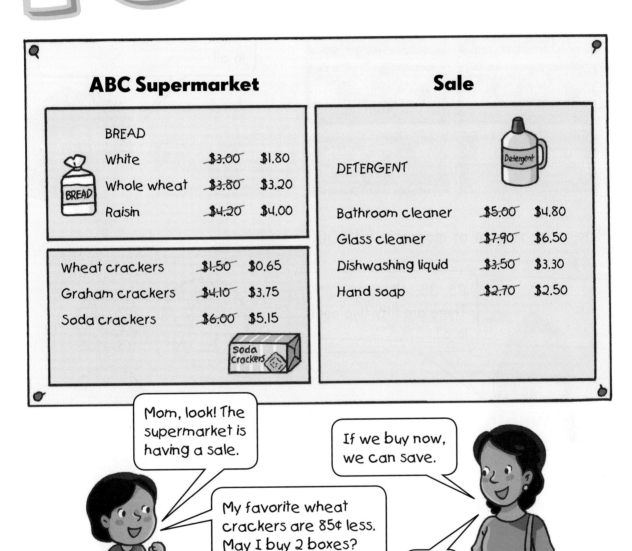

Recall Prior Knowledge

Counting to find the value

10, 20, 25, 30, 31, 32, 33.
There are thirty-three dollars in all.

The total amount of money is $33.00.

25, 35, 45, 50, 51, 52.
There are fifty-two cents in all.

The total amount of money is $0.52.

Changing dollars and cents to cents

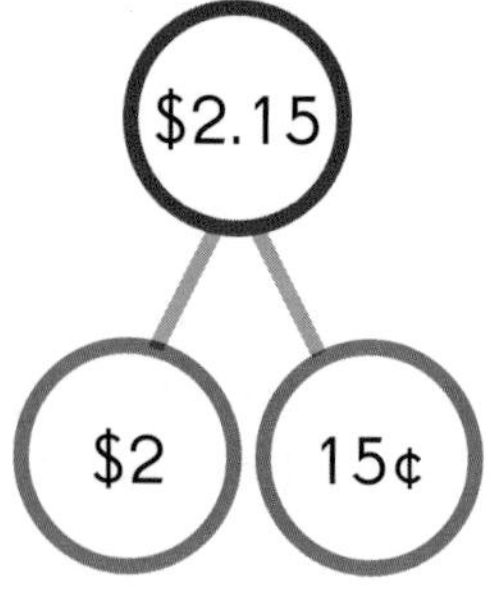

$1 = 100¢
$2 = 200¢
$2.15 = 200¢ + 15¢
= 215¢

Changing cents to dollars and cents

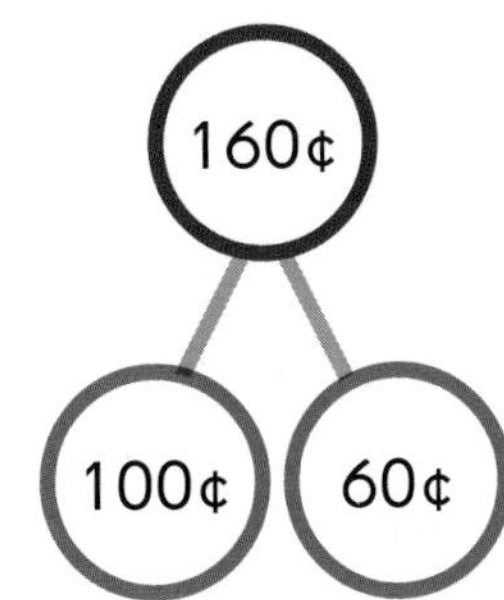

100¢ = $1
160¢ = $1.60

Adding and subtracting

$$\begin{array}{r} 417 \\ +\ 302 \\ \hline 719 \end{array} \qquad \begin{array}{r} \overset{1}{1}85 \\ +\ 762 \\ \hline 947 \end{array} \qquad \begin{array}{r} 895 \\ -\ 534 \\ \hline 361 \end{array} \qquad \begin{array}{r} \overset{5}{\cancel{6}}\,\overset{13}{\cancel{4}}\,{}^{1}4 \\ -\ 3\ 7\ 8 \\ \hline 2\ 6\ 6 \end{array}$$

✔Quick Check

Change dollars and cents to cents.

1. $5.05 = ☐ ¢
2. $12.90 = ☐ ¢

Change cents to dollars and cents.

3. 180¢ = $ ☐
4. 3045¢ = $ ☐

Add.

5. 56 + 865 = ☐
6. 308 + 596 = ☐

Subtract.

7. 485 − 32 = ☐
8. 310 − 172 = ☐

Addition

Lesson Objectives

- Add money in different ways without regrouping.
- Add money in different ways with regrouping.

Learn

Add the dollars using number bonds.

Dad buys a pack of cheese for \$5.35.
He also buys a jar of peanut butter for \$2.00.
How much does Dad spend in all?

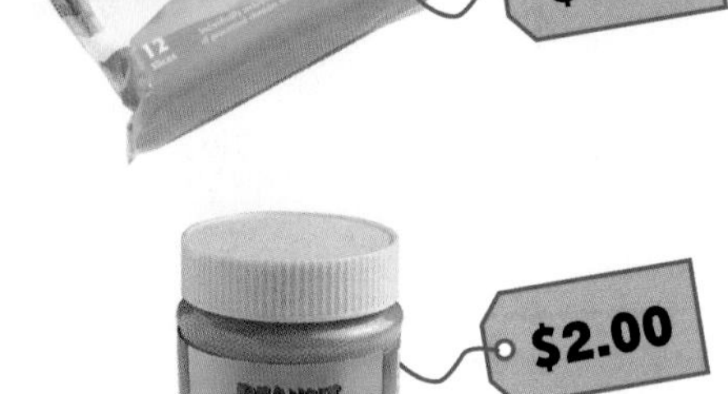

+

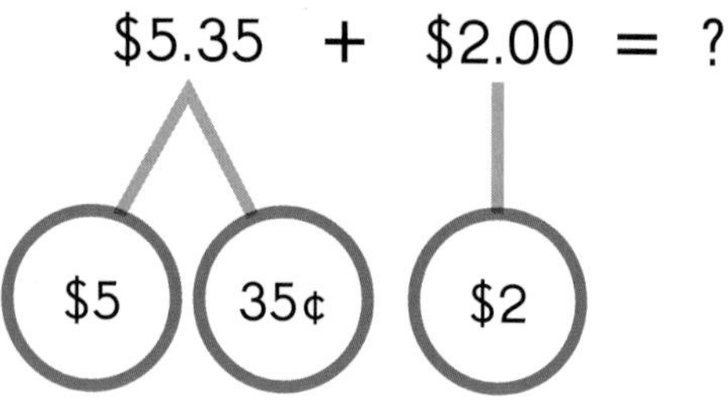

STEP 1 Add the dollars.

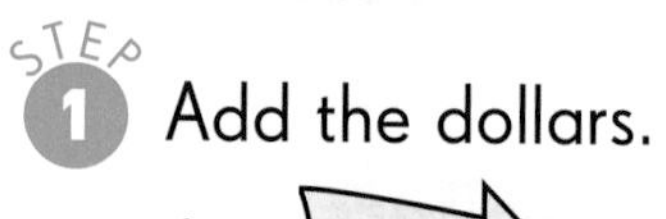

STEP 2 Add 35¢ to \$7.

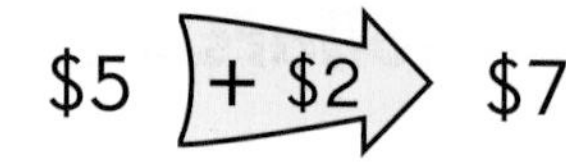

Dad spends \$7.35 in all.

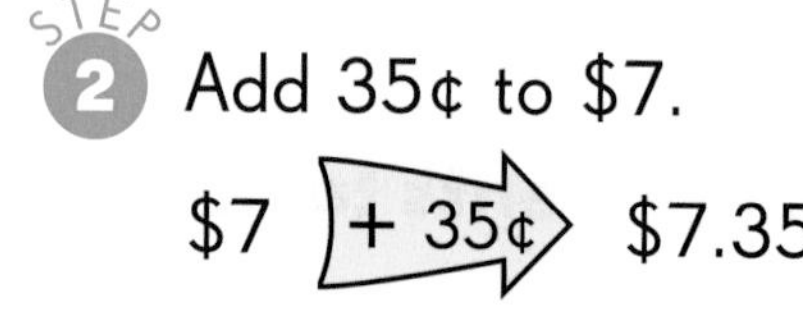

Guided Learning

Add the dollars. Then add the cents to the dollars.

1. \$2.15 + \$7.00 = \$ ____
2. \$5.00 + \$3.75 = \$ ____
3. \$6.45 + \$4.00 = \$ ____
4. \$12.35 + \$8.00 = \$ ____

Learn: Add the cents using number bonds.

Mary buys a basket of apples for $3.20.
She also buys an orange for $0.55.
How much does Mary spend in all?

+

$3.20 + $0.55 = ?

($3.20 → $3 and 20¢; $0.55 → 55¢)

STEP 1 Add the cents.

20¢ → + 55¢ → 75¢

STEP 2 Add $3 to 75¢.

75¢ → + $3 → $3.75

Mary spends $3.75 in all.

Guided Learning

Add the cents. Then add the dollars to the cents.

5. $0.40 + $4.25 = $ ____

6. $5.40 + $0.55 = $ ____

7. $15.25 + $0.15 = $ ____

8. $3.25 + $0.65 = $ ____

Learn

Add dollars and cents using number bonds.

A DVD costs \$12.35. A book costs \$4.95.
What is the total cost of the DVD and the book?

\$12.35 + \$4.95 = ?

\$12.35 → \$12.30 and 5¢; \$4.95

STEP 1 Add 5¢ to \$4.95.

\$4.95 → + 5¢ → \$5

STEP 2 Add \$12.30 to \$5.

\$5 → + \$12.30 → \$17.30

The DVD and book cost \$17.30.

Guided Learning

Add. Use number bonds to help you.

17 \$3.55 + \$4.95 = \$ ____

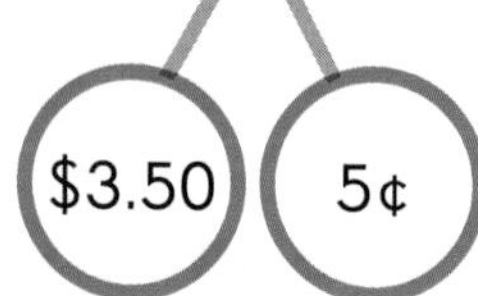

18 \$6.25 + \$8.90 = \$ ____

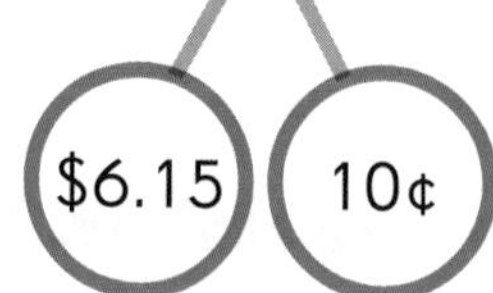

19 \$12.75 + \$3.80 = \$ ____

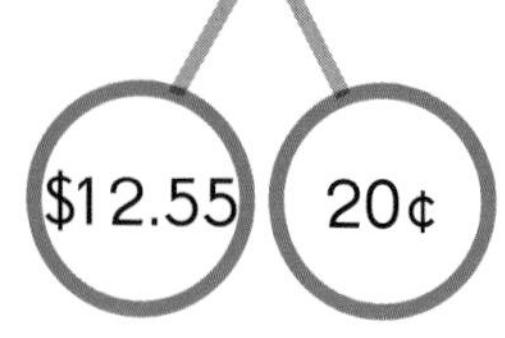

20 \$15.65 + \$4.85 = \$ ____

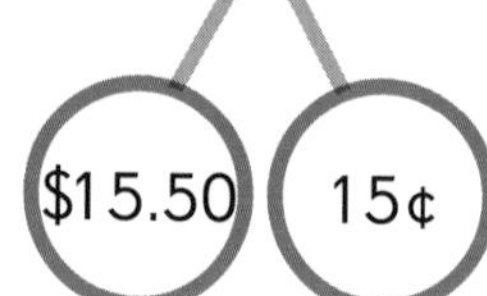

Learn

Add using the 'adding one dollar and subtracting the extra cents' strategy.

A tub of colored chalk costs \$6.70.
A sketchpad costs \$0.80.
What is the total cost of the chalk and the sketchpad?

\$6.70 + \$0.80 = ?

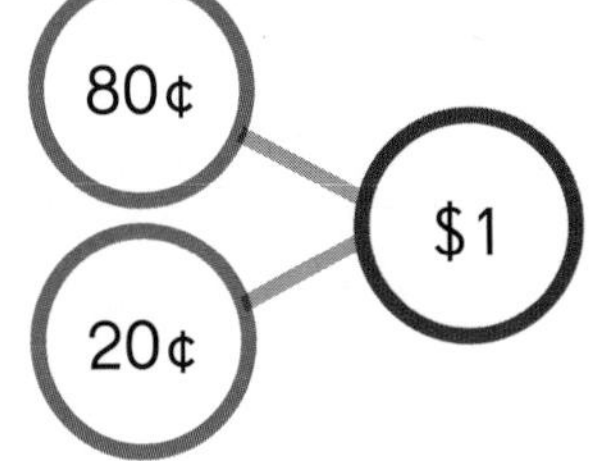

Adding 80¢ is the same as adding \$1 and subtracting 20¢.

STEP 1 \$6.70 → + \$1 → \$7.70

STEP 2 \$7.70 → − 20¢ → \$7.50

The chalk and the sketchpad cost \$7.50.

Guided Learning

Find each missing amount.

21 \$4.80 + \$0.90 = ?

\$4.80 → + \$ ____ → \$ ____

\$ ____ → − ____ ¢ → \$ ____

\$4.80 + \$0.90 = \$ ____

22 \$23.65 + \$0.95 = ?

\$23.65 → + \$ ____ → \$ ____

\$ ____ → − ____ ¢ → \$ ____

\$23.65 + \$0.95 = \$ ____

Learn

Add using the 'adding whole dollars and subtracting the extra cents' strategy.

Mrs. Rodgers buys a dollhouse and a stuffed animal for her children. The dollhouse costs \$15.80 and the stuffed animal costs \$7.95. How much does she spend for the two toys?

\$15.80 + \$7.95 = ?

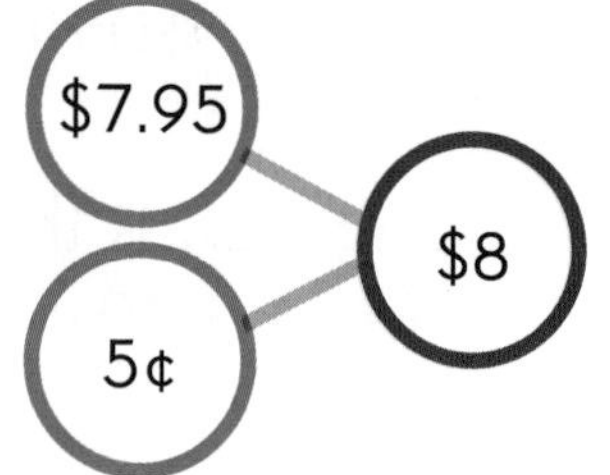

Adding \$7.95 is the same as adding \$8 and subtracting 5¢.

STEP 1 \$15.80 → + \$8 → \$23.80

STEP 2 \$23.80 → − 5¢ → \$23.75

Mrs. Rodgers spends \$23.75 for the two toys.

Guided Learning

Find each missing amount.

23 \$16.70 + \$5.85 = ?

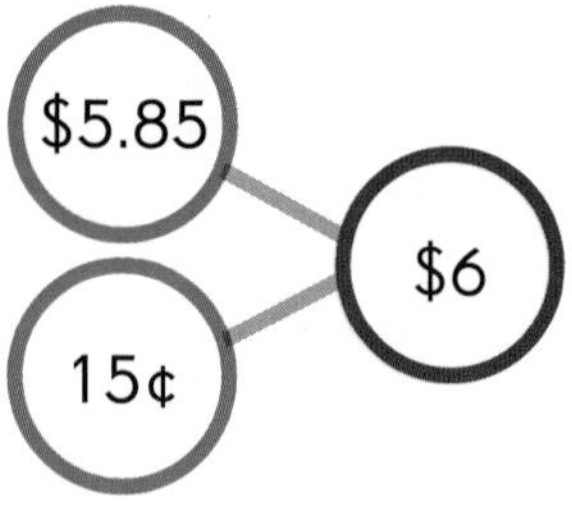

\$16.70 + \$5.85 = \$

 \$27.85 + \$7.65 = ?

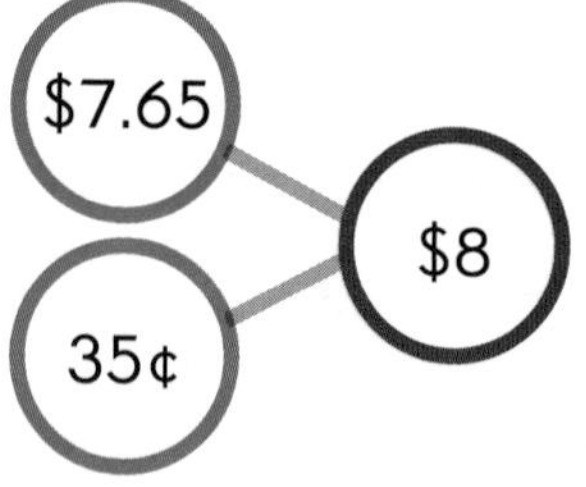

\$27.85 + \$7.65 = \$

Learn

Change dollars and cents to cents. Then add.

$8.75 + $2.20 = ?

$$\begin{array}{r} \$8.75 \\ +\ \$2.20 \\ \hline \end{array}$$

This is one way of adding dollars and cents.

STEP 1 Change the dollars and cents to cents.

$$\begin{array}{r} 875¢ \\ +\ 220¢ \\ \hline \end{array}$$

STEP 2 Add the cents.

$$\begin{array}{r} 875¢ \\ +\ 220¢ \\ \hline 1{,}095¢ \end{array}$$

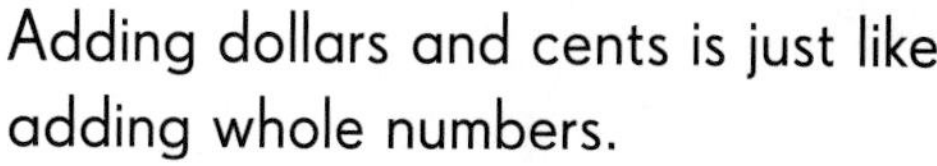

Adding dollars and cents is just like adding whole numbers.

$$\begin{array}{r} 875 \\ +\ 220 \\ \hline 1{,}095 \end{array}$$

STEP 3 Write the sum as dollars and cents.

1,095¢ = $10.95

$8.75 + $2.20 = $10.95

Guided Learning

Find each missing amount.

25 $9.30 + $15.45 = ?

$$\begin{array}{r} \$\ \ 9.30 \\ +\ \$15.45 \\ \hline \$24.75 \end{array} \longrightarrow \begin{array}{r} \square¢ \\ +\ \square¢ \\ \hline \square¢ \end{array}$$

$\square$¢ = $$\square$

$9.30 + $15.45 = $$\square$

Learn Add money.

Find the sum of \$8.35 and \$2.85.

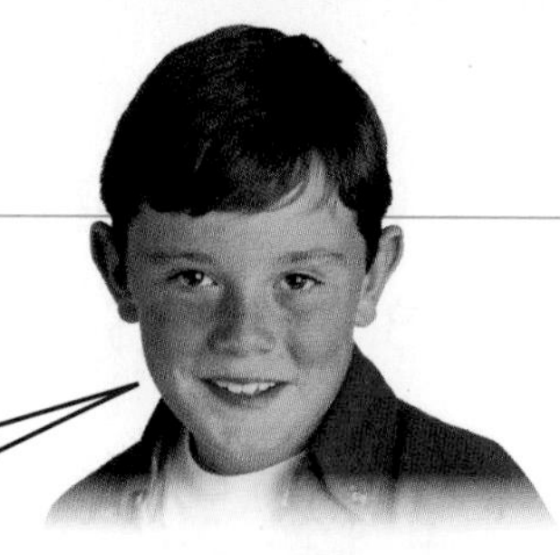

Here is another way of adding dollars and cents.

+

\$8.35 + \$2.85 = ?

Add as you would whole numbers.

$$\begin{array}{r} \overset{1}{8}\,\overset{1}{3}\,5 \\ +\ 2\,8\,5 \\ \hline 1{,}1\,2\,0 \end{array}$$

STEP 1 Add the cents.

$$\begin{array}{r} \$\ \overset{1}{8}.\overset{1}{3}5 \\ +\ \$\ 2.85 \\ \hline \$\ \ .20 \end{array}$$

STEP 2 Add the dollars.

$$\begin{array}{r} \$\ \overset{1}{8}.\overset{1}{3}5 \\ +\ \$\ 2.85 \\ \hline \$11.20 \end{array}$$

\$8.35 + \$2.85 = \$11.20

Guided Learning

Add.

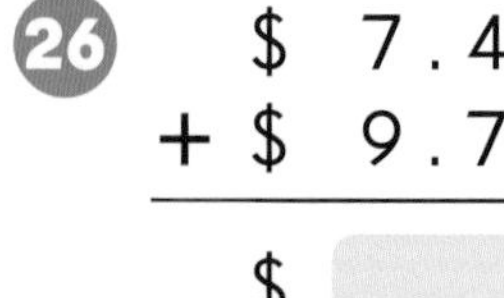

26
$$\begin{array}{r} \$\ 7.45 \\ +\ \$\ 9.75 \\ \hline \$\ \square \end{array}$$

27
$$\begin{array}{r} \$16.05 \\ +\ \$28.95 \\ \hline \$\ \square \end{array}$$

Materials:
- a set of coins
- a set of bills

Look at the advertisement.

Weekend Specials
Popcorn $4.50
Cat Food 60¢
POPCORN
Batteries $3.85
Raincoat $16.70
MP3 Player $85.40
Umbrella $9.30
Comb $1.10

STEP 1 Find each cost.

1. A can of cat food and a box of popcorn $ ______
2. An MP3 player and a pack of batteries $ ______
3. Two combs $ ______
4. A raincoat and an umbrella $ ______
5. A raincoat and an MP3 player $ ______
6. Two MP3 players $ ______

STEP 2 Your partner checks each amount using the set of money.

STEP 3 Take turns doing **STEP 1** and **STEP 2**.

Let's Practice

Add.

1. $7.35 + $6.00 = $ ___
2. $5.45 + $0.35 = $ ___
3. $9.30 + $2.55 = $ ___
4. $25.35 + $24.65 = $ ___

Find each missing amount.

5. $7.50 + $4.90 = $ ___

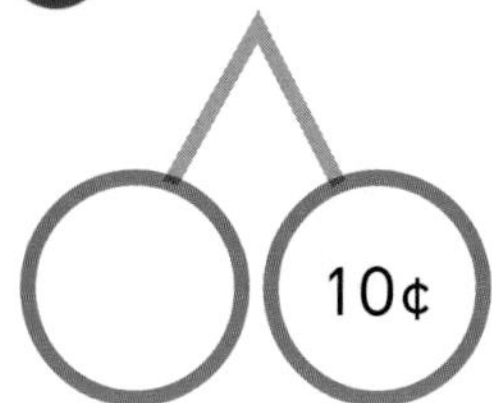

6. $8.35 + $0.75 = ?

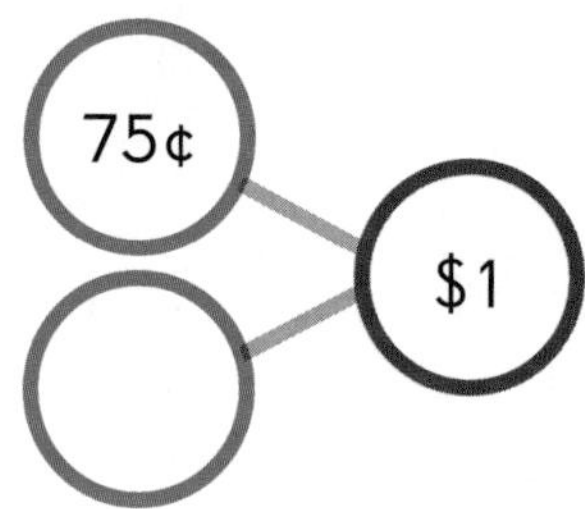

$8.35 + $0.75 = $ ___

Add.

7.
```
   $  3.25
 + $  5.70
 ---------
   $ ___
```

8.
```
   $35.65
 + $54.20
 ---------
   $ ___
```

Add.

9.
```
   $  6.45
 + $  8.55
 ---------
   $ ___
```

10.
```
   $56.75
 + $24.95
 ---------
   $ ___
```

Adding money is just like adding whole numbers.

ON YOUR OWN

Go to Workbook B: Practice 1 to 3, pages 1–6

Lesson 10.2 Subtraction

Lesson Objectives

- Subtract money in different ways without regrouping.
- Subtract money in different ways with regrouping.

Learn **Subtract the dollars using number bonds.**

Tristan has $32.25.
He buys a pair of shoes for $21.00
How much money does Tristan have left?

−

$32.25 − $21.00 = ?

$32 | 25¢ | $21

STEP 1 Subtract the dollars.

$32 → − $21 → $11

STEP 2 Add 25¢ to $11.

$11 → + 25¢ → $11.25

Tristan has $11.25 left.

Guided Learning

Subtract the dollars. Then add the cents to the dollars.

1. $17.85 − $4.00 = $ ____
2. $15.45 − $8.00 = $ ____

Learn Subtract the cents using number bonds.

Kay had $28.95.
After buying a blouse, she had $0.50 left.
How much did she pay for the blouse?

−

$28.95 − $0.50 = ?

$28 | 95¢ | 50¢

STEP 1 Subtract the cents.

95¢ → − 50¢ → 45¢

STEP 2 Add 45¢ to $28.

$28 → + 45¢ → $28.45

She paid $28.45 for the blouse.

Guided Learning

Subtract the cents. Then add the dollars and cents.

3. $21.75 − $0.30 = $ ______

4. $18.80 − $0.50 = $ ______

5. $23.95 − $0.70 = $ ______

6. $32.50 − $0.40 = $ ______

Learn Subtract dollars and cents using number bonds.

Alex buys a jacket for \$79.65.
He also buys a shirt for \$43.25.
How much more does the jacket cost than the shirt?

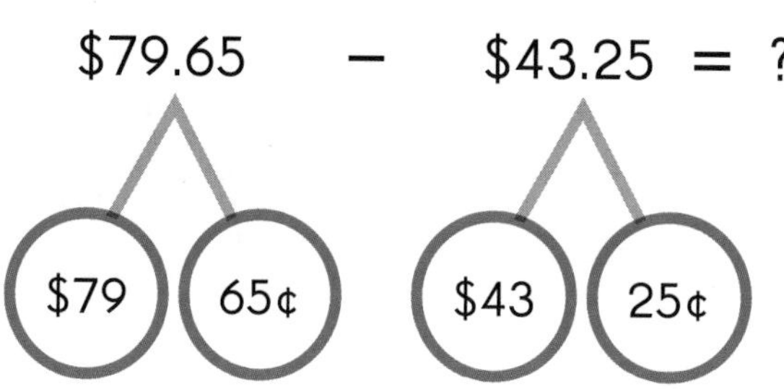

STEP 1 Subtract the dollars.

\$79 → − \$43 → \$36

STEP 2 Subtract the cents.

65¢ → − 25¢ → 40¢

STEP 3 Add 40¢ to \$36.

\$36 → + 40¢ → \$36.40

The jacket costs \$36.40 more than the shirt.

Guided Learning

Subtract the dollars. Subtract the cents. Then add the dollars to the cents.

7. \$65.75 − \$12.45 = \$ ____
8. \$78.65 − \$23.05 = \$ ____
9. \$49.80 − \$27.70 = \$ ____
10. \$83.95 − \$31.50 = \$ ____

Learn Subtract using the 'subtracting one dollar and adding the extra cents' strategy.

A watermelon costs $4.70.
An apple costs $0.80.
How much less does the apple cost than the watermelon?

$4.70 − $0.80 = ?

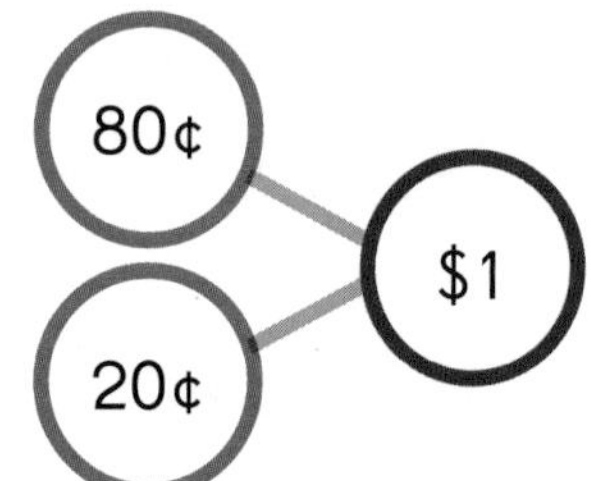

Subtracting 80¢ is the same as subracting $1 and adding 20¢.

STEP 1 $4.70 → − $1 → $3.70

STEP 2 $3.70 → + 20¢ → $3.90

The apple costs $3.90 less than the watermelon.

Guided Learning

Find each missing amount.

11 $5.60 − $0.90 = ?

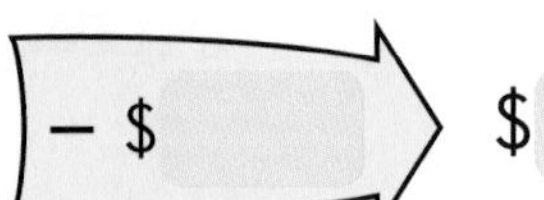

$5.60 → − $ ____ → $ ____

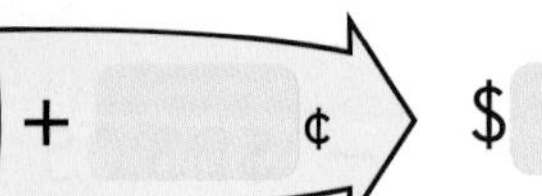

$ ____ → + ____ ¢ → $ ____

$5.60 − $0.90 = $ ____

12 $12.55 − $0.95 = ?

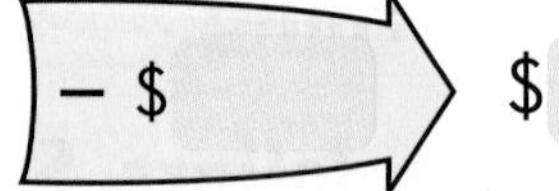

$12.55 → − $ ____ → $ ____

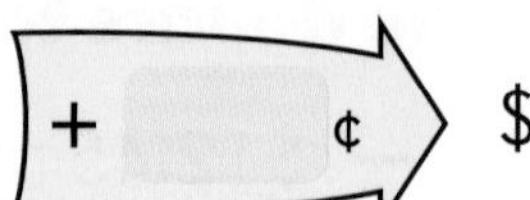

$ ____ → + ____ ¢ → $ ____

$12.55 − $0.95 = $ ____

Learn: Subtract using the 'subtracting whole dollars and adding the extra cents' strategy.

Tim had \$9.70.
He bought a cup for \$4.90.
How much does Tim have left?

\$9.70 − \$4.90 = ?

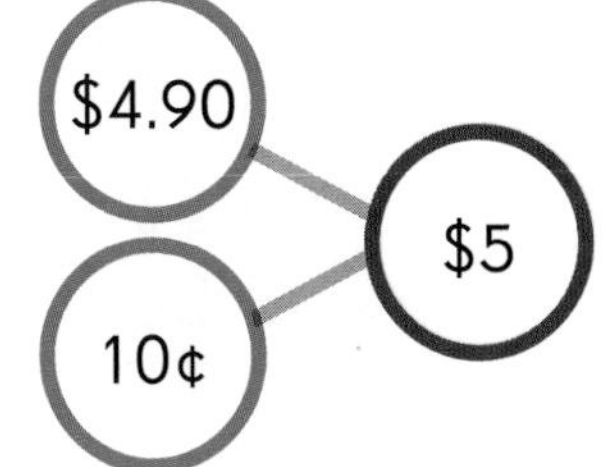

Subtracting \$4.90 is the same as subtracting \$5 and adding 10¢.

STEP 1 \$9.70 → − \$5 → \$4.70

STEP 2 \$4.70 → + 10¢ → \$4.80

Tim has \$4.80 left.

Guided Learning

Find each missing amount.

13 \$8.40 − \$5.80 = ?

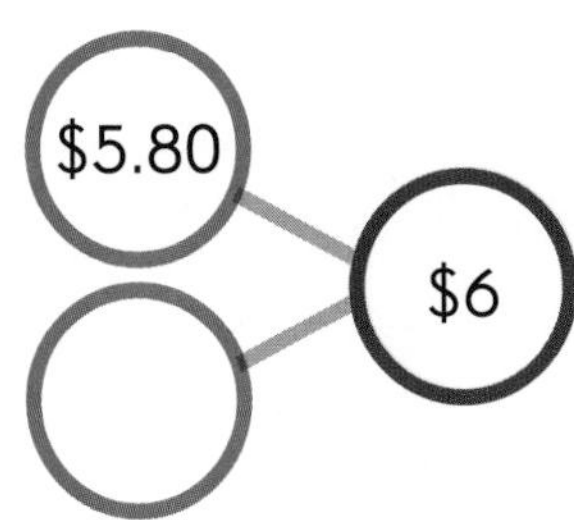

\$8.40 − \$5.80 = \$ ____

14 \$15.45 − \$8.95 = ?

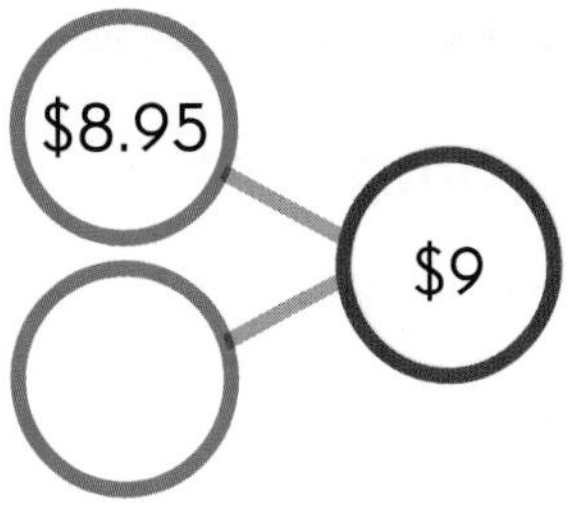

\$15.45 − \$8.95 = \$ ____

Learn Change dollars and cents to cents. Then subtract.

$\$9.65 - \$4.30 = ?$

$$\begin{array}{r} \$9.65 \\ -\ \$4.30 \\ \hline \end{array}$$

This is one way of subtracting dollars and cents.

Change the dollars and cents to cents.

$$\begin{array}{r} 965¢ \\ -\ 430¢ \\ \hline \end{array}$$

Subtract the cents.

$$\begin{array}{r} 965¢ \\ -\ 430¢ \\ \hline 535¢ \end{array}$$

Subtracting dollars and cents is just like subtracting whole numbers.

$$\begin{array}{r} 965 \\ -\ 430 \\ \hline 535 \end{array}$$

Write the difference as dollars and cents.

535¢ = \$5.35

\$9.65 − \$4.30 = \$5.35

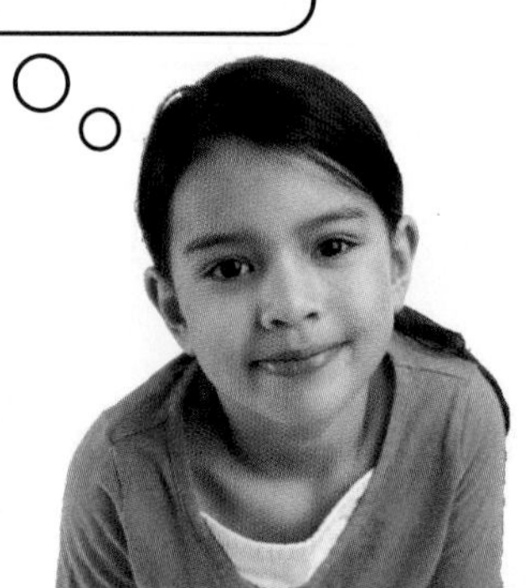

Guided Learning

Find each missing amount.

15 $\$11.85 - \$4.55 = ?$

$$\begin{array}{r} \$11.85 \\ -\ \$\ \ 4.55 \\ \hline \$\ \ 7.30 \end{array} \longrightarrow \begin{array}{r} \_\_\_¢ \\ -\ \_\_\_¢ \\ \hline \_\_\_¢ \end{array}$$

___¢ = \$___

\$11.85 − \$4.55 = \$___

Learn Subtract money.

Find the difference between $27.30 and $15.40.

Here is another way of subtracting dollars and cents.

−

$\$27.30 - \$15.40 = ?$

Step 1 Regroup $27.30.

$\$27.30 = \$26 + 130¢$

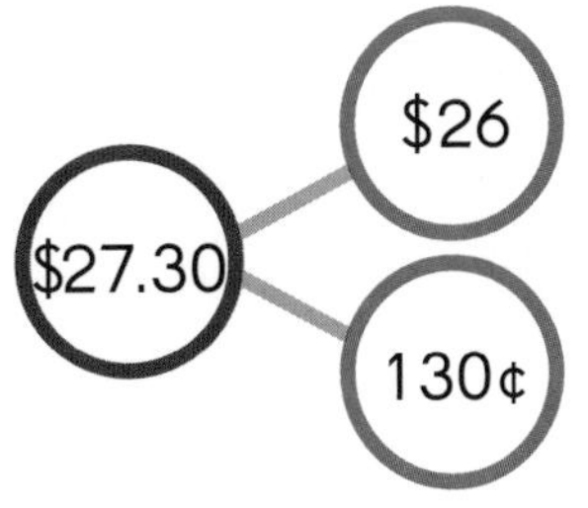

Step 2 Subtract the cents.

$$\begin{array}{r} \$2\overset{6}{\cancel{7}}.{}^{1}30 \\ -\ \$15.40 \\ \hline \$\ \ \ .90 \end{array}$$

Subtract as you would whole numbers.

$$\begin{array}{r} 2,\overset{6}{\cancel{7}}\,{}^{1}30 \\ -1,5\ 40 \\ \hline 1,1\ 90 \end{array}$$

Step 3 Subtract the dollars.

$$\begin{array}{r} \$2\overset{6}{\cancel{7}}.{}^{1}30 \\ -\ \$15.40 \\ \hline \$11.90 \end{array}$$

Guided Learning

Subtract. Use number bonds to help you.

16

$$\begin{array}{r} \$18.30 \\ -\ \$\ \ 2.40 \\ \hline \$\ \square \end{array}$$

Regroup.

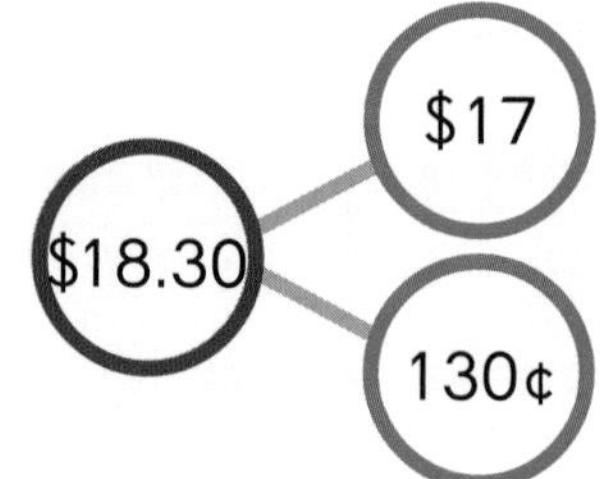

17

$$\begin{array}{r} \$11.25 \\ -\ \$\ \ 3.15 \\ \hline \$\ \square \end{array}$$

Regroup.

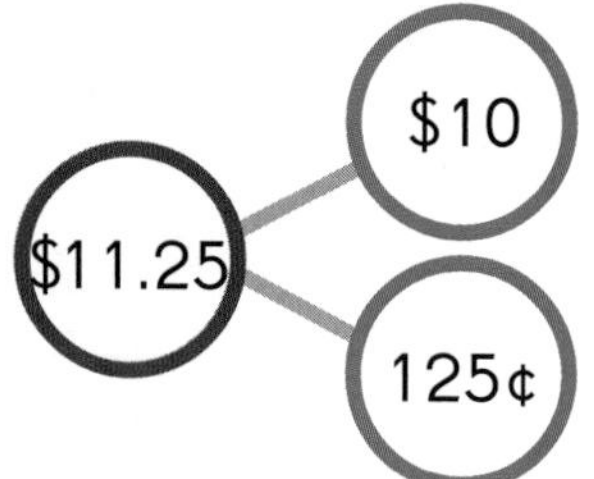

18

$$\begin{array}{r} \$25.00 \\ -\ \$\ \ 7.85 \\ \hline \$\ \square \end{array}$$

Regroup.

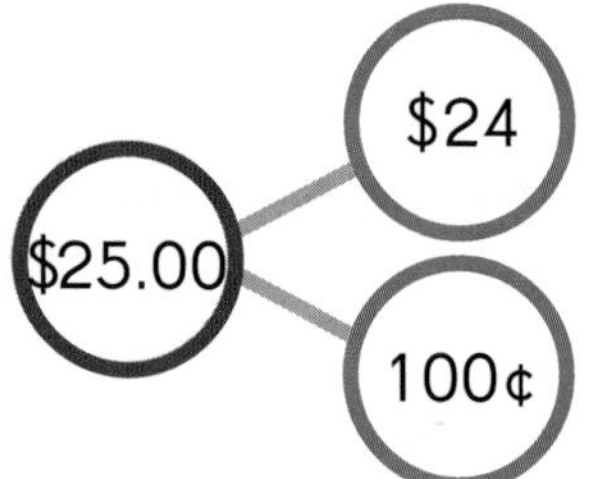

19

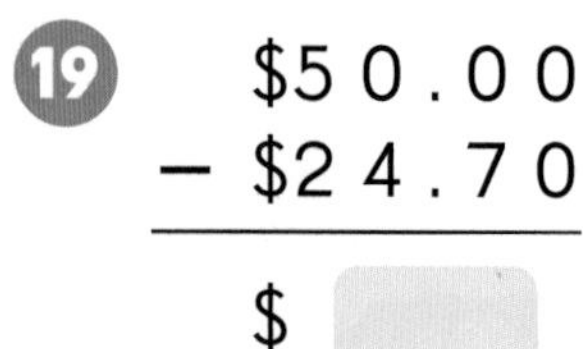

$$\begin{array}{r} \$50.00 \\ -\ \$24.70 \\ \hline \$\ \square \end{array}$$

Regroup.

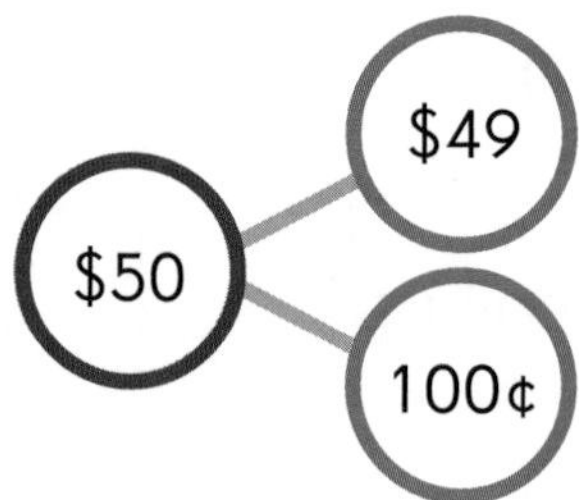

Let's Practice

Subtract mentally.

1. $9.45 − $5.00 = $ ____
2. $12.65 − $0.20 = $ ____
3. $23.85 − $0.40 = $ ____
4. $48.70 − $15.45 = $ ____

Find each missing amount.

5. $7.50 − $0.80 = ?

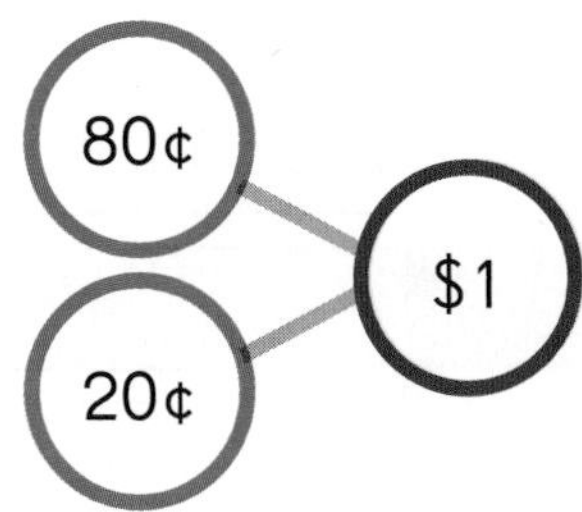

$7.50 − $0.80 = $ ____

6. $15.35 − $6.75 = ?

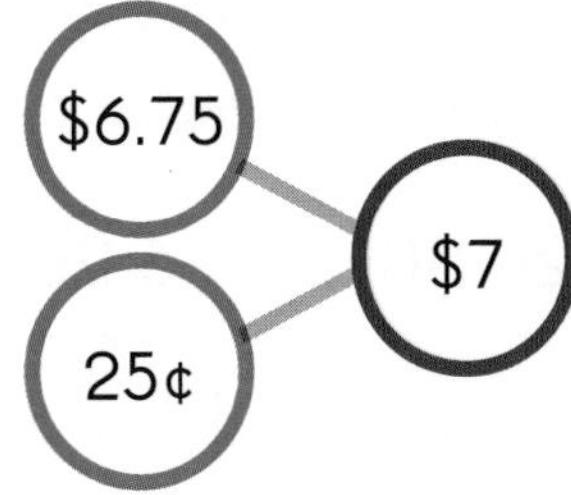

$15.35 − $6.75 = $ ____

Subtract.

7.
```
  $1 2 . 6 5
− $1 1 . 3 0
  $ ____
```

8.
```
  $2 8 . 8 0
− $1 6 . 5 0
  $ ____
```

Subtracting money is just like subtracting whole numbers.

Subtract.

9.
```
  $8 . 2 5
− $3 . 6 0
  $ ____
```

10.
```
  $4 5 . 4 5
− $2 7 . 7 5
  $ ____
```

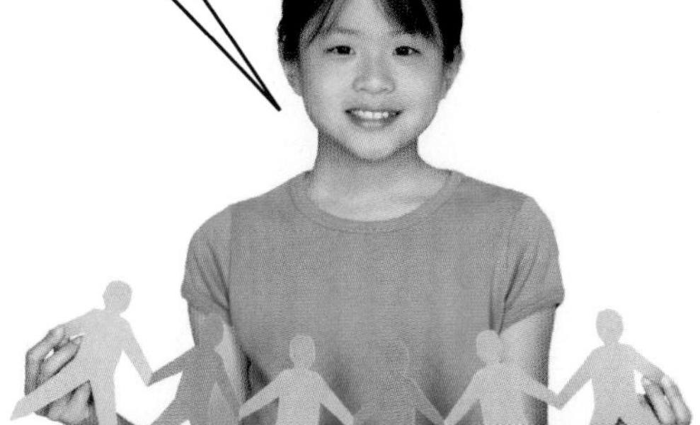

ON YOUR OWN

Go to Workbook B: Practice 4 to 6, pages 7–12

Lesson 10.3 Real-World Problems: Money

Lesson Objectives

- Solve up to two-step real-world problems involving addition and subtraction of money.
- Write real-world problems for given situations.

Learn Solve real-world problems using bar models.

Nancy has $35.50.
She buys a necklace and has $29.30 left.
How much does Nancy spend on the necklace?

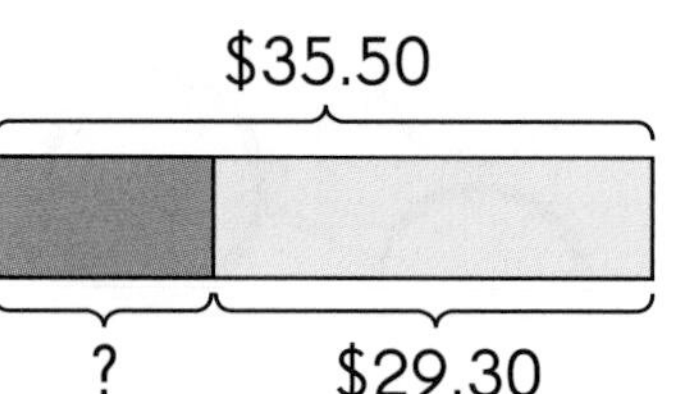

$35.50 – $29.30 = $6.20

Nancy spends $6.20 on the necklace.

Jim has $12 in his wallet. He buys a carton of fruit juice for $2.50 and a sandwich for $7.90. How much money does he have left?

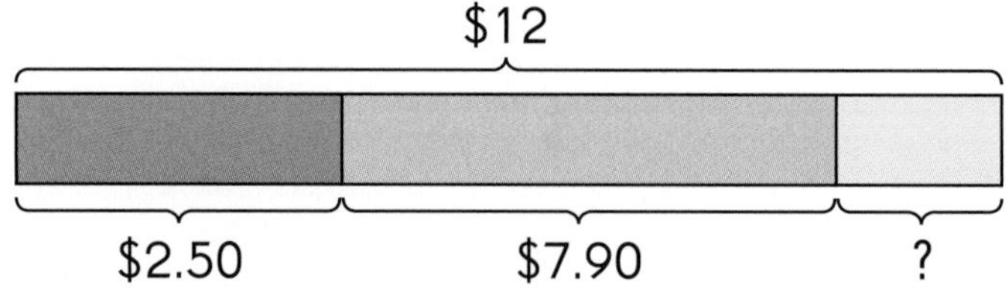

First, find the amount of money Jim spent.

$2.50 + $7.90 = $10.40

Then subtract this amount.

$12.00 – $10.40 = $1.60

Jim has $1.60 left.

Guided Learning

Solve.

1. Peter has $25.50. Sue has $18.75.
How much more money does Peter have than Sue?

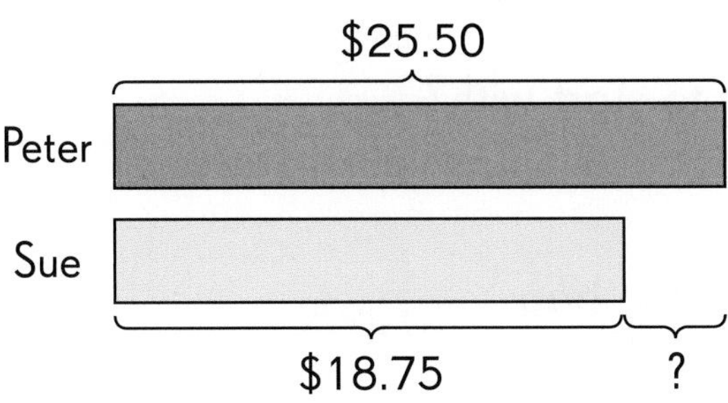

$ ___ − $ ___ = $ ___

Peter has $ ___ more than Sue.

2. A school sweatshirt costs $24.85.
A T-shirt is $3.40 less than the sweatshirt.
How much do the sweatshirt and the T-shirt cost in all?

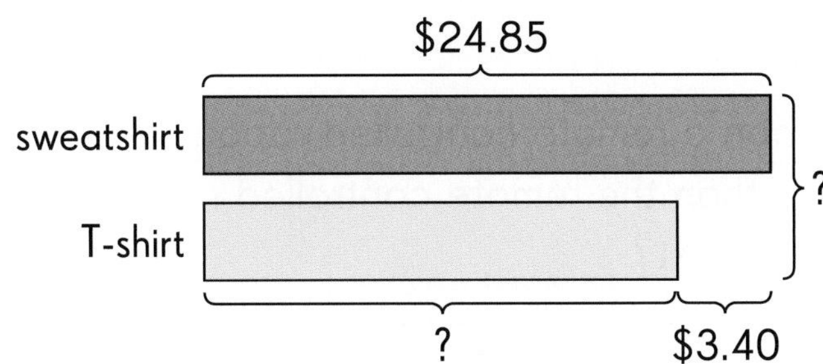

$ ___ ◯ $ ___ = $ ___

The T-shirt costs $ ___ .

$ ___ ◯ $ ___ = $ ___

The sweatshirt and the T-shirt cost $ ___ .

Let's Practice

Solve. Use bar models to help you.

1. Katherine bought a towel for \$7.90.
   She has \$18.75 left.
   How much money did she have to start with?

2. A bag costs \$12.35.
   A T-shirt costs \$2.65 more than the bag.
   How much does the T-shirt cost?

3. Pele wants to buy a clock that costs \$28.45.
   He needs \$2.20 more to buy it.
   How much money does he have now?

4. Carrie buys a bunch of bananas for \$3.80 and some mangoes for \$5.45. She has \$16.50 left.
   a. How much do the bananas and mangoes cost?
   b. How much money did she have to start with?

5. A stuffed animal costs \$28.45.
   It is \$15.20 more expensive than a remote controlled robot.
   A comic book costs \$7.90 less than the remote controlled robot.
   How much does the comic book cost?

6. Kevin buys a CD-ROM and has \$7.50 left.
   If he buys a watch instead, how much money does he have left?

ON YOUR OWN

Go to Workbook B:
Practice 7 and 8, pages 13–18

CRITICAL THINKING SKILLS

Put On Your Thinking Cap!

PROBLEM SOLVING

Solve.

1. Grandma buys some tomatoes and carrots.
The total cost is $18.
The tomatoes cost $2 more than the carrots.
How much does she spend on the carrots?

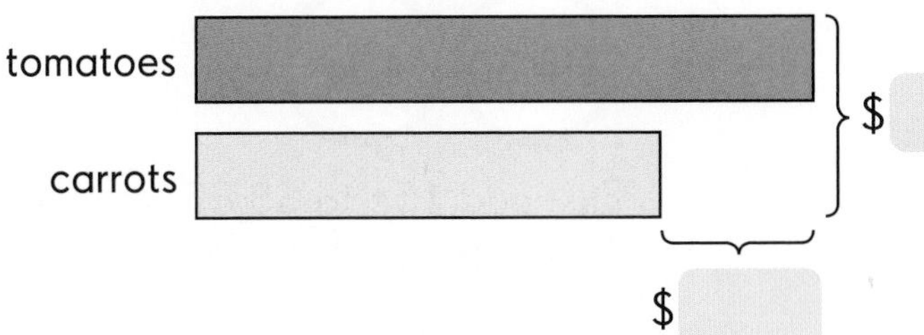

2. Winona buys some pencils and erasers.
She spends $1.20 altogether.
The pencils cost $0.40 more than the erasers.
How much does she spend on the erasers?
Give your answers in cents.

ON YOUR OWN

Go to Workbook B: Put On Your Thinking Cap! pages 21–22

Chapter Wrap Up

Study Guide

You have learned...

Money

Addition

1. \$6.25 + \$2 = ?
   First add the dollars: \$6 + \$2 = \$8
   Then add the cents to the dollars:
   25¢ + \$8 = \$8.25

2. \$5.60 + 25¢ = ?
   First add the cents: 60¢ + 25¢ = 85¢
   Then add the dollars to the cents:
   \$5 + 85¢ = \$5.85

3. \$7.25 + \$2.60 = ?
   First add the dollars: \$7 + \$2 = \$9
   Then add the cents:
   25¢ + 60¢ = 85¢
   Then add the cents to the dollars:
   \$9 + 85¢ = \$9.85

4. \$12.35 + \$6.65 = ?
   First add the cents to make one dollar:
   35¢ + 65¢ = \$1

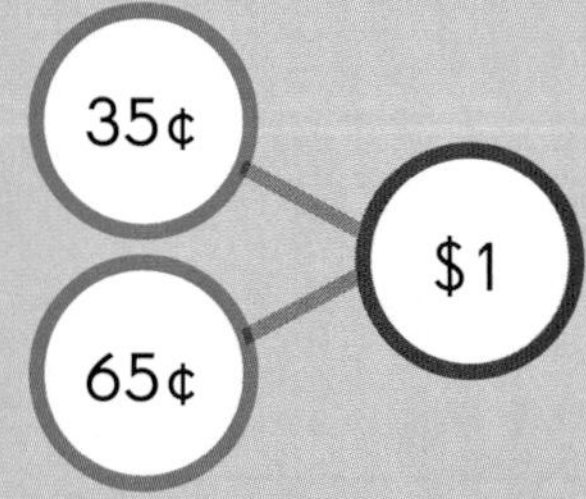

   Then add the dollars:
   \$1 + \$12 + \$6 = \$19

5. Use number bonds to add.
   \$14.45 + \$3.85 = ?

   First add 15¢ to \$3.85 = \$4
   Then add \$14.30 to \$4 = \$18.30

6. Use number bonds to add.
   \$5.60 + 80¢ = ?
   Adding 80¢ is the same as adding \$1 and subtracting 20¢.
   \$5.60 + \$1 = \$6.60
   Then subtract 20¢ from \$6.60:
   \$6.60 − 20¢ = \$6.40

   20¢
   80¢
   \$1

7. \$6.60 + \$3.25 = ?

$$\begin{array}{r} \$6\,.\,6\,0 \\ +\,\$3\,.\,2\,5 \\ \hline \end{array} \rightarrow \begin{array}{r} 6\,6\,0¢ \\ +\,3\,2\,5¢ \\ \hline 9\,8\,5¢ \end{array}$$

   985¢ = \$9.85

8. \$16.15 + \$5.95 = ?

$$\begin{array}{r} {}^{1}\,{}^{1}\,\,\,{}^{1}\,\, \\ \$1\,6\,.\,1\,5 \\ +\,\$\,\,\,5\,.\,9\,5 \\ \hline \$2\,2\,.\,1\,0 \end{array}$$

▶ You can add and subtract money the same way you add and subtract whole numbers.

Subtraction

1 $\$14.25 - \$9 = ?$
Subtract the dollars: $\$14 - \$9 = \$5$
Add the dollars and cents:
$\$5 + 25¢ = \$5.25$

2. $\$26.85 - \$0.60 = ?$
Subtract the cents: $85¢ - 60¢ = 25¢$
Add the dollars and cents:
$\$26 + 25¢ = \$26.25$

3. $\$99.45 - \$56.25 = ?$
Subtract the dollars:
$\$99 - \$56 = \$43$
Subtract the cents:
$45¢ - 25¢ = 20¢$
Add 20¢ to $\$43 = \$43.20$

4. Use number bonds to subtract.
$\$14.70 - \$0.90 = ?$
Subtracting 90¢ is the same as subtracting \$1 and adding10¢.
First subtract \$1 from $\$14.70 = \$13.70$
Then add 10¢ to \$13.70:
$10¢ + \$13.70 = \$13.80$

Number bond: 90¢, 10¢ → \$1

5. Use number bonds to subtract.
$\$11.70 - \$8.90 = ?$
Subtracting \$8.90 is the same as subtracting \$9 and adding 10¢.
First subtract \$9 from \$11.70:
$\$11.70 - \$9 = \$2.70$
Then add 10¢ to \$2.70:
$\$2.70 + 10¢ = \$2.80$

Number bond: \$8.90, 10¢ → \$9

6. $\$8.95 - \$6.30 = ?$

$$\begin{array}{r} \$8.95 \\ -\ \$6.30 \\ \hline \end{array} \rightarrow \begin{array}{r} 895¢ \\ -\ 630¢ \\ \hline 265¢ \end{array}$$

$265¢ = \$2.65$

7. $\$17.30 - \$12.50 = ?$
Regroup \$17.30.
$\$17.30 = \$16 + \$1.30$

$$\begin{array}{r} \$1\overset{6}{\not{7}}.{}^{1}30 \\ -\ \$12.50 \\ \hline \$\ \ 4.80 \end{array}$$

Chapter Review/Test

Concepts and Skills

Add mentally.

1. $3.45 + $8.00 = $ ___
2. $6.25 + $0.35 = $ ___
3. $2.55 + $6.20 = $ ___
4. $15.60 + $3.40 = $ ___
5. $8.35 + $1.95 = $ ___
6. $12.70 + $0.90 = $ ___
7. $11.30 + $3.85 = $ ___

Subtract mentally.

8. $16.78 − $9.00 = $ ___
9. $6.45 − $0.20 = $ ___
10. $8.65 − $7.25 = $ ___
11. $5.40 − $0.90 = $ ___
12. $5.70 − $4.80 = $ ___

Add or subtract.

13.
```
   $70.48
 + $ 9.65
 --------
   $ ___
```

14.
```
   $10.00
 − $ 7.38
 --------
   $ ___
```

Problem Solving

Solve. Use bar models to help you.

15. Randy wants to buy a calculator that costs $36.42.
He has only $27.09.
How much more money does he need? ___

16. Melvin gives $16.20 to his teacher for a book.
He pays $3.85 less for another book.
How much do the two books cost? ___

17. Sally and Joshua have the same amount of money.
Joshua pays $9.10 for a bag and has $16.25 left.
Sally buys a pen and has $19.60 left.
How much does the pen cost? ___

Metric Length, Mass, and Volume

Lessons

11.1 Meters and Centimeters
11.2 Kilometers and Meters
11.3 Kilograms and Grams
11.4 Liters and Milliliters

▶ Length, mass, and volume can be measured using metric units of measurement.

Recall Prior Knowledge

Using number bonds

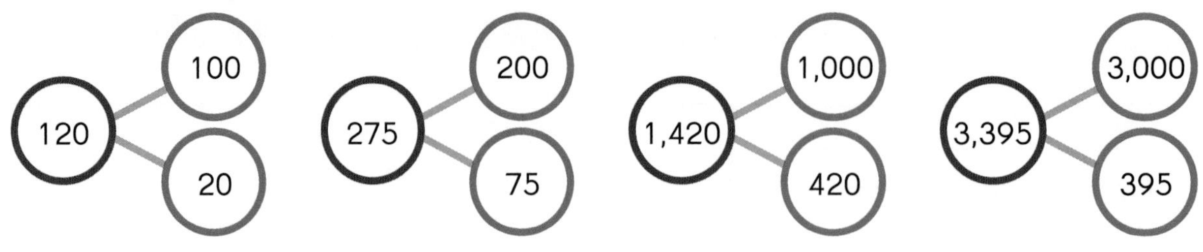

Measuring length in meters and centimeters

The meter is a unit of length.
It is a little longer than 3 feet.
It is used to measure length and height.

Stanley jumped 1 meter.

The cupboard is 2 meters tall.

The centimeter is also a unit of length.
It is used to measure shorter lengths.

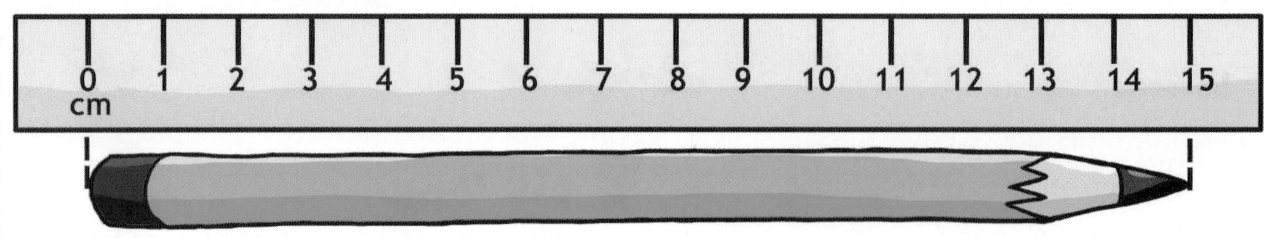

The pencil is 15 centimeters long.

Measuring mass in kilograms and grams

The kilogram is used to measure the mass of heavier objects.
The gram is used to measure the mass of lighter objects.

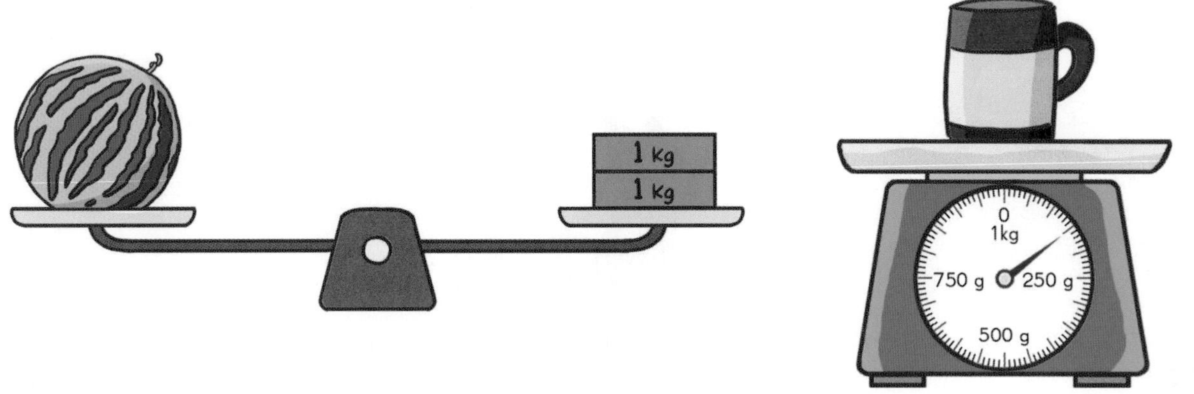

The mass of the watermelon is 2 kilograms.
The mug has a mass of 150 grams.

Measuring volume in liters

You can use liters to measure volume.

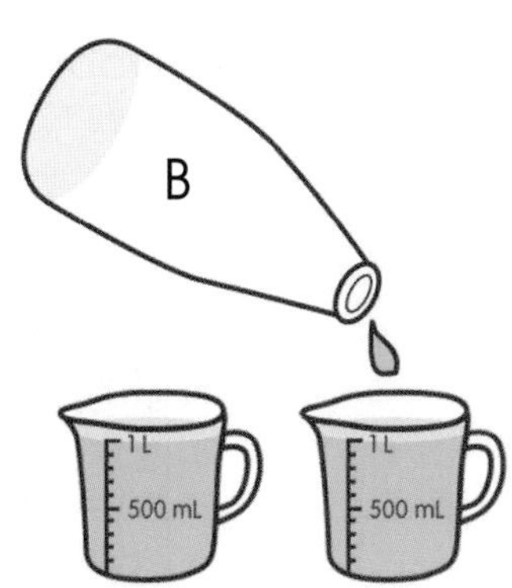

Bottle A contains 4 liters of water.
Bottle B contains 2 liters of water.
Bottle A contains more water than Bottle B.

1 The dog is ___ meter tall.

2

The mass of the flower pot is ___ grams.

3

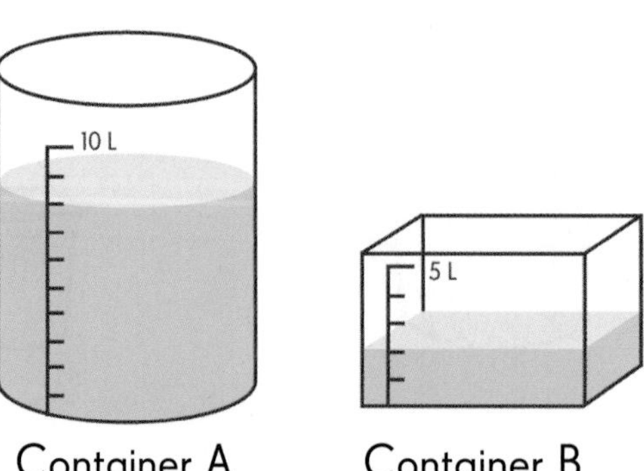

Container A Container B

Container A has ___ liters of water.

Container B has ___ liters of water.

Lesson

11.1 Meters and Centimeters

Lesson Objectives

- Use meters and centimeters as units of measurement of length.
- Estimate and measure length.
- Convert units of measurement.

Vocabulary
meter (m)
centimeter (cm)

Learn

Use meters to measure length.

The length of the ribbon is 1 meter.

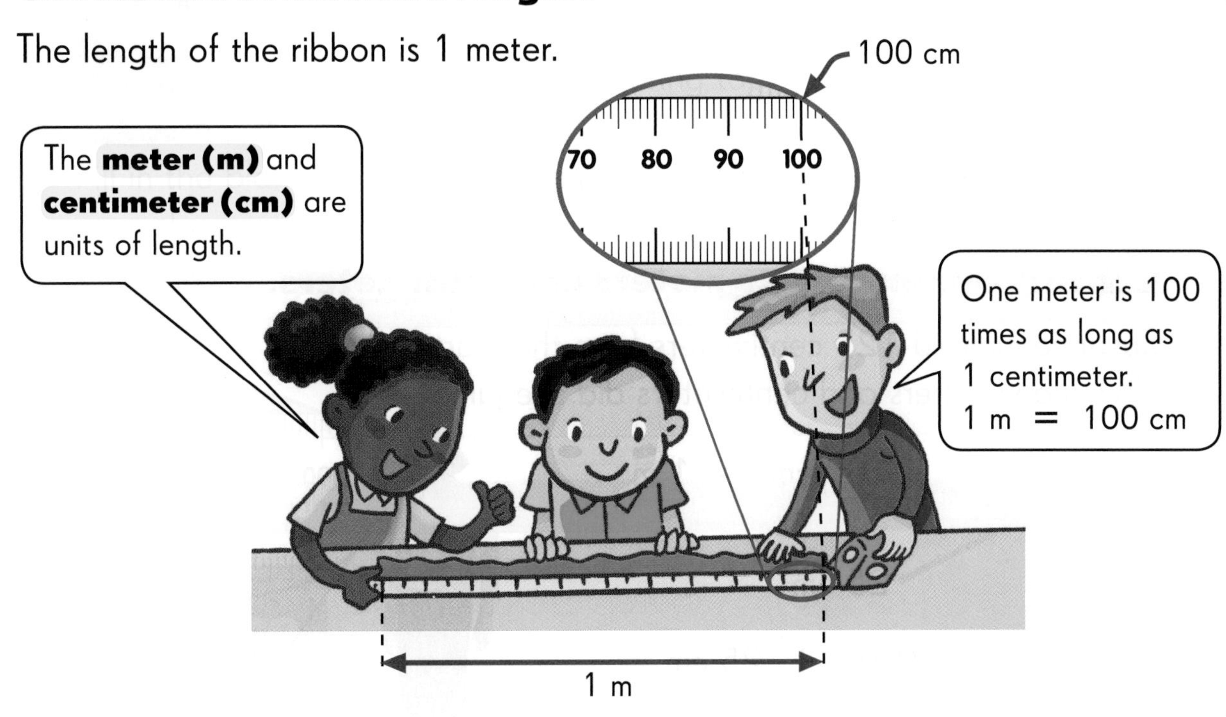

100 cm
70
80
90
100
The **meter (m)** and **centimeter (cm)** are units of length.
One meter is 100 times as long as 1 centimeter.
1 m = 100 cm
1 m

Learn

Convert meters and centimeters to centimeters.

Kate's height is 1 meter 38 centimeters.
What is her height in centimeters?

1 m 38 cm → 1 m = 100 cm; 38 cm

1 m 38 cm = 100 cm + 38 cm
= 138 cm

Kate's height is 138 centimeters.

Learn: Convert meters to kilometers and meters.

A plane flies 2,790 meters above the ground.
How high is the plane above the ground?
Express your answer in kilometers and meters.

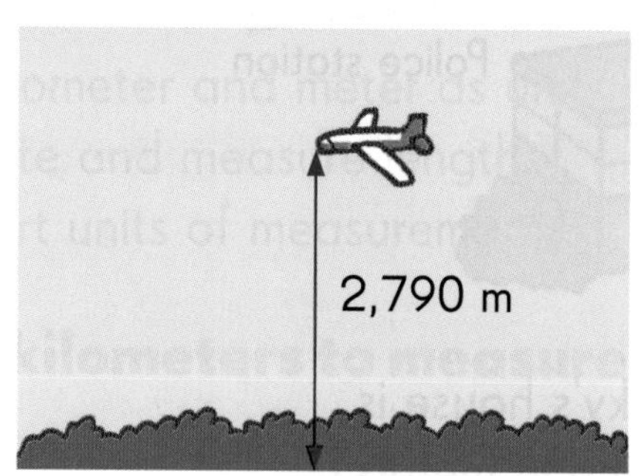

2,790 m → 2,000 m = 2 km; 790 m

2,790 m = 2 km + 790 m
= 2 km 790 m

The plane is 2 kilometers 790 meters above the ground.

Guided Learning

Complete.

3. The distance from Zack's home to school is 5,275 meters.
He bikes to school every morning.
What is the distance he bikes in kilometers and meters?

5,275 m = ____ m + ____ m
= ____ km + ____ m
= ____ km ____ m

5,275 m → 5,000 m; 275 m

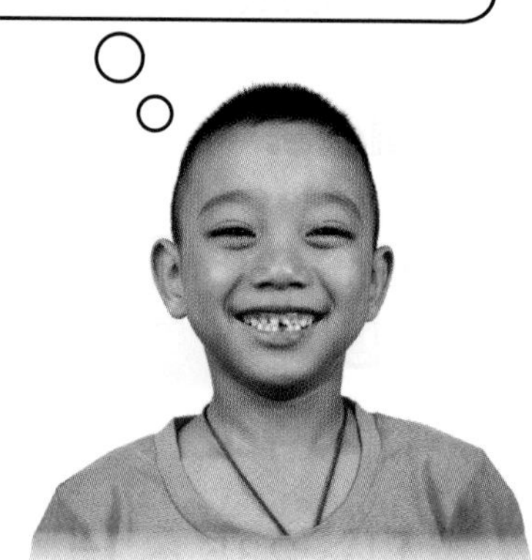

The distance he bikes is 5 kilometers 275 meters.

4. 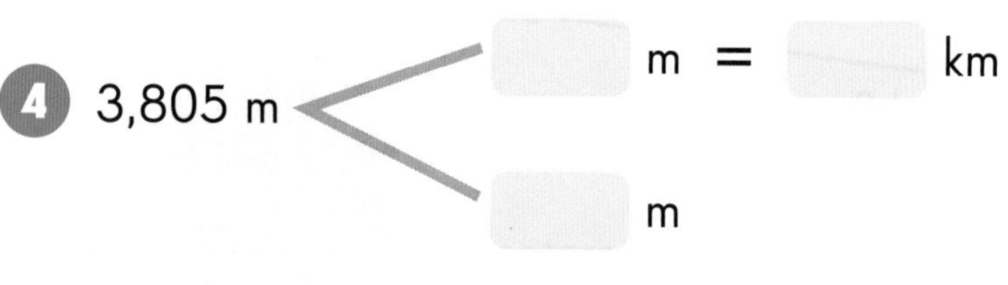

3,805 m → ____ m = ____ km; ____ m

3,805 m = ____ km ____ m

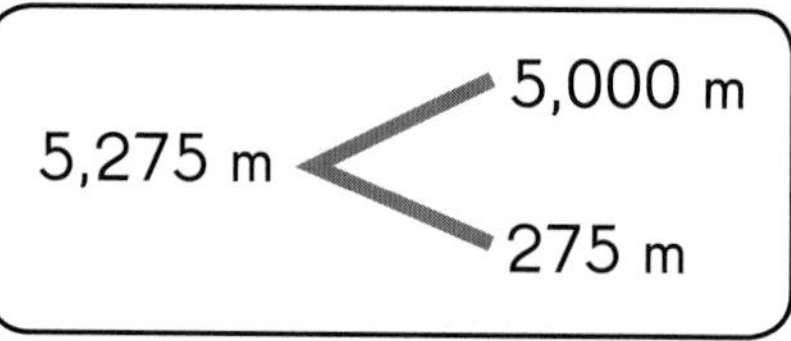

Let's Practice

The map is not drawn to scale. Find each distance.

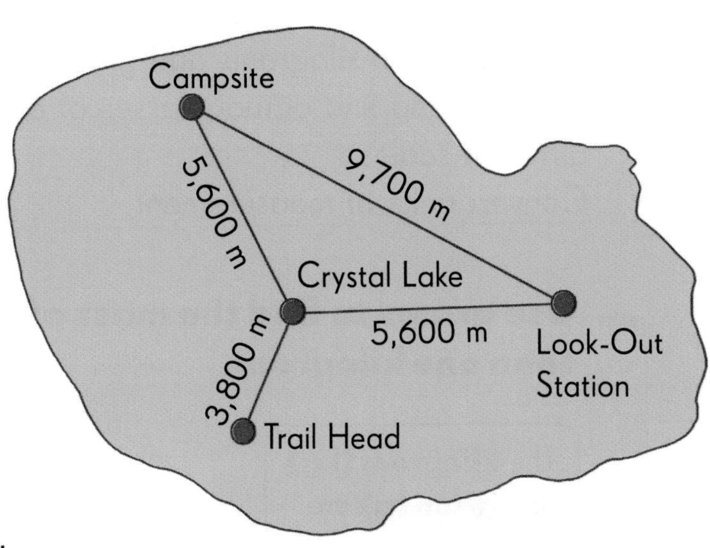

1. The distance between Crystal Lake and the Campsite is about ___ kilometers ___ meters.

2. The distance between Trail Head and Crystal Lake is about ___ kilometers ___ meters.

3. The distance from the Campsite to Look-Out Station is about ___ kilometers and ___ meters.

Convert kilometers and meters to meters.

4. 4 km = ___ m
5. 6 km 128 m = ___ m
6. 8 km 700 m = ___ m
7. 2 km 49 m = ___ m
8. 5 km 80 m = ___ m
9. 3 km 7 m = ___ m

Convert meters to kilometers and meters.

10. 5,000 m = ___ km ___ m
11. 1,465 m = ___ km ___ m
12. 5,400 m = ___ km ___ m
13. 2,084 m = ___ km ___ m
14. 7,090 m = ___ km ___ m
15. 9,009 m = ___ km ___ m

ON YOUR OWN

Go to Workbook B: Practice 2, pages 27–30

Lesson 11.3 Kilograms and Grams

Lesson Objectives
- Read scales in kilograms and grams.
- Estimate and find actual masses of objects by using different scales.
- Convert units of measurement.

Vocabulary
kilogram (kg)
gram (g)

Learn Use grams to find the mass of items that are less than one kilogram.

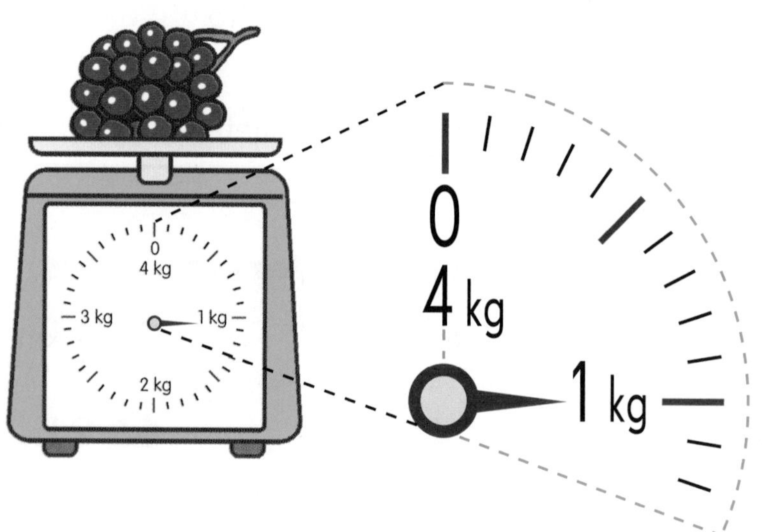

The **kilogram (kg)** and **gram (g)** are units of mass.

The bunch of grapes has a mass of 1 kilogram.

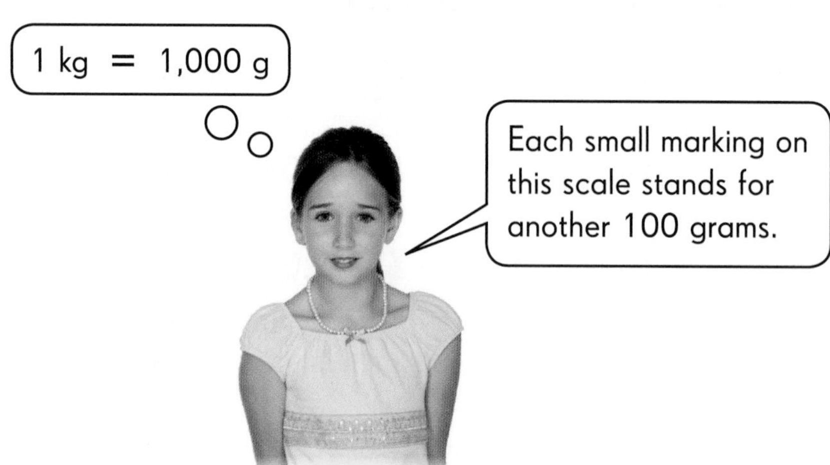

1 kg = 1,000 g
Each small marking on this scale stands for another 100 grams.

Luis uses this scale to find the mass of items that are light.

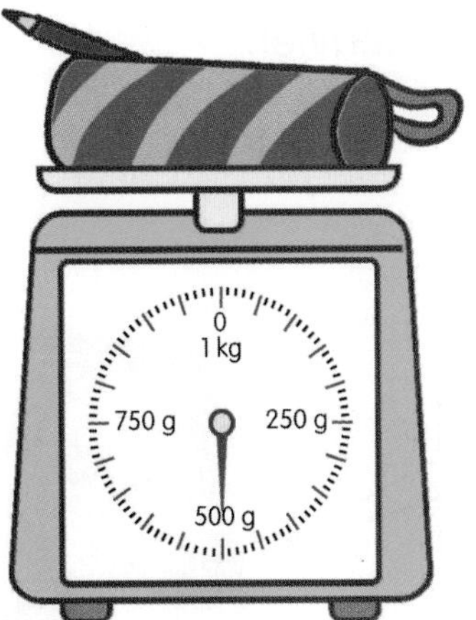

Use this scale to measure mass 1 kilogram or less. Each small marking stands for another 10 grams.

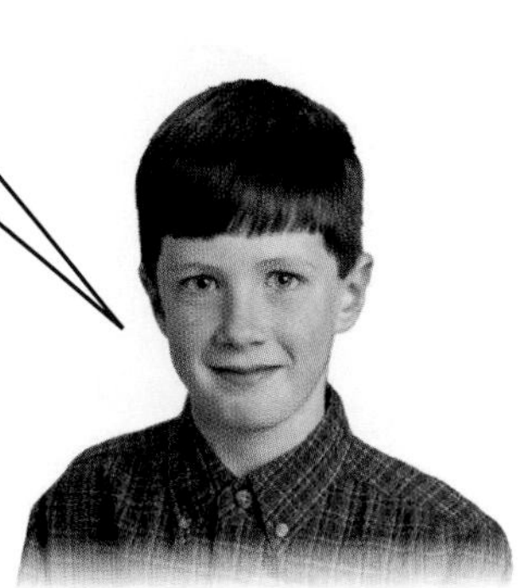

The pencil case has a mass of 500 grams.

Guided Learning

Complete.

1 The carrots have a mass of 600 grams.
What is the mass of the pumpkin?

The mass of the pumpkin is ______ grams.

Learn

Use kilograms to find the mass of items that are more than one kilogram.

Celia uses this scale to find the mass of items that are heavier.

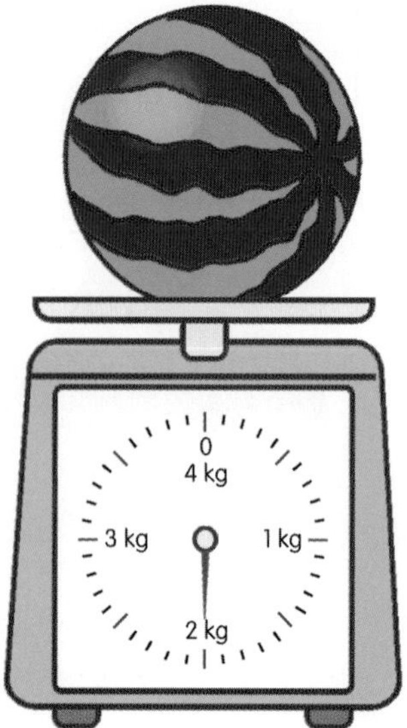

Use this scale to measure mass 4 kilograms or less. Each small marking stands for another 100 grams.

The mass of the watermelon is 2 kilograms.

The cabbage has a mass of 1 kilogram 500 grams.
What is the mass of the apples?

The mass of the apples is 2 kilograms 300 grams.

Guided Learning

Read each scale to find the mass.

2

The mass of the apples is

[ ] grams.

3

The mass of the vegetables is

[ ] grams.

The mass of the pineapple is

[ ] grams.

5

The mass of the melon is

[ ] grams.

Learn Convert kilograms and grams to grams.

The mass of a bag of potatoes is 1 kilogram 250 grams.
What is the mass of the bag of potatoes in grams?

1 kg 250 g → 1 kg = 1,000 g
1 kg 250 g → 250 g

1 kg 250 g = 1,000 g + 250 g
= 1,250 g

The mass of the bag of potatoes is 1,250 grams.

Guided Learning

Complete.

6. 8 kg 405 g → ___ kg = ___ g
8 kg 405 g → ___ g

8 kg 405 g = ___ g

8 kg = 8 × 1,000 g

Learn Convert grams to kilograms and grams.

The mass of a bag of coffee beans is 3,450 grams.
What is its mass in kilograms and grams?

3,450 g = 3,000 g + 450 g
= 3 kg 450 g

3,450 g → 3,000 g = 3 kg
3,450 g → 450 g

The mass of the bag of coffee beans is 3 kilograms 450 grams.

Guided Learning

Complete.

7. 5,805 g → ____ g = ____ kg; ____ g

5,805 g = ____ kg ____ g

Let's Practice

Complete.

1.

____ kg ____ g

2. 5 kg = ____ g
3. 4 kg 830 g = ____ g
4. 5 kg 208 g = ____ g
5. 3 kg 40 g = ____ g
6. 9 kg 6 g = ____ g
7. 7,000 g = ____ kg ____ g
8. 2,479 g = ____ kg ____ g
9. 2,900 g = ____ kg ____ g
10. 3,085 g = ____ kg ____ g
11. 8,025 g = ____ kg ____ g
12. 6,008 g = ____ kg ____ g

ON YOUR OWN

Go to Workbook B: Practice 3, pages 31–34

CRITICAL THINKING SKILLS

Put On Your Thinking Cap!

PROBLEM SOLVING

1. How much oil is in the beaker?
Express your answer in mL.

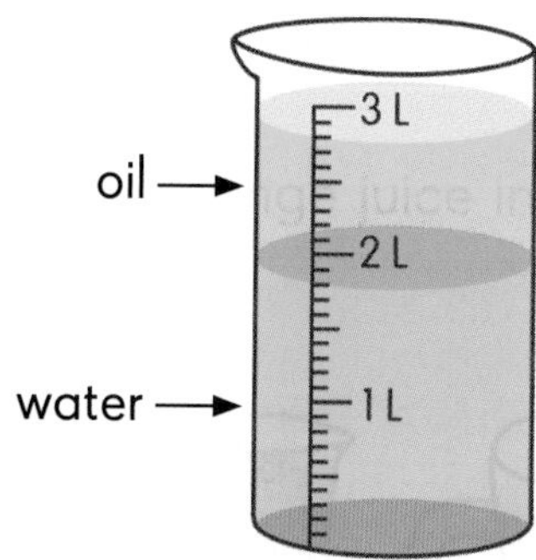

2. Mr. Smith has three coins. One out of the three is a fake coin. It is lighter than a real coin. With the help of a balance, how can you tell which is the fake coin?

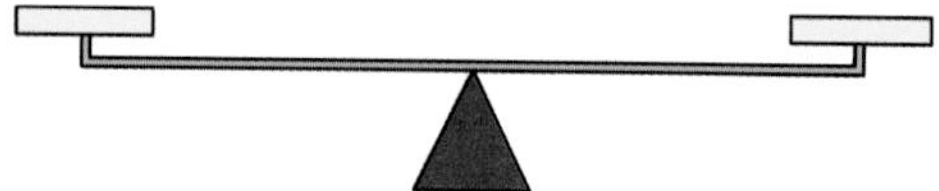

Explain what happens if you:

a. choose the two real coins first.

b. choose one real coin and one fake coin first.

3. Show how these two containers can be used to measure 200 milliliters of water exactly.

ON YOUR OWN

**Go to Workbook B:
Put On Your Thinking Cap!
pages 39–40**

Chapter Wrap Up

Study Guide

You have learned...

▶ Length, mass, and volume can be measured using metric units of measurement.

Measurement of

Length

Use a ruler or measuring tape to find length.

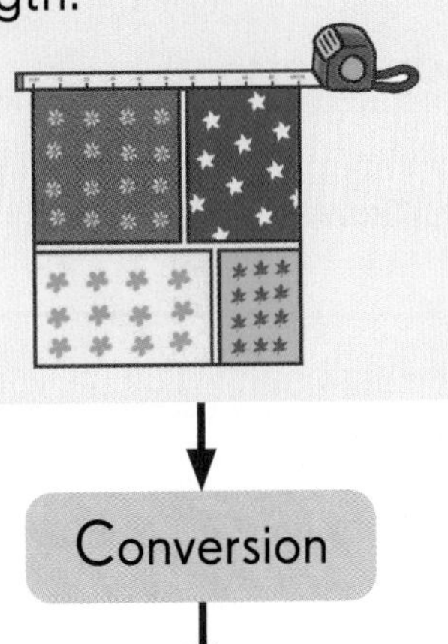

Conversion

Convert measurements of length:

100 cm = 1 m
835 cm = 8 m 35 cm

1,000 m = 1 km
5,890 m = 5 km 890 m

Mass

Use a weighing scale to find mass.

Conversion

Convert measurements of mass:

1,000 g = 1 kg
1,750 g = 1 kg 750 g

Volume

Volume is the amount of liquid in a container.

Capacity is the amount of liquid a container can hold.

Use measuring cups to find volume.

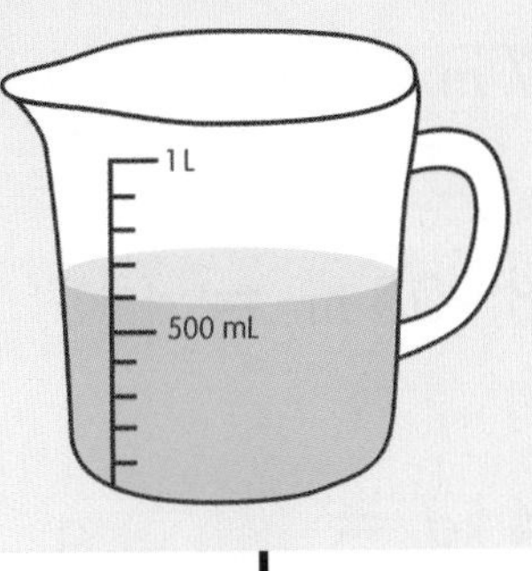

Conversion

Convert measurements of volume:

1,000 mL = 1 L
1,270 mL = 1 L 270 mL

Chapter Review/Test

Vocabulary

Choose the correct word.

kilometers
milliliters
length
mass
liters

1. Ariel has two pieces of fabric. The total ____ of the two pieces of fabric is ____ 5 meters 92 centimeters.

2. Mabel will be traveling soon. She is weighing her luggage. The total ____ of her luggage is 55 kilograms.

3. Nathan wants to know how much water his new fish tank can hold. He measures its capacity to be 30 ____ 500 ____.

4. Caleb has to travel several ____ by train to visit his grandparents.

Concepts and Skills

Complete.

5. 7 m 69 cm = ____ cm

6. 641 cm = ____ m ____ cm

7. 8,905 m = ____ km ____ m

8. 3 km 509 m = ____ m

9. 4 kg = ____ g

10. 8,555 g = ____ kg ____ g

11. 3 L = ____ mL

12. 6,924 mL = ____ L ____ mL

Real-World Problems: Measurement

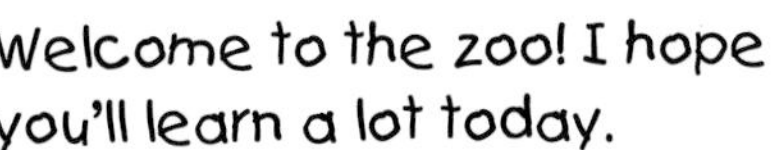

Lessons

BIG IDEA

- Bar models can be used to solve one- and two-step problems on measurements.

Recall Prior Knowledge

Adding, subtracting, multiplying, and dividing

$$\begin{array}{r} \overset{1}{3},\overset{1}{2}78 \\ +2,831 \\ \hline 6,109 \end{array} \qquad \begin{array}{r} \overset{7}{\cancel{8}},\overset{12}{\cancel{3}}\overset{14}{\cancel{5}}\,{}^{1}0 \\ -\ \ 956 \\ \hline 7,394 \end{array} \qquad \begin{array}{r} \overset{2}{1}\overset{1}{8}5 \\ \times\ \ 3 \\ \hline 555 \end{array} \qquad \begin{array}{r} 15 \\ 4\overline{)60} \\ 40 \\ \hline 20 \\ 20 \\ \hline 00 \end{array}$$

Using bar models

- to show comparison

Crate A has 100 apples.
Crate B has 90 apples.
How many more apples does Crate A have?

100 − 90 = 10

Crate A has 10 more apples.

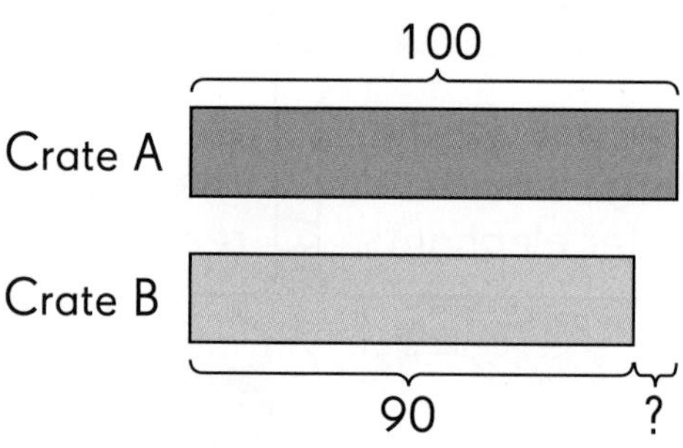

- to show multiplication

Adam has 2 pencils. Brad has 3 times as many pencils as Adam. How many pencils does Brad have?

3 × 2 = 6

Brad has 6 pencils.

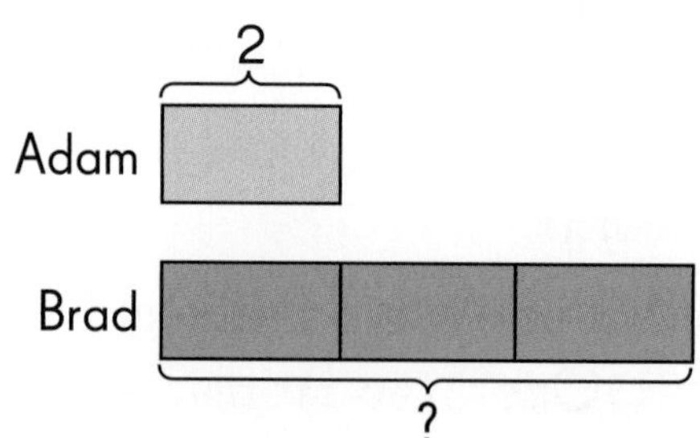

- to show division

A box has 45 strawberries. Laura shares the strawberries equally among 5 friends. How many strawberries does each person get?

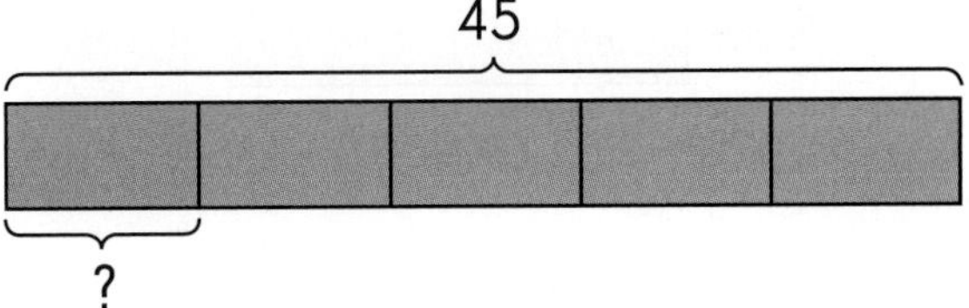

45 ÷ 5 = 9

Each person gets 9 strawberries.

Tyrone has 24 yogurt bars.
He puts them in boxes of 4.
How many boxes does he need?

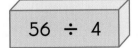

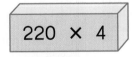

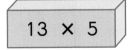

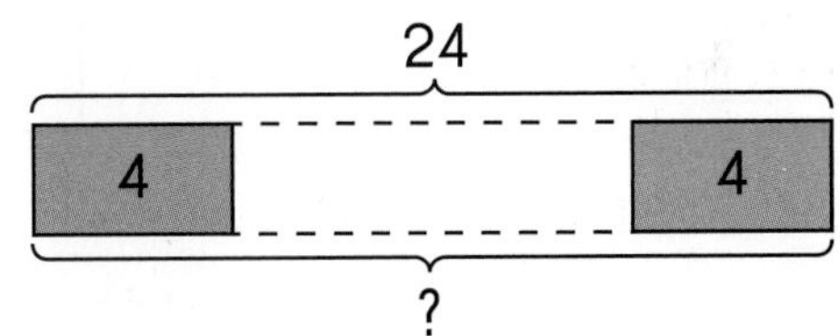

24 ÷ 4 = 6

He needs 6 boxes.

✔Quick Check

Complete.

1. 1,234 + 3,789 = ▭
2. 6,325 − 5,236 = ▭

Choose the boxes that match.

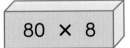

3. 880 — 80 × 8 | 220 × 4 | 440 × 2
4. 14 — 56 ÷ 4 | 13 × 5 | 42 ÷ 3

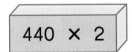

Decide which situation describes the bar models.

5

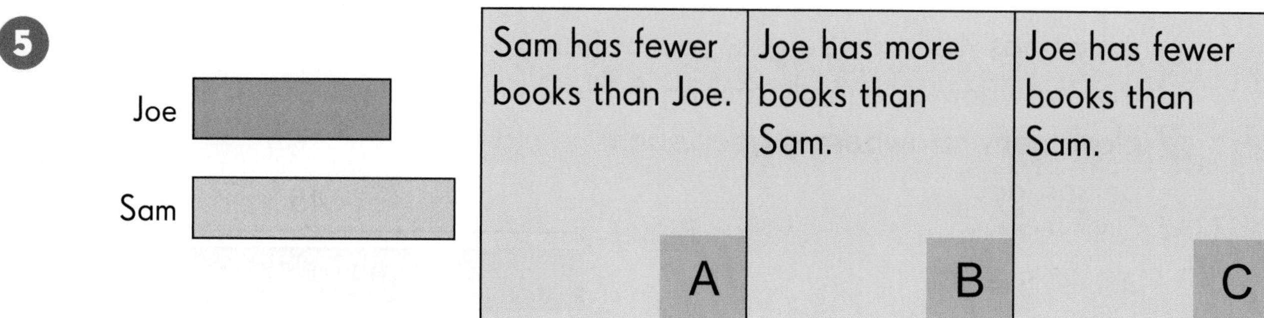

Joe
Sam
Sam has fewer books than Joe.
A
Joe has more books than Sam.
B
Joe has fewer books than Sam.
C

6

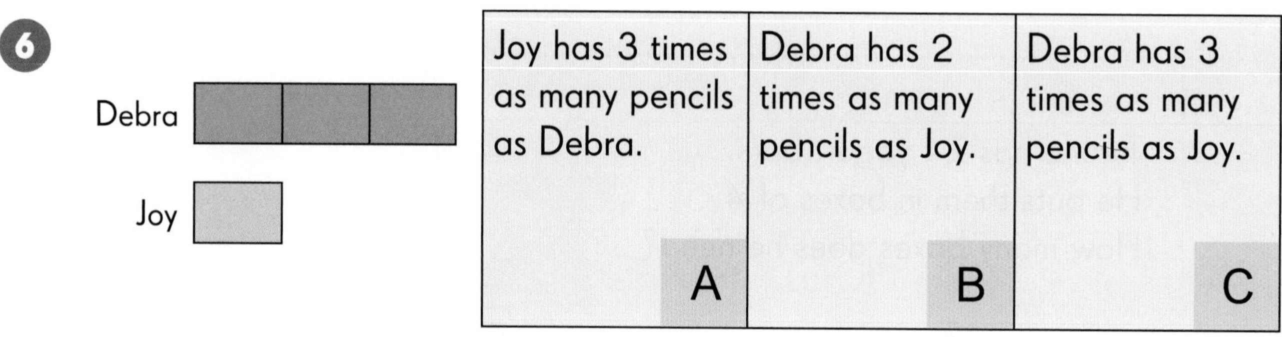

Debra
Joy
Joy has 3 times as many pencils as Debra.
A
Debra has 2 times as many pencils as Joy.
B
Debra has 3 times as many pencils as Joy.
C

7

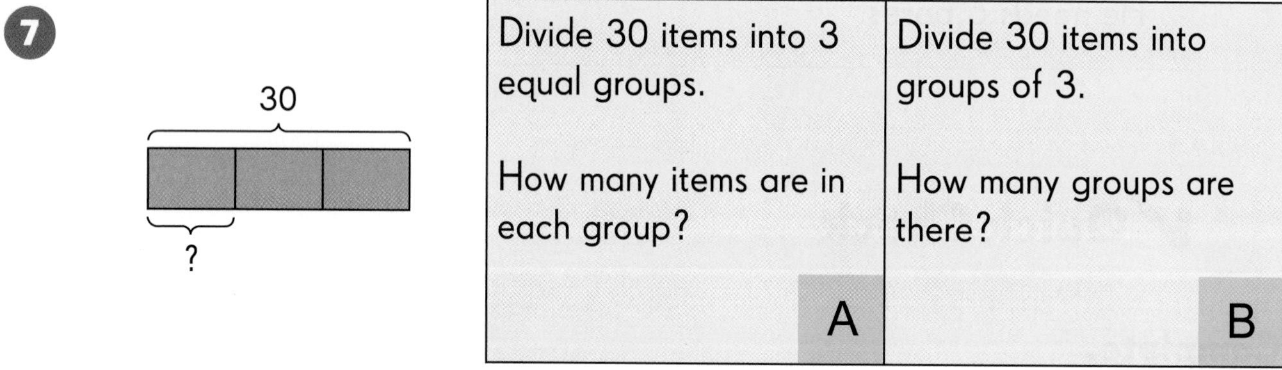

30
?
Divide 30 items into 3 equal groups.
How many items are in each group?
A
Divide 30 items into groups of 3.
How many groups are there?
B

8

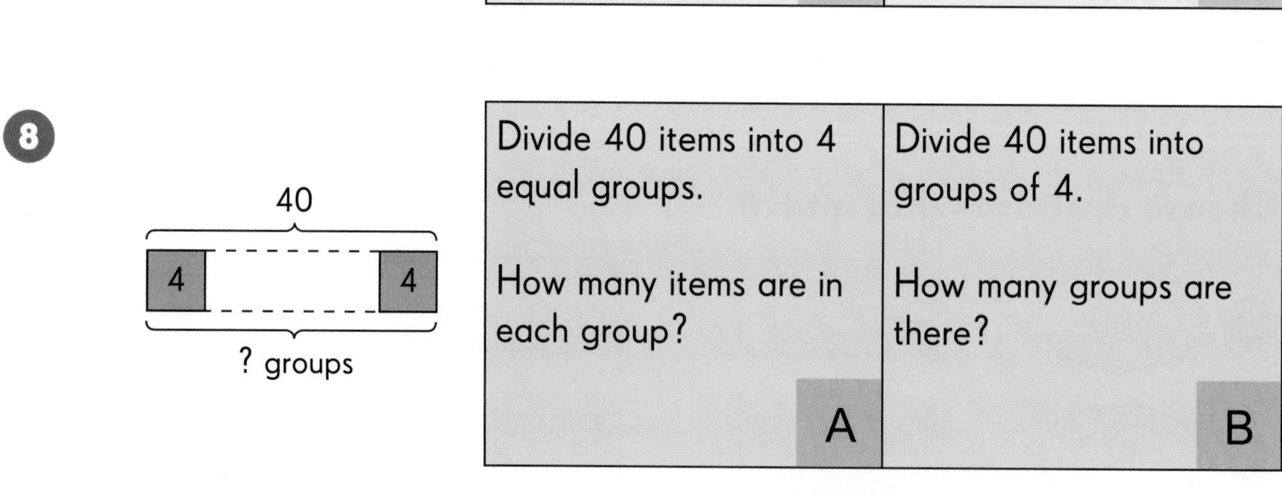

40
4
4
? groups
Divide 40 items into 4 equal groups.
How many items are in each group?
A
Divide 40 items into groups of 4.
How many groups are there?
B

Real-World Problems: One-Step Problems

Lesson Objectives

- Draw bar models to solve one-step measurement problems.
- Choose the operation to solve one-step problems.

Learn

Use addition to solve measurement problems.

Keisha ties a package with a string 75 centimeters long.
She ties another package with a string 255 centimeters long.
What is the total length of the two strings she uses?
Give your answer in meters and centimeters.

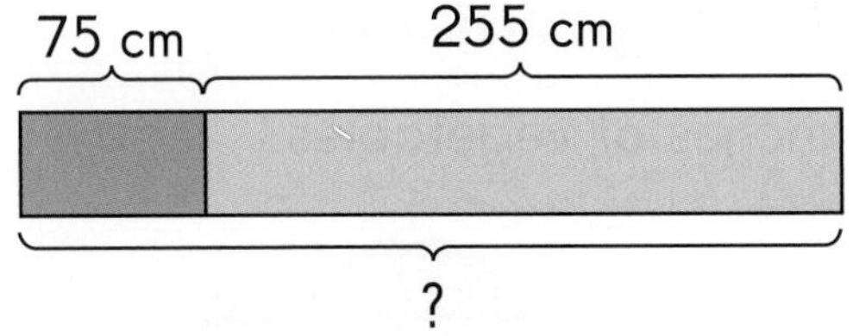

$$\begin{array}{r} \scriptstyle{1\ 1} \\ 75 \\ +\ 255 \\ \hline 330 \end{array}$$

$75 + 255 = 330$
$330 \text{ cm} = 3 \text{ m } 30 \text{ cm}$

The total length of the two strings is 3 meters 30 centimeters.

100 cm = 1 m
300 cm = 3 m
330 cm = 3 m 30 cm

Guided Learning

Solve.

1 Abel tied a gift box with a ribbon 56 centimeters long.
He tied another gift box with a ribbon 184 centimeters long.
What was the total length of ribbon that he used?
Give your answer in meters and centimeters.

56 cm | 184 cm

?

___ ○ ___ = ___

___ cm = ___ m ___ cm

The total length of ribbon that Abel used was ___ meters ___ centimeters.

Learn Use addition to solve measurement problems.

What is the total mass of the two bunches of vegetables?

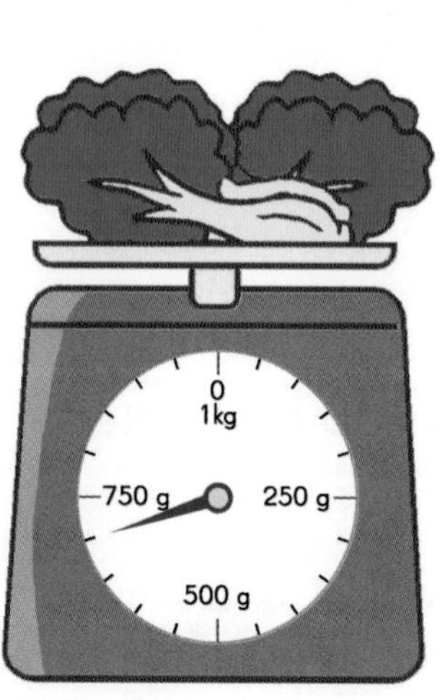

700 + 800 = 1,500

1,500 g = 1 kg 500 g

1,000 g = 1 kg
1,500 g = 1 kg 500 g

The total mass of the two bunches of vegetables is 1 kilogram 500 grams.

Guided Learning

Solve.

2. Sonia walks 650 meters to her friend's house.
She takes a longer route home and walks 740 meters.
What is the total distance she walked?
Give your answer in kilometers and meters.

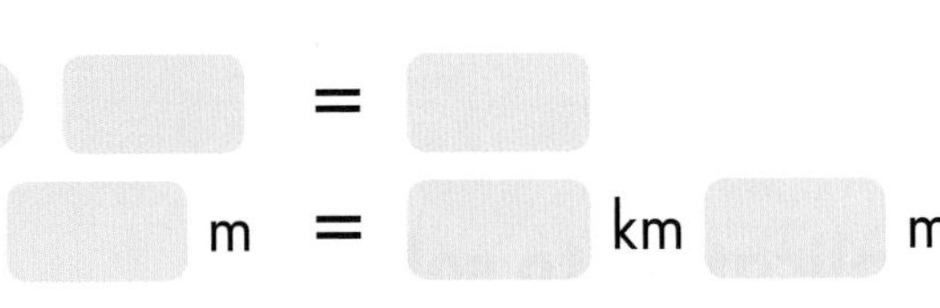

m = km m

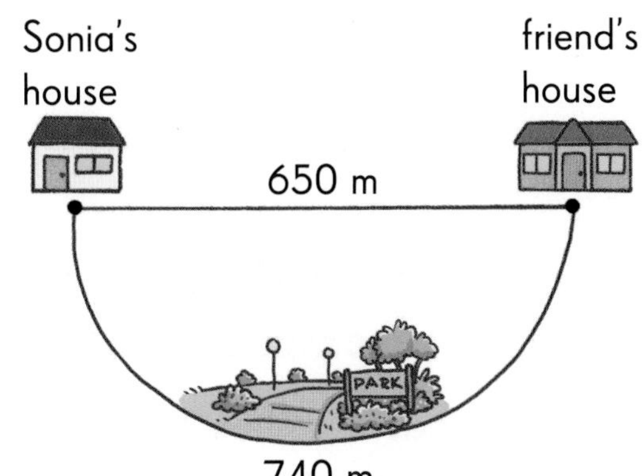

The total distance she walked is

kilometer meters.

Learn Use subtraction to solve measurement problems.

The distance between Town A and Town B is 420 kilometers.
The distance between Town B and Town C is 28 kilometers.
What is the difference between the two distances?

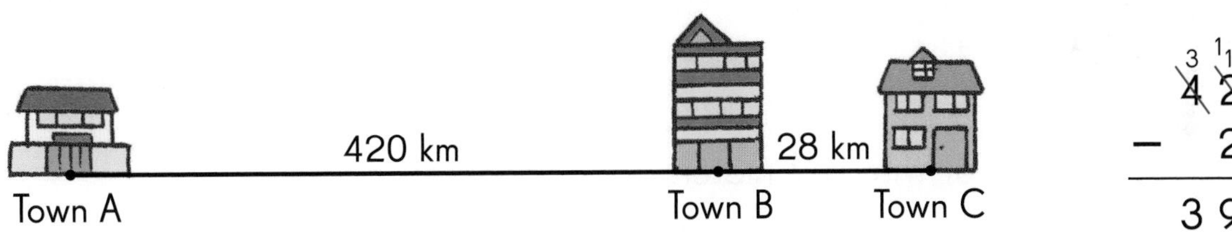

$$\begin{array}{r} \overset{3}{\not{4}}\,\overset{11}{\not{2}}\,{}^{1}0 \\ -\quad 2\;8 \\ \hline 3\;9\;2 \end{array}$$

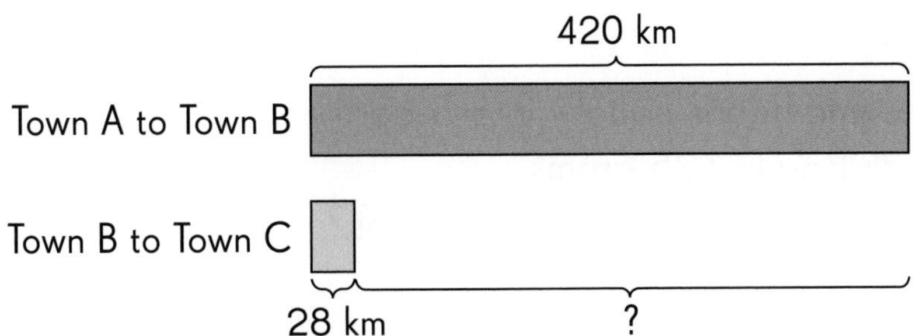

420 − 28 = 392

The difference between the two distances is 392 kilometers.

Guided Learning

3 An inflatable pool contains 356 liters of water.
15 liters of water leaks from it.
Find the volume of water that is left.

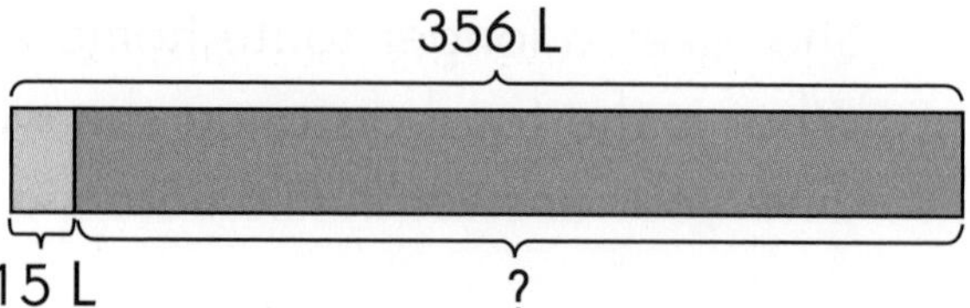

☐ ◯ ☐ = ☐

☐ liters of water is left.

Learn Use bar models and multiplication to solve measurement problems.

Julio has 4 pieces of wire each 178 centimeters long.
What is the total length of wire?
Give your answer in meters and centimeters.

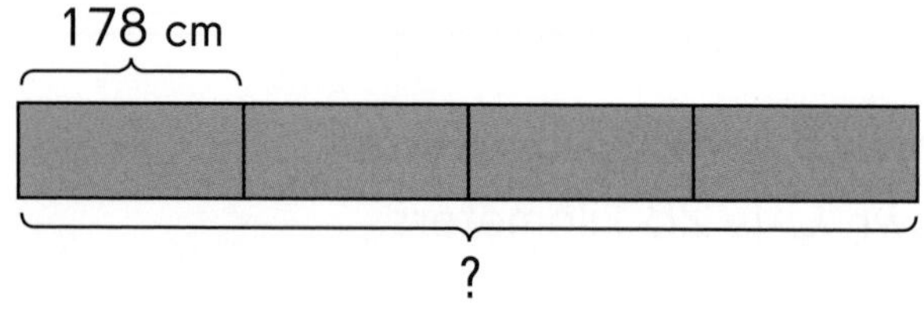

$$\begin{array}{r} \overset{3}{1}\overset{3}{7}8 \\ \times \quad 4 \\ \hline 712 \end{array}$$

$4 \times 178 = 712$
$712 \text{ cm} = 7 \text{ m } 12 \text{ cm}$

The total length of wire is 7 meters 12 centimeters.

Guided Learning

4 A teacher puts some beans equally into 5 bags.
The mass of each bag is 125 grams.
What is the total mass of the 5 bags of beans?

☐ ◯ ☐ = ☐

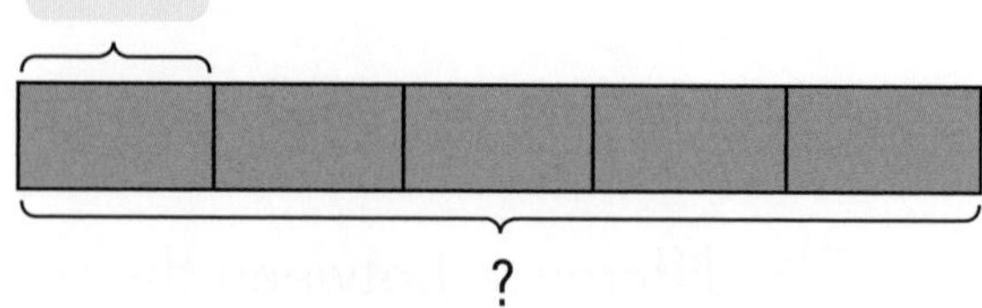

The total mass of the 5 bags of beans is ☐ grams.

Learn

Use bar models and division to solve measurement problems.

An oil delivery truck has 96 liters of fuel.
The fuel is pumped equally into 3 tanks.
How many liters of fuel are in each tank?

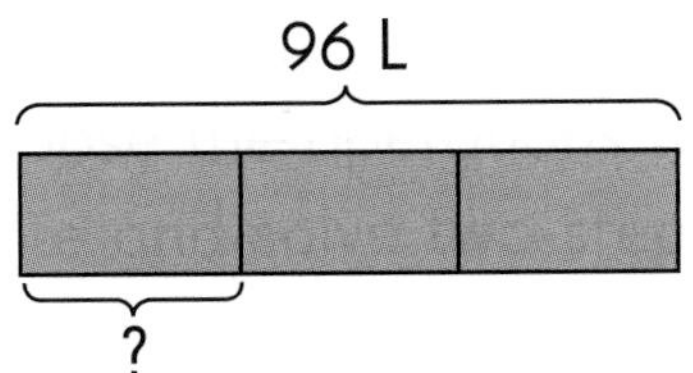

$$
\begin{array}{r}
32 \\
3\overline{)96} \\
\underline{90} \\
6 \\
\underline{6} \\
0
\end{array}
$$

$96 \div 3 = 32$

There are 32 liters of fuel in each tank.

Guided Learning

5 Janice cuts a ribbon that is 90 centimeters long into 5 equal pieces. How long is each piece?

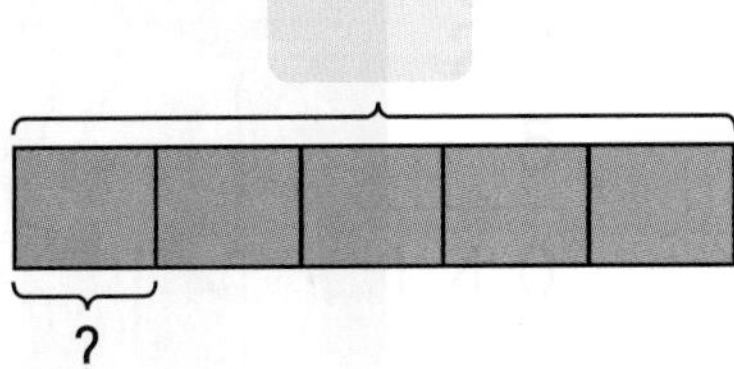

Each piece of ribbon is ___ centimeters long.

6 A grocer buys 850 kilograms of granola.
He repacks the granola equally into 5-kilogram bags.
How many bags are there?

___ ___ ___ = ___ tens ___ ___

= ___ tens

= ___

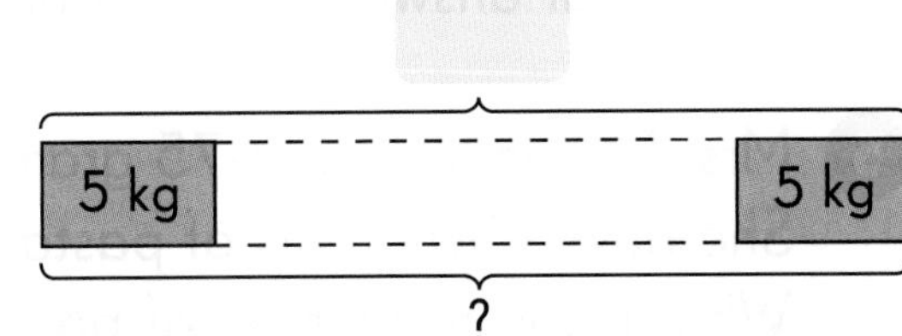

There are ___ bags.

Guided Learning

1 Alex and Billy compete in a bike race.
Each of them bikes from Point A to Point B and back again.
The distance between Point A and Point B is 54 meters.
When Alex completes the race, Billy has only biked 36 meters.
How much farther does Billy have to bike to complete the race?

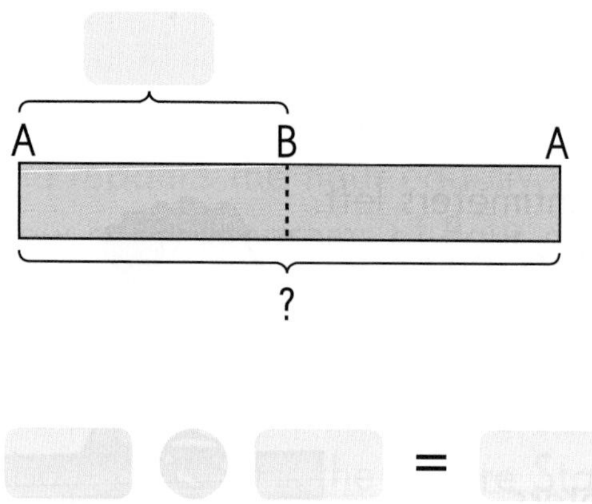

First, find the distance of the whole race.

The distance for the whole race is ___ meters.

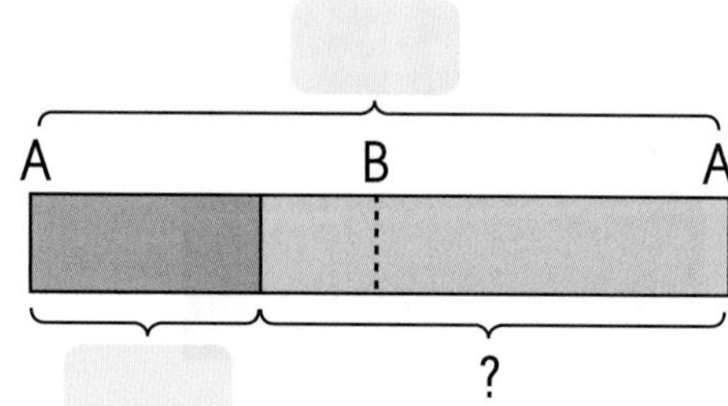

Billy has to bike another ___ meters to complete the race.

Learn Solve measurement problems using two operations.

Dylan buys 3 bags of beans and 1 bottle of cooking oil.
The mass of each bag of beans is 500 grams.
The 3 bags of beans are 475 grams lighter than the bottle of oil.

a What is the mass of the 3 bags of beans?

b What is the mass of the bottle of cooking oil?
Give your answer in kilograms and grams.

a

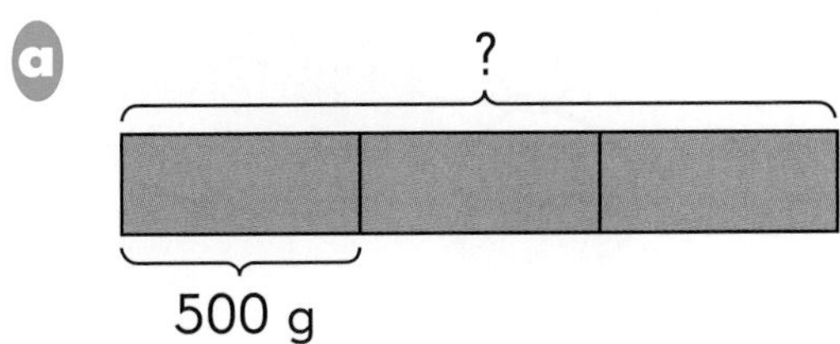

$3 \times 500 = 1{,}500$

The mass of the 3 bags of beans is 1,500 grams.

3 × 5 hundreds = 15 hundreds
15 hundreds = 1,500

b

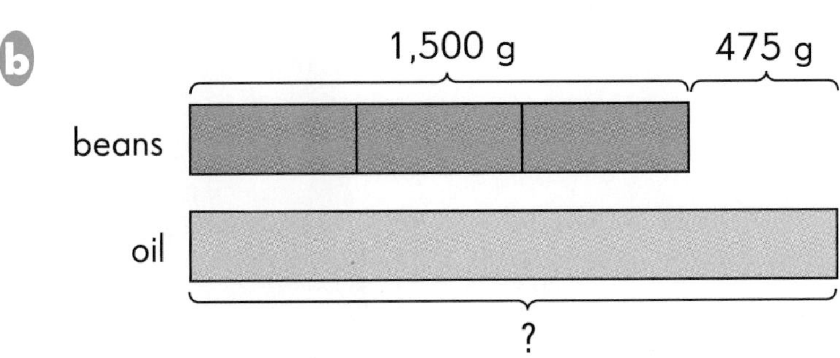

$1{,}500 + 475 = 1{,}975$

$1{,}975 \text{ g} = 1 \text{ kg } 975 \text{ g}$

The mass of the bottle of oil is 1 kilogram 975 grams.

Guided Learning

2 Liza has 780 grams of dried peas.
She uses 330 grams to make pea soup.
Then she packs the remaining peas equally into 5 bags.
Find the mass of each bag of peas.

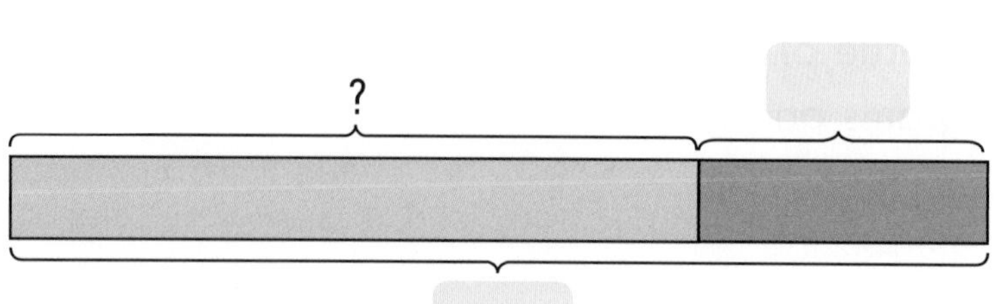

First, find the mass of the remaining peas.

▢ ◯ ▢ = ▢

The mass of the remaining peas is ▢ grams.

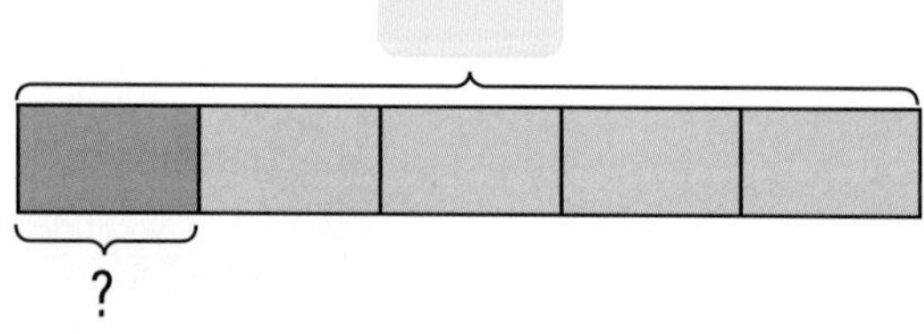

▢ ◯ ▢ = ▢ tens ◯ ▢

= ▢ tens

= ▢

The mass of each bag of peas is ▢ grams.

Learn Solve measurement problems using two operations.

A water cooler contains 27 liters of water.
A teacher uses all the water to completely fill several 3-liter bottles for a science experiment.

a How many bottles does the teacher fill?

b The teacher uses 5 bottles of water for one experiment.
How many bottles of water are left?

a

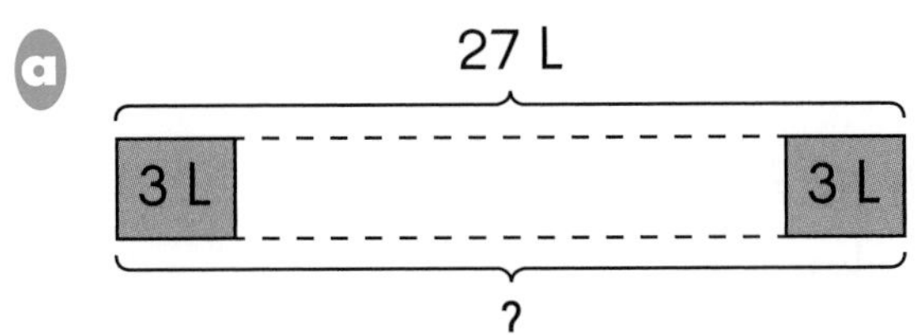

$27 \div 3 = 9$

The teacher fills 9 bottles.

b

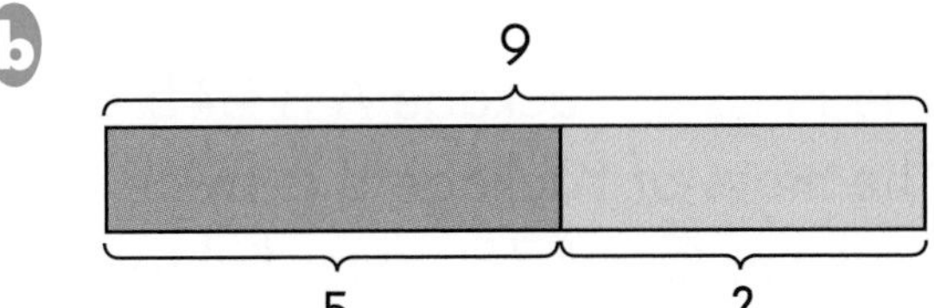

$9 - 5 = 4$

4 bottles of water are left.

Guided Learning

Complete.

3 Ian stacks 5 glasses of juice.
Each glass contains 185 milliliters of juice.

a Find the total volume of juice in the 5 glasses.

b Ian drinks one glass of juice.
How much juice is left?

a 

The total volume of juice in the 5 glasses is ____ milliliters.

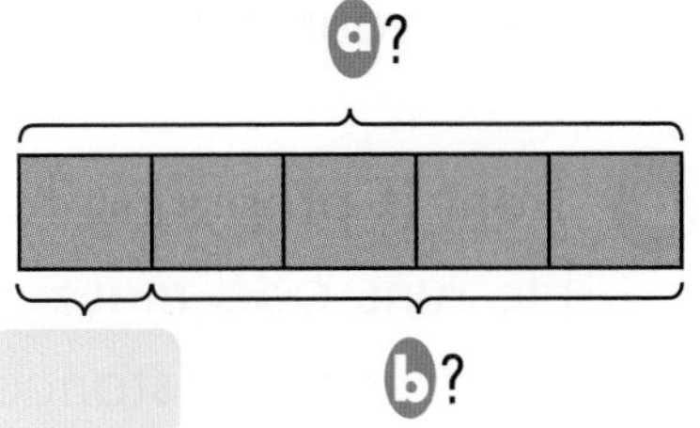

b 

____ milliliters of juice is left.

Let's Practice

Solve. Use bar models to help you.

1. Matt has 95 centimeters of rope.
He cuts 14 centimeters from it.
He then cuts the rest into 3 equal pieces.
What is the length of each piece?

2. The mass of Package A is 245 grams.
The mass of Package B is twice as much as Package A.
Package C is 175 grams lighter than Package B.
Find the mass of Package C.

3. A barrel has 49 liters of water.
Erin adds another 14 liters into the barrel.
She then pours all the water equally into 7 pails.
How much water is in each pail?

4. A green ribbon is 4 meters long.
A red ribbon is 6 times as long as the green ribbon.
Martin cuts the red ribbon into 3 equal pieces.
What is the length of each piece of red ribbon?

5. Mrs. Lee buys a bag of beans and a bag of flour.
The bag of beans is 230 grams.
The bag of flour is 4 times as heavy as the bag of beans.
Find the total mass of the flour and the beans.
Give your answer in kilograms and grams.

6. Trent is preparing for an endurance race.
He runs 685 meters, swims 490 meters, and cycles 900 meters.
What is the distance he covers?
Give your answer in kilometers and meters.

ON YOUR OWN

Go to Workbook B:
Practice 2, pages 45–50

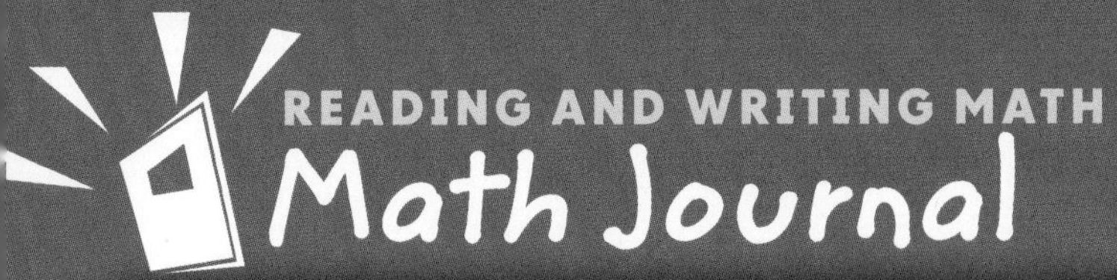

READING AND WRITING MATH

Math Journal

Read the real-world problem. Study the bar models. Then answer the questions.

There are 3 pitchers of cranberry juice on a table.
Each pitcher has 800 milliliters of juice.
All the juice in the 3 pitchers is poured equally into 8 glasses.
How much juice is in each glass?

Dana draws these bar models to solve the real-world problem.

Total amount of juice

800 mL

Amount of juice in each glass

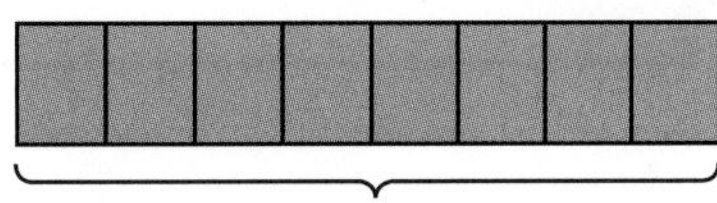

800 mL

Are the bar models correct? Explain your answer.
If the bar models are not correct, draw the correct bar models.

CRITICAL THINKING SKILLS

Put On Your Thinking Cap!

PROBLEM SOLVING

1. Lucas has a 12-liter pail and a 5-liter pail. Explain how he can get the following amount of water using these pails.

   a. 2 liters

   b. 3 liters

ON YOUR OWN

Go to Workbook B: Put On Your Thinking Cap! pages 51—52

Chapter Wrap Up

Study Guide

You have learned...

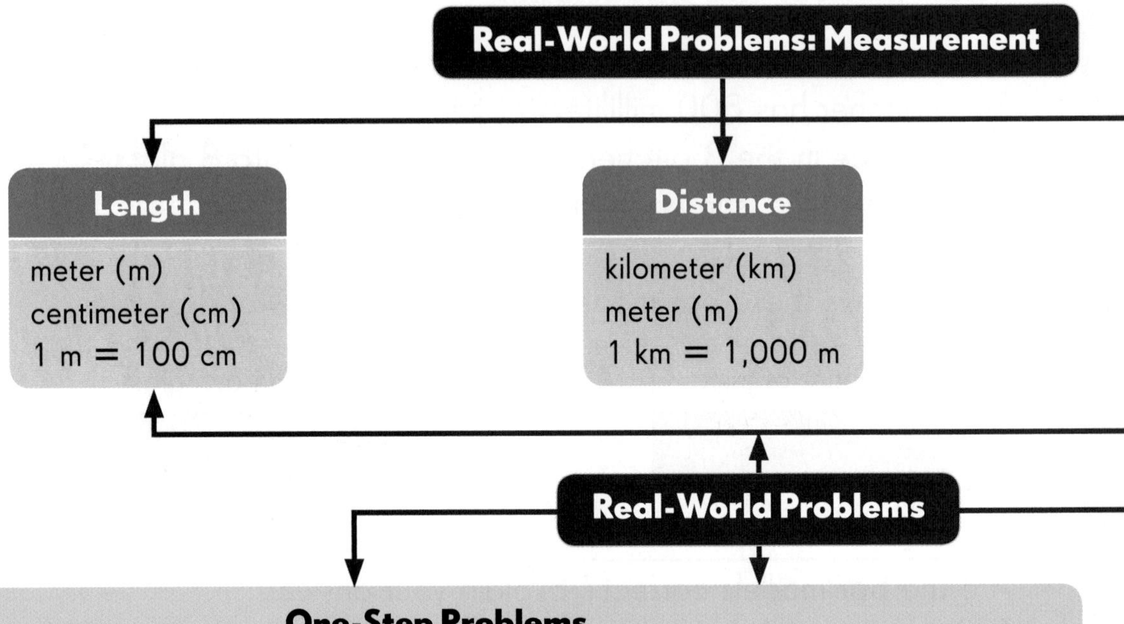

One-Step Problems

Length
Pole A is 134 centimeters long.
Pole B is 103 centimeters long.
Both poles are placed end to end.
What is the total length of both poles?

$134 + 103 = 237$

The total length of both poles is 237 centimeters.

Distance
The distance between Sam's house and his school is 455 meters. The distance between Sam's house and the library is 280 meters. How much nearer is the library than the school to Sam's house?

$455 - 280 = 175$

The library is 175 meters nearer.

Mass
The mass of a block of cheese is 2 kilograms.
Chef Clark buys 16 such blocks of cheese.
What is the mass of cheese Chef Clark buys?

$16 \times 2 = 32$

He buys 32 kilograms of cheese.

Volume
Chloe fills 4 identical tanks completely with 112 liters of water.
What is the volume of water in each tank?

$112 \div 4 = 28$

The volume of water in each tank is 28 liters.

▶ Bar models can be used to solve one- and two-step problems on measurements.

Mass

kilogram (kg)
gram (g)
1 kg = 1,000 g

Volume

liter (L)
milliliter (mL)
1 L = 1,000 mL

Two-Step Problems

Sally has a length of ribbon 2 meters long. She cuts 6 equal pieces from the ribbon and has 110 centimeters left.
What is the length of each of the 6 pieces of ribbon?

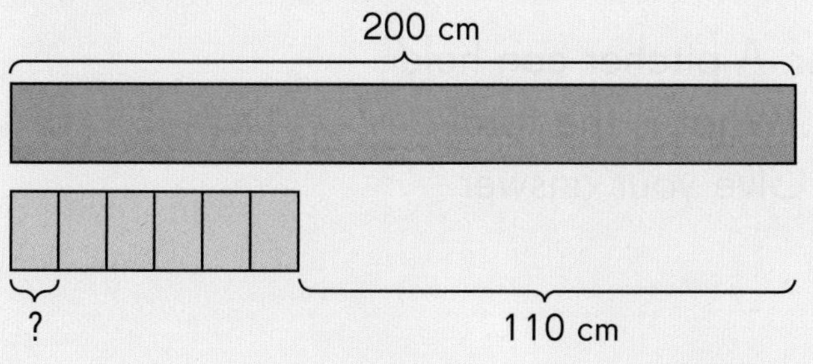

2 m = 200 cm
200 − 110 = 90
90 ÷ 6 = 15

The length of each piece is 15 centimeters.

Joan buys 3 cans of oatmeal and 2 bottles of liquid detergent. The mass of each can of oatmeal is 3 kilograms.
The mass of each bottle of liquid detergent is 500 grams. What is the total mass of the items?

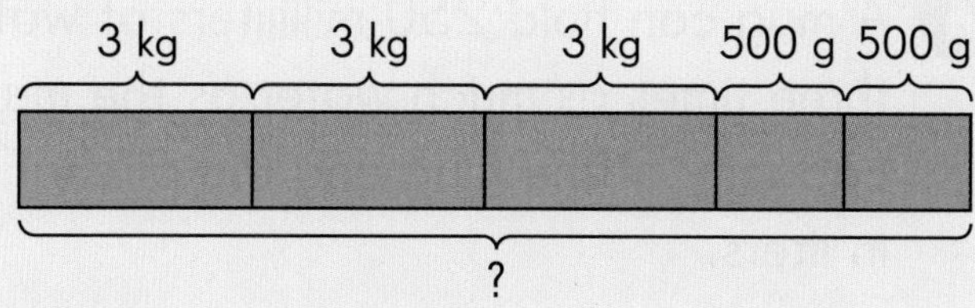

2 × 500 = 1,000
3 + 3 + 3 + 1 = 10

1,000 g = 1 kg

The total mass is 10 kilograms.

Chapter Review/Test

Problem Solving

Solve. Use bar models to help you.

1. The Benaro family is going camping. They want to place two sleeping bags end to end. The lengths of the sleeping bags are 153 centimeters and 167 centimeters. How long does the tent need to be? Give your answer in meters and centimeters.

2. On a road trip, Mr. Stewart drives 850 kilometers from Chicago to Kansas City. He drives another 1,280 kilometers from Kansas City to Houston. What is the total distance he drives?

3. The mass of a package is 210 grams. What is the mass of 4 similar packages?

4. A pot has 950 milliliters of soup. The chef pours all the soup equally into 5 bowls. How much soup is there in each bowl?

5. Mr. Geller pours 135 liters of water equally into 3-liter pails. How many pails does he fill up?

6. A mug can hold 250 milliliters of water. A pitcher can hold three times as much water as the mug. What is the total capacity of the mug and the pitcher? Give your answer in liters.

7. A piece of fabric is 1,030 centimeters long. Mrs. Grey uses some of it to sew 4 similar table runners. There is 190 centimeters of fabric left.

   a. What is the length of fabric used by Mrs. Grey?

   b. What is the length of fabric used for each table runner? Give your answer in meters and centimeters.

Bar Graphs and Line Plots

Lessons

13.1 Making Bar Graphs with Scales
13.2 Reading and Interpreting Bar Graphs
13.3 Line Plots

▶ Bar graphs and line plots help to organize data. Bar graphs are used to compare data. Line plots show how data is spread out.

Recall Prior Knowledge

Using a picture graph to represent data

Four friends made some posters.

The picture graph shows the number of posters made by the four friends.

Number of Posters Made

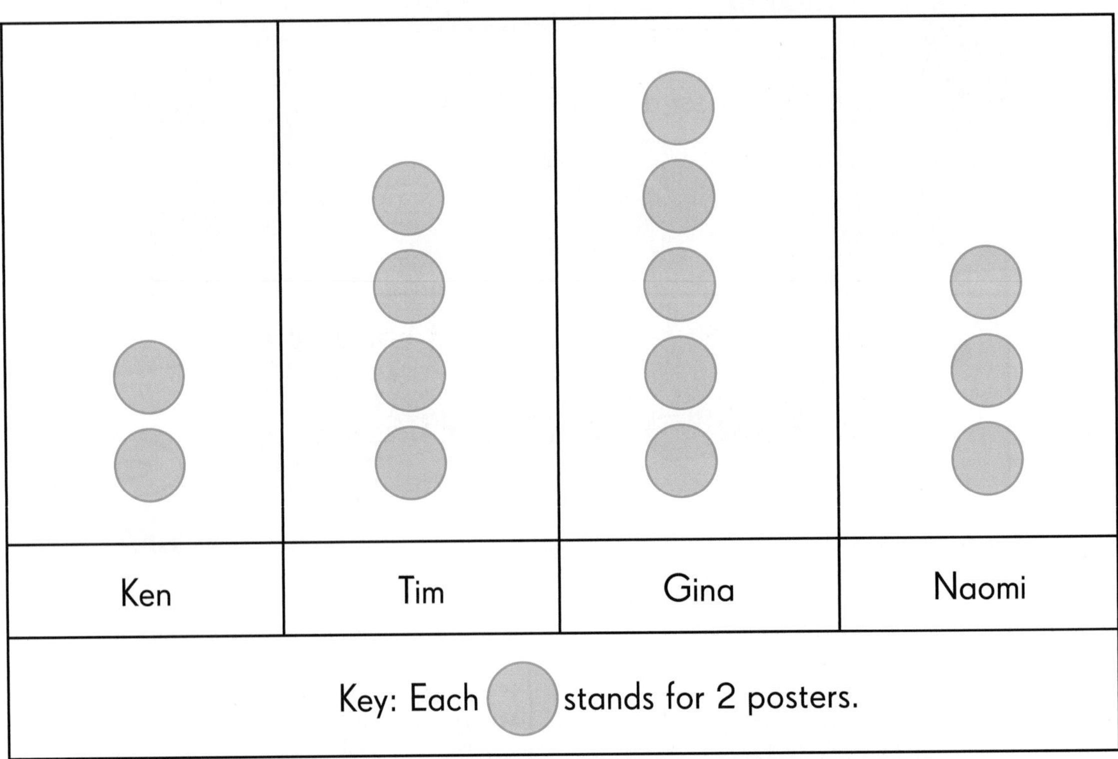

A picture graph shows information (data) using pictures and symbols.
The key shows what each symbol, or picture, stands for.

Ken made 4 posters.
Tim made 8 posters.
Gina made 4 more posters than Naomi.
The four friends made 28 posters in all.

Using a bar graph to represent data

The tally chart shows the kinds of fruits in Sara's picnic basket.

Fruits in Sara's Picnic Basket

Kind of Fruit	Tally	Number of Fruits
plum	///	3
pear	////	4
orange	~~////~~ //	7

She used the data in the tally chart to draw a bar graph.

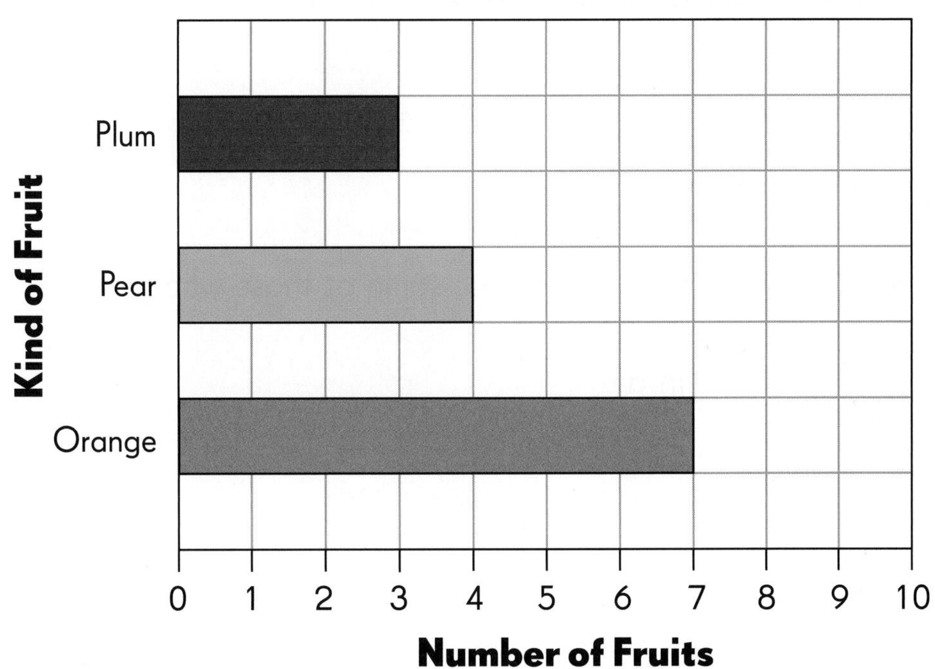

The bar graphs shows that Sara has 4 pears and 3 plums. She has a total of 14 pieces of fruit in her picnic basket.

Miguel is helping his teacher to find his classmates' favorite colors. The picture graph shows the number of classmates who like each color.

Favorite Colors

Red	Green	Blue	Purple

Key: Each stands for 3 friends.

Complete. Use the picture graph to help you.

1. ____ is the color chosen most often.
2. There are ____ classmates who like purple.
3. The number of classmates who like ____ is the same as those who like ____ .
4. Miguel has ____ classmates in all.

The tally chart shows the kinds and number of animals that are found at a zoo.

Complete the tally chart.

5 **Animals in the Zoo**

Kind of Animal	Tally	Number of Animals
Polar Bear	//	
Elephant	////	
Penguin	~~////~~ ///	
Dolphin	~~////~~	

Complete the bar graph. Use the data in the tally chart.

6

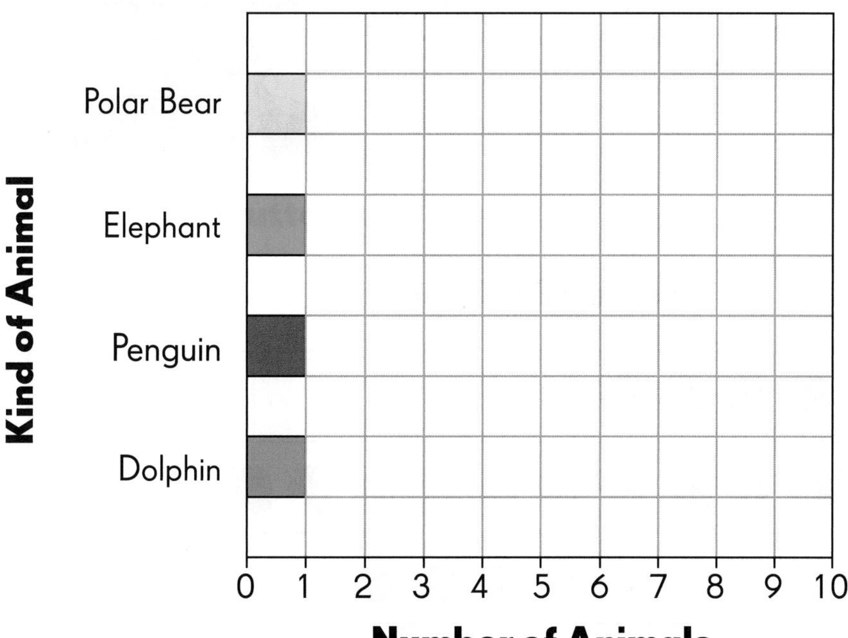

Read and interpret the bar graph.

7 There are ______ more penguins than elephants.

8 There are ______ fewer polar bears than dolphins.

9 There are ______ elephants and polar bears in the zoo.

Then Linda redraws Melissa's vertical graph as a **horizontal** graph.

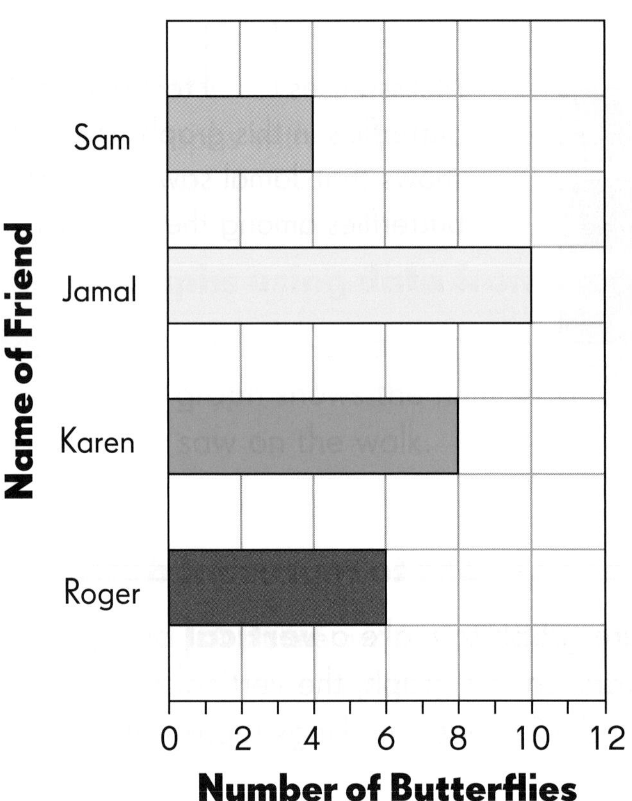

A bar graph uses vertical or horizontal bars to show data. The length of each bar represents a value. This can be read from the scale marked on the axis of the graph.

Linda's graph uses a scale of 2. It starts with 0 and skips in twos. The greatest number on the scale is 12 because it needs to include all the data.

Guided Learning

The bar graph shows the data in the tally chart.

Our Model Cars

Name	Tally	Number of Model Cars
Ken	~~IIII~~ I	6
Tasha	~~IIII~~ III	8
Bryan	~~IIII~~ ~~IIII~~ II	12
Pat	II	2

Find the missing data.

1

Our Model Cars

The scale on the bar graph has skips of ____.

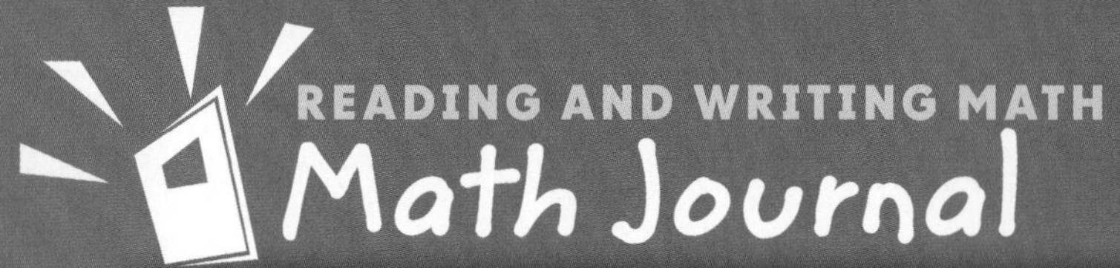

King Elementary School has a field day each year. Groups of students take part in the field day. The table shows the number of medals won by each group.

Medals Won

Group	Number of Medals
Evergreen	10
Birch	14
Maple	18
Gum	12
Bay	16

Make a bar graph that displays the data in the table.

Follow the steps to make your graph.

STEP 1 Use grid paper.
Give the bar graph a title.
Label the vertical and horizontal axes of the graph.

STEP 2 Choose a suitable scale to show the number of medals won.
Start with 0 and then complete the scale.

STEP 3 Draw the bars.
Choose a different color for each bar.

STEP 4 Check the length of the bars against the data to be sure the lengths are correct.

Answer each question.

1. How did you decide on a scale for your graph? Explain your answer.

2. What is the greatest number for your scale? Explain why.

3. Only groups that won 10 or more medals are shown in the table on page 88. In all, 100 medals were won. How many medals are not shown in the table? Explain your answer.

Conduct a survey within each group to find the total number of letters found in each classmate's whole name. (This includes the family name.)

Tally the results and record the findings below.

Letters in Each Classmate's Whole Name

Name of Student	Tally	Number of Letters

On a grid paper, make a bar graph that displays the above data effectively.

Ask your classmates questions based on your bar graph.

Let's Practice

Justin and his friends are folding paper objects.

The number of each type of paper object made is shown below.

18 paper airplanes

15 paper balls

21 paper boats

12 paper cranes

6 paper frogs

Use a copy of the bar graph.

Help Justin show the number of paper objects on the graph.

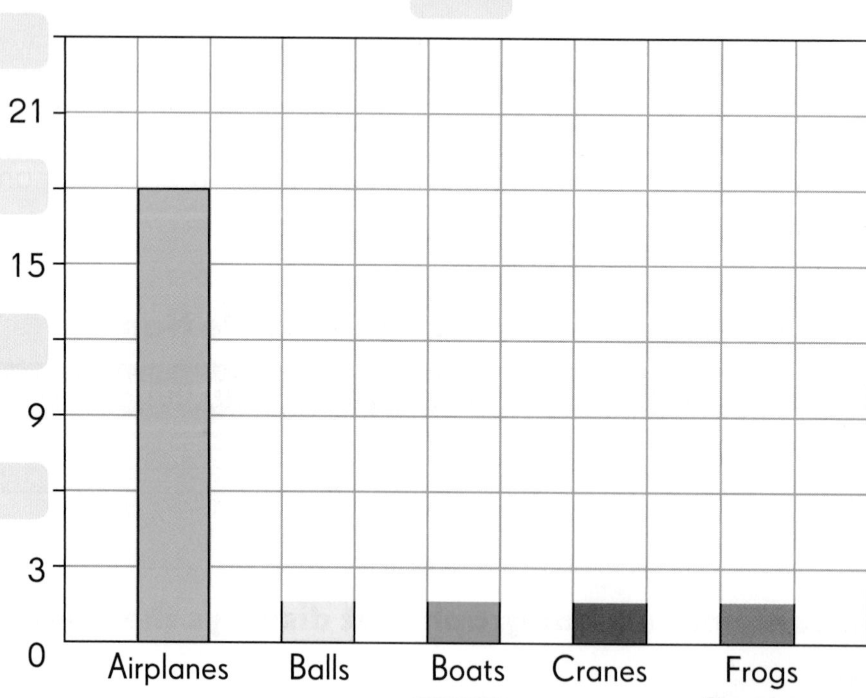

2 What number does the scale skip by?

ON YOUR OWN

Go to Workbook B: Practice 1, pages 61–68

Reading and Interpreting Bar Graphs

Lesson Objectives

- Read and interpret data from bar graphs.
- Solve problems using bar graphs.

Learn Read and interpret bar graphs to solve problems.

Tricia sold tickets from Monday to Friday last week.
She drew a bar graph to show the number of tickets she sold each day.

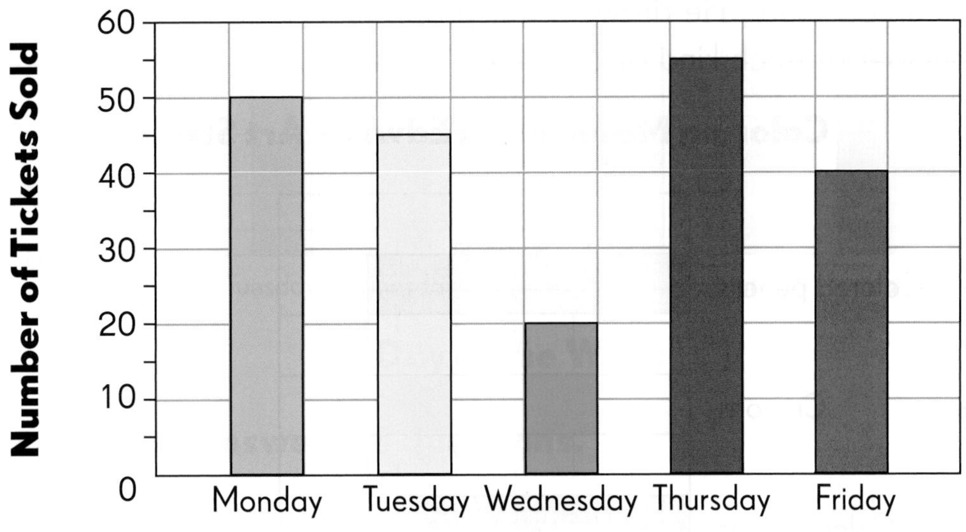

a. How many tickets did Tricia sell on Monday?
Tricia sold 50 tickets on Monday.

b. On which day did Tricia sell 45 tickets?
She sold 45 tickets on Tuesday.

c. On which day did she sell the least number of tickets?
She sold the least on Wednesday.

Use line plots to organize data.

Martha conducted a survey. She wanted to find out the number of hours her classmates spent on homework each day. She recorded her data in a table.

Number of Hours Spent on Homework

Number of Hours	Number of Classmates
1	2
2	3
3	5
4	2

A line plot is an easy way to organize data. It makes it easy to see how the data is grouped, compared, and spread.

Then she displayed her data in a line plot.

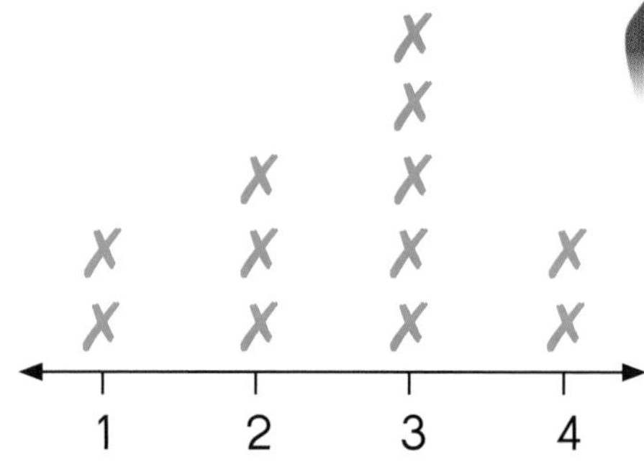

Number of Hours Spent on Homework

Martha found that five of her classmates spent 3 hours on their homework each day.

Five classmates spent less than 3 hours on their homework. Martha surveyed a total of 12 classmates.

The greatest number of hours spent on homework is 4. The same number of classmates spent the least and greatest number of hours on their homework.

Guided Learning

A carnival recorded the number of games won by each player at one booth.
Numbers of games won — 3, 5, 2, 1, 3, 1, 3, 3, 3, 2, 2, 1, 1, 1, 2, 4, 4, 3.

Complete the table.

Number of Games Won

Number of Games Won	Number of People
1	
	4
3	
4	
	1

8. **Show the data in a line plot. Remember to give your line plot a title.**

Answer each question. Use the data in your line plot.

9. How many people won exactly 2 games? ______ people

10. How many people won more than 1 game? ______ people

11. How many people were surveyed in all? ______ people

12. What is the most frequent number of games won? ______ games

13. ______ as many people won 2 games as the number of people who won 4 games.

14. Three times as many people won ______ games as the number of people who won ______ games.

Hands-On Activity

WORKING TOGETHER

Conduct a survey to find the number of pieces of fruit your classmates eat in a week.

1. Use the tally chart to record your findings.

Number of pieces of ___	Tally	Number of ___

2. Then show the data in a line plot.
   Remember to give it a title.

3. Write three statements about the data shown in the line plot.

What does each ✗ stand for?
What do the numbers on the number line stand for?

What is the greatest number of pieces of fruit eaten in a week?
What is the least number of pieces of fruit eaten in a week?

Let's Practice

Solve.

The tally chart shows the number of football games a group of people watched in a season.

Complete the tally chart.

1 **Number of Football Games Watched**

Number of Football Games	Tally	Number of People
0	𝍸	5
1					
2						
3			
4				

2 **Show the data in a line plot. Remember to give it a title.**

Answer each question. Use the data in your line plot.

3 How many people watched three or more football games? ____ people

4 How many people did not watch any football games? ____ people

5 **a** Did more people watch 2 football games or 4 football games in a season?

____ football games

b How many more? ____ more

6 What was the most common number of football games watched?

____ football games

Kim conducted a survey to find the number of paintbrushes her friends use for an art lesson. The table shows the results of her survey.

Number of Paintbrushes Used for Art Lesson

Name of Friend	Number of Paintbrushes
Renee	3
Lynn	5
Sam	2
Joy	2
Debra	2
Joe	5

7 **Show the data on a line plot.**
Remember to give it a title.

Answer each question. Use your line plot to help you.

8 Which numbers will she mark on the horizontal line of the line plot? ____

9 What do the Xs on the line plot stand for? ____

10 How many Xs are marked on the line plot? ____

11 How many friends use 5 paintbrushes? ____ friends

12 How many paintbrushes do most friends use?
____ paintbrushes

13 **a** Look at the tally chart. Find the total number of paintbrushes used by Kim's friends. ____ paintbrushes

b If each paintbrush costs \$2, how much was spent in all? \$____

ON YOUR OWN

Go to Workbook B:
Practice 3, pages 75–82

CRITICAL THINKING SKILLS

Put On Your Thinking Cap!

PROBLEM SOLVING

Study the information.

Mary Lou noticed that 18 classmates are wearing yellow shirts. There were 7 more classmates wearing red shirts than blue shirts. There were 10 fewer classmates wearing blue shirts than yellow shirts.

Read bar graphs A, B, and C carefully. Which of the bar graphs shows **all** the given information **correctly**? Explain your answer.

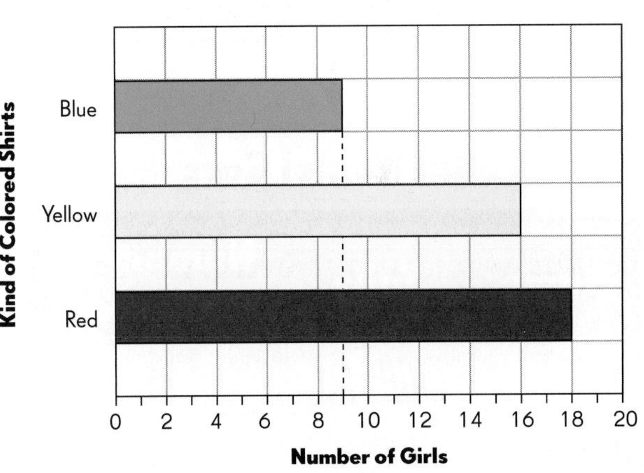

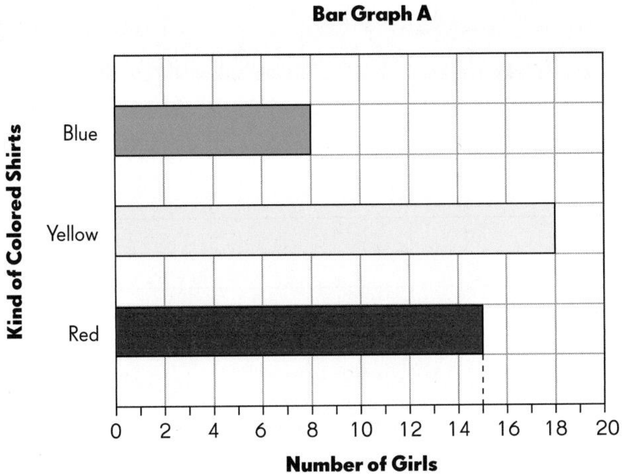

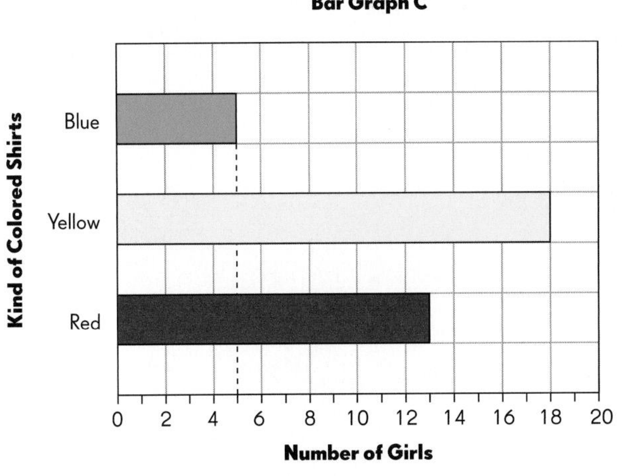

ON YOUR OWN

Go to Workbook B: Put On Your Thinking Cap! pages 87–90

Chapter Wrap Up

Study Guide

You have learned...

Bar Graphs and Line Plots

Tally Chart

A tally chart is used to record and organize data. A tally mark on the chart stands for 1 of something.

Our Model Cars

Name	Tally	Number of Model cars
Ken	~~////~~ /	6
Tasha	///	3
Bryan	~~////~~ ////	9
Pat	///	3

Line Plots

A line plot is used to show the spread of data points.

Number of birthday cards received – 4, 5, 5, 6, 6, 6

Number of Birthday Cards Received

Number of Birthday Cards	Number of Friends
4	1
5	2
6	3

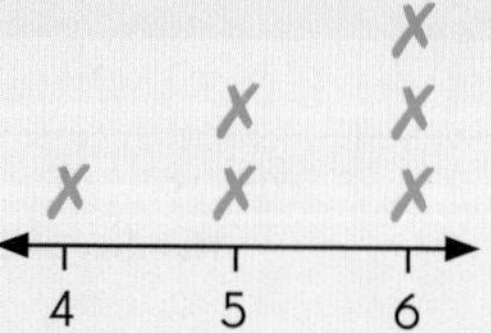

Number of Birthday Cards Received

Each ✗ stands for 1 friend.
The numbers 4 to 6 show the number of birthday cards received.

▶ Bar graphs and line plots help to organize data. Bar graphs are used to compare data. Line plots show how data is spread out.

Bar Graph

A bar graph uses bars to show data. The scales show the value of the bars.

Favorite Fruits

Favorite Fruit	Apple	Peach	Orange	Pear
Number of Children	10	15	25	20

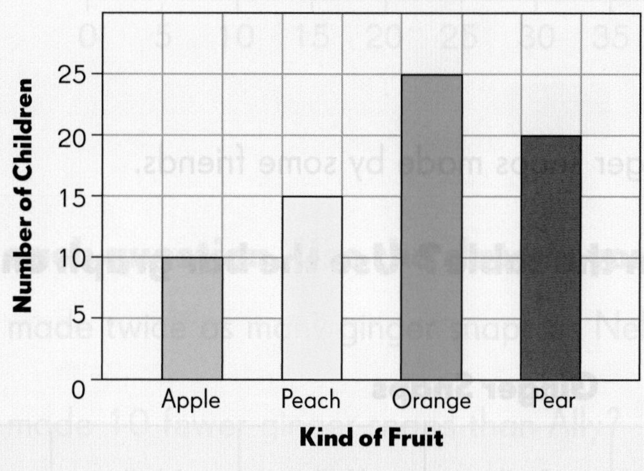

Read and interpret data.

Guided Learning

Complete.

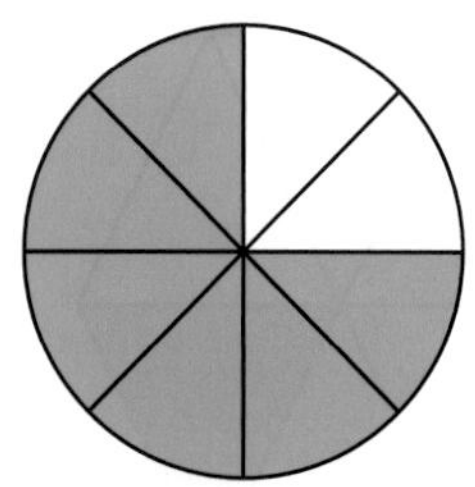

11 ___ of the circle is shaded.

12 The numerator of the fraction is ___ .

13 The denominator of the fraction is ___ .

Let's Practice

What fraction is shaded? Choose the correct answers.

1 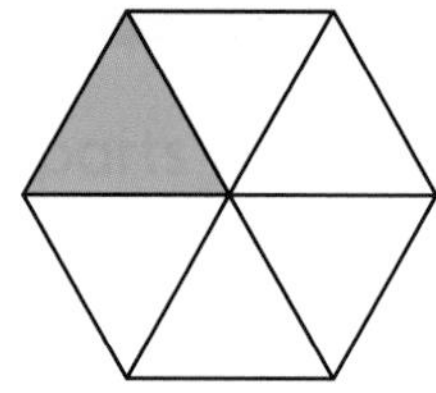

$\frac{1}{6}$	one-seventh	one-sixth	$\frac{1}{7}$

Complete.

Jane wants to make a number train with 10 . She starts by connecting 7 .

2 She needs to connect ___ more  to complete the train.

3 What fraction of the number train has she already connected? ___

4 What fraction of the cubes has she not yet connected? ___

5 ___ and ___ together make 1 whole.

ON YOUR OWN

Go to Workbook B: Practice 1, pages 91–92

Lesson

14.2 Understanding Equivalent Fractions

Lesson Objectives

- Use models to identify equivalent fractions.
- Use a number line to identify equivalent fractions.

Vocabulary
equivalent fractions
number line

Learn

What are equivalent fractions?

Look at the fraction strips.

1							
$\frac{1}{2}$				$\frac{1}{2}$			
$\frac{1}{4}$		$\frac{1}{4}$		$\frac{1}{4}$		$\frac{1}{4}$	
$\frac{1}{8}$	$\frac{1}{8}$	$\frac{1}{8}$	$\frac{1}{8}$	$\frac{1}{8}$	$\frac{1}{8}$	$\frac{1}{8}$	$\frac{1}{8}$

One whole

1 out of 2 equal parts $= \frac{1}{2}$

2 out of 4 equal parts $= \frac{2}{4}$

4 out of 8 equal parts $= \frac{4}{8}$

The fractions $\frac{1}{2}$, $\frac{2}{4}$, and $\frac{4}{8}$ have different numerators and denominators.

But $\frac{1}{2}$ is equal to $\frac{2}{4}$.

$\frac{1}{2}$ is also equal to $\frac{4}{8}$.

$\frac{1}{2}$, $\frac{2}{4}$, and $\frac{4}{8}$ are called **equivalent fractions**.

$\frac{1}{2}$, $\frac{2}{4}$, and $\frac{4}{8}$ name the same parts of a whole.

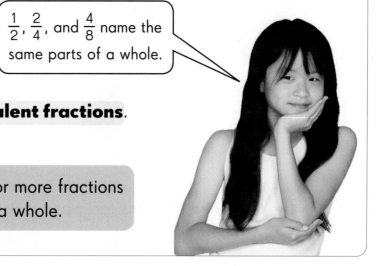

Equivalent fractions are two or more fractions that name the same parts of a whole.

Hands-On Activity

WORK IN PAIRS

Materials:
- 3 paper strips of the same size

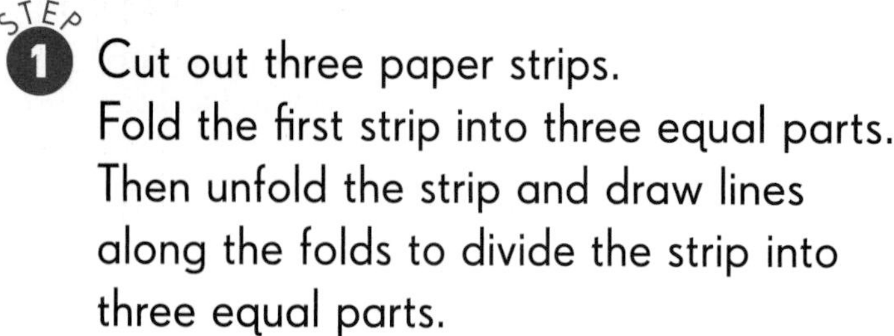

STEP **1** Cut out three paper strips.
Fold the first strip into three equal parts.
Then unfold the strip and draw lines along the folds to divide the strip into three equal parts.

STEP **2** Shade one part of the strip.

You get the shaded fraction $\frac{1}{3}$.

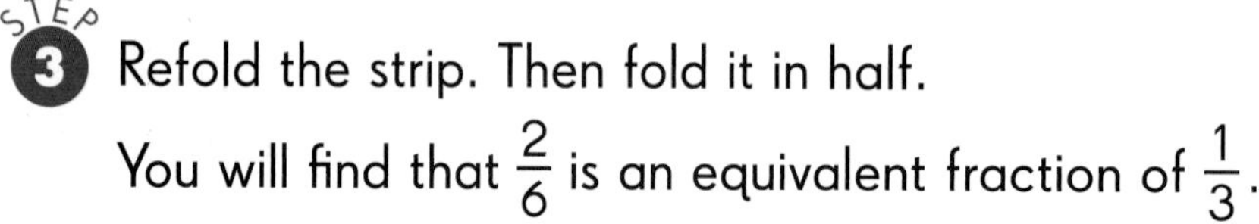

STEP **3** Refold the strip. Then fold it in half.

You will find that $\frac{2}{6}$ is an equivalent fraction of $\frac{1}{3}$.

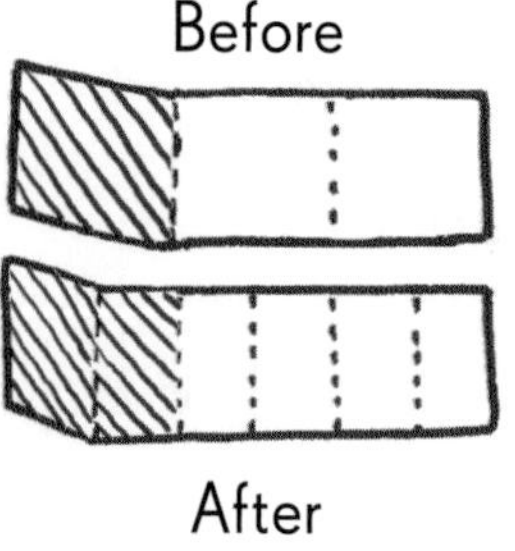

STEP **4** Make shaded fractions for $\frac{1}{4}$ and $\frac{3}{4}$ with the remaining paper strips.

Fold these strips again to find equivalent fractions.

Guided Learning

Find the equivalent fractions.

$\frac{2}{3}$ of the bar is shaded.

1. $\frac{2}{3} = \frac{\square}{6}$

2. $\frac{2}{3} = \frac{\square}{9}$

Find the missing numerators and denominators.

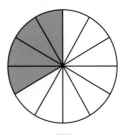

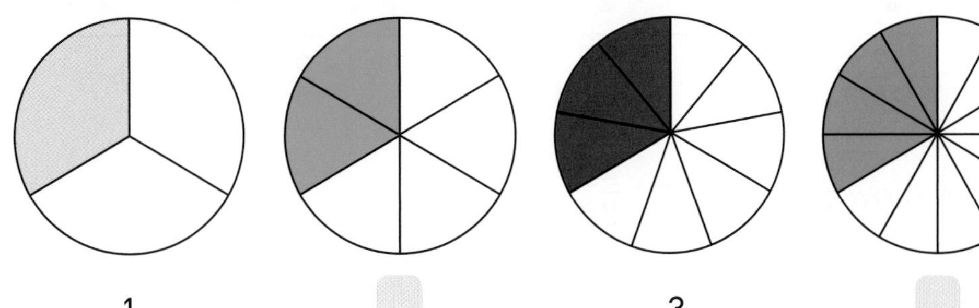

3. $\frac{1}{3} = \frac{\square}{6} = \frac{3}{\square} = \frac{\square}{\square}$

Hands-On Activity

Use grid paper.

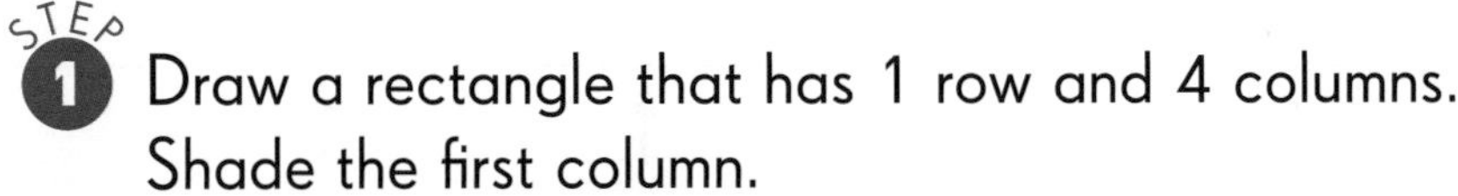

STEP 1 Draw a rectangle that has 1 row and 4 columns. Shade the first column.

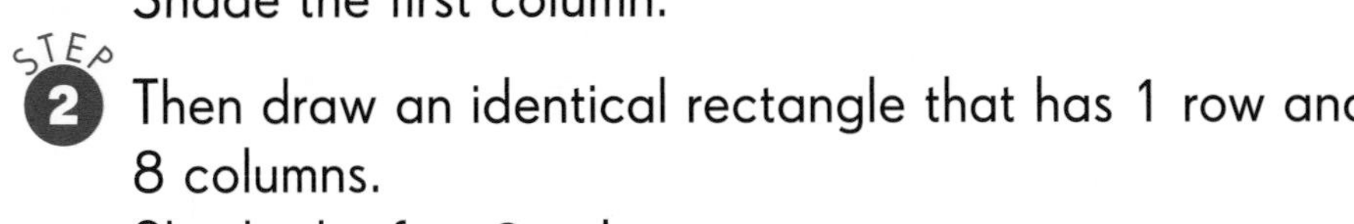

STEP 2 Then draw an identical rectangle that has 1 row and 8 columns. Shade the first 2 columns.

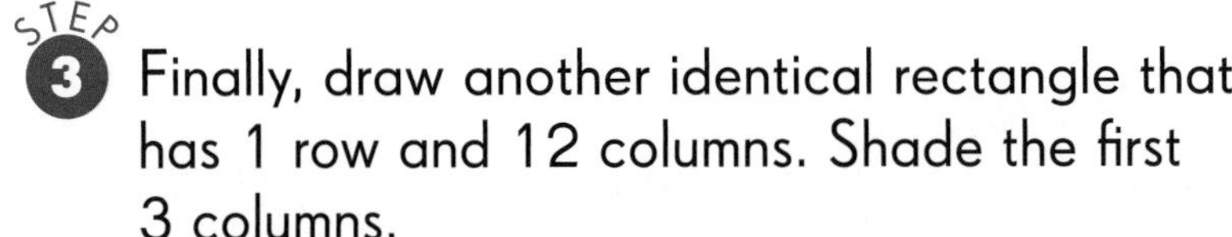

STEP 3 Finally, draw another identical rectangle that has 1 row and 12 columns. Shade the first 3 columns.

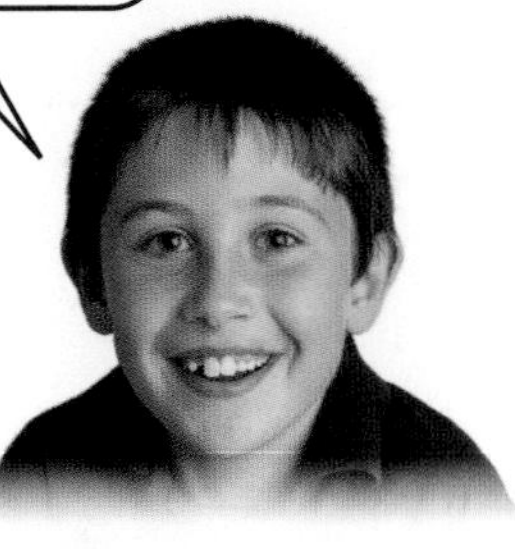

All three rectangles should be of the same width and height.

What do you notice about the shaded parts?
What fraction of each rectangle is shaded?

Learn Use a number line to find equivalent fractions.

Look at the **number lines**.

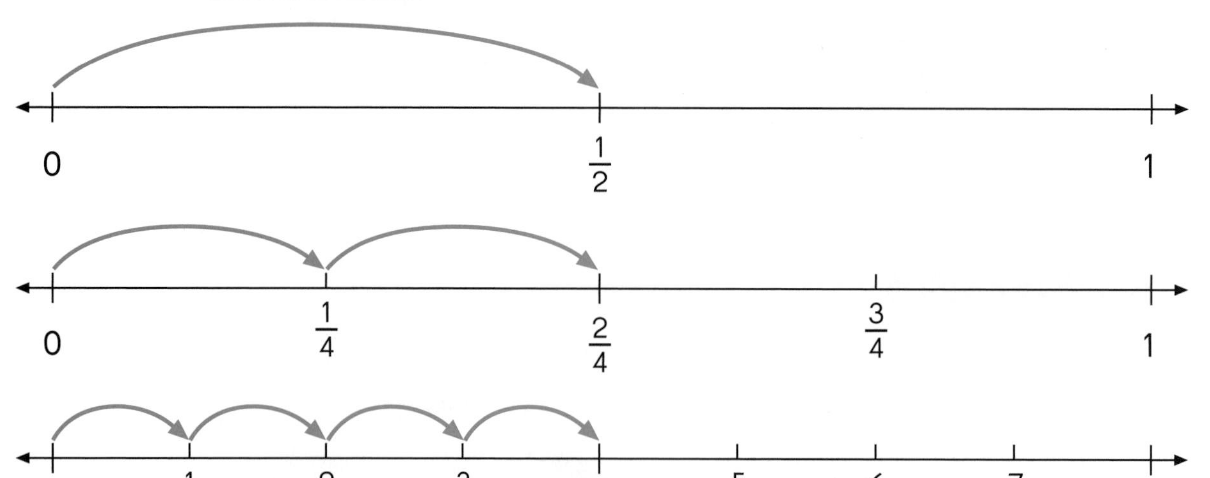

The number lines show $\frac{1}{2} = \frac{2}{4} = \frac{4}{8}$.

Guided Learning

Copy the number lines on grid paper.
Fill in the missing fractions on the number lines.
Use the number lines to find the equivalent fractions.

4

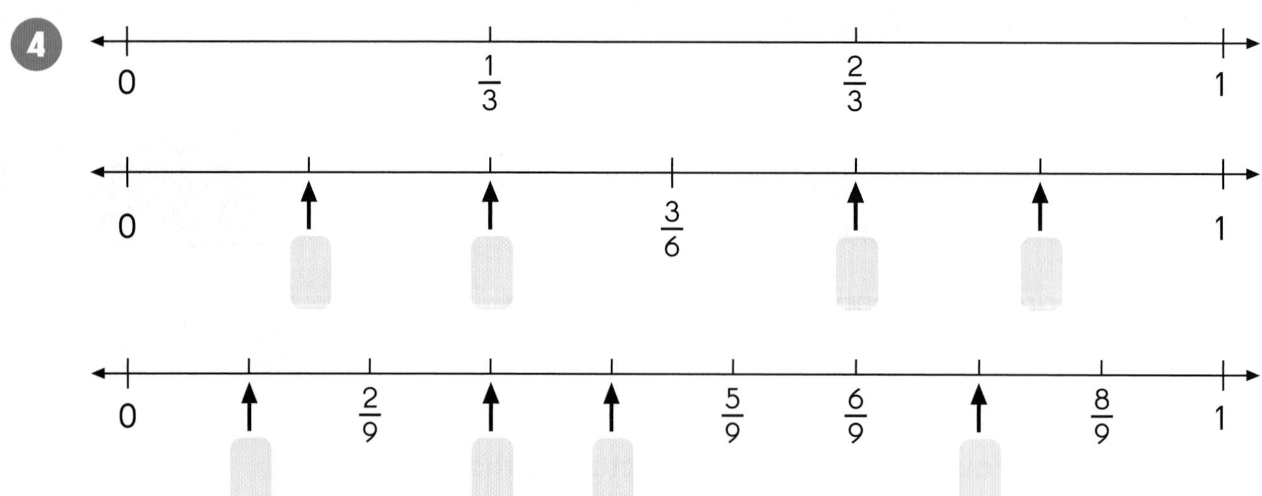

5 $\frac{1}{3} = \frac{?}{?} = \frac{?}{?}$

6 $\frac{2}{3} = \frac{?}{?} = \frac{?}{?}$

Let's Practice

Find equivalent fractions of $\frac{2}{5}$.

1 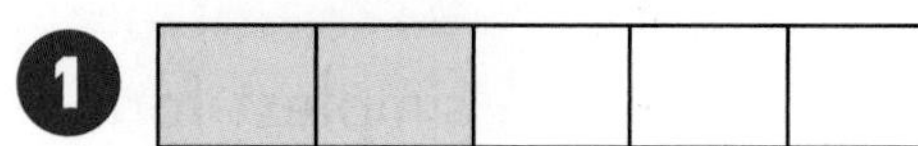 $\frac{2}{5}$

$\frac{2}{5} = \frac{\square}{\square}$

$\frac{2}{5} = \frac{\square}{\square}$

Use a fraction strip to find two fractions equivalent to $\frac{1}{6}$.

2 

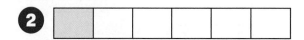

Use the number lines to find equivalent fractions of $\frac{1}{5}$.

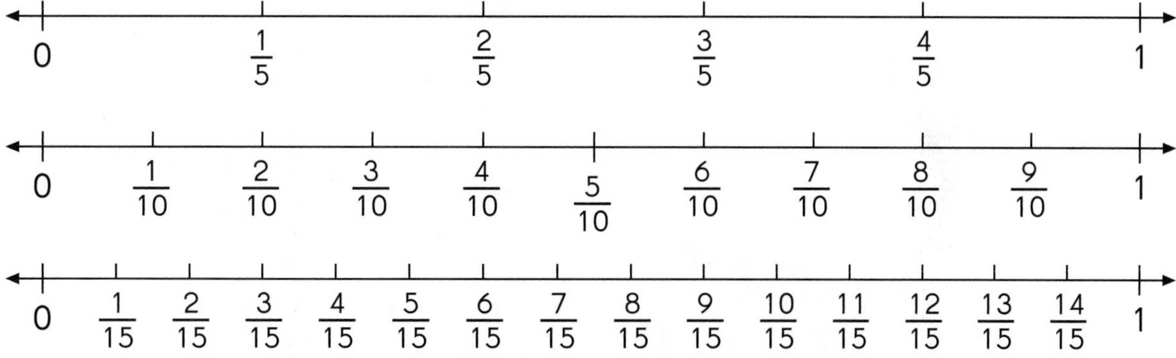

3 $\frac{1}{5} = \frac{\square}{10} = \frac{\square}{15}$

ON YOUR OWN

Go to Workbook B: Practice 2, pages 93–96

Lesson 14.3

More Equivalent Fractions

Lesson Objectives

- Use multiplication and division to find equivalent fractions.
- Write fractions in simplest form.

Vocabulary
simplest form

Learn

Use multiplication to find equivalent fractions.

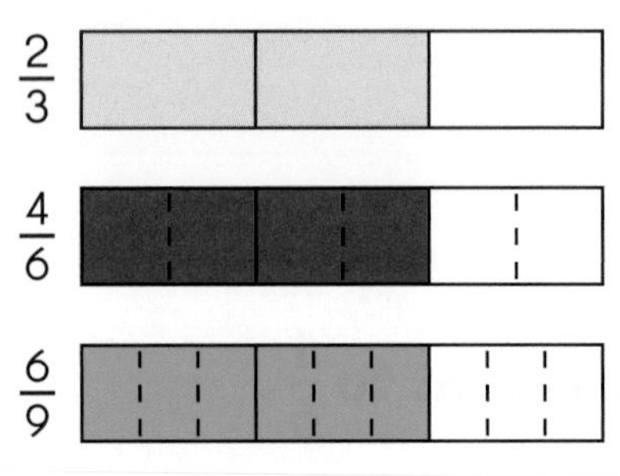

The models show that $\frac{2}{3} = \frac{4}{6} = \frac{6}{9} = \frac{8}{12}$.

I know another way to find an equivalent fraction. Multiply the numerator and the denominator by the same number.

$$\frac{2}{3} = \frac{2 \times 2}{3 \times 2} = \frac{4}{6}$$

$$\frac{2}{3} = \frac{2 \times 3}{3 \times 3} = \frac{6}{9}$$

Multiply the numerator and denominator of $\frac{2}{3}$ by 4 to get $\frac{8}{12}$.

Guided Learning

Use models and multiplication to find equivalent fractions.

1 models

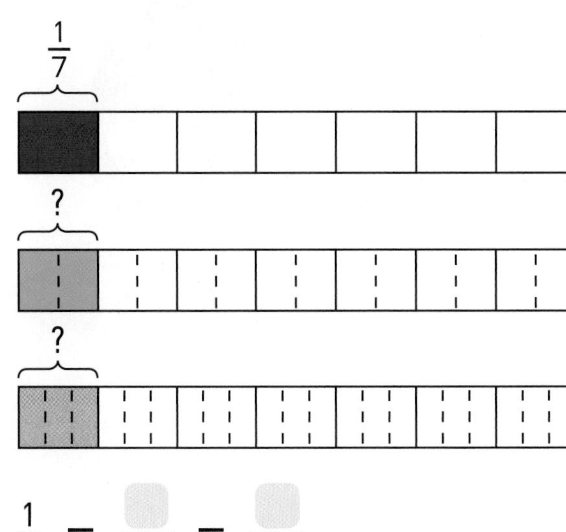

$\frac{1}{7} = \frac{\square}{\square} = \frac{\square}{\square}$

2 multiplication

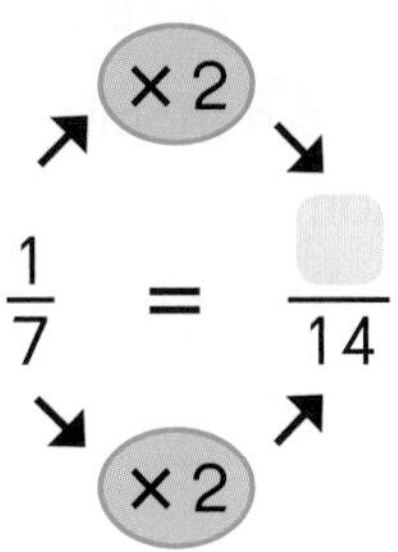

×3

$\frac{1}{7} = \frac{\square}{21}$

×3

$\frac{1}{7} = \frac{\square}{\square} = \frac{\square}{\square}$

Learn Use division to find a fraction in simplest form.

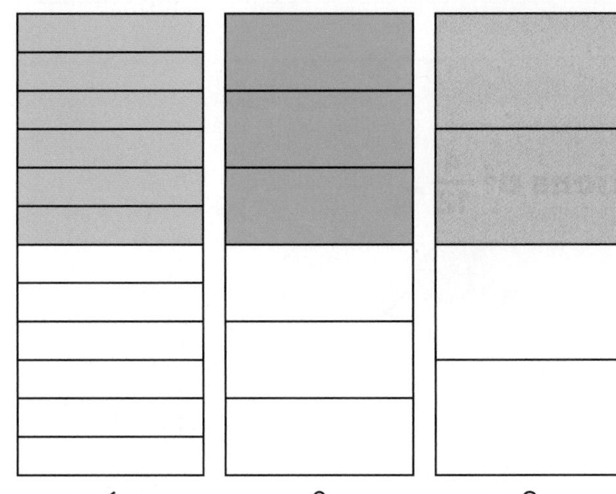

$\frac{6}{12}$ $\frac{3}{6}$ $\frac{2}{4}$

The models show that $\frac{6}{12} = \frac{3}{6} = \frac{2}{4}$.

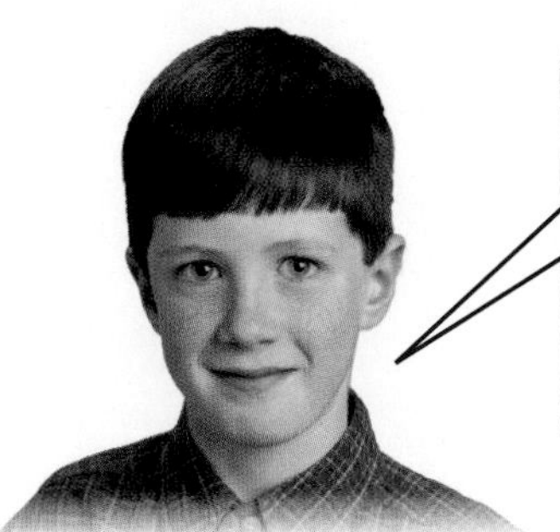

Here is another way to find equivalent fractions. Divide the numerator and the denominator by the same number.

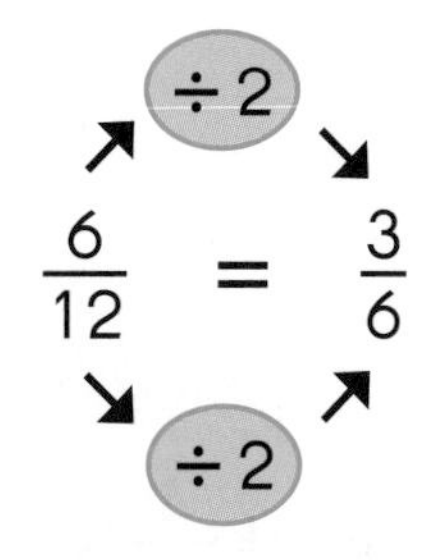

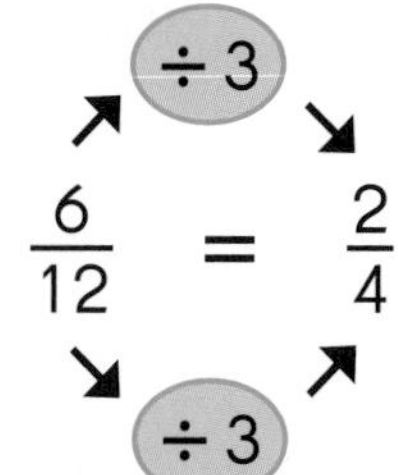

Continued on next page

Is $\frac{2}{4}$ the simplest fraction equivalent to $\frac{6}{12}$?

$$\frac{2}{4} \xrightarrow{\div 2} \frac{1}{2}$$

$$\frac{2}{4} = \frac{1}{2}$$

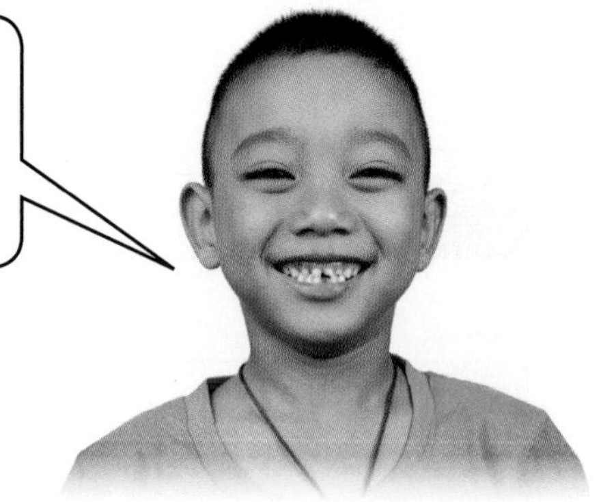

No, you can divide the numerator and denominator of $\frac{2}{4}$ by the same number further.

$\frac{1}{2}$ is the **simplest form** of $\frac{2}{4}$.

The simplest fraction equivalent to $\frac{6}{12}$ is $\frac{1}{2}$.

Use division to find a fraction in its simplest form.

Guided Learning

Divide to find the equivalent fractions of $\frac{4}{12}$.

3 ÷ 2 (numerator and denominator)

$$\frac{4}{12} = \frac{\square}{6}$$

÷ 4 (numerator and denominator)

$$\frac{4}{12} = \frac{1}{\square}$$

$$\frac{4}{12} = \frac{\square}{6} \qquad \frac{4}{12} = \frac{1}{\square}$$

The simplest form of $\frac{4}{12}$ is $\square$.

Let's Practice

Find the equivalent fractions.

1

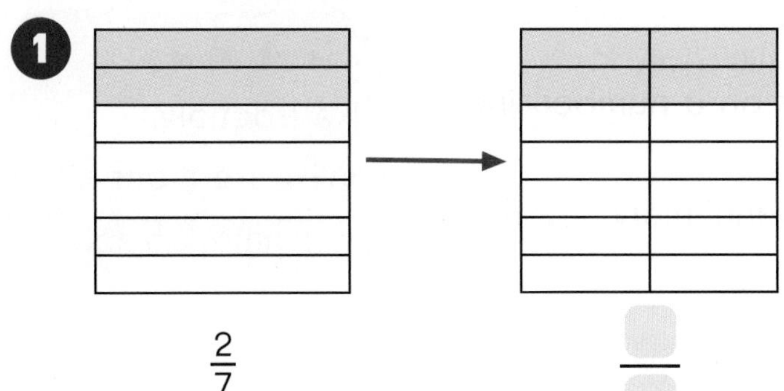

$\frac{2}{7}$ → $\frac{\square}{\square}$

$\frac{2}{7} \xrightarrow{\times 2} \frac{\square}{\square}$ (numerator × 2, denominator × 2)

$\frac{2}{7}$ is equivalent to $\frac{\square}{\square}$.

2

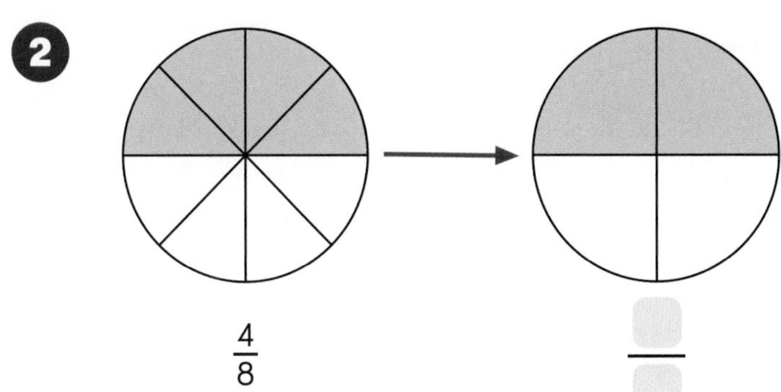

$\frac{4}{8}$ → $\frac{\square}{\square}$

$\frac{4}{8} \xrightarrow{\div 2} \frac{\square}{\square}$ (numerator ÷ 2, denominator ÷ 2)

$\frac{4}{8}$ is equivalent to $\frac{\square}{\square}$.

Find the first eight fractions equivalent to $\frac{5}{6}$.

3 $\frac{5}{6} = \frac{\square}{\square} = \frac{\square}{\square} = \frac{\square}{\square} = \frac{\square}{\square} = \frac{\square}{\square} = \frac{\square}{\square} = \frac{\square}{\square} = \frac{\square}{\square}$

ON YOUR OWN

Go to Workbook B: Practice 3, pages 97–100

Lesson

14.4 Comparing Fractions

Lesson Objectives

- Show fractions as points or distances on a number line.
- Compare and order fractions.
- Compare and order fractions using benchmark fractions.

Vocabulary
like fractions
unlike fractions
benchmark fraction

Learn

Fractions on a Number Line

A rectangle is divided into 4 equal parts.

Each part is $\frac{1}{4}$.

$\frac{1}{4}$	$\frac{1}{4}$	$\frac{1}{4}$	$\frac{1}{4}$

This fraction bar is shown on the number line.

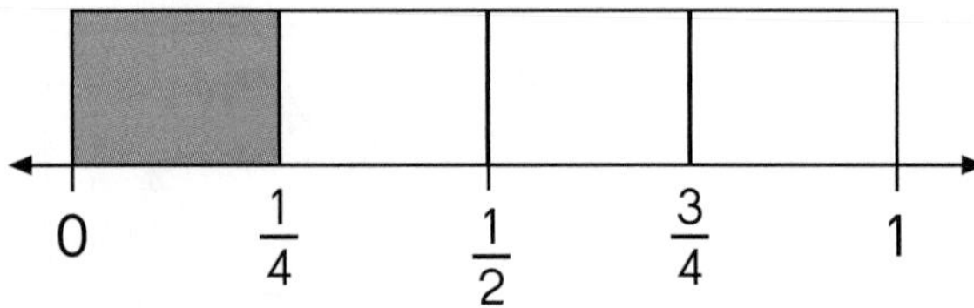

Guided Learning

Complete.

1. Show $\frac{4}{5}$ on the number line using fraction bars.

   $\frac{4}{5}$ is the same as 4 groups of $\frac{1}{5}$.

   Complete the number line to show $\frac{4}{5}$.

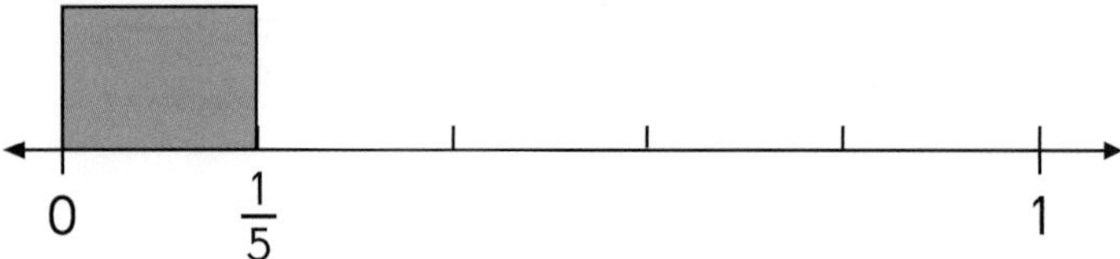

Learn: Compare fractions using pictures and number lines.

Zoe served $\frac{1}{2}$ of a vegetarian pie.

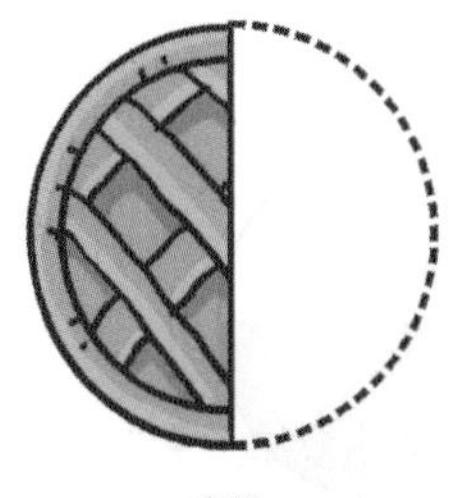

$\frac{1}{2}$

You can only compare fractions from the same whole or equal-sized wholes.

Lisa served $\frac{3}{4}$ of an equal-sized vegetarian pie.

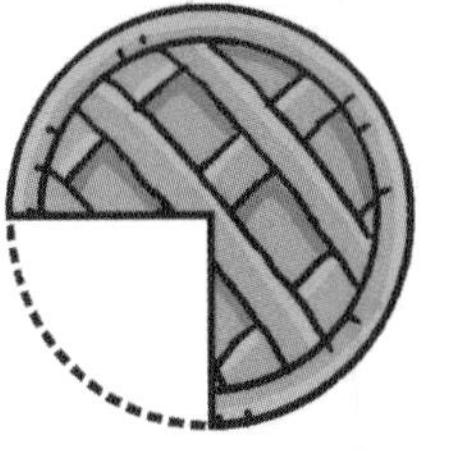

$\frac{3}{4}$

Abby served $\frac{1}{4}$ of another equal-sized vegetarian pie.

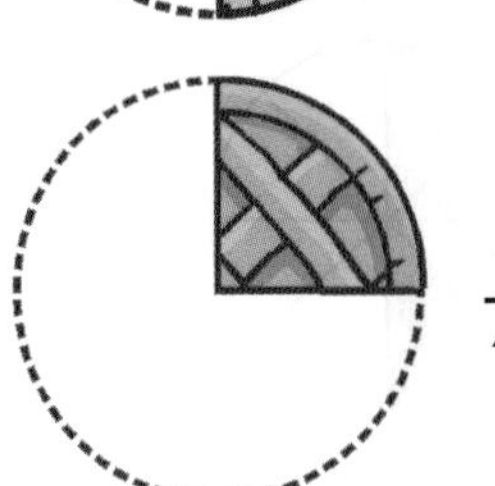

$\frac{1}{4}$

Lisa had a bigger part than Zoe.
$\frac{3}{4}$ is greater than $\frac{1}{2}$.

Abby had a smaller part than Zoe.
$\frac{1}{4}$ is less than $\frac{1}{2}$.

$\frac{3}{4} > \frac{1}{2}$

$\frac{1}{4} < \frac{1}{2}$

The number lines show $\frac{1}{2}$, $\frac{1}{4}$, and $\frac{3}{4}$.

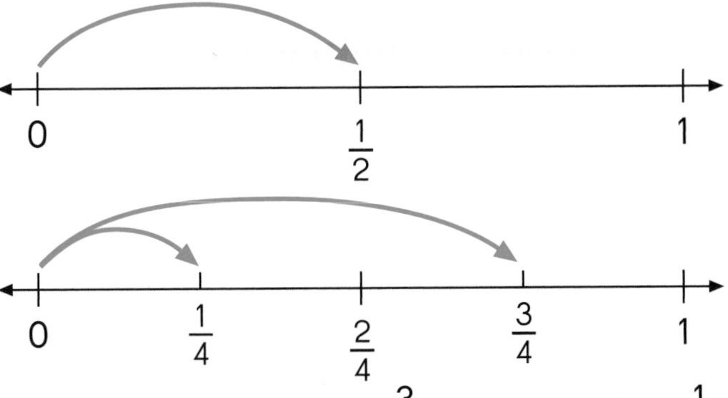

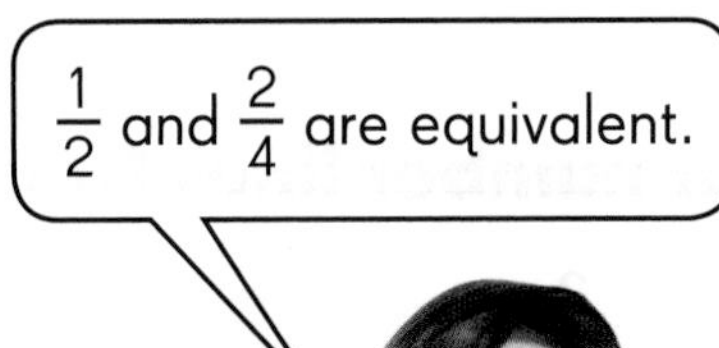

From the number lines, $\frac{3}{4}$ is greater than $\frac{1}{2}$.

$\frac{1}{4}$ is less than $\frac{1}{2}$.

17 Which is greater, $\frac{2}{5}$ or $\frac{5}{8}$?

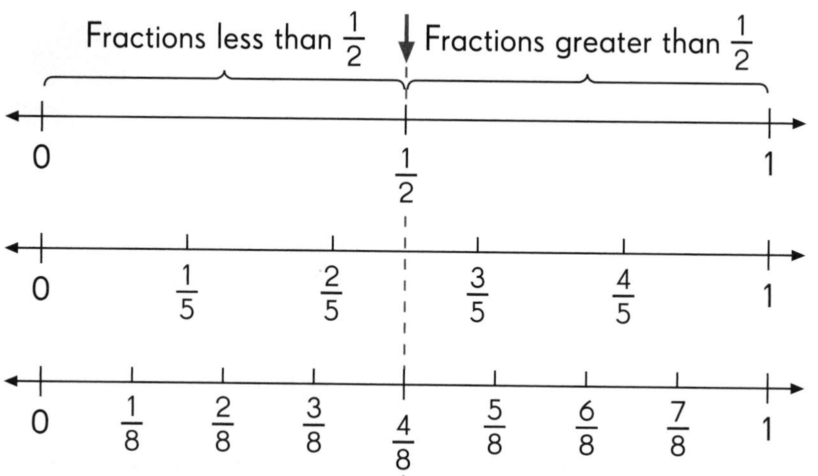

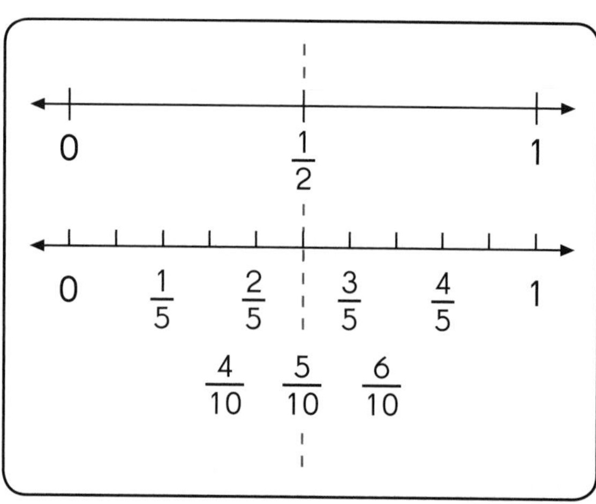

Do these.

18 Write three fractions, two of which are less than than $\frac{3}{4}$.

19 Write three fractions, two of which are greater than $\frac{1}{2}$.

Use benchmark fractions and number lines to help you.

Learn

Compare and order unlike fractions.

Method 1. Use a number line.

Order $\frac{1}{2}$, $\frac{5}{6}$, and $\frac{1}{12}$ from least to greatest.

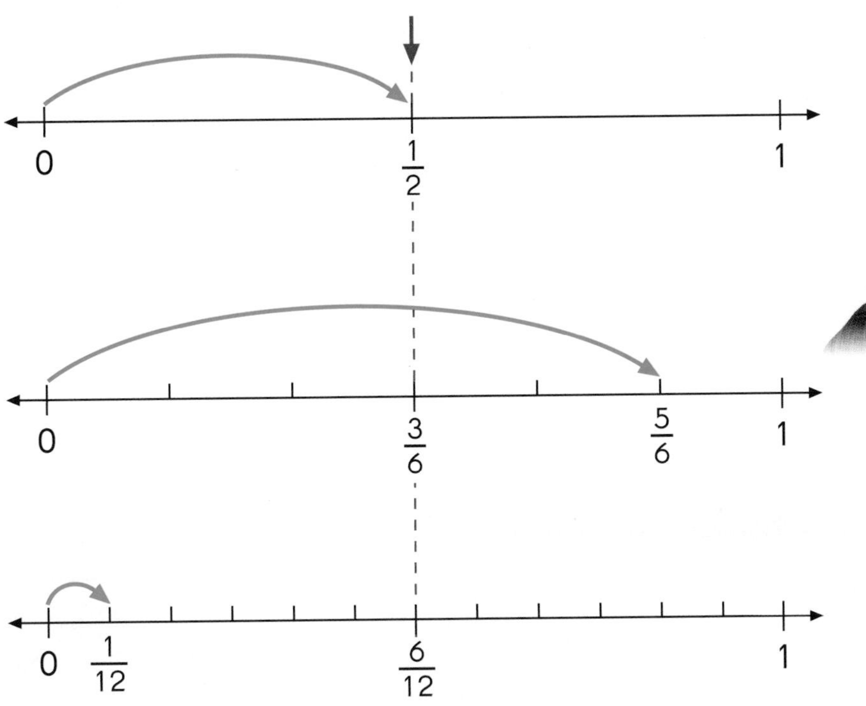

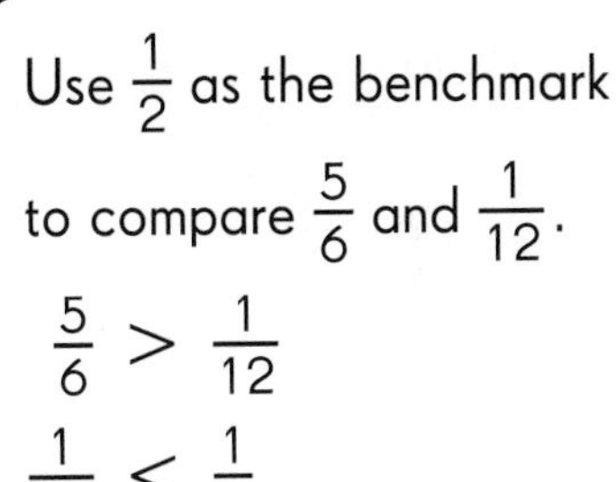

Use $\frac{1}{2}$ as the benchmark to compare $\frac{5}{6}$ and $\frac{1}{12}$.
$\frac{5}{6} > \frac{1}{12}$
$\frac{1}{12} < \frac{1}{2}$

From the number line, $\frac{5}{6}$ is the greatest and $\frac{1}{12}$ is the least.

In order from least to greatest, they are:

$\frac{1}{12}$, $\frac{1}{2}$, $\frac{5}{6}$

least

Continued on next page

Method 2. Use models.

Compare $\frac{5}{6}$ and $\frac{1}{12}$ with $\frac{1}{2}$.

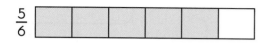

$\frac{5}{6}$ is greater than $\frac{1}{2}$.

$\frac{1}{12}$ is less than $\frac{1}{2}$.

$\frac{1}{12}$, $\frac{1}{2}$, $\frac{5}{6}$

least

Method 3. Use multiplication and division.

Express each fraction with a denominator 12.

$\frac{1}{2} = \frac{6}{12}$

$\frac{5}{6} = \frac{10}{12}$

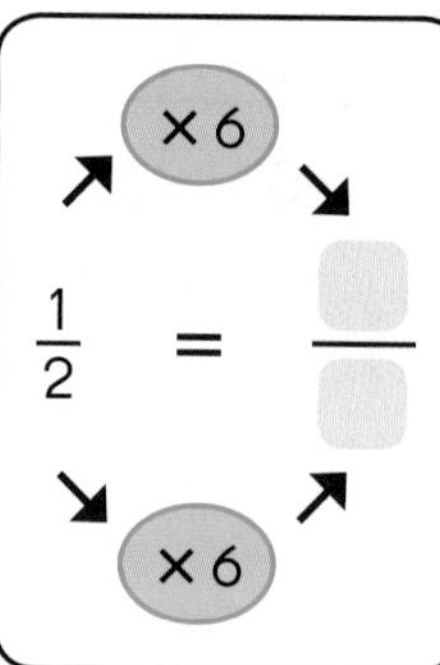

$\frac{1}{12}$ is less than $\frac{1}{2}$.

$\frac{5}{6}$ is greater than $\frac{1}{2}$.

$\frac{1}{12}$, $\frac{1}{2}$, $\frac{5}{6}$

least

Guided Learning

Order the fractions from least to greatest.

20. $\frac{7}{8}$, $\frac{1}{4}$, $\frac{1}{2}$ ___, ___, ___

21. $\frac{7}{8}$, $\frac{5}{7}$, $\frac{1}{2}$ ___, ___, ___

Order the fractions from greatest to least.

22. $\frac{1}{2}$, $\frac{9}{10}$, $\frac{2}{5}$ ___, ___, ___

23. $\frac{2}{3}$, $\frac{1}{2}$, $\frac{5}{6}$ ___, ___, ___

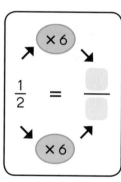

Let's Practice

Draw fraction bars to show the following fractions on number lines.

1. $\frac{4}{7}$

2. $\frac{1}{2}$

Compare.

3. Which is greater, $\frac{3}{8}$ or $\frac{1}{2}$? ____

4. Which is less, $\frac{1}{2}$ or $\frac{7}{10}$? ____

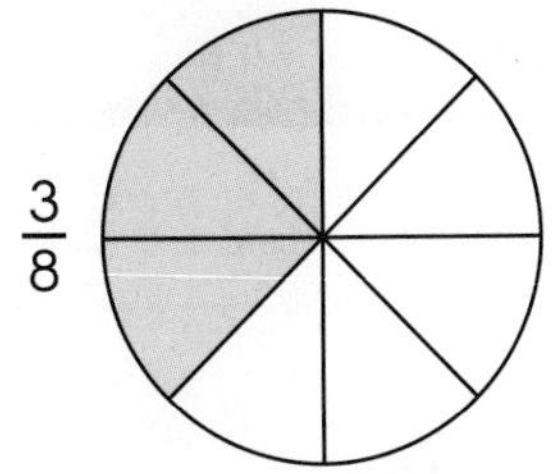

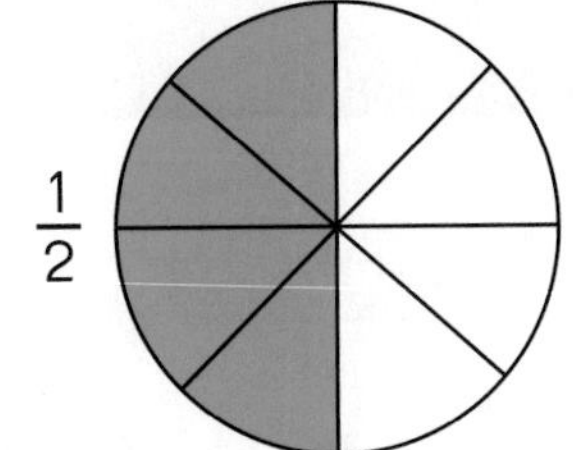

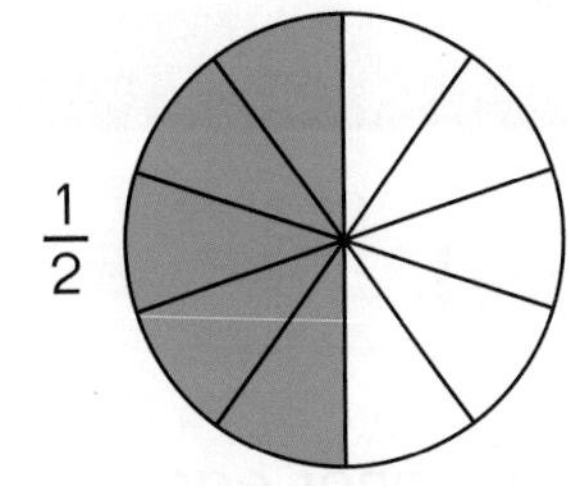

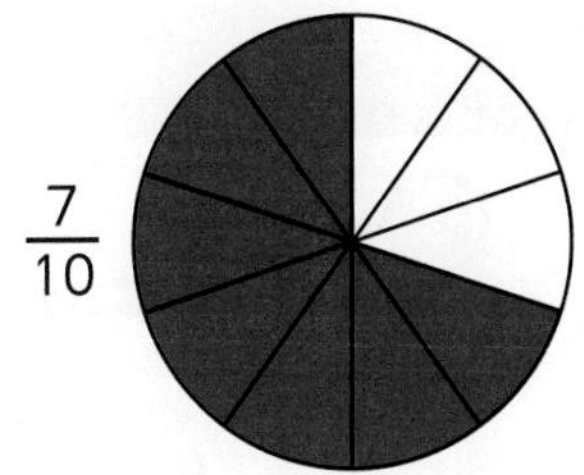

Compare. Choose > or <.

5. Which is greater, $\frac{1}{2}$ or $\frac{5}{8}$?

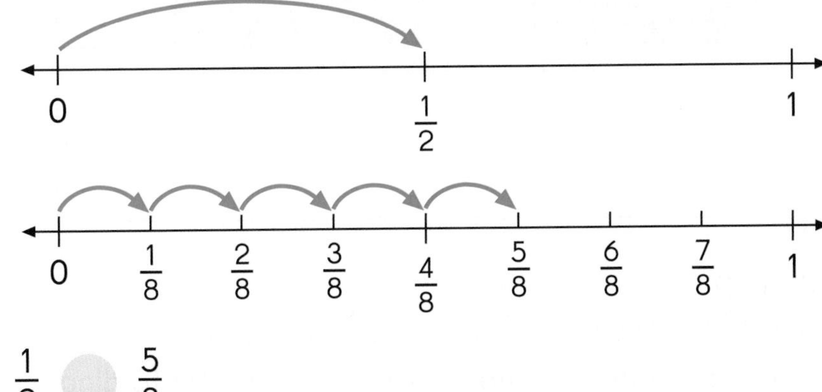

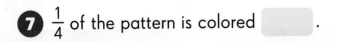

$\frac{1}{2}$ ◯ $\frac{5}{8}$

Complete the sentences.

6. More than $\frac{1}{2}$ of the pattern is colored ____.

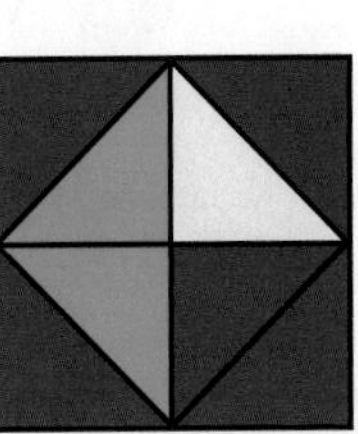

7. $\frac{1}{4}$ of the pattern is colored ____.

Compare.

8. Which is less, $\frac{3}{10}$ or $\frac{3}{5}$?

9. Which is greater, $\frac{1}{3}$ or $\frac{2}{5}$?

Order the fractions from least to greatest.

10. $\frac{5}{12}$, $\frac{5}{6}$, $\frac{1}{2}$ ___, ___, ___

11. $\frac{3}{4}$, $\frac{7}{12}$, $\frac{2}{3}$ ___, ___, ___

Order the fractions from greatest to least.

12. $\frac{1}{6}$, $\frac{4}{9}$, $\frac{7}{12}$ ___, ___, ___

ON YOUR OWN

Go to Workbook B:
Practice 4, pages 101–106

Let's Explore!

Alex, Ben, and Connor each have an equal-sized fraction strip.

Alex's fraction is greater than Ben's and Connor's.
Ben's fraction is less than Connor's.

Alex	■	■	■	■	■	■	■	□
Ben								
Connor								

Look at Alex's fraction strip.
Trace and cut Ben's and Connor's strips on a piece of paper.
Then divide each bar into a different number of equal parts by folding.

1. What could Ben's and Connor's fractions be?
Shade the parts of each bar to show possible answers.

2. Write the fractions and check your answers.

3 Are there any other possible answers? If so, what are they?

Copy the number line on grid paper.

Compare fractions with common benchmarks of 0, $\frac{1}{2}$, and 1.

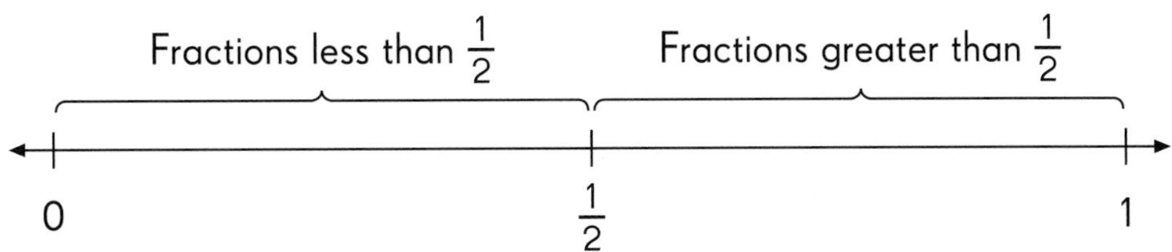

The clues are as follows:

$\frac{2}{11}$ is closer to 0 than to $\frac{1}{2}$.

$\frac{8}{9}$ is closer to 1 than to $\frac{1}{2}$.

$\frac{5}{12}$ is closer to $\frac{1}{2}$ than to 0, but is less than $\frac{1}{2}$.

$\frac{4}{7}$ is closer to $\frac{1}{2}$ than to 1, but is greater than $\frac{1}{2}$.

4 Explore and order these fractions using these benchmarks.

Start with the least. ___, ___, ___, ___
least

5 Name another fraction closer to 0 than to $\frac{1}{2}$.

6 Name another fraction closer to $\frac{1}{2}$ than to 0, but less than $\frac{1}{2}$.

7 Name another fraction closer to $\frac{1}{2}$ than to 1, but greater than $\frac{1}{2}$.

8 Name another fraction closer to 1 than to $\frac{1}{2}$.

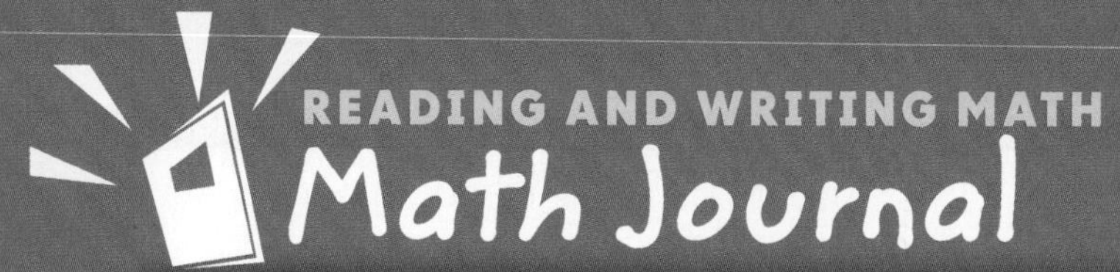

Solve.

Matthew, Jacob, and Ethan each have an equal-sized fraction strip.
Matthew folds his fraction strip into 8 equal parts and shades 7 parts.
The fraction he shades is greater than Jacob's and Ethan's.
Jacob's fraction is less than Ethan's.
How would you fold and shade Jacob's and Ethan's fraction strip?

First, I fold Jacob's strip into half and shade one part.

I must shade a fraction less than $\frac{7}{8}$.

I check my answer: $\frac{1}{2} = \frac{4}{8}$.

So, $\frac{1}{2}$ is less than $\frac{7}{8}$.

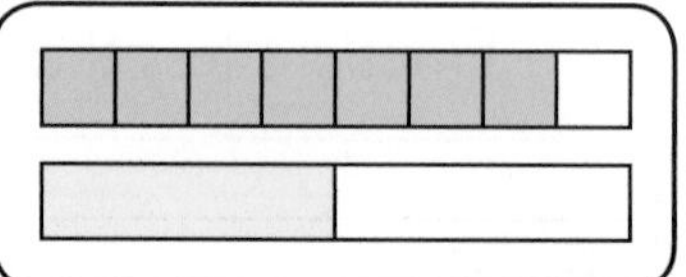

1. Now, list all the steps to your answers on a piece of paper to compare the fractions $\frac{1}{2}$, $\frac{4}{6}$, and $\frac{7}{8}$.

2. Which halves can be compared? Explain your answer.

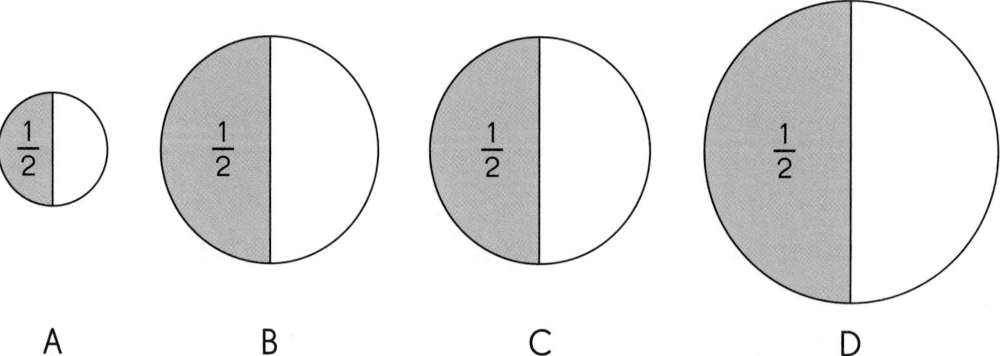

Fraction as a Whole or Set

Lesson Objectives

- Read, write, and identify fractions of a set.
- Find the number of items in a fraction of a set.
- Express whole numbers as fractions.
- Recognize fractions that are equal to whole numbers.

Learn **Use pictures to show fractions as part of a set of objects.**

There are 4 apples.
3 out of the 4 apples are red.

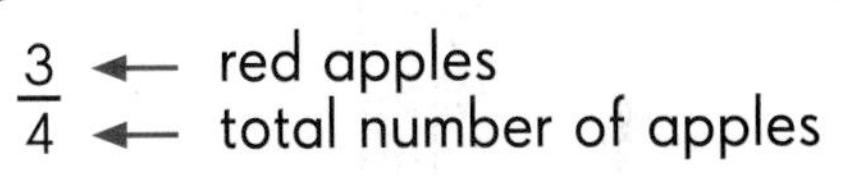

What fraction of the apples are red?
$\frac{3}{4}$ of the apples are red.

Guided Learning

Find the fractions of a set.

There are 10 flowers.

1. What fraction of the flowers are red?
2. What fraction of the flowers are purple?
3. What fraction of the flowers are yellow?
4. What fraction of the flowers are not red?

Learn Find the fraction of a part of objects.

Here is a set of 12 apples.
The set of apples is divided into 4 equal groups.
3 out of 4 groups of apples are red.

$\frac{3}{4}$ is 3 out of 4 equal groups.

What fraction of the apples are red?

$\frac{3}{4}$ of the apples are red.

Guided Learning

Complete.

5. The set of ducks is divided into ☐ equal groups.

6. What fraction of the ducks are yellow?
☐ of the ducks are yellow.

7. What fraction of the ducks are purple?
☐ of the ducks are purple.

Let's Explore!

Whole numbers can be written as fractions.

The number $1 = \frac{1}{1}$ $1 \div 1 = 1$

1. $3 = \frac{3}{1}$, $4 =$ ▢

2. $5 =$ ▢

Whole numbers can be written as other fractions.

The number 1 can also be written as $\frac{2}{2}$ because $2 \div 2 = 1$.

3. Write another fraction for 1.

What do you notice about the fractions $\frac{4}{2}$, $\frac{8}{4}$, and $\frac{6}{3}$?

4. Write another fraction for 2.

Write two fractions to show each of these numbers.

5. $5 =$ ▢ $=$ ▢

6. $6 =$ ▢ $=$ ▢

What numbers are shown by these fractions?

7. $\frac{7}{1}$

8. $\frac{10}{2}$

9. $\frac{21}{7}$

10. $\frac{111}{111}$

Learn Find the fractional part of a set.

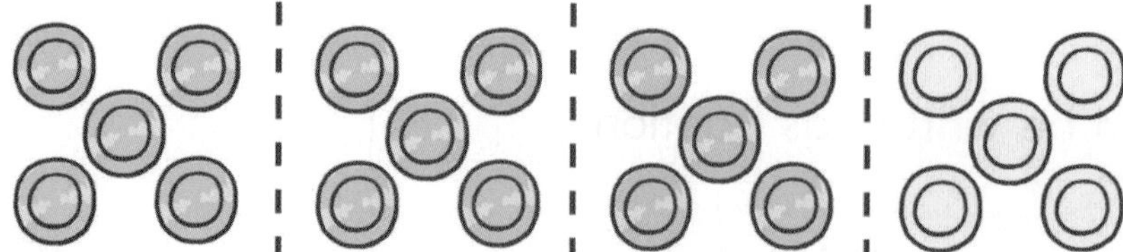

There are 20 plates in the set.
15 of the 20 plates are blue.
$\frac{3}{4}$ of the plates are blue.

So, $\frac{3}{4}$ of 20 is 15.

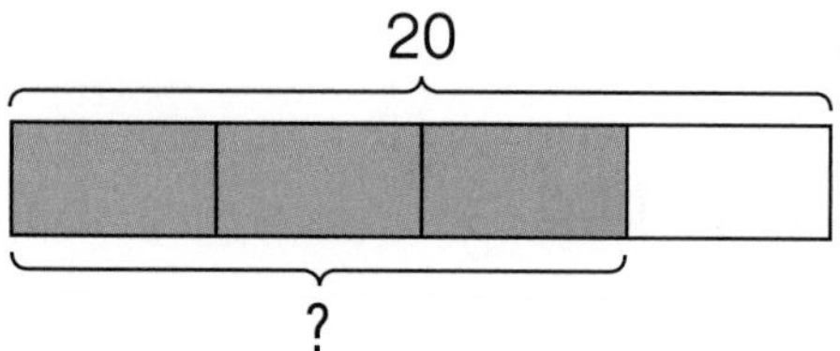

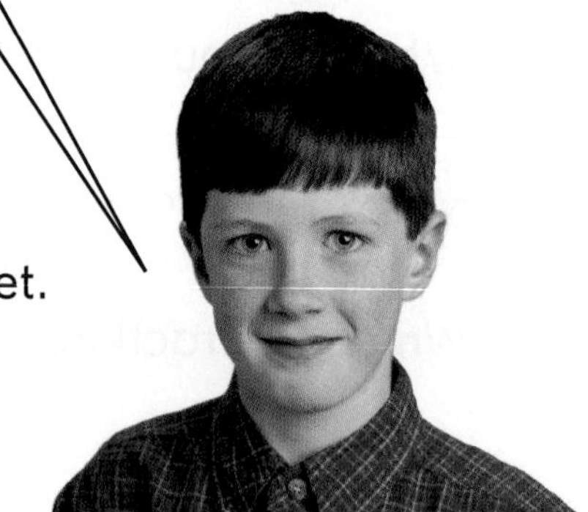

You can find the items in the fractional part of a set by using a bar model.

The shaded parts in the bar model show $\frac{3}{4}$ of the set.

Find $\frac{3}{4}$ of 20.

4 units → 20
1 unit → 20 ÷ 4 = 5
3 units → 5 × 3 = 15

So, $\frac{3}{4}$ of 20 is 15.

Guided Learning

Complete.

8 John has 20 toy cars.
$\frac{3}{5}$ of the toy cars are yellow.
How many toy cars are yellow?

___ toy cars are yellow.

9 Find $\frac{3}{5}$ of 20 to find how many cars are yellow.

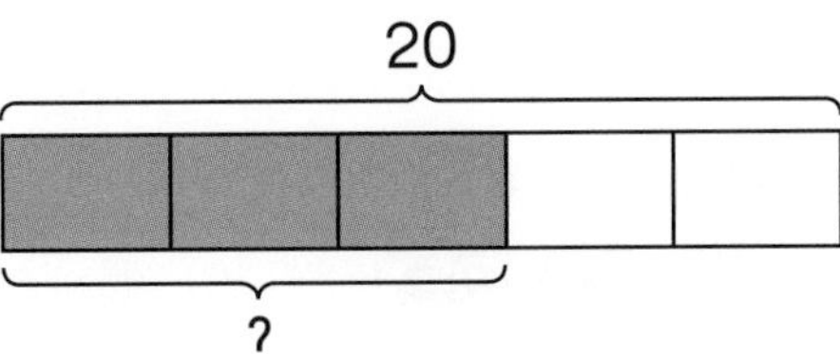

Draw a bar model.
Divide it into 5 parts.
Shade 3 parts.

5 units → ___

1 unit → ___

3 units → ___

So, $\frac{3}{5}$ of 20 = ___

___ toy cars are yellow.

Let's Practice

Solve.

There are 15 fruits.

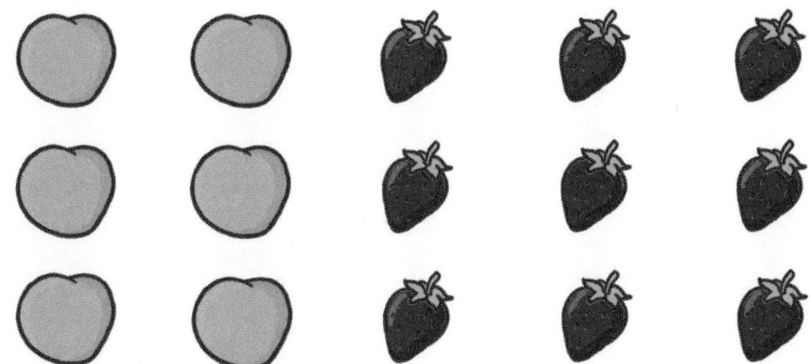

1 What fraction of the fruits are peaches? ___

2 What fraction of the fruits are strawberries? ___

Complete. Mark the correct answer with a tick (✓).

3. Which of the following sets shows the fraction $\frac{3}{4}$?

4. Jerry had 15 granola bars.
$\frac{2}{3}$ of them were eaten by his friends.
How many granola bars did his friends eat?
Find $\frac{2}{3}$ of 15 to find how many granola bars his friends ate.

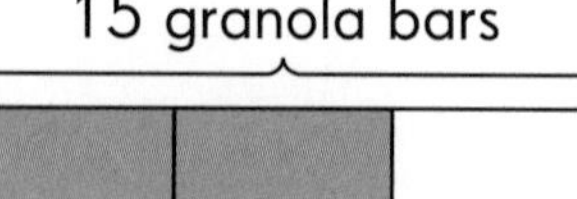

3 units → ☐ granola bars

1 unit → ☐ granola bars

2 units → ☐ granola bars

So, $\frac{2}{3}$ of 15 = ☐ granola bars

His friends ate ☐ granola bars.

Complete.

5. $1 = \frac{5}{\square}$

6. $1 = \frac{\square}{7}$

7. $1 = \frac{\square}{\square}$

8. $4 \div 2 = \square$

9. $6 \div 3 = \square$

10. $2 = \frac{\square}{4}$

11. $2 = \frac{\square}{5}$

12. $2 = \frac{\square}{6}$

Write two fractions that show each of these whole numbers.

13. $4 = \square = \square$

14. $9 = \square = \square$

ON YOUR OWN

Go to Workbook B: Practice 5, pages 107–111

CRITICAL THINKING SKILLS

Put On Your Thinking Cap!

PROBLEM SOLVING

1. The model shows $\frac{3}{4}$.

   How much of the shading must be erased so that the remaining shaded part is $\frac{3}{8}$ of the strip?

Try drawing the model in another way.

2. Gary, Joey, and Kylie shared a vegetarian pizza.
   The pizza was divided into 9 equal slices.

   Gary ate $\frac{2}{9}$ of the pizza.

   Joey ate more pizza than Kylie.
   Together they finished the whole pizza.

   What are some possible fractions that show the part of the pizza that Joey and Kylie each ate?

   What is the greatest possible fraction that describes the part of the pizza that Kylie ate?

Try drawing a model first.

ON YOUR OWN

Go to Workbook B: Put On Your Thinking Cap! pages 112–114

Chapter Wrap Up

Study Guide

You have learned...

BIG IDEA

▶ Fractions can be used to describe parts of a region or parts of a set.

Understanding fractions, numerator, and denominator:

Unit fractions

$\frac{1}{6}$ is one-sixth. $\frac{1}{7}$ is one-seventh. $\frac{1}{8}$ is one-eighth.

$\frac{1}{9}$ is one-ninth. $\frac{1}{10}$ is one-tenth. $\frac{1}{11}$ is one-eleventh.

$\frac{1}{12}$ is one-twelfth.

Identifying fractions to make a whole

$\frac{2}{5}$ and $\frac{3}{5}$ make 1 whole.

Numerator and Denominator

2 ⟵ Numerator: The number of equal parts shaded.
4 ⟵ Denominator: The number of equal parts the whole is divided into.

Equivalent fractions:

Using a model

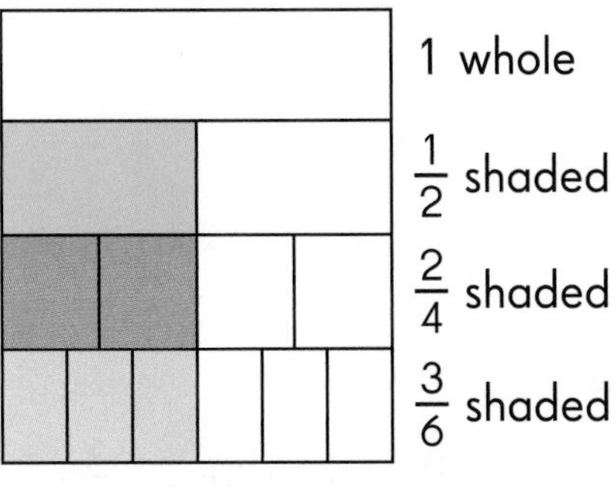

Using a number line

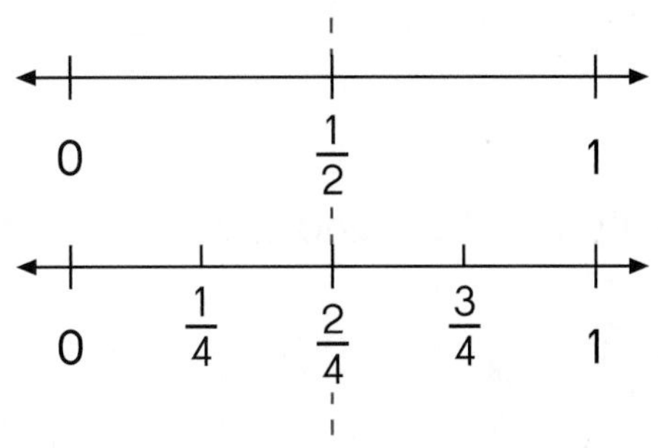

Continued on next page

Using multiplication and division:

$$\frac{1}{2} \xrightarrow{\times 2} \frac{2}{4}$$

$$\frac{1}{2} = \frac{2}{4}$$

$\frac{1}{2}$ and $\frac{2}{4}$ are equivalent fractions.

Comparing and ordering fractions:

Like fractions are fractions with the same denominators and unlike fractions are fractions with different denominators.

Comparing like fractions

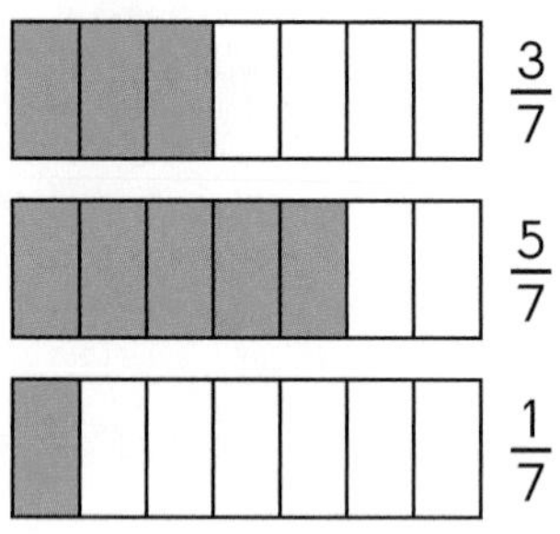

$\frac{5}{7}$ is the greatest.

$\frac{1}{7}$ is the least.

$\frac{5}{7}$, $\frac{3}{7}$, $\frac{1}{7}$

greatest

When the denominators are the same, compare the numerators.

Comparing unlike fractions with the same numerator

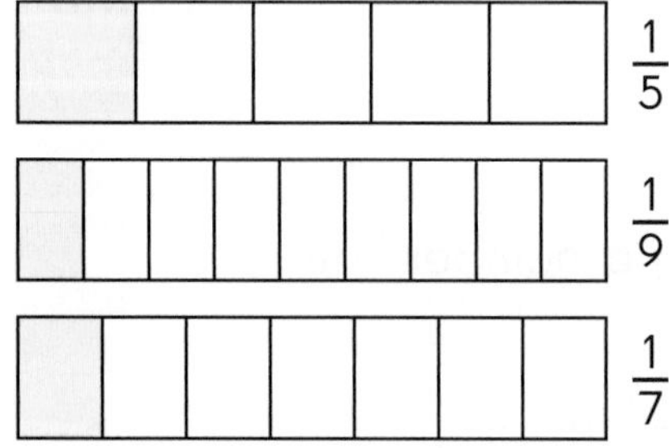

$\frac{1}{9}$ is less than $\frac{1}{7}$.

$\frac{1}{5}$ is greater than $\frac{1}{9}$.

$\frac{1}{5}$, $\frac{1}{7}$, $\frac{1}{9}$

greatest

Using multiplication and division to compare

$$\frac{1}{3} \xrightarrow{\times 2} \frac{2}{6}$$

$$\frac{1}{3} = \frac{2}{6}$$

$\frac{1}{3}$ is less than $\frac{5}{6}$.

$$\frac{6}{12} \xrightarrow{\div 3} \frac{2}{4}$$

$$\frac{6}{12} = \frac{2}{4}$$

$\frac{6}{12}$ is less than $\frac{3}{4}$.

Using number lines and a benchmark of $\frac{1}{2}$:

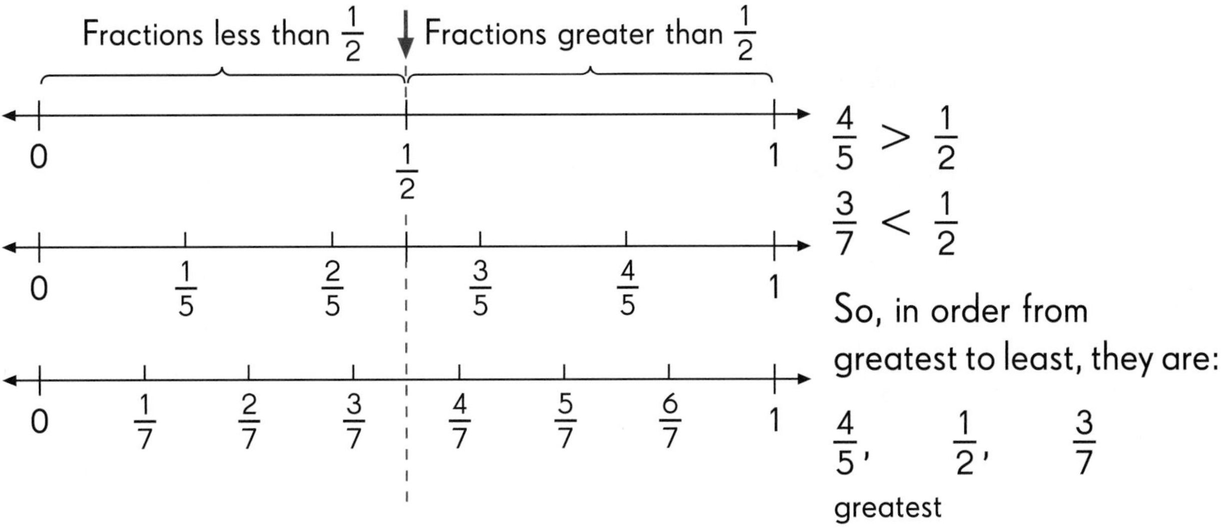

Writing whole numbers as fractions:

$0 = \frac{0}{4}$ $\quad 1 = \frac{3}{3}$ $\quad 2 = \frac{2}{1} = \frac{4}{2} = \frac{6}{3}$

Finding fractions of a set using models:

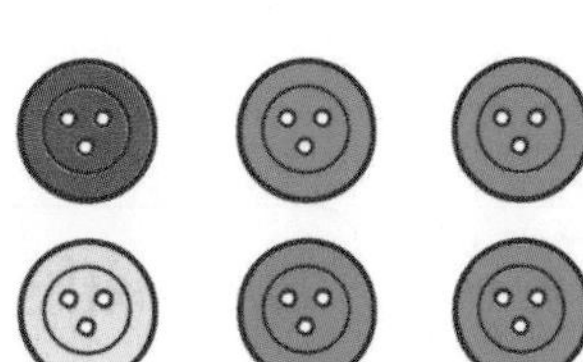

$\frac{4}{6}$ of the buttons are blue.

$\frac{2}{6}$ of the buttons are not blue.

$\frac{6}{6}$ of the buttons are round.

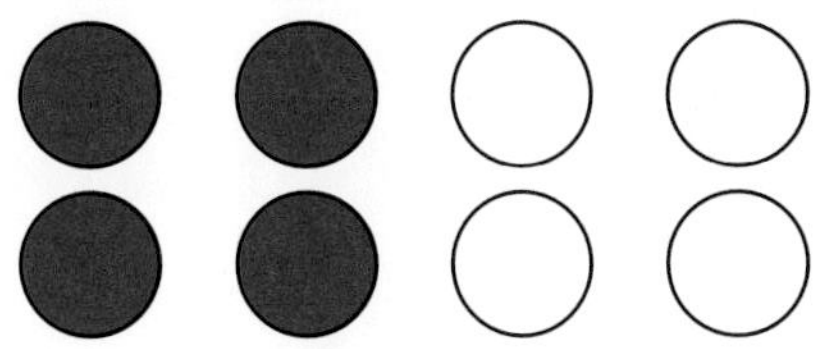

$\frac{1}{2}$ of the set of circles is red.

$\frac{1}{2}$ of 8 is 4.

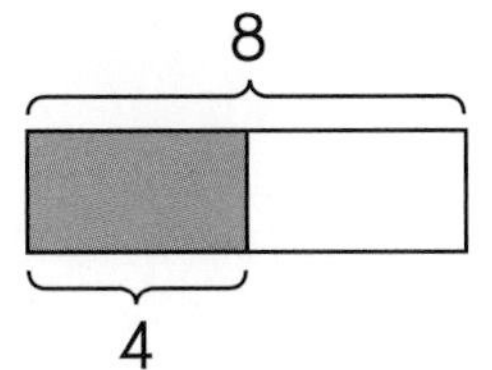

$\frac{1}{2}$ of the bar model is shaded.

$\frac{1}{2}$ of 8 is 4.

Chapter Review/Test

Vocabulary

Choose the correct word.

1. In the fraction $\frac{4}{5}$, 4 is the ______, and 5 is the ______.

denominator
simplest form
numerator
whole
equivalent fractions
like fractions
unlike fractions

2. 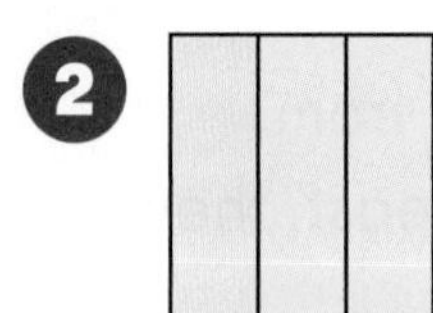

$\frac{1}{3}$ and $\frac{2}{3}$ make a ______.

3. $\frac{1}{3}$ and $\frac{3}{9}$ are ______.

4. $\frac{2}{8}$ and $\frac{3}{12}$ are equivalent to $\frac{1}{4}$ in ______.

5. ______ have the same denominators and ______ have different denominators.

Concept and Skills

Match the fraction names to the models.

two-sixths
three-eighths
six-twelfths

6. 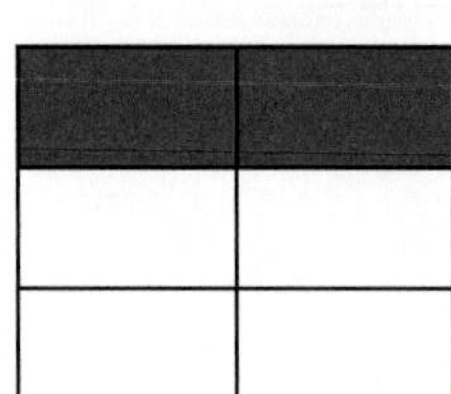

______

7. 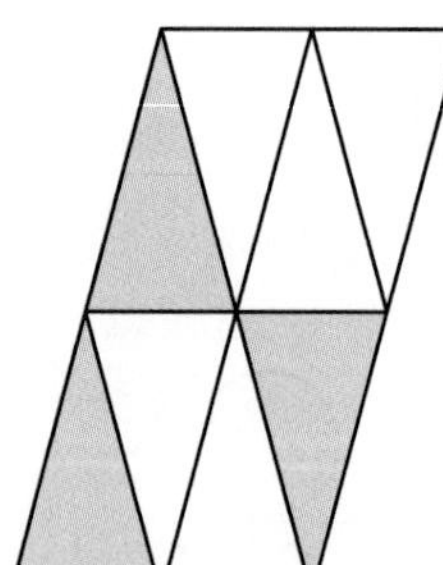

______

8. 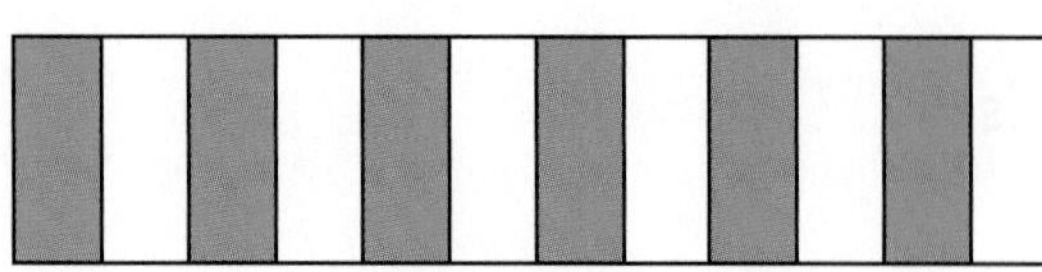

______

Complete.

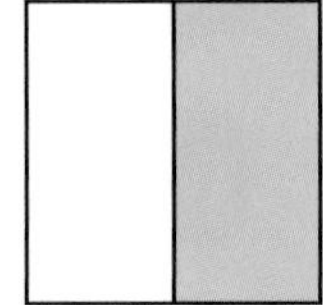

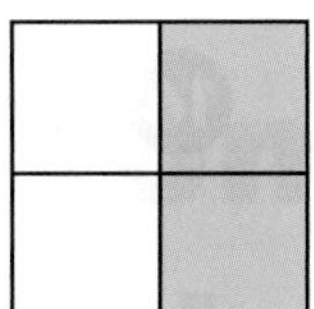

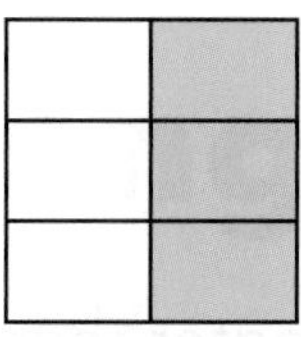

$\frac{1}{2}$ = $\frac{\square}{4}$ = $\frac{\square}{\square}$

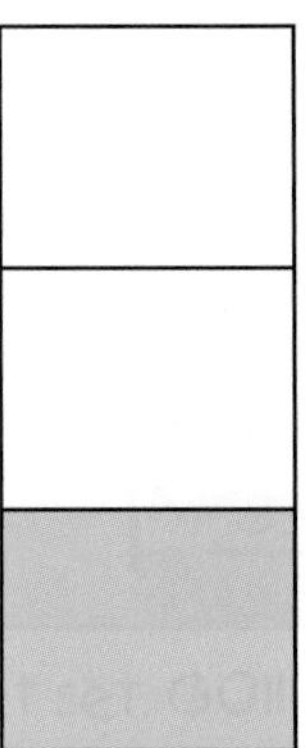

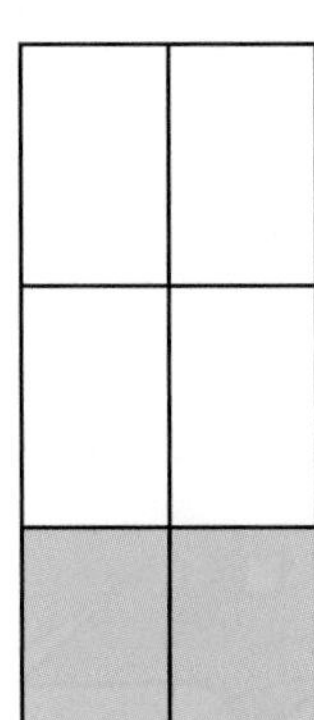

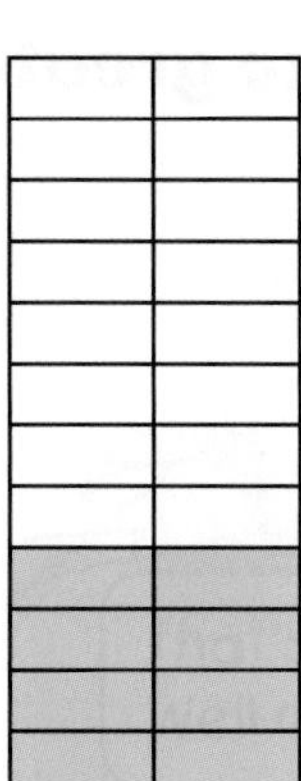

$\frac{1}{3}$ = $\frac{\square}{6}$ = $\frac{\square}{\square}$

11

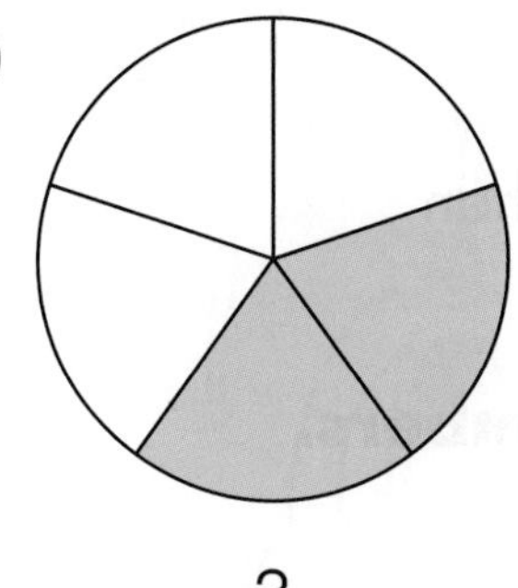

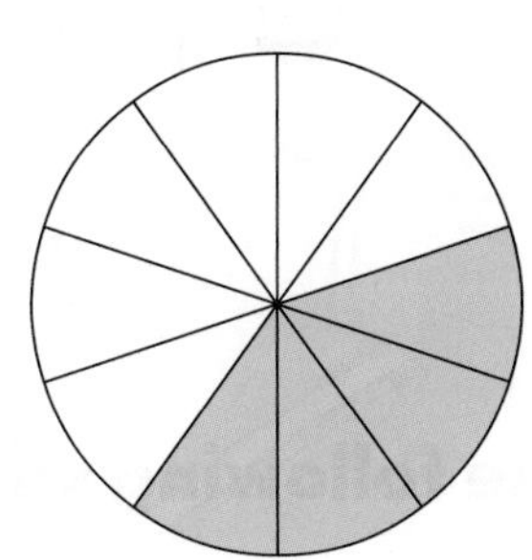

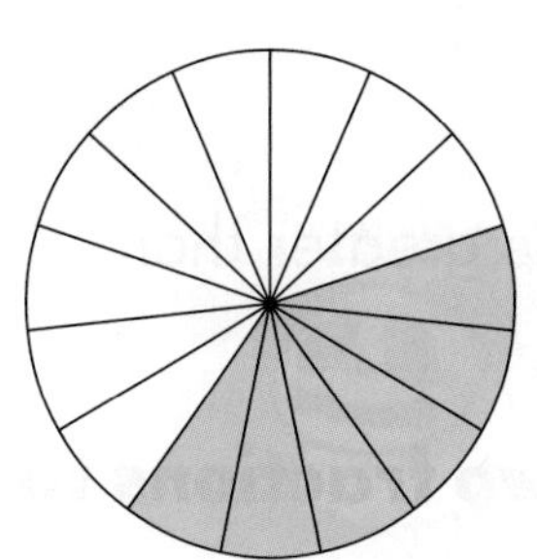

$\frac{2}{5}$ = $\frac{4}{\square}$ = $\frac{\square}{\square}$

Find equivalent fractions.

12 $\frac{3}{4} = \frac{\square}{8} = \frac{\square}{12}$

13 $\frac{2}{3} = \frac{\square}{6} = \frac{\square}{9}$

Simplify the fraction.

14 $\frac{8}{12} = \frac{\square}{\square} = \frac{\square}{\square}$

Recall Prior Knowledge

Identify fractions on a number line

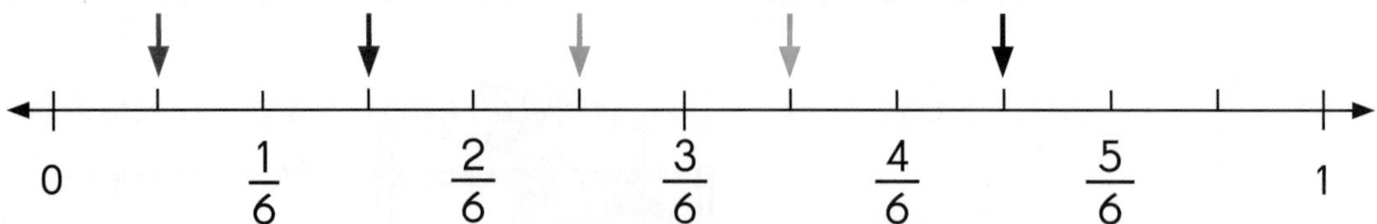

The red arrow points to one-twelfth $\left(\frac{1}{12}\right)$.

The purple arrow points to three-twelfths or one-fourth $\left(\frac{3}{12} \text{ or } \frac{1}{4}\right)$.

The green arrow points to five-twelfths $\left(\frac{5}{12}\right)$.

The blue arrow points to seven-twelfths $\left(\frac{7}{12}\right)$.

The black arrow points to nine-twelfths or three-fourths $\left(\frac{9}{12} \text{ or } \frac{3}{4}\right)$.

As you move along the number line, the fraction increases by one-twelfth $\left(\frac{1}{12}\right)$.

Fractions and whole numbers

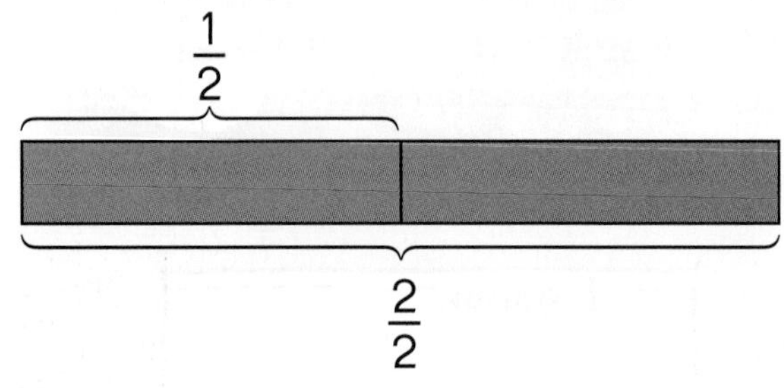

$\frac{1}{2} + \frac{1}{2} = \frac{2}{2}$

$= 1$

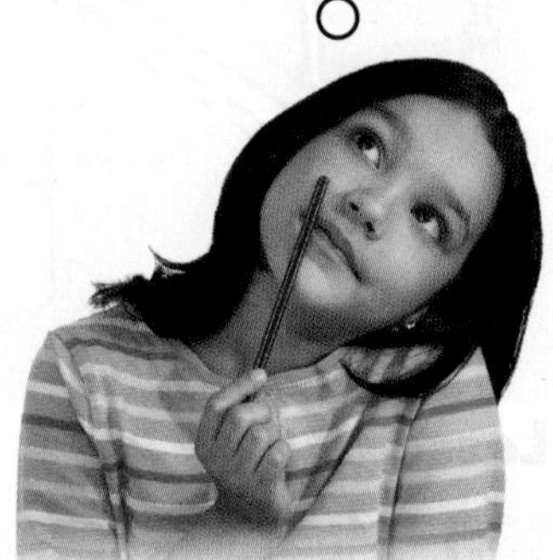

Measuring length in feet (ft) and inches (in.)

Both feet (ft) and inches (in.) are customary units of length.

1 foot (ft) = 12 inches (in.)

Feet are used to measure longer lengths.
Inches are used to measure shorter lengths.
Inch-rulers are used for measuring customary lengths.

The arrow points to 1 inch (in.).

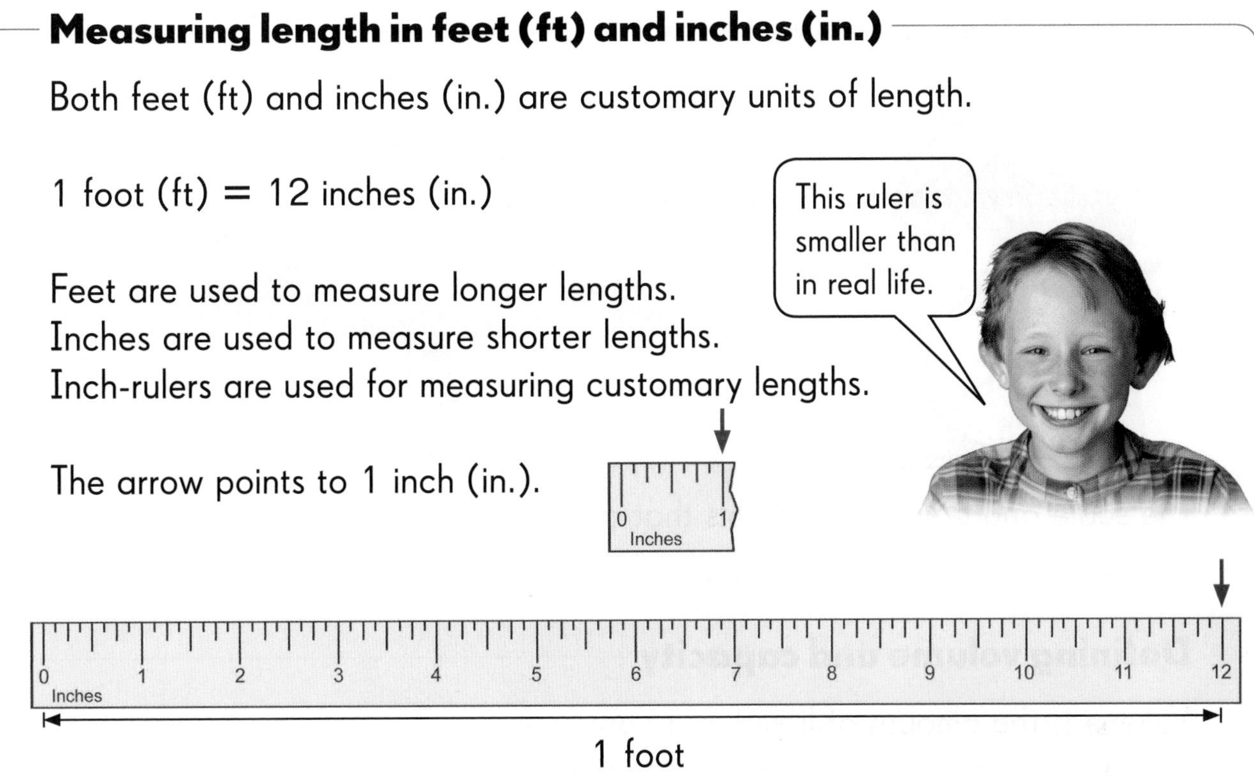

Comparing lengths using feet (ft) and inches (in.)

Math

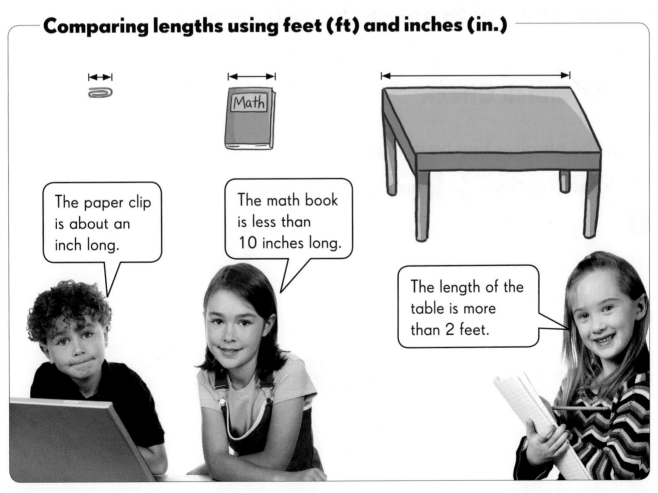

The paper clip is about an inch long.

The math book is less than 10 inches long.

The length of the table is more than 2 feet.

Using tools to measure mass

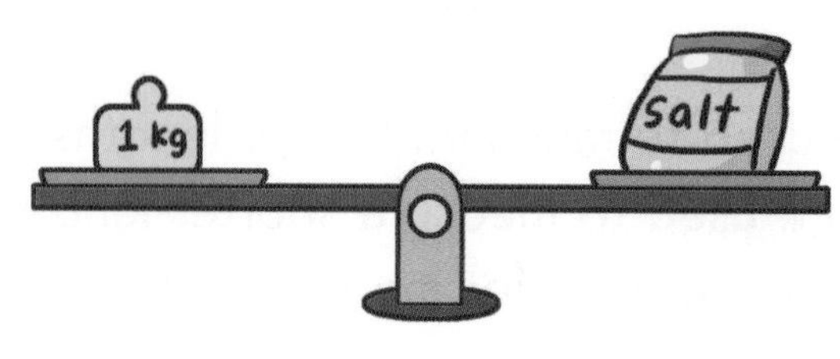

The scale and balance are tools that are used for measuring mass.

Defining volume and capacity

Volume is the amount of liquid in a container.
Capacity is the amount of liquid a container can hold.

Larger containers have a greater capacity than smaller containers.

Copy the number line on grid paper.

Mark the fractions $\frac{3}{8}$, $\frac{5}{8}$, and $\frac{7}{8}$ on the number line.

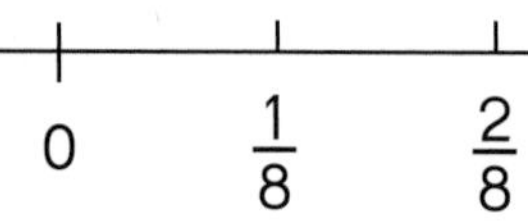

0, $\frac{1}{8}$, $\frac{2}{8}$, ▢, $\frac{4}{8}$, ▢, $\frac{6}{8}$, ▢, 1

Complete.

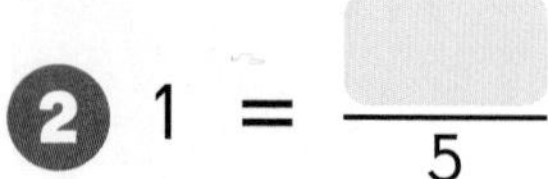

$1 = \frac{\square}{5}$

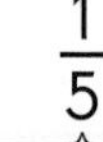

$\frac{1}{5}$

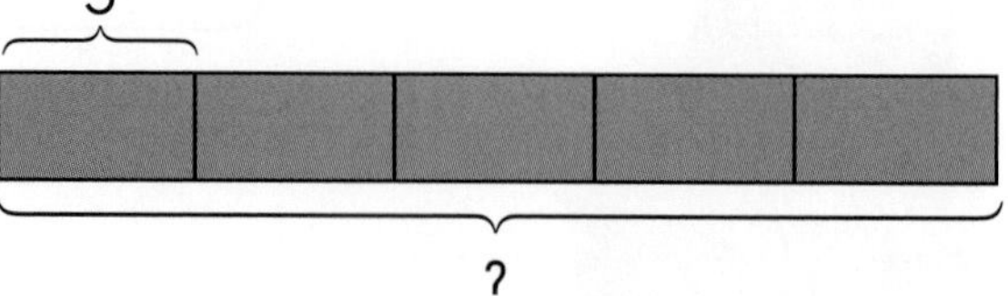

?

Complete. Use shorter or longer.

3. Feet are used to measure ______ lengths.

4. Inches are used to measure ______ lengths.

Name two objects for each measure.

5. About 1 inch long ______

6. More than 1 foot long ______

7. Less than 1 foot long ______

Choose the correct unit of measure for each object. Use inches or feet.

8. 

______

9. 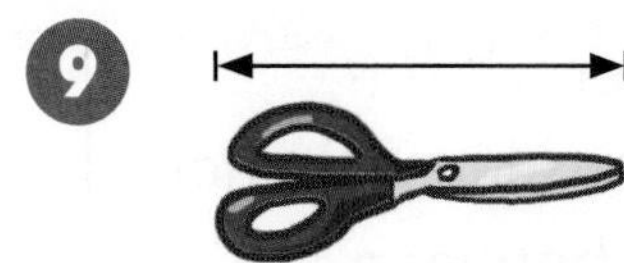

______

Fill in the blanks.

10. You use a ______ for measuring mass.

11. Container ______ has a greater capacity.

A

B

Measuring Length

Lesson Objectives

- Use inch, foot, yard, and mile as units of measurement for lengths.
- Estimate and measure given lengths in inches, in halves, and in fourths of an inch.
- Use referents to estimate lengths.

Vocabulary

inch (in.)	mile (mi)
half inch	quarter inch
foot (ft)	three quarter inch
yard (yd)	

Learn

Estimate and measure length to the nearest inch.

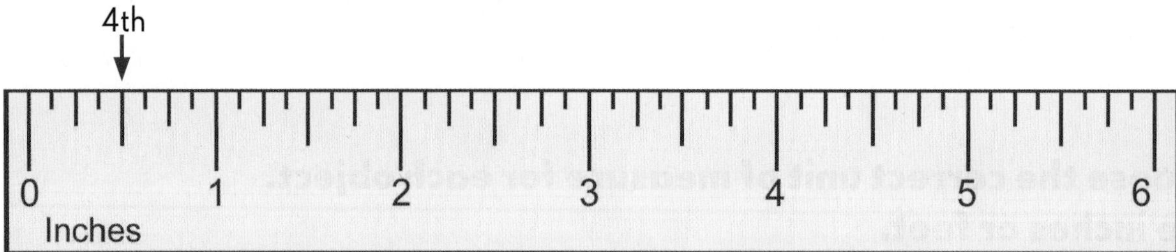

This is an **inch** ruler.
There are 8 divisions in each inch.
The mark halfway between two inch marks is $\frac{1}{2}$ inch.

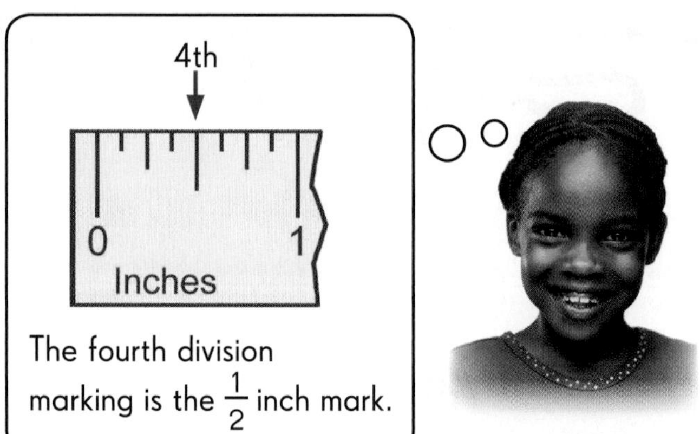

The fourth division marking is the $\frac{1}{2}$ inch mark.

Sally wants to measure the length of these objects.

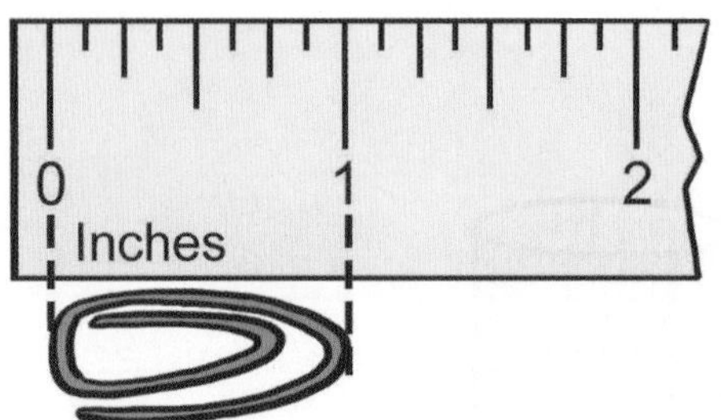

Line up one end of the paper clip with the zero mark.

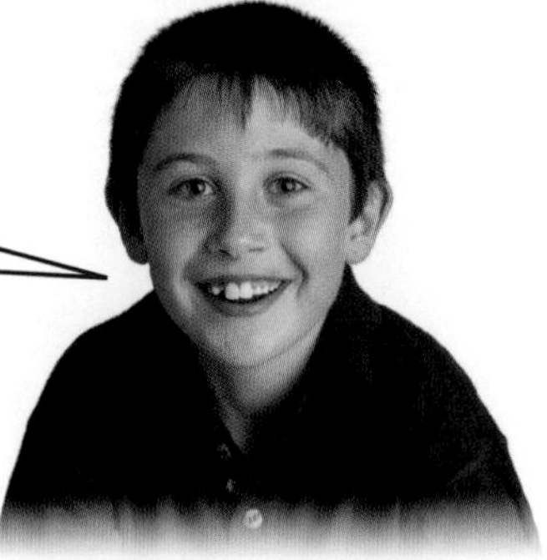

The length of the paper clip is 1 inch.
You can use this paper clip to estimate short lengths in inches.

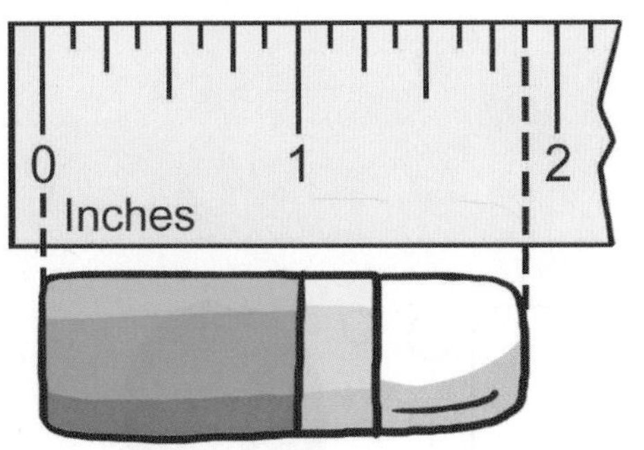

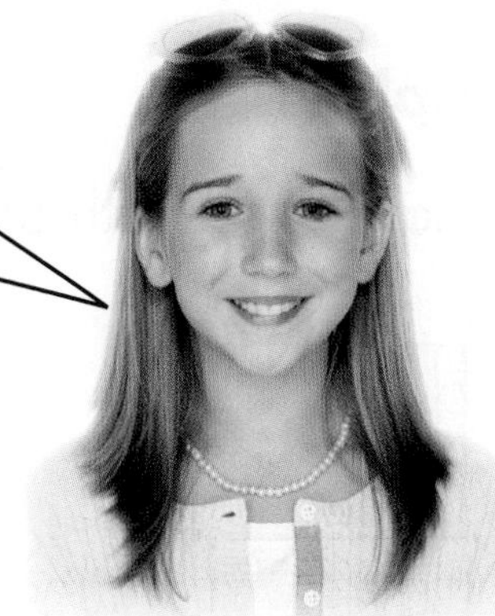

The length of the eraser is 2 inches measured to the nearest inch.

The length of the eraser is more than 1 inch but less than 2 inches.
It is nearer to 2 inches than to 1 inch.
So, the length of the eraser is about 2 inches.

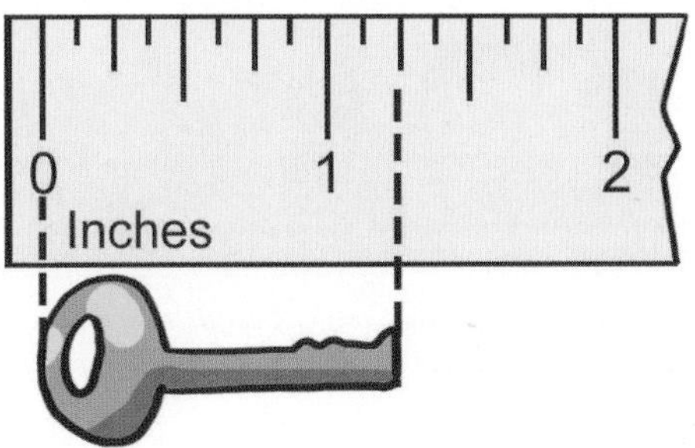

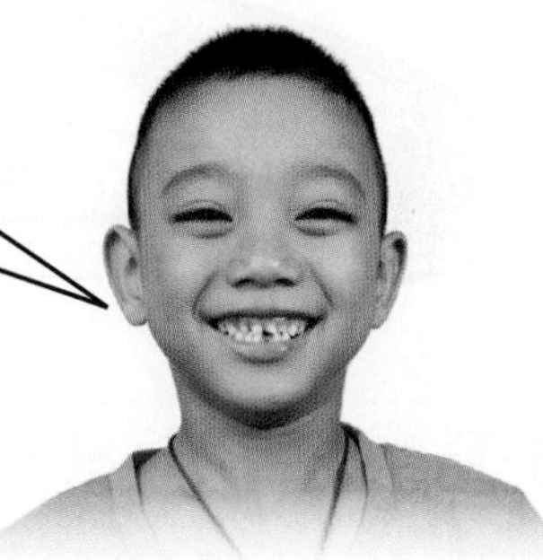

The length of the key is 1 inch, measured to the nearest inch.

The length of the key is more than 1 inch but less than 2 inches.
It is nearer to 1 inch than to 2 inches.
So, the length of the key is about 1 inch.

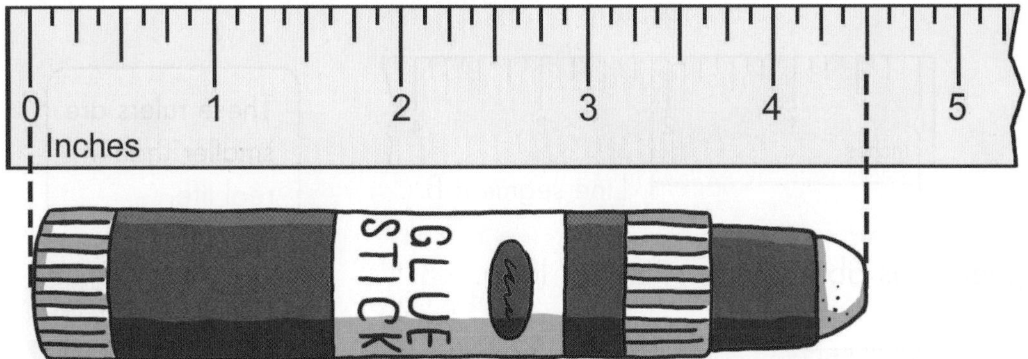

The length of the glue stick is more than 4 inches but less than 5 inches.
It is 4 inches and $\frac{1}{2}$ inch long.
So, the length of the glue stick is about 5 inches.

Guided Learning

Complete.

Estimate the length of the stapler mentally.

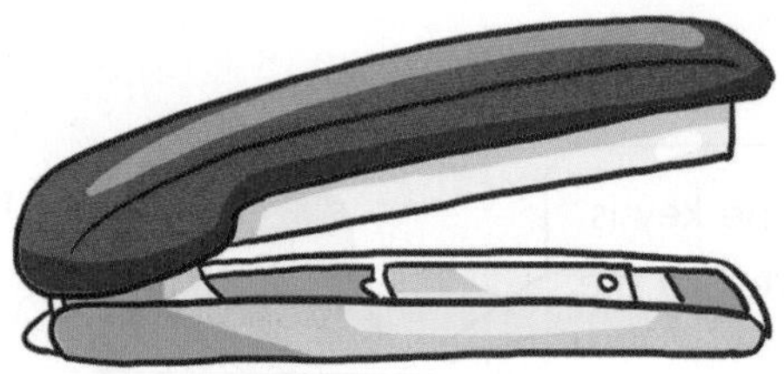

1. The stapler is about ______ inches long.

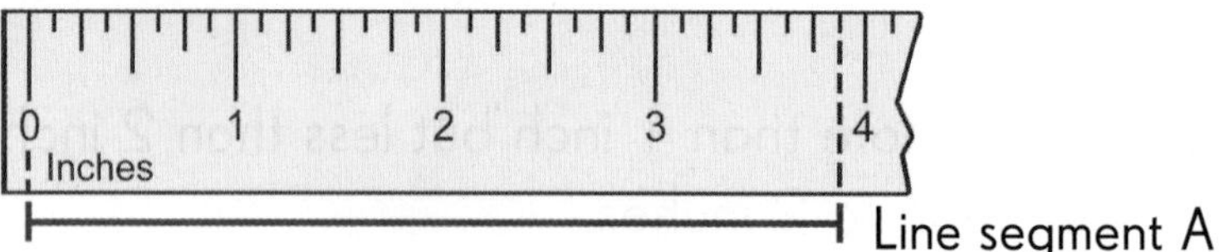

2. Line segment A is about ______ inches long.

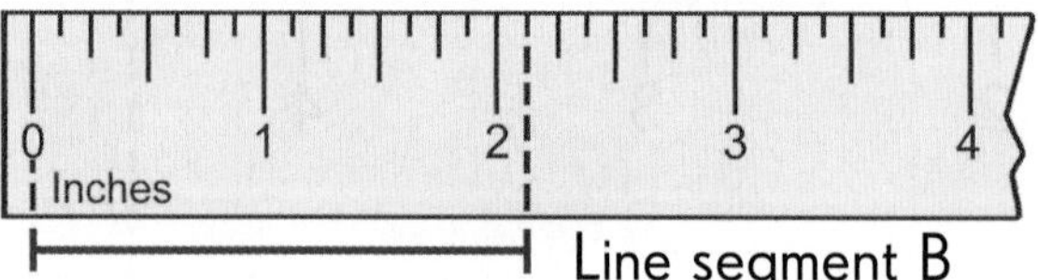

3. Line segment B is about ______ inches long.

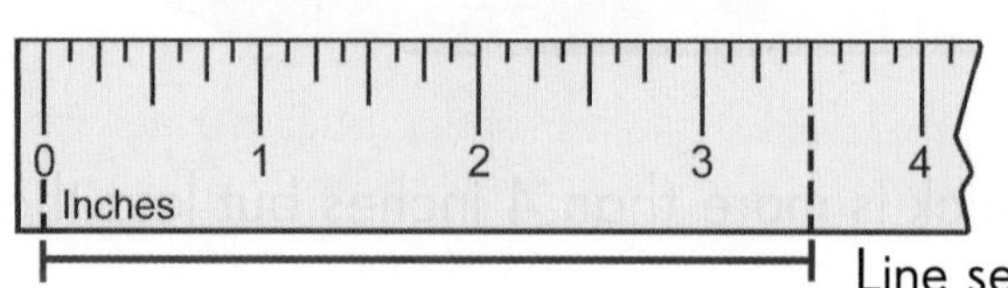

4. Line segment C is about ______ inches long.

These rulers are smaller than in real life.

Learn

Estimate and measure length to the nearest half inch.

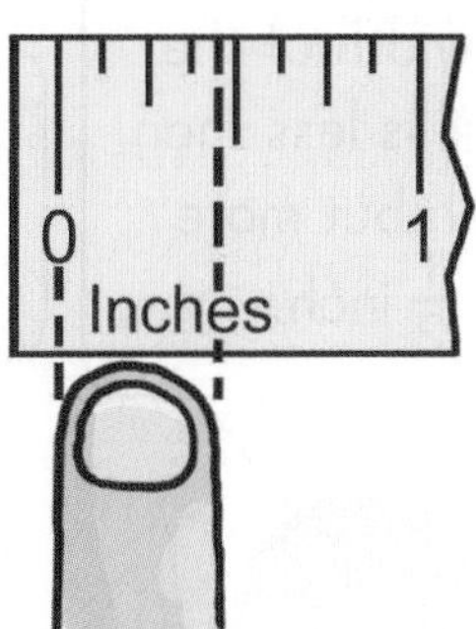

The width of the finger is about $\frac{1}{2}$ inch.
You can use the width of a finger to estimate short lengths.

This is an eraser.
Now measure the eraser with a ruler.

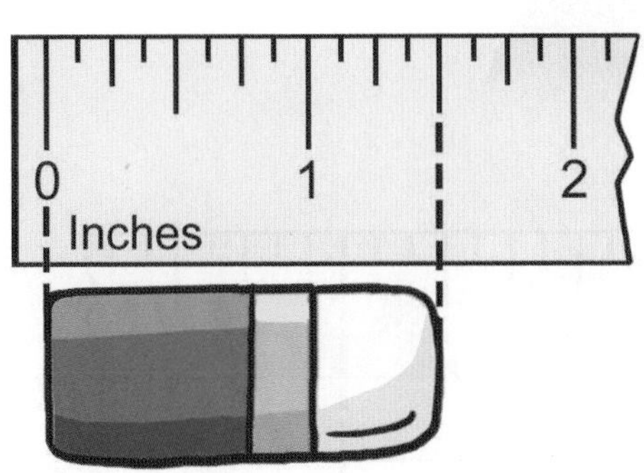

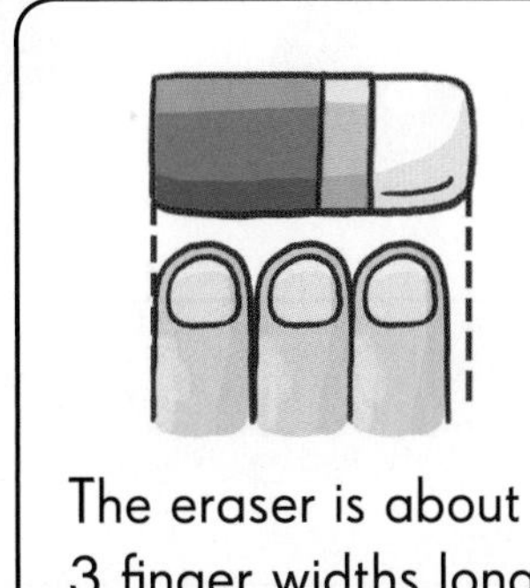

The length of the eraser is $1\frac{1}{2}$ inches to the nearest **half inch**.

$1\frac{1}{2}$ inches is read as "one and one-half inches".

$1\frac{1}{2}$ is a mixed number. It means a half more than one.
It is halfway between 1 and 2.

$2\frac{1}{2}$ means a half more than two. It is halfway between 2 and 3.

How do you read these mixed numbers? What do they mean?

$3\frac{1}{2}$: three and one half

$4\frac{1}{2}$: four and one half

Continued on next page

Gita wants to measure the width and length of a pencil.

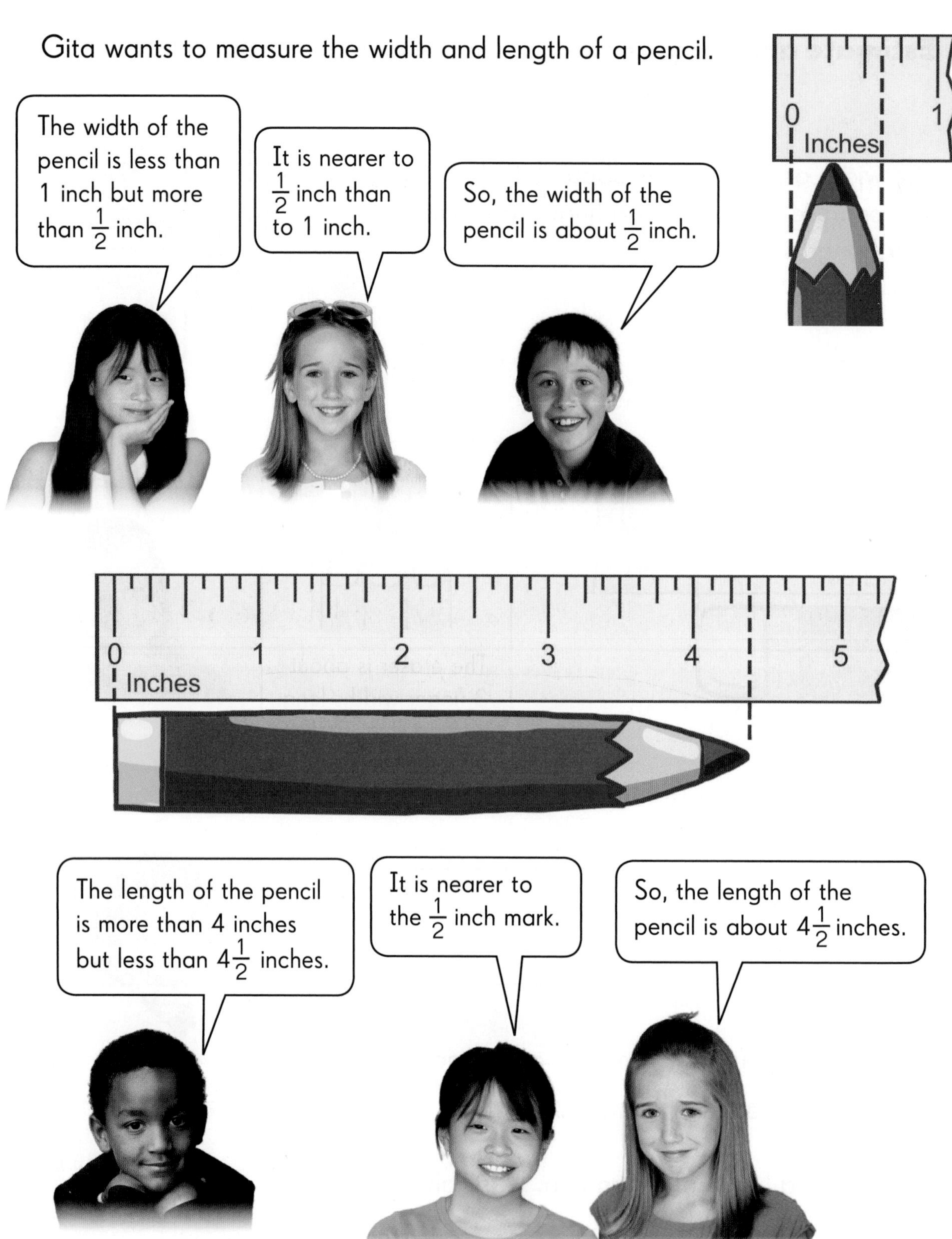

The width of the pencil is less than 1 inch but more than $\frac{1}{2}$ inch.
It is nearer to $\frac{1}{2}$ inch than to 1 inch.
So, the width of the pencil is about $\frac{1}{2}$ inch.
0
1
Inches
0
1
2
3
4
5
Inches
The length of the pencil is more than 4 inches but less than $4\frac{1}{2}$ inches.
It is nearer to the $\frac{1}{2}$ inch mark.
So, the length of the pencil is about $4\frac{1}{2}$ inches.

The width of the pencil is $\frac{1}{2}$ inch, measured to the nearest $\frac{1}{2}$ inch.

The length of the pencil is $4\frac{1}{2}$ inches, measured to the nearest $\frac{1}{2}$ inch.

Gita also wants to estimate the length of 3 ribbons.

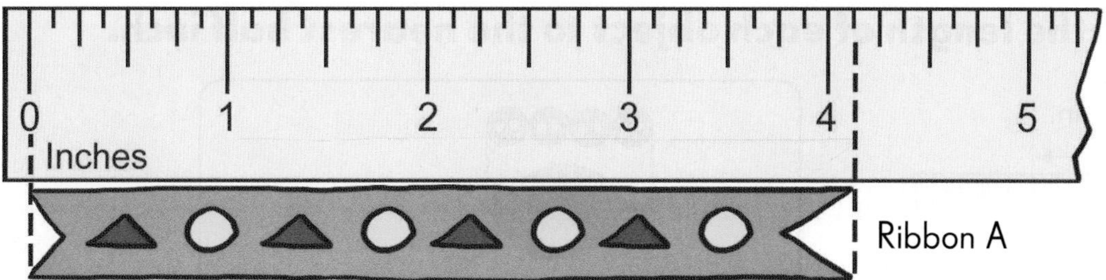

Ribbon A is more than 4 inches but less than $4\frac{1}{2}$ inches long.

It is nearer to 4 inches than to $4\frac{1}{2}$ inches.

So, the length of Ribbon A is 4 inches to the the nearest half inch.

Ribbon B is more than $2\frac{1}{2}$ inches but less than 3 inches long.

It is nearer to 3 inches than to $2\frac{1}{2}$ inches.

So, the length of Ribbon B is 3 inches to the nearest half inch.

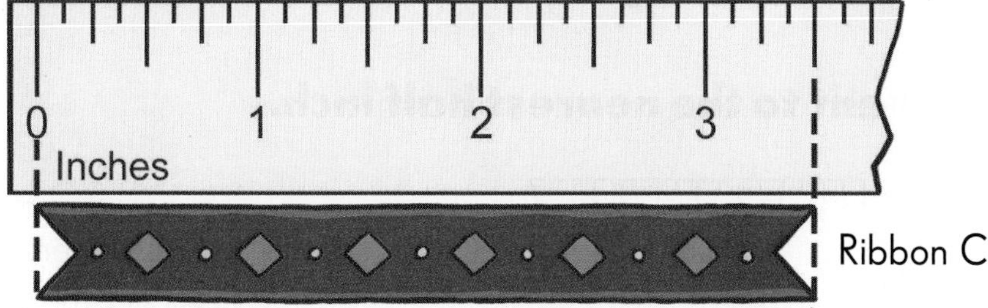

Ribbon C is more than 3 inches but less than 4 inches long.

It is $3\frac{1}{2}$ inches long.

So, the length of Ribbon C is $3\frac{1}{2}$ inches to the nearest half inch.

The lengths of Ribbon A, Ribbon B, and Ribbon C are measured to the nearest half inch.

Guided Learning

Estimate the length of each object to the nearest half inch.

5 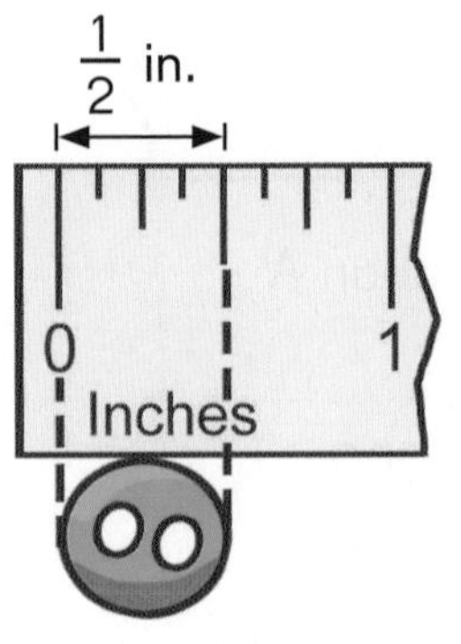

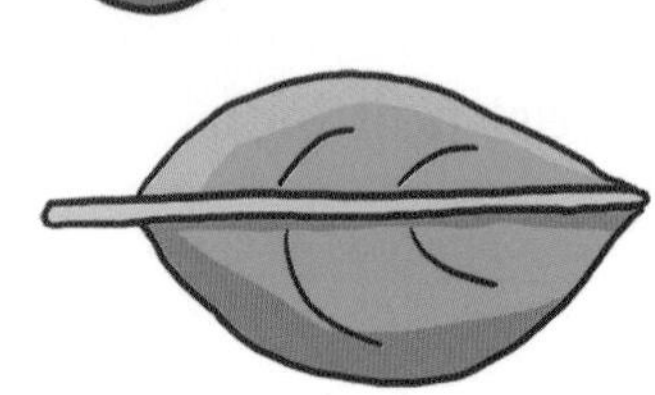

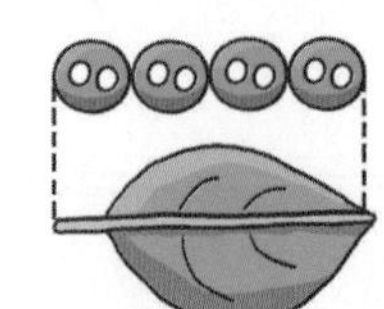

1 button is $\frac{1}{2}$ inch long.

$\frac{1}{2} + \frac{1}{2} = 1$

So, 2 buttons are 1 inch long.

The leaf is about 4 buttons long.

$\frac{1}{2} + \frac{1}{2} + \frac{1}{2} + \frac{1}{2} = 1 + 1$

So, 4 buttons are ____ inches long.

The leaf is about ____ inches long.

6 

The marker is about 8 buttons long.

The marker is about ____ inches long.

Measure each line segment to the nearest half inch.

7 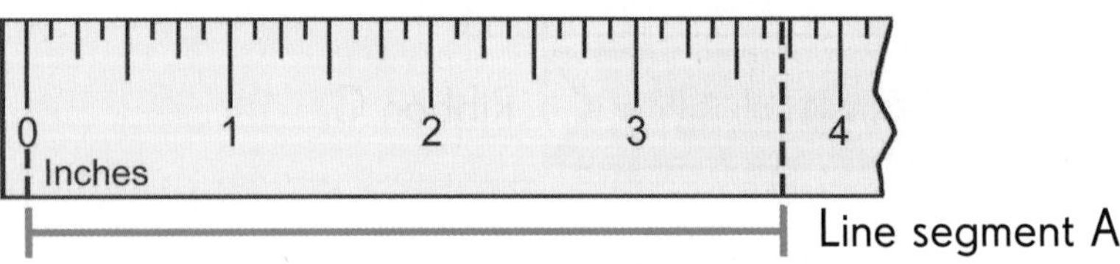

These rulers are smaller than in real life.

Line segment A is more than ____ inches but less than ____ inches.

It is nearer to ____ inches than to ____ inches.

Line segment A is ____ inches to the nearest half inch.

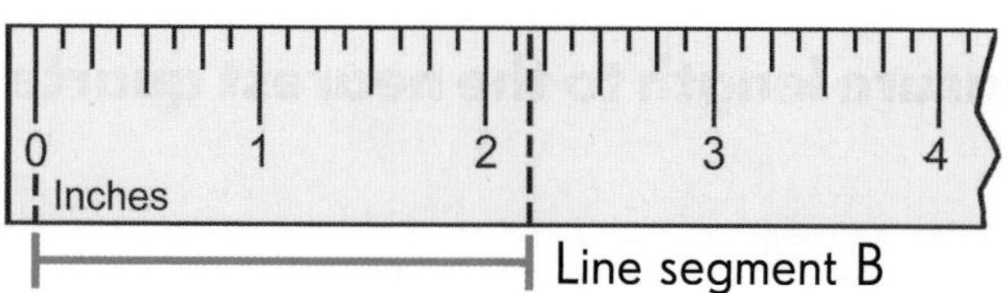

Line segment B is more than ______ inches but less than ______ inches.

It is nearer to ______ inches than to ______ inches.

Line segment B is ______ inches to the nearest half inch.

These rulers are smaller than in real life.

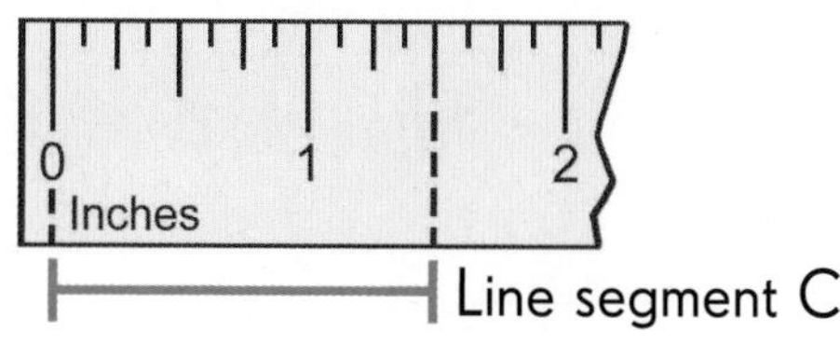

Line segment C is more than ______ inch but less than ______ inches.

It is ______ inches long.

Line segment C is ______ inches to the nearest half inch.

Find the length of each object to the nearest half inch.

10 The length of the scissors is about ______ inches.

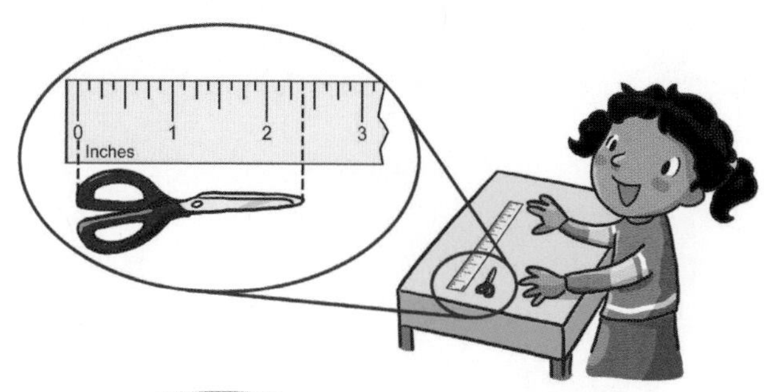

11 The length of the scissors is about ______ inches.

Learn Estimate and measure length to the nearest quarter inch.

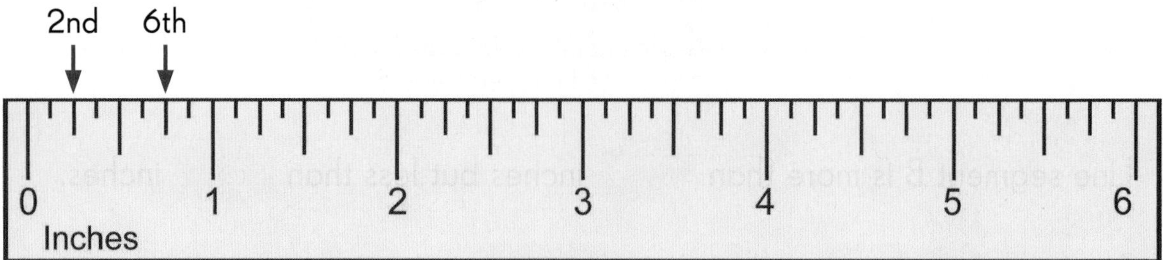

The second division marking is the $\frac{1}{4}$ inch mark.

The sixth division marking is the $\frac{3}{4}$ inch mark.

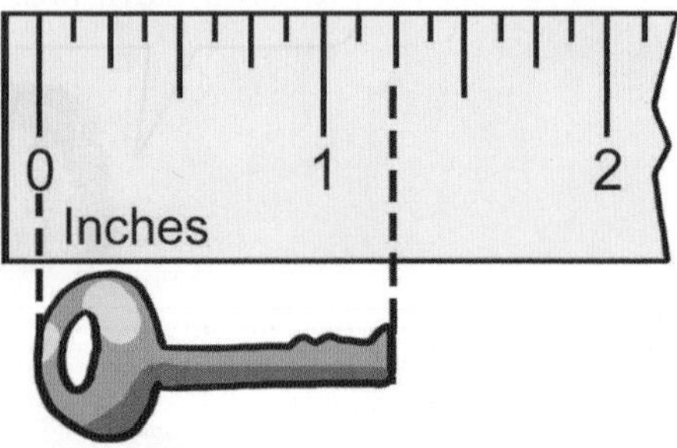

The length of the key is $1\frac{1}{4}$ inches to the nearest **quarter inch**.

It is halfway between 1 and $1\frac{1}{2}$.

$1\frac{3}{4}$ is halfway between $1\frac{1}{2}$ and 2.

$\frac{2}{4}$ is two quarters $\left(\frac{2}{4}\right)$ or one half $\left(\frac{1}{2}\right)$.

Guided Learning

Measure the length of the object to the nearest quarter inch.

12 The length of the scissors is ________ inches long.

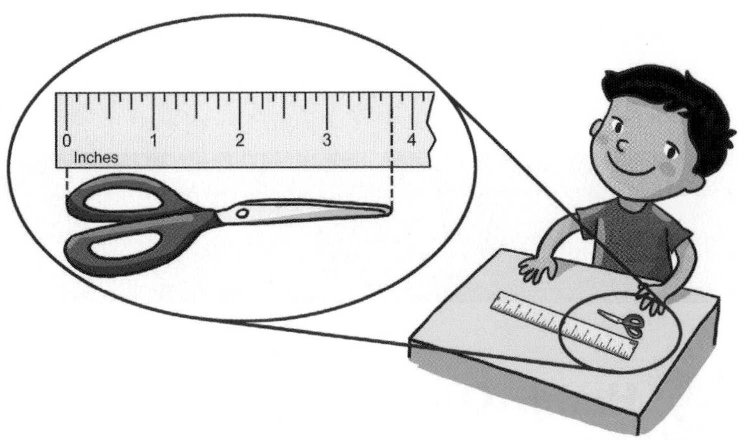

Measure each line segment to the nearest quarter inch.

13 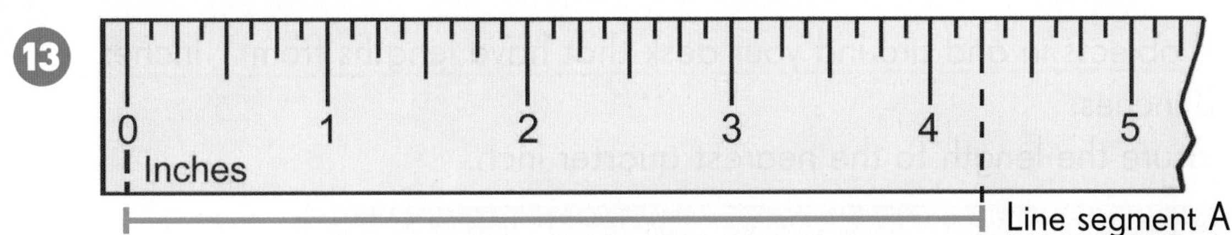

Line segment A is ________ inches long.

14 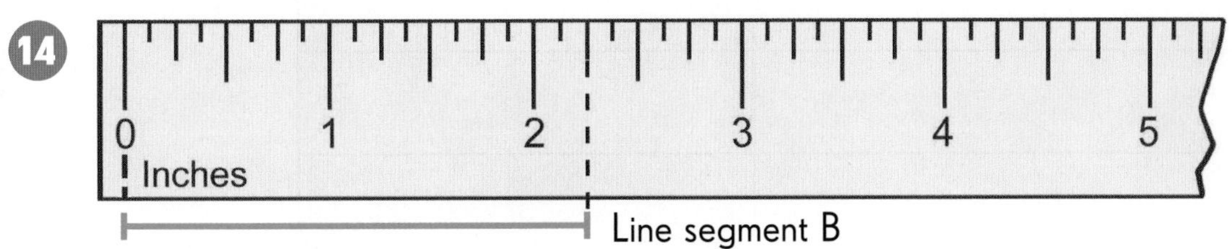

Line segment B is ________ inches long.

15

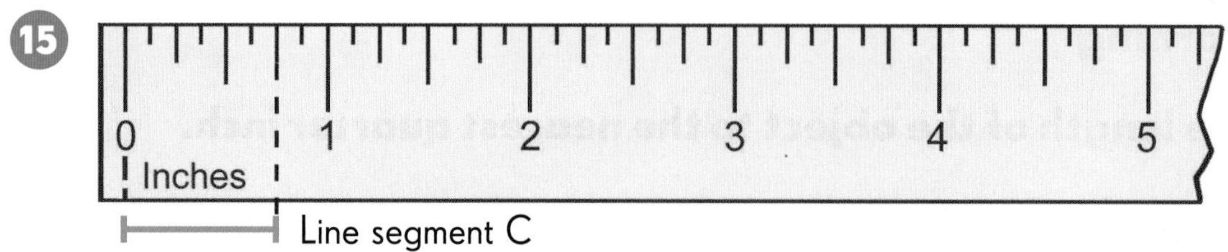

Line segment C is __________ inch long.

Materials:

• 12-inch rulers

STEP 1 Find objects in and around your desk that have lengths from 1 inches to 3 inches.
Measure the length to the nearest quarter inch.

Object	Measured Length (in.)

STEP 2 Ask two friends for their measurements.
Record all your data in a tally chart.

Number of Objects at Each Length

Measured Length (in.)	Tally	Number of Items
1		
$1\frac{1}{4}$		
$1\frac{1}{2}$		
$1\frac{3}{4}$		
2		
$2\frac{1}{4}$		
$2\frac{1}{2}$		
$2\frac{3}{4}$		
3		

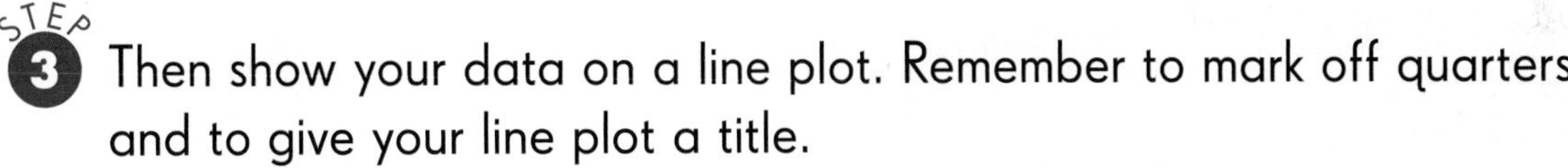

STEP 3 Then show your data on a line plot. Remember to mark off quarters and to give your line plot a title.

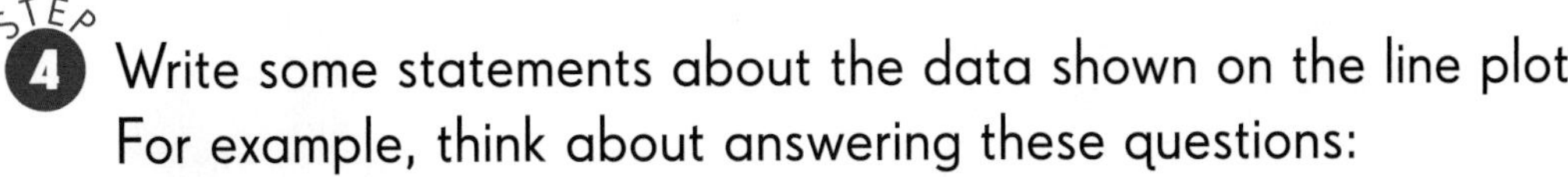

STEP 4 Write some statements about the data shown on the line plot. For example, think about answering these questions:

- What does each × stand for?
- How long is the greatest number of objects?

Use feet to measure length.

The length of this picture frame is about 1 foot. Use feet to measure longer objects.

The **foot** is another standard unit of length.
ft stands for foot.
Read 1 ft as 1 foot.
Read 2 ft as 2 feet.
1 foot (ft) = 12 inches (in.)

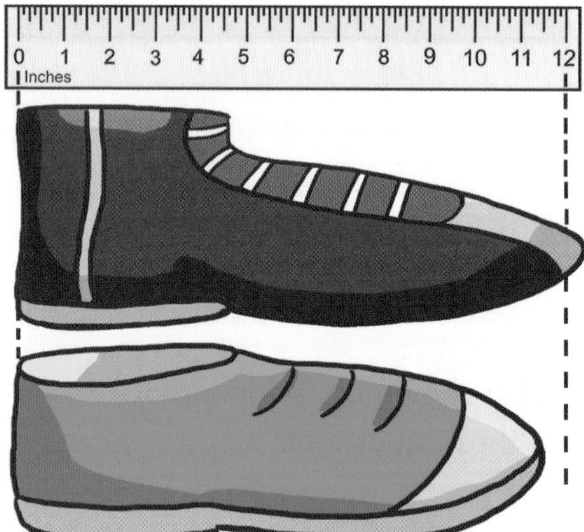

Large envelopes, a sheet of paper, and a football are about 1 foot long.

The length of the boot is more than 1 foot.
The length of the shoe is less than 1 foot.

The lengths of both the boot and the shoe are close to 1 foot. So, the boot and the shoe are each about 1 foot long.

Guided Learning

Complete.

The length of each shoe is about 12 inches.

16 The length of the tennis racket is about ______ feet.

17 The width of the tennis racket is about ______ foot.

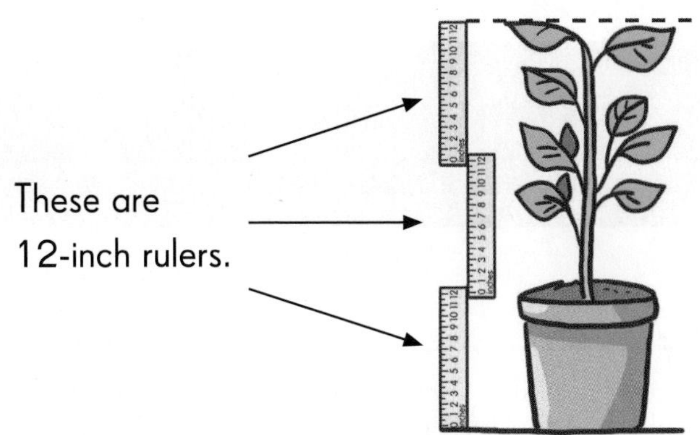
These are
12-inch rulers.

18 The plant is about ______ feet tall.

Complete. Use taller or shorter.

19 The plant is ______ than 2 feet.

Estimate the width or length of each object to the nearest foot.

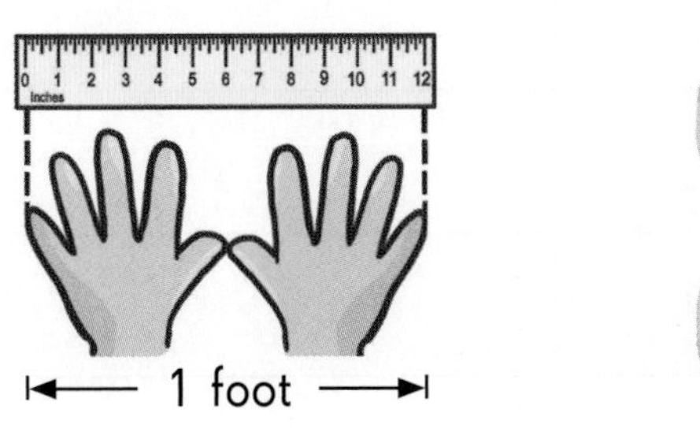
1 foot

20 The place mat is about ______ foot long.

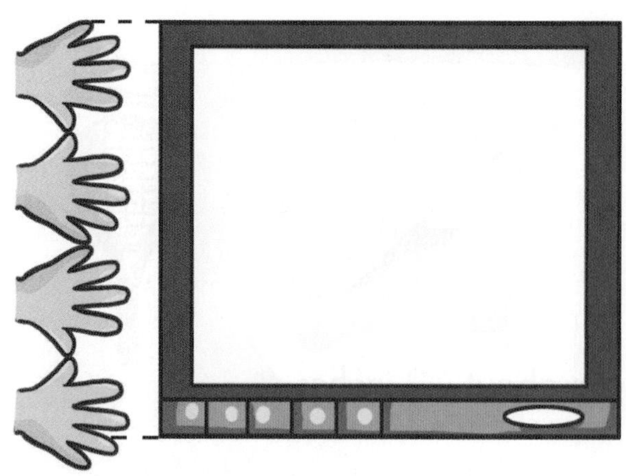

21 The height of the television set is about ____ feet.

Hands-On Activity

Materials:
- 12-inch rulers

First, estimate the length of each object in feet.
Then use rulers to measure the length.

Object	Estimate (ft)	Measured Length (in.)
Length of a bulletin board		
Height of the teacher's desk		
Length of your desk		
Height of your chair		
Length of the whiteboard		

Learn

Use yards to measure length.

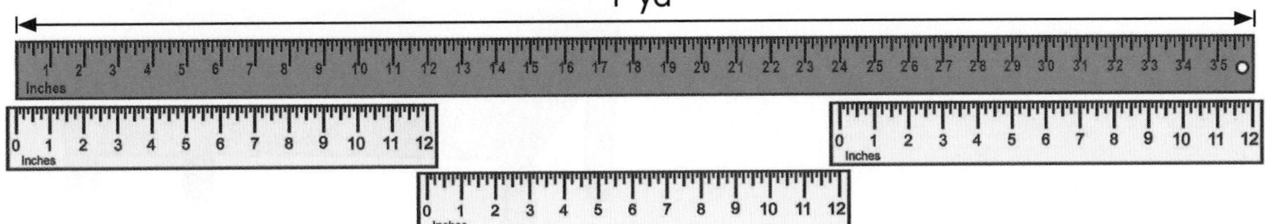

A yardstick is 3 times as long as a 12-inch ruler.

The **yard** is another standard customary unit of length.
It is used for measuring long lengths and short distances.
yd stands for yard.
1 yard (yd) = 3 feet (ft)
1 yard (yd) = 36 inches (in.)

A baseball bat is about 1 yard long.
A doorway is about 1 yard wide.

1 ft = 12 in.
3 ft = 12 × 3
= 36 in.

The height of a doorway is about 2 yards. The length of my garden is about 10 yards. The distance from my house to my neighbor's house is about 40 yards.

The boy is shorter than 1 yard.
The girl is taller than 1 yard.

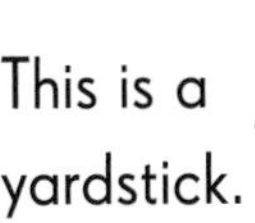

This is a yardstick.

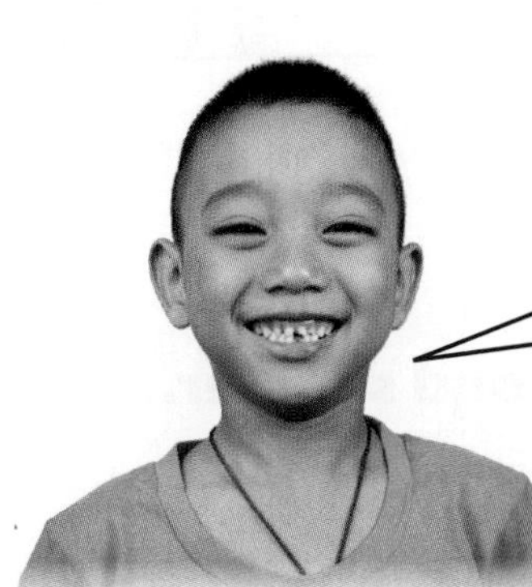

The heights of both the boy and the girl are close to 1 yard. So, they are about 1 yard tall.

Continued on next page

The length of the table is 1 yard.

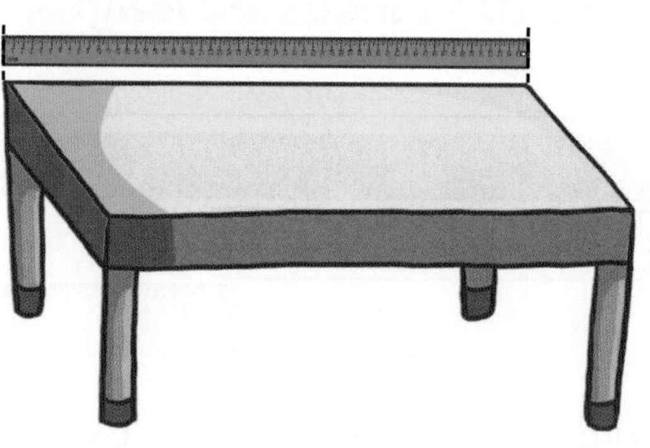

Guided Learning

Estimate the height of each object to the nearest yard.

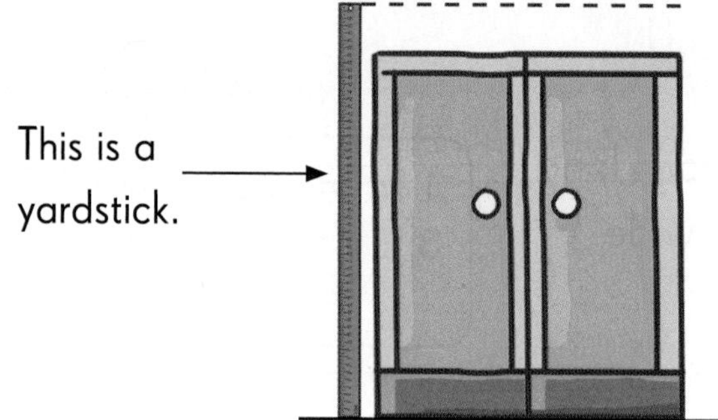
This is a
yardstick.

22 The height of the cupboard is about ______ yard.

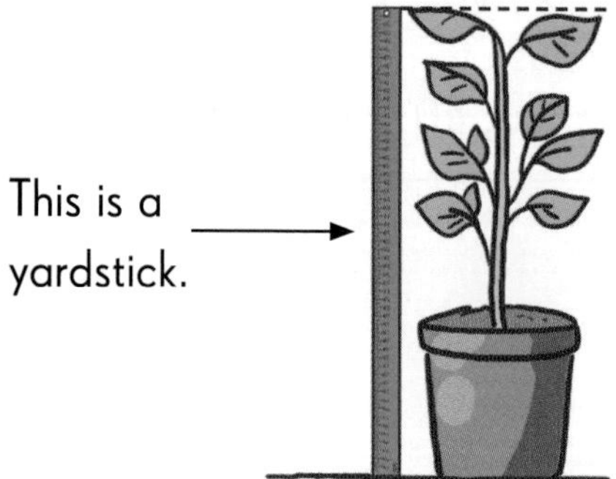
This is a
yardstick.

23 The height of the plant is ______ yard.

Complete. Use taller and shorter.

24 A chair is ______ than 3 yards.

25 A house is ______ than 2 yards.

Estimate the length of each object to the nearest yard.

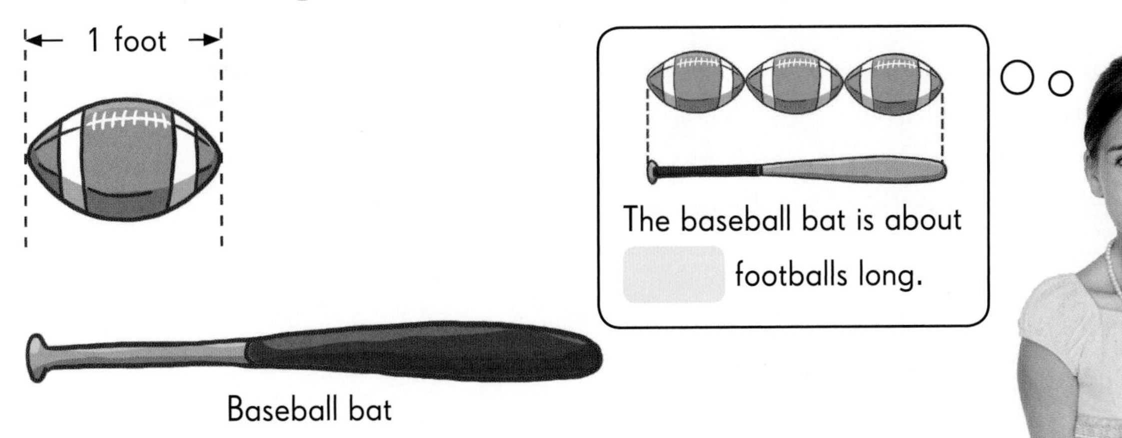
1 foot
The baseball bat is about
footballs long.

Baseball bat

26 The length of the baseball bat is about ______ yard.

27 The length of a car is about ______ yards.

Hands-On Activity

Material:
- 1-yard measuring tape

Estimate the length of each object in yards. Then use a 1-yard measuring tape to measure each object.

Object	Estimate (yd)	Measured Length (yd)
Length of your classroom		
Width of your classroom		
Height of a door		
Width of a door		
Length of a hallway		
Width of a hallway		

Learn Use miles to measure length.

The standard customary unit for measuring distance is the **mile**.
mi stands for mile.
The distance you can briskly walk in 20 minutes is about 1 mile.
Jerome estimates that the distance between his home and school is 1 mile.

1 mile (mi) = 1,760 yards (yd)
1 mile (mi) = 5,280 feet (ft)

There are 1,760 yards, or 1 mile, between my home and the school.

1 yd = 3 ft

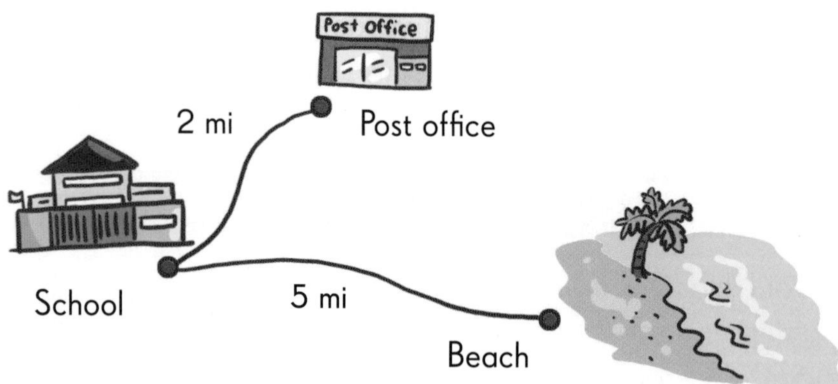

The distance between the school and the post office is 2 miles.

Is the school about 3,500 yards from the post office?

Yes. The post office is also about 10,000 feet away from the school.

The distance between the school and the beach is 5 miles.

Is the school about 5,000 yards from the beach?

No. It is further than 5,000 yards away. It is 5 miles. So, it is about 8,800 yards from the beach.

Guided Learning

Complete.

28 A helicopter is flying at a height of 5,257 feet.

It is about ___ mile high.

1 mi = 5,280 ft

Rebecca estimated the distance between her home and the school to be about 1 mile.

29 Give two possible distances in feet that are about 1 mile.

They are ___ and .

30 Give two possible distances in yards that are about 2 miles.

They are  and ___.

31 A 3-mile brisk walk will usually take about ___ minutes.

Let's Practice

Measure the line segment to the nearest inch.

1. 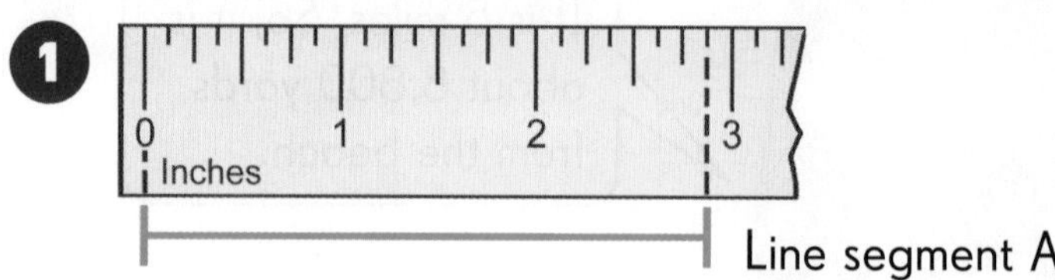

Line segment A is about ______ inches.

Measure the line segment to the nearest half inch.

2. 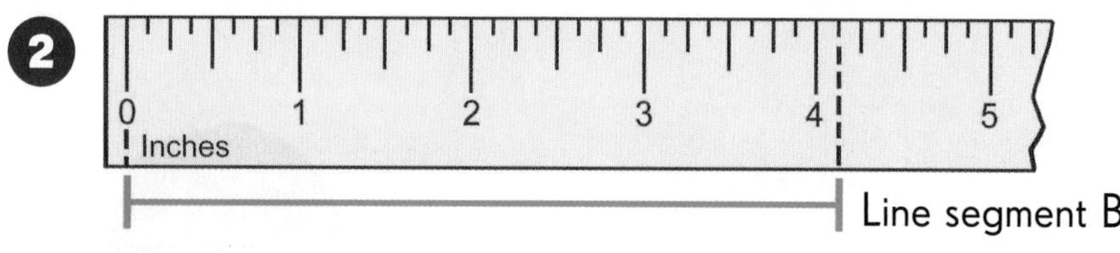

Line segment B is about ______ inches.

These rulers are smaller than in real life.

Measure the line segment to the nearest quarter inch.

3. 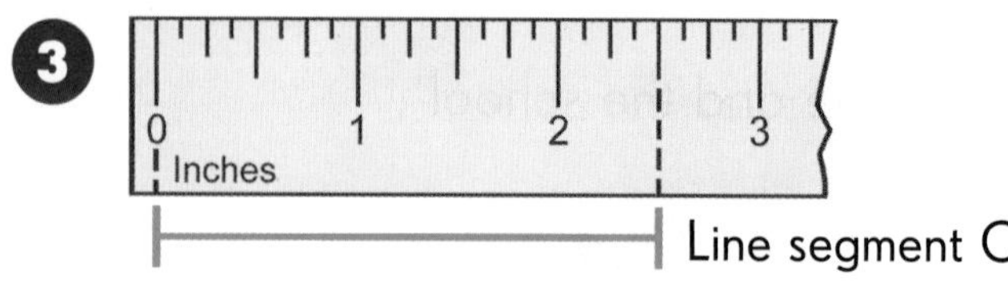

Line segment C is about ______ inches.

Choose the answer.

4. The width of 2 fingers is about 1 inch.
Which of these objects is about 1 inch long?

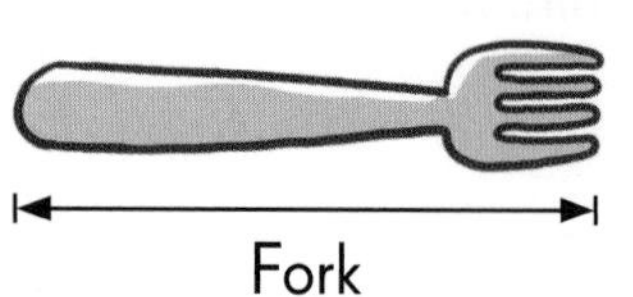
Fork

Bottle cap

Exercise book

Choose the unit you would use to measure each object.
Use inch, foot, yard, or mile.

5. the length of a pair of glasses

6. the length of a football field

Choose the best estimate of the objects.

7. The length of two footballs is about 2 inches / feet / yards / miles.

8. The distance a person might travel to school is about 2 inches / feet / yards / miles.

Choose the answer.

9. 1 foot is equal to 12 inches.
Which of these objects is about 1 foot long?

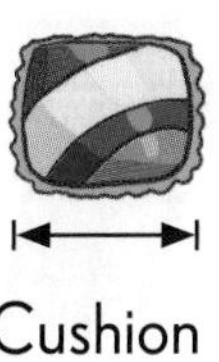
Cushion

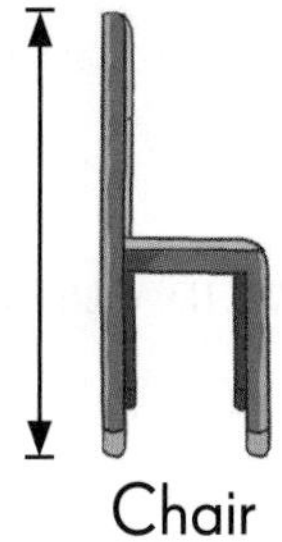
Chair

Tree

10. 1 yard is equal to 3 feet, or 36 inches.
Which of these objects is about 1 yard long?

Bottle

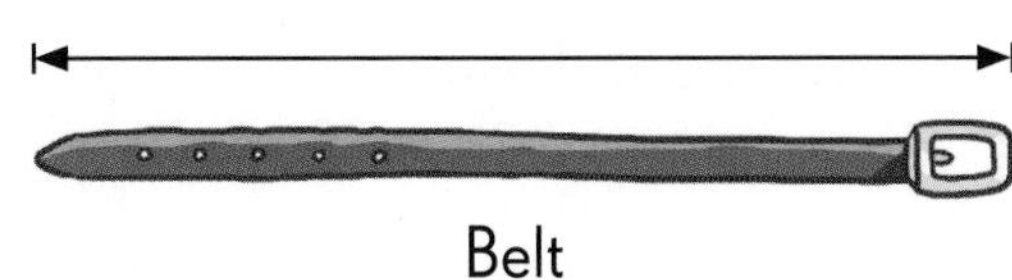
Belt

House

11. How long will it take you to briskly walk 2 miles?

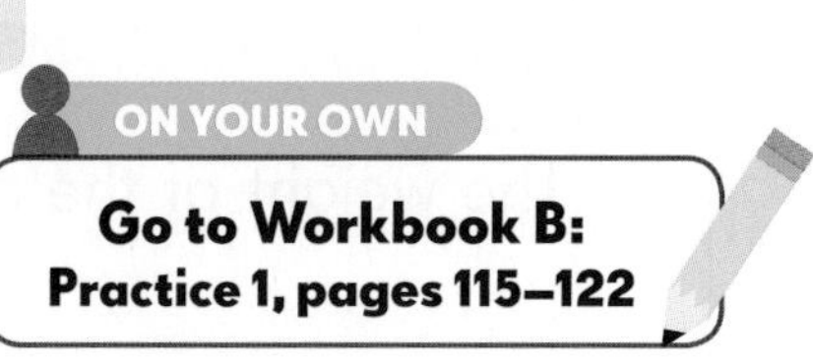

ON YOUR OWN
Go to Workbook B:
Practice 1, pages 115–122

Lesson

15.2 Measuring Weight

Lesson Objectives

- Use ounce, pound, and ton as units of measurement for weight.
- Read scales in ounces (oz) and pounds (lb).
- Estimate and find actual weights of objects by using different scales.
- Use referents to estimate weight.

Vocabulary
ounce (oz)
pound (lb)
ton (T)

Learn

Use ounces to measure weight.

The **ounce** is a standard customary unit of weight.
It is used for measuring light objects.
oz stands for ounce.

This is a scale that measures light objects in ounces.

The scale shows the weight of 1 slice of bread.
The weight of the slice of bread is about 1 ounce.

The balance shows the weight of some carrots.

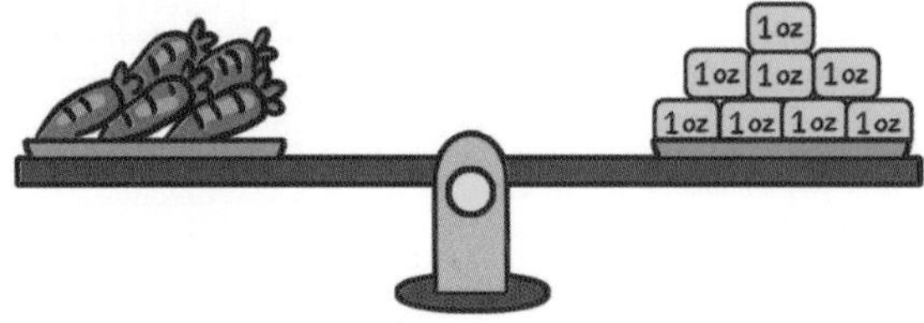

The weight of the carrots is about 8 ounces.

Guided Learning

Complete.

The scale shows the weight of 5 grapes.
The weight of the grapes is 1 ounce.

1. Make a guess. What is the weight of a bunch of grapes? ____

2. The weight of the bunch of grapes above is ____ ounces.

Learn: Weigh objects to the nearest ounce.

The pencils weigh more than 3 ounces
but less than 4 ounces.
The pencils weigh about 3 ounces.

The pointer on the scale is nearer to the 3 ounce mark.

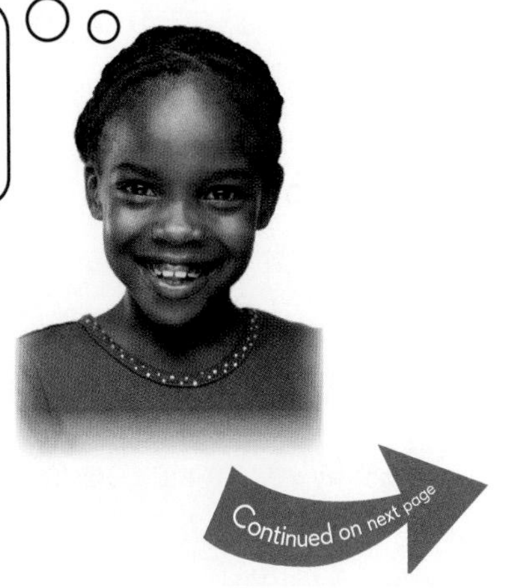

Continued on next page

The cherries weigh more than 9 ounces but less than 10 ounces.

The pointer on the scale is nearer to the 10 ounce mark.

The cherries weigh about 10 ounces.

A slice of bread weighs about 1 ounce. You can use the slice of bread to estimate the weights of other light objects.

1 slice of bread weighs about 1 ounce.
4 slices of bread weigh about 4 ounces.

The apple is about 4 ounces.

Guided Learning

Complete.

3 What is the weight of the 3 apples? ____ ounces

4 What is the weight of the tube of toothpaste? About ____ ounces

5 What is the weight of 2 tennis balls? About ____ ounces

6 A slice of cheese weighs about 1 ounce.

The 2 limes weigh about ____ ounces.

Chapter Wrap Up

Study Guide

You have learned...

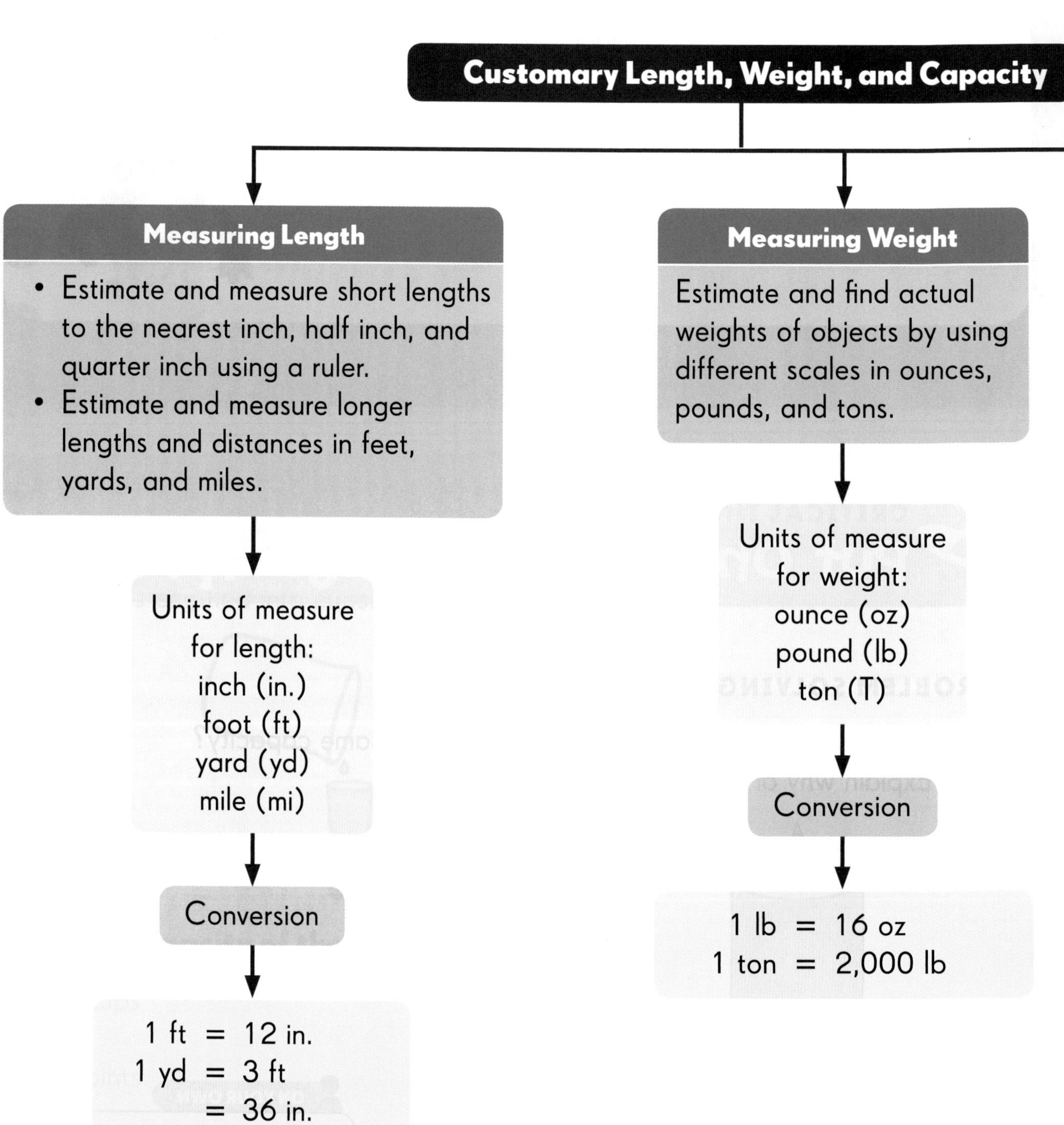

Customary Length, Weight, and Capacity
Measuring Length
• Estimate and measure short lengths to the nearest inch, half inch, and quarter inch using a ruler.
• Estimate and measure longer lengths and distances in feet, yards, and miles.
Units of measure for length:
inch (in.)
foot (ft)
yard (yd)
mile (mi)
Conversion
1 ft = 12 in.
1 yd = 3 ft
= 36 in.
1 mi = 1,760 yd
1 mi = 5,280 ft
Measuring Weight
Estimate and find actual weights of objects by using different scales in ounces, pounds, and tons.
Units of measure for weight:
ounce (oz)
pound (lb)
ton (T)
Conversion
1 lb = 16 oz
1 ton = 2,000 lb

▶ Length, weight, and capacity can be measured using customary units.

Measuring Capacity

Estimate and find actual capacity using standard measuring cups.

Units of measure for capacity:
cup (c)
pint (pt)
quart (qt)
gallon (gal)

Conversion

1 pt = 2 c
1 qt = 2 pt
= 4 c
1 gal = 4 qt
= 8 pt
= 16 c

Farmer Fred travels to his orchard barn each day. Help him to find the distance he travels each day.

Complete the sentences.

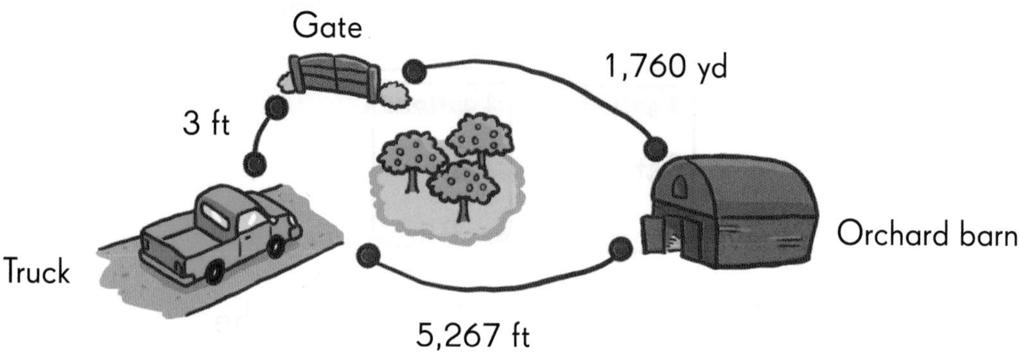

23 Farmer Fred travels ___ yard to the gate from his truck each day.

24 He travels ___ mile from the gate to the orchard barn.

25 On his way back to the truck from the orchard barn, he travels about ___ mile.

Problem Solving

Solve.

26 Farmer Fred has a container of orange juice that has a capacity of 4 quarts. He has 2 pints of orange juice in it now. How much more orange juice does he need to completely fill the container? ___

27 Farmer Fred makes 4 quarts of orange juice on Monday. He makes 2 quarts more orange juice on Tuesday than on Monday. He makes 2 more quarts on Wednesday than on Tuesday. He carries on making 2 more quarts of orange juice every day than the day before. In how many days will he make a total of 80 pints of orange juice? ___ days

Time and Temperature

Lessons

16.1 Telling Time
16.2 Converting Hours and Minutes
16.3 Adding Hours and Minutes
16.4 Subtracting Hours and Minutes
16.5 Elapsed Time
16.6 Measuring Temperature
16.7 Real-World Problems: Time and Temperature

- Time can be used to tell when activities start and end, or how long an activity will last.
- Temperature can be used to understand what the weather will be like.

Recall Prior Knowledge

Skip counting by 5s to find minutes

5 10 15 20 25 30 35

$7 \times 5 = 35$
The minute hand shows 35 minutes.

Knowing that 60 minutes is 1 hour

60 minutes = 1 hour

The minute hand moves one complete round in 60 minutes.
The hour hand moves from one number to the next number in 1 hour.

Telling time

Read 2:30 as two thirty.

A.M. shows the time after midnight but before noon.
P.M. shows the time after noon but before midnight.

Finding elapsed time

8:00 A.M. is 1 hour after 7:00 A.M.
7:00 A.M. is 1 hour before 8:00 A.M.

10:30 A.M. is 30 minutes or half an hour after 10 A.M.
10:30 A.M. is 30 minutes or half an hour before 11 A.M.

Reading numbers on a number line

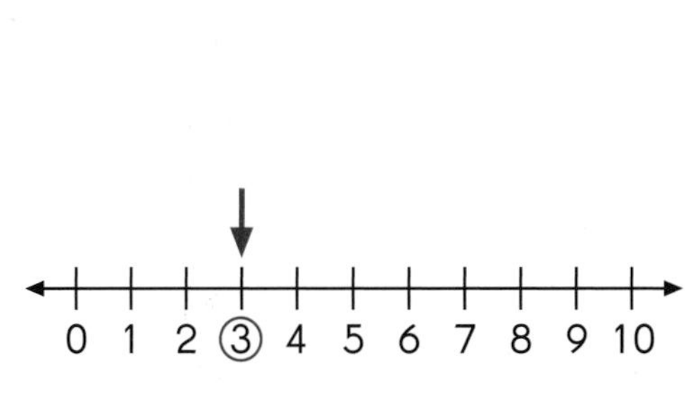

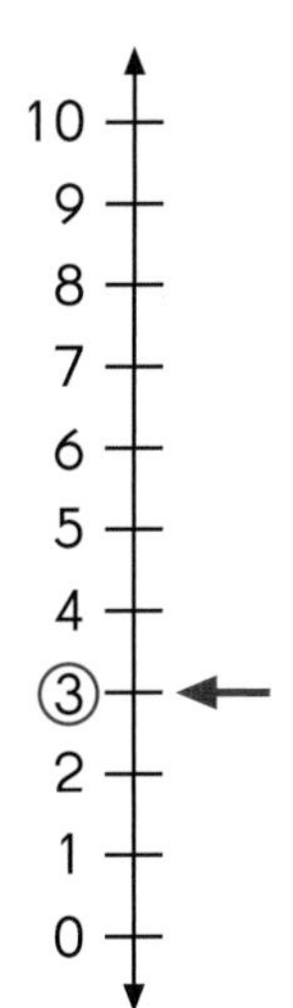

The arrow points to (3) on the number lines.

✔ Quick Check

Look at each clock. Then decide which number is missing.

1

The minute hand shows ___ minutes after the hour.

2

The minute hand shows ___ minutes after the hour.

Tell the time.

___

4

___

5 The time is 20 minutes past 7.

6 The time is 45 minutes before 10.

Complete the sentences with A.M. or P.M.

7

Robin eats breakfast at 7:50 ____

8

He eats dinner at 8:00 ____

Find the length of time.

9 3 P.M. is ____ after 2 P.M.

10 4:30 A.M. is ____ before 5 A.M.

11 Noon is ____ after 11:30 A.M.

Lesson 16.1 Telling Time

Lesson Objectives

- Tell time to the minute.
- Read time on a digital clock.

Vocabulary
hour
past
minute
to

Learn Tell time to the nearest minute.

Each small mark stands for 1 **minute**.

The minute hand shows 5 minutes.

Students are in the auditorium at 9:20 A.M. for an assembly.

9:20
It is 20 minutes after 9 o'clock.
You can also say the time is 20 minutes **past** 9.
The time is nine twenty.

Continued on next page

At 7:40 P.M., a group of people visit the Community Center for a charity dinner.

It is 20 minutes before 8 o'clock.
60 − 40 = 20
The time is seven forty.
You can also say the time is 20 minutes **to** 8.

Guided Learning

Find the missing numbers.

1

The time is six fifteen.
It is ___ minutes after 6.

6:15 is ___ minutes past 6.

2

The time is five forty-five.
It is ___ minutes before 6.

5:45 is ___ minutes to 6.

3 3:25

The time is three twenty-five.

It is ____ minutes after 3.

4 3:30

The time is half past three.

It is ____ minutes before 4.

Complete using past or to.

5

8:07 is 7 minutes ____ 8.

6

2:37 is 23 minutes ____ 3.

7

5:05 is 5 minutes ____ 5.

8

____ − 30 = ____

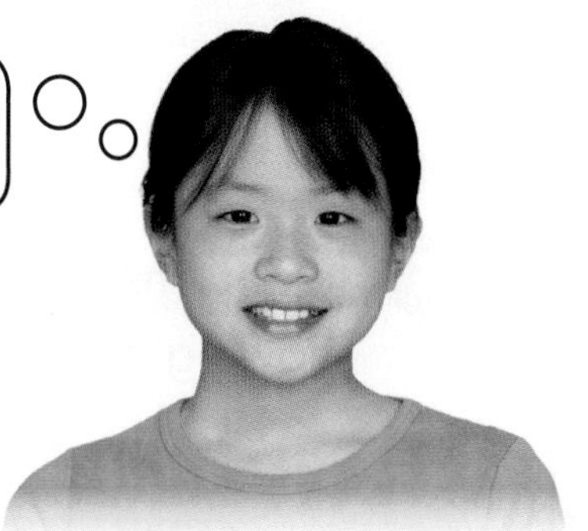

7:30 is 30 minutes ____ 8.

WORKING TOGETHER **Game**

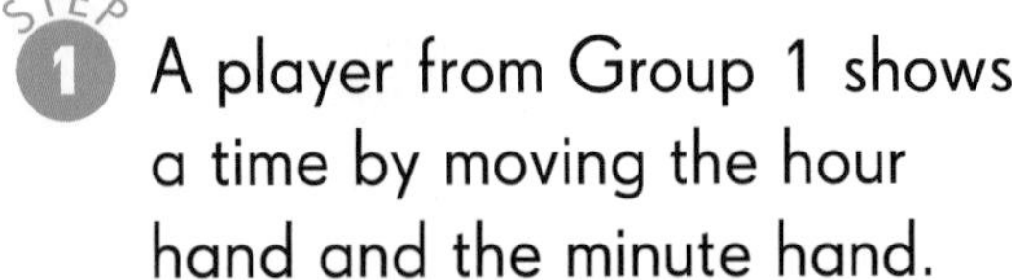

Show and Tell Time!

Players: 2 groups of students

Material:

- a clock with movable hands

STEP 1 A player from Group 1 shows a time by moving the hour hand and the minute hand.

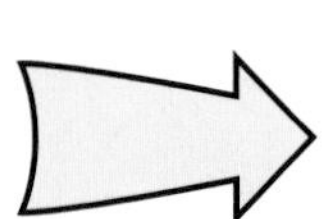

STEP 2 A player from Group 2 tells the time in two ways.

- two fifty
- 10 minutes to 3

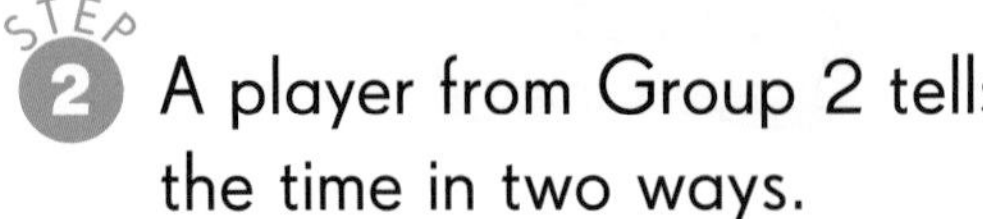

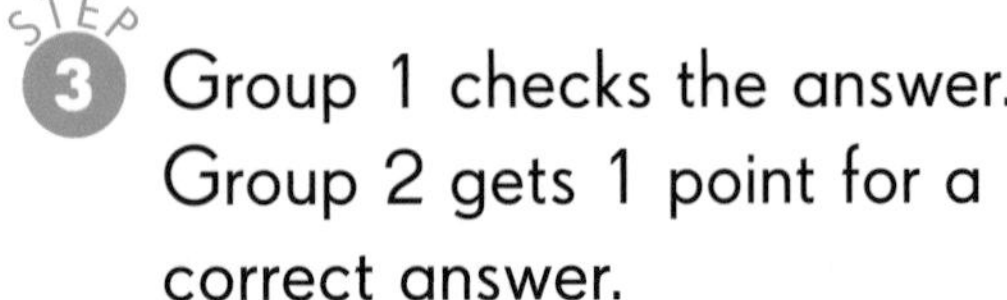

STEP 3 Group 1 checks the answer. Group 2 gets 1 point for a correct answer.

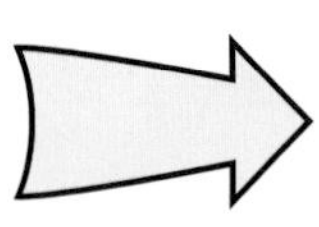

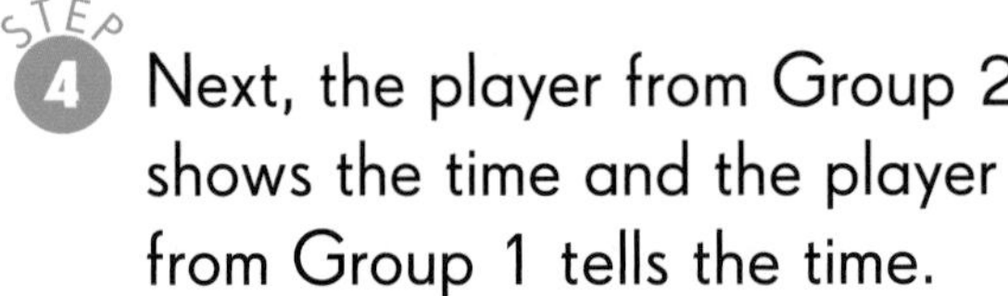

STEP 4 Next, the player from Group 2 shows the time and the player from Group 1 tells the time.

- five seventeen
- 17 minutes past 5

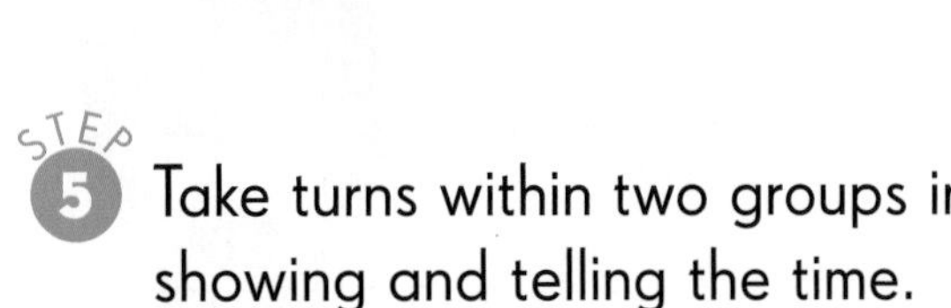

STEP 5 Take turns within two groups in showing and telling the time.

The group with the most points wins!

Let's Practice

Tell the time in two ways.

1. 

2. 

3. 

4. 

Tell the time in a different way.

5. 5 minutes past 11 is ______.

6. 5 minutes to 11 is ______.

7. 12 minutes past 6 is ______.

8. 15 minutes to 8 is ______.

Fill in the blanks.

9. 3:20 is ______ minutes past ______.

10. 12:35 is ______ minutes to ______.

ON YOUR OWN

Go to Workbook B: Practice 1, pages 143–146

Converting Hours and Minutes

Vocabulary
hours (h)
minutes (min)

Lesson Objective

- Change minutes to hours or hours to minutes.

Learn

Convert hours (h) to minutes (min).

Jerry rides for 2 **hours**.
How many **minutes** are in 2 hours?

1 h = 60 min
2 h = 60 min + 60 min = 120 min

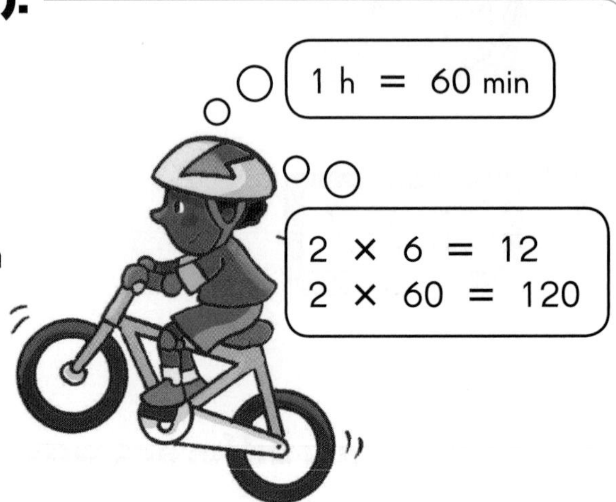

You can also multiply to find the number of minutes.

2 h = 2 × 60 min = 120 min

There are 120 minutes in 2 hours.

h stands for hour.
min stands for minutes.
Read 1 h as one hour.
Read 30 min as thirty minutes.

Guided Learning

Express the time in minutes.

1. Jerry took 3 hours to do his homework.
How many minutes are in 3 hours?

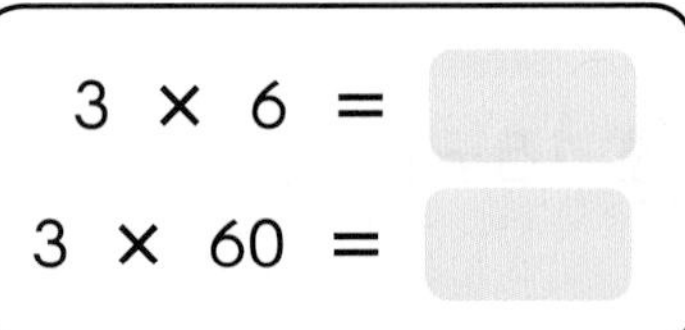

3 h = ____ min + ____ min + ____ min
= ____ min

You can also multiply.

3 h = ____ × 60 min
= ____ min

There are ____ minutes in 3 hours.

Learn Convert hours and minutes to minutes.

Matt plays basketball for 1 hour 10 minutes.
How many minutes are in 1 hour 10 minutes?

1 h 10 min = 60 min + 10 min
= 70 min

1 h 10 min → 1 h = 60 min, 10 min

There are 70 minutes in 1 hour 10 minutes.

Guided Learning

Express the time in minutes.

2 Kevin's baseball game lasts for 2 hours 30 minutes.
How many minutes are in 2 hours 30 minutes?

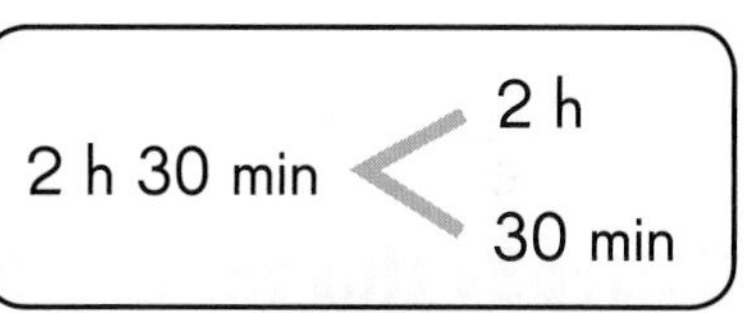

2 hour 30 minutes
= ___ min + ___ min + ___ min
= ___ min

There are ___ minutes in 2 hours 30 minutes.

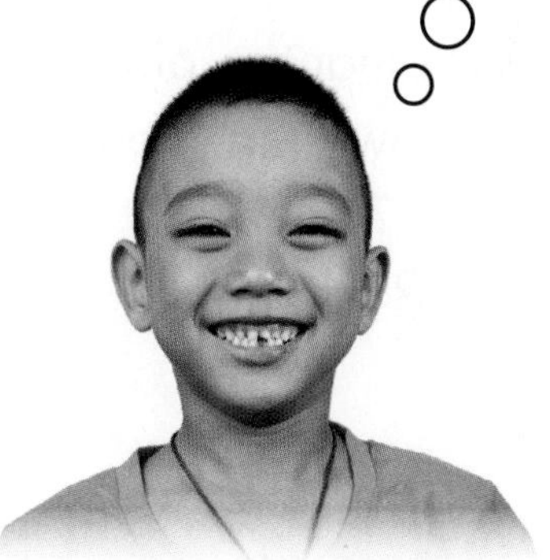

Express the time in minutes.

3 2 h 45 min
= ___ min + ___ min
= ___ min

4 4 h 28 min
= ___ min + ___ min
= ___ min

1 h = 60 min
2 h = 2 × ___ min
= ___ min

1 h = 60 min
4 h = 4 × ___ min
= ___ min

Learn Convert minutes to hours and minutes.

Marshall takes 135 minutes to mow the lawn.
How many hours and minutes are in 135 minutes?

135 min = 120 min + 15 min
= 2 h 15 min

1 h = 60 min
1 × 60 = 60
2 × 60 = 120 ✓
3 × 60 = 180

135 min → 120 min = 2 h
→ 15 min

There are 2 hours 15 minutes in 135 minutes.

Guided Learning

Express the time in hours and minutes.

5. Samantha plays the piano for 82 minutes.
How many hours and minutes are in 82 minutes?

82 min = ___ min + ___ min
= ___ h ___ min

There are ___ hour ___ minutes in 82 minutes.

Express the time in hours and minutes.

6. 90 min = ___ min + ___ min
= ___ h ___ min

7. 130 min = ___

8. 145 min = ___

9. 192 min = ___

WORKING TOGETHER **Game**

Let's Play Time Bingo!

Players: 2 groups of 2 students

Materials:
- Time Cards
- Bingo Board

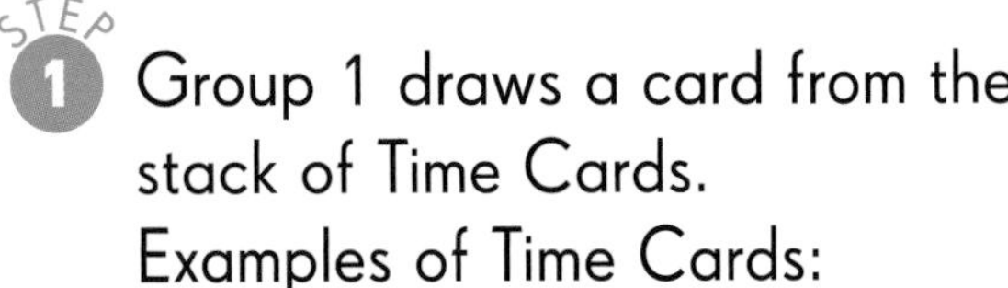

STEP 1 Group 1 draws a card from the stack of Time Cards.
Examples of Time Cards:

1 h 25 min = ☐ min

75 min = ☐ h ☐ min

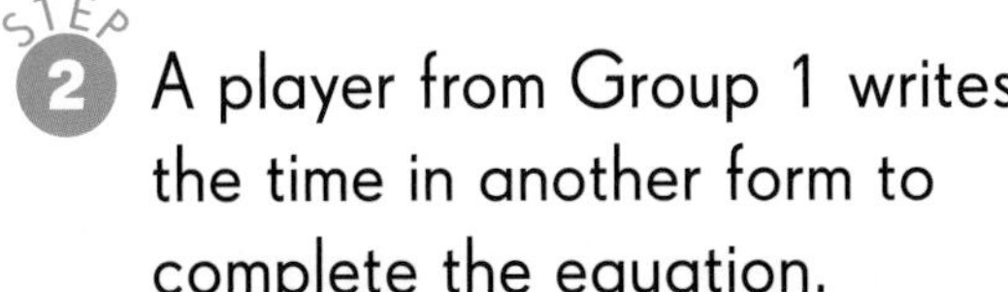

STEP 2 A player from Group 1 writes the time in another form to complete the equation.

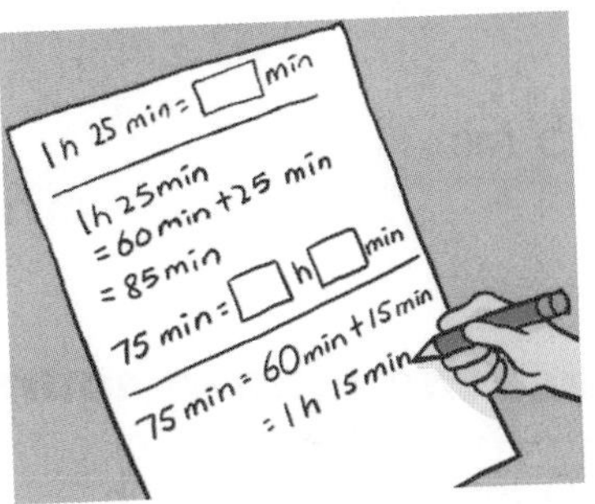

STEP 3 Groups take turns. Group 1 marks their answers on their Bingo Board with an X. Group 2 marks their answers with an O.

100 min	60 min	240 min
1 h 15 min	2 h 5 min	~~85 min~~
130 min	63 min	3 h

The first group to mark three correct answers in a straight line (↕, ↔, ↖↘, ↙↗) on the Bingo Board wins!

Let's Practice

Complete each number bond.

1. 1 h 45 min < ___ h, ___ min

2. 3 h 40 min < ___ h, ___ min

Complete each number bond.

3. 75 min < ___ h, ___ min

4. 140 min < ___ h, ___ min

Express the time in hours.

5. 60 min = ___ h

6. 120 min = 60 min + ___ min
   = ___ h

7. 180 min = 60 min + 60 min + ___ min
   = ___ h

120 min
= ___ × 60 min

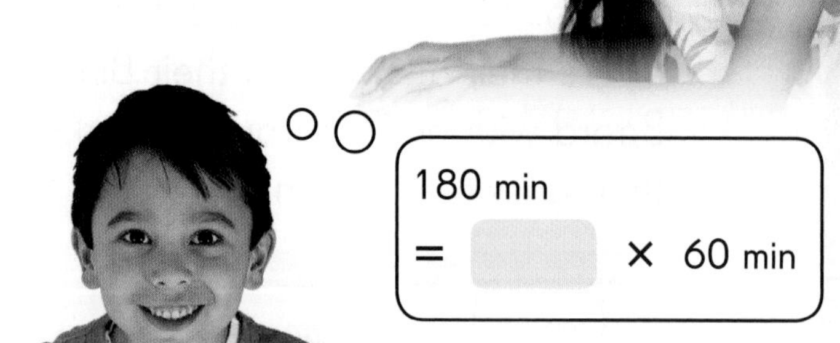

Express the time in minutes.

8. 4 h 33 min = ___ min

9. 3 h 54 min = ___ min

ON YOUR OWN

Go to Workbook B: Practice 2, pages 147–150

Lesson 16.3 Adding Hours and Minutes

Lesson Objective

- Add time with and without regrouping.

Learn Add time without regrouping.

Today, Mr. Carlson works 2 hours 15 minutes in the morning.
He works 5 hours 10 minutes in the afternoon.
How long did he work today?

2 h 15 min + 5 h 10 min = ?

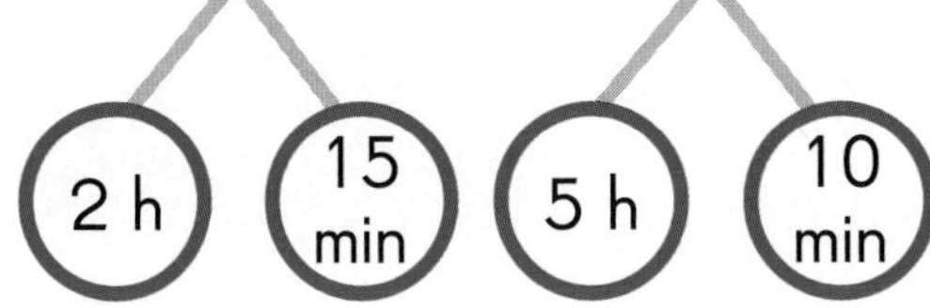

Add the hours.

2 h → + 5 h → 7 h

Add the minutes.

15 min → + 10 min → 25 min

2 h 15 min + 5 h 10 min = 7 h 25 min

Mr. Carlson worked 7 hours 25 minutes today.

Guided Learning

Complete.

1 3 h 20 min + 4 h 15 min = ?

3 h 20 min + 4 h 15 min

= ____ h ____ min

3 h + 4 h = ____

20 min + 15 min = ____

Learn Add time with regrouping.

Emily takes a flight from Chicago to New York.
She waits 40 minutes to check her luggage.
Then she waits 1 hour 55 minutes before boarding the airplane.
How long does she wait in all?

40 min + 1 h 55 min = ?

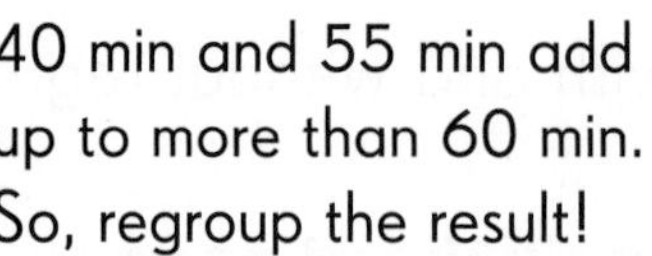

40 min and 55 min add up to more than 60 min. So, regroup the result!

 STEP 1 Add the minutes.

40 min + 55 min = 95 min
95 min = 1 h 35 min

 STEP 2 Add the hours.

1 h 35 min + 1 h = 2 h 35 min

She waits 2 hours 35 minutes in all.

Guided Learning

Complete.

 2 h 45 min + 5 h 35 min = ?

First, add the minutes.

45 min + 35 min = ____ min

____ min = ____ h ____ min

Then, add the hours.

2 h + 5 h + ____ h ____ min = ____ h ____ min

WORK IN PAIRS **Game**

Let's Play Time Shuffle!

Players: 2

Materials:

- a counter
- game board

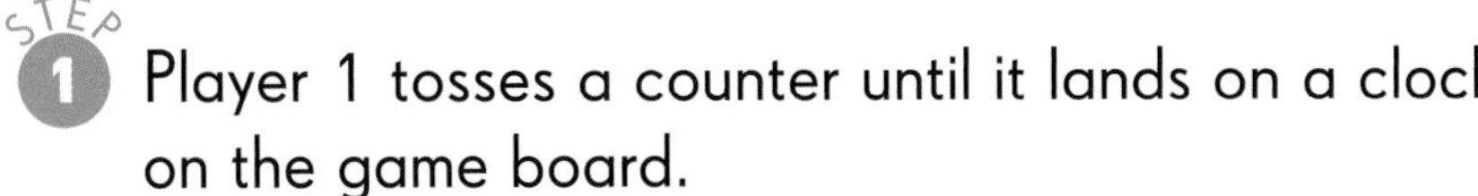

STEP 1 Player 1 tosses a counter until it lands on a clock on the game board.

STEP 2 The player writes a time that is shown on the clock picture.
For example, the player gets 50 minutes if the counter lands on the clock showing 50 minutes.

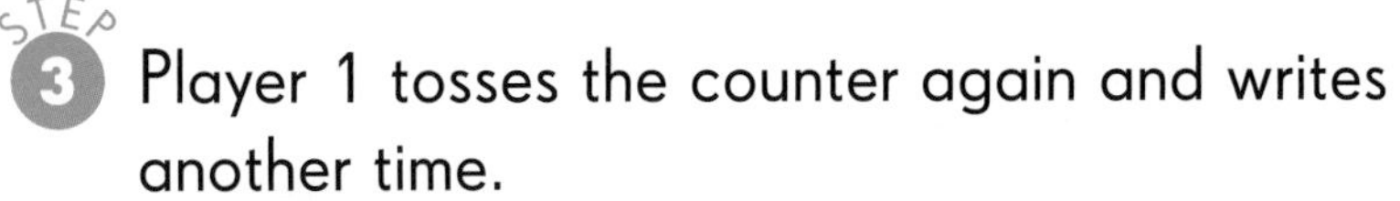

STEP 3 Player 1 tosses the counter again and writes another time.
For example, the player gets 2 hours.
The player then adds the two times.
50 min + 2 h = 2 h 50 min

STEP 4 Player 2 checks the answer.
Player 1 gets 1 point for a correct answer.

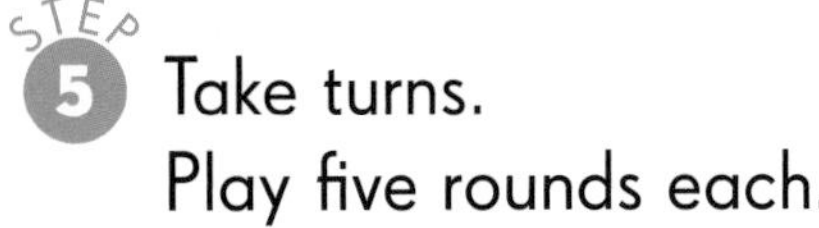

STEP 5 Take turns.
Play five rounds each.

The player with the most points wins!

Let's Practice

Add. Use number bonds to help you.

1. 4 h 15 min + 5 h 30 min
2. 7 h 10 min + 2 h 45 min
3. 2 h 35 min + 2 h 20 min
4. 4 h 25 min + 1 h 15 min
5. 1 h 40 min + 2 h 10 min
6. 6 h 5 min + 1 h 35 min

Add. Use number bonds to help you.

7. 3 h 40 min + 5 h 25 min
8. 4 h 55 min + 6 h 15 min
9. 2 h 57 min + 2 h 8 min
10. 3 h 45 min + 1 h 40 min

57 min + 8 min = ___ min
= ___ h ___ min

11. 3 h 45 min + 4 h 50 min
12. 5 h 35 min + 1 h 37 min
13. 3 h 25 min + 3 h 45 min

ON YOUR OWN

Go to Workbook B: Practice 3, pages 151–152

Subtracting Hours and Minutes

Lesson Objective

- Subtract time with and without regrouping.

Subtract time without regrouping.

Mr. Jackson takes 2 hours 15 minutes to paint his bedroom.
He takes 1 hour 5 minutes to paint his dining room.
How much longer does he take to paint the bedroom than dining room?

2 h 15 min − 1 h 5 min = ?

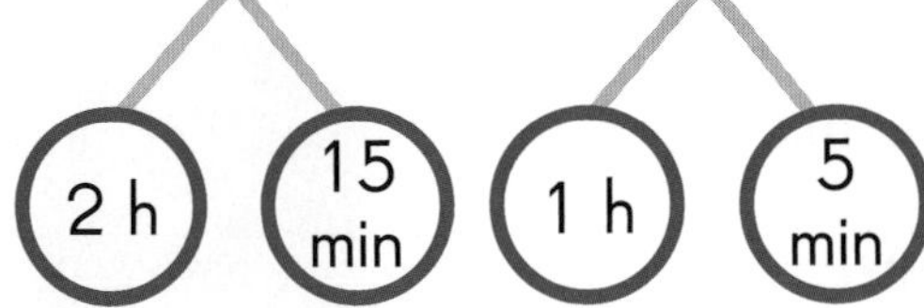

STEP 1 Subtract the hours.

2 h → (− 1 h) → 1 h

STEP 2 Subtract the minutes.

15 min → (− 5 min) → 10 min

2 h 15 min − 1 h 5 min = 1 h 10 min

He takes 1 hour 10 minutes longer to paint the bedroom than the dining room.

Guided Learning

8 h − 3 h = ☐ h
45 min − 20 min = ☐ min

Complete.

1 8 h 45 min − 3 h 20 min = ?

8 h 45 min − 3 h 20 min

= ☐ h ☐ min

Learn Subtract time with regrouping.

Kyle bikes for 4 hours 30 minutes.
Joey bikes for 2 hours 50 minutes.
How much longer does Kyle bike than Joey?

4 h 30 min − 2 h 50 min = ?

STEP 1 Regroup 4 h 30 min.

4 h 30 min = 3 h 90 min

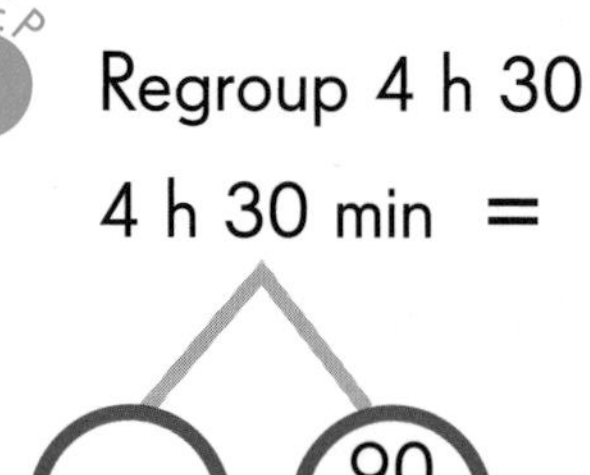

STEP 2 Subtract.

3 h 90 min − 2 h 50 min = 1 h 40 min

Kyle bikes 1 hour 40 minutes longer than Joey.

You cannot subtract 50 minutes from 30 minutes. So regroup 4 hours 30 minutes.

Guided Learning

Complete.

2 7 h 20 min − 4 h 45 min = ?

First, regroup 7 h 20 min.

7 h 20 min = 6 h ___ min

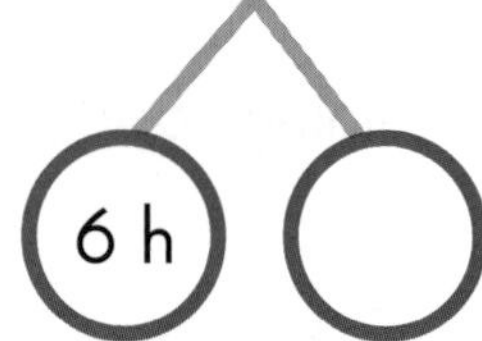

Then, subtract.

6 h ___ min − 4 h ___ min = ___ h ___ min

Subtract.

3 4 h 30 min – 2 h 45 min

___

4 8 h 35 min − 4 h 50 min

___

WORKING TOGETHER **Game**

Let's Subtract!

Players: 4
Materials:
- paper strips
- a bag

1 Each player writes four time subtraction problems on separate strips of paper.

Example

2 h 15 min − 1 h 20 min =

2 Players put their problems in a bag.

3 Player 1 picks a problem from the bag and solves it.

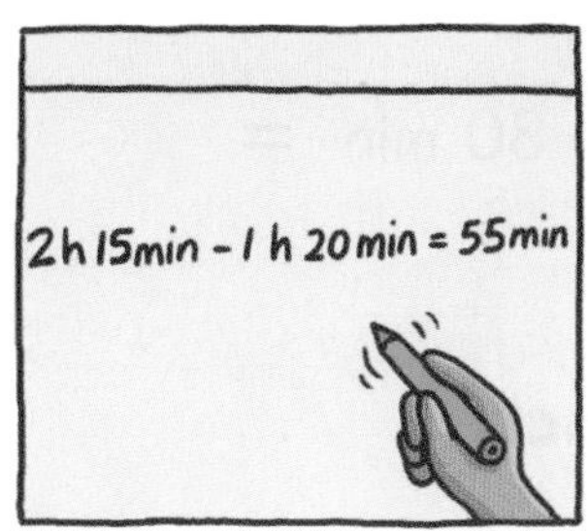
2 h 15 min - 1 h 20 min = 55 min

I got it correct!

4 The other players check the answer.
Player 1 gets 1 point for a correct answer.
The player with the greatest difference in time in each round also gets an extra point.

5 Players take turns.
Play four rounds.

The player with the most points wins!

Let's Practice

Subtract.

1. 12 h 35 min − 7 h 10 min = ___ h ___ min
2. 15 h 40 min − 9 h 25 min = ___ h ___ min
3. 3 h 20 min − 2 h 10 min = ___ h ___ min
4. 5 h 15 min − 1 h 5 min = ___ h ___ min

Regroup.

5. 3 h 20 min = 2 h ___ min
6. 8 h 25 min = ___ h 85 min
7. 5 h 15 min = ___ h 75 min
8. 2 h 30 min = ___ h 90 min

Subtract.

9. 5 h 38 min − 1 h 55 min
10. 3 h 20 min − 1 h 45 min
11. 9 h 15 min − 8 h 35 min
12. 8 h 20 min − 6 h 24 min
13. 3 h − 1 h 30 min
14. 5 h 46 min − 55 min

ON YOUR OWN

Go to Workbook B: Practice 4, pages 153–154

Lesson 16.5 Elapsed Time

Lesson Objective

- Find elapsed time.

Vocabulary
elapsed time
timeline

Learn Introduction to finding elapsed time.

Tom's soccer practice started at 3:00 P.M.
It ended at 5:00 P.M.
How long was his soccer practice?

Start:

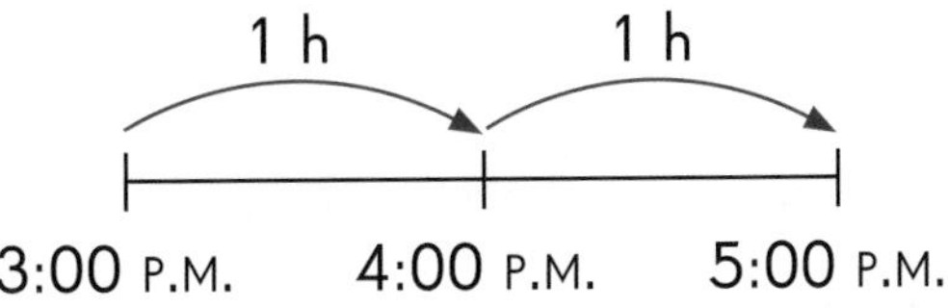

The soccer practice lasted 2 hours.

Elapsed time is the amount of time that has passed between the start and the end of an activity.

Anita started her dinner at 6:45 P.M.
She finished at 7:20 P.M.
How long did her dinner last?

Start:

15 min 20 min

6:45 P.M. 7:00 P.M. 7:20 P.M.

End:

15 min + 20 min = 35 min

Anita ate dinner for 35 minutes.

Guided Learning

Answer each question.

1. What time is 3 hours after 7:00 P.M.?
2. What time is 2 hours after 7:15 P.M.?
3. How many hours are there from 9:00 to noon?
4. How many hours are there from 2:30 P.M. to 4:30 P.M.?
5. What time is 15 minutes after 11:00 A.M.?
6. What time is 45 minutes after 11:30 A.M.?
7. How many minutes are there from 11:50 A.M. to 12:25 P.M.?

Learn

Find elapsed time in hours and minutes.

Rachel and Shannon went to a fair.
They arrived at 7:50 P.M. and left at 9:15 P.M.
How long were they at the fair?

Arrived:
7:50 P.M. or
10 minutes to 8.

Left:
9:15 P.M. or
15 minutes past 9.

You can use a **timeline** to find elapsed time.

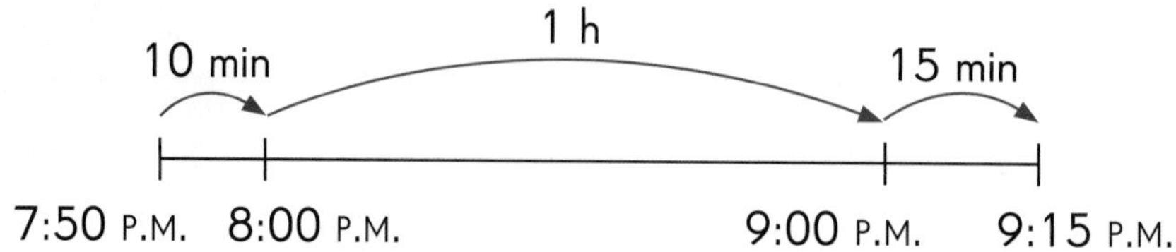

10 min + 1 h + 15 min
= 1 h 25 min

or

10 min + 15 min = 25 min
1 h + 25 min = 1 h 25 min

They were at the fair for 1 hour 25 minutes.

Guided Learning

8 Kevin had a birthday party.
What time did the guests arrive?
What time did the guests leave?
Look at the clocks. Complete the times.
Use past or to.

Arrive:
25 minutes ______ 3
or 2:35 P.M.

Leave:
20 minutes ______ 5
or 5:20 P.M.

How long did the party last?

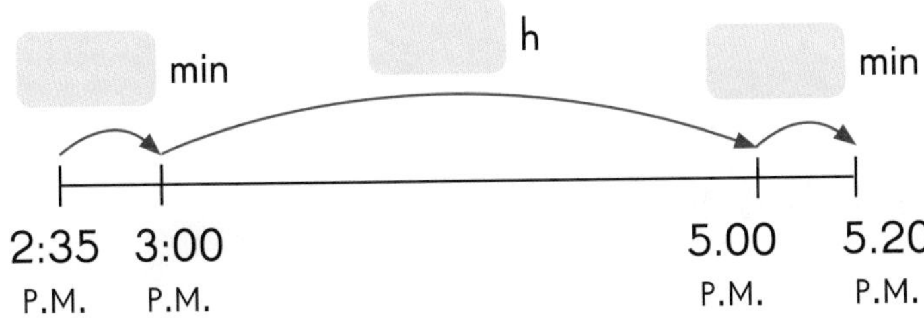

______ min + ______ h + ______ min = ______ h ______ min

The party lasted ______ hours ______ minutes.

Learn

Find the end time given the start time and elapsed time.

After a party, Emily cleans her house.
She starts cleaning at 10:30 P.M. and finishes in 1 hour 45 minutes.
What time did she finish cleaning the house?

Emily works past midnight. So, P.M. time becomes A.M. time.

Count on the hours and minutes from 12 A.M.

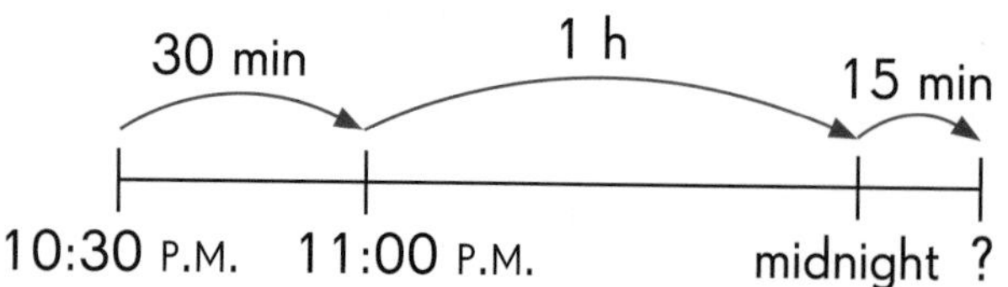

30 minutes after 10:30 P.M. is 11:00 P.M.
1 hour after 11:00 P.M. is midnight.
So, midnight is 12 A.M.
15 minutes after midnight is 12:15 A.M.

Emily finished cleaning the house at 12:15 A.M.

Check:
1 hour before 12:15 A.M. is 11:15 P.M.
45 minutes before 11:15 P.M. is 10:30 P.M.

Guided Learning

Complete. Use the timeline to help you.

9 Taylor makes posters for his family.
He takes 2 hours and 35 minutes to make the posters.
He started making them at 10:10 A.M.
When did he finish making them?

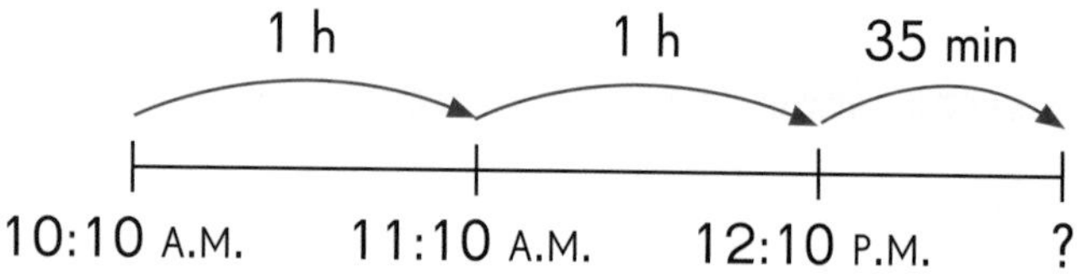

2 hours after 10:10 A.M. is 12:10 P.M.

35 minutes after 12:10 P.M. is ______.

He finished making them at ______.

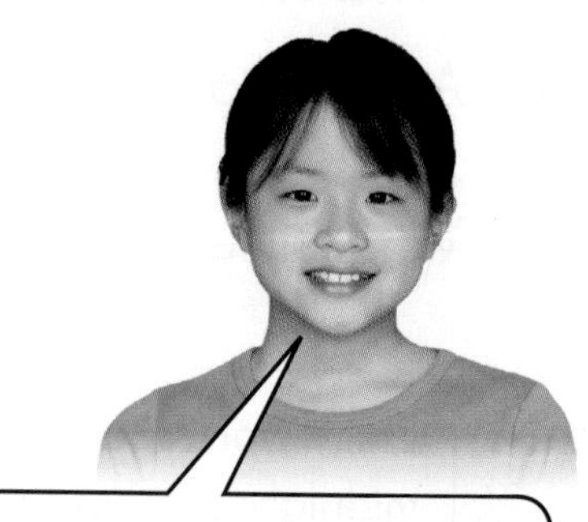

Taylor works past noon. So, A.M. time becomes P.M. time.

Learn

Find the start time given the elapsed time and end time.

Brooke was painting a sign. She finished painting it at 3 P.M. She took 1 hour 50 minutes to paint it. When did she begin?

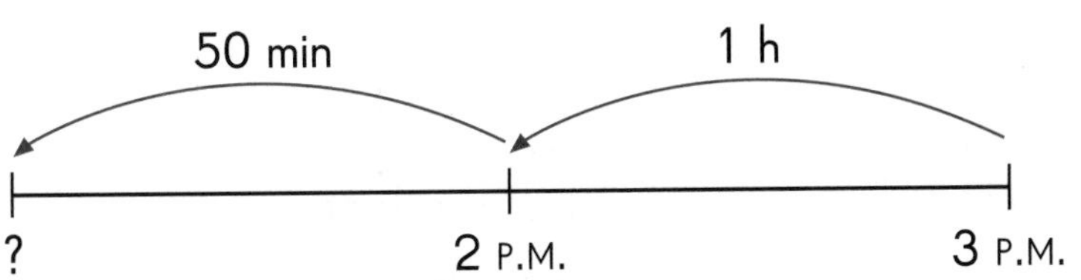

Count back!

1 hour before 3 P.M. is 2 P.M.
50 minutes before 2 P.M. is 1:10 P.M.
Brooke began painting at 1:10 P.M.

50 minutes after 1:10 P.M. is 2 P.M.
1 hour after 2 P.M. is 3 P.M.

Guided Learning

Complete using the timeline.

10 Jamal spent 45 minutes opening his birthday gifts. He finished opening his gifts at 12:05 A.M. What time did he start?

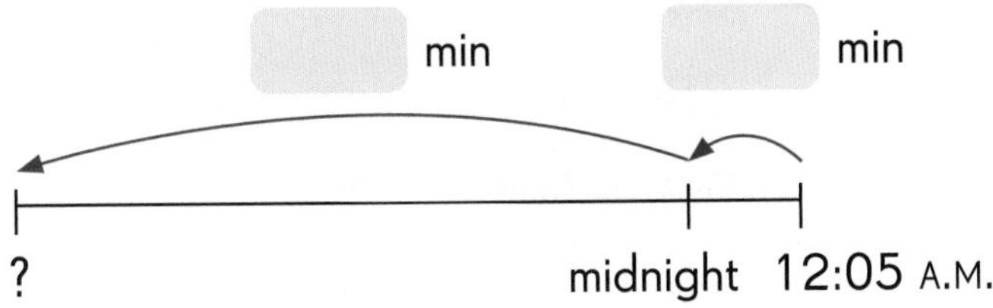

Jamal started opening his gifts at ______.

Hands-On Activity

WORKING TOGETHER

1. In groups of four, take turns telling one another the last time you did each activity. Include the time you think you started and ended each one.

Reading a story

Playing a game

Having lunch

2. Write down your start time and end time for each activity.

3. Draw a timeline for each activity. Then find the elapsed time.

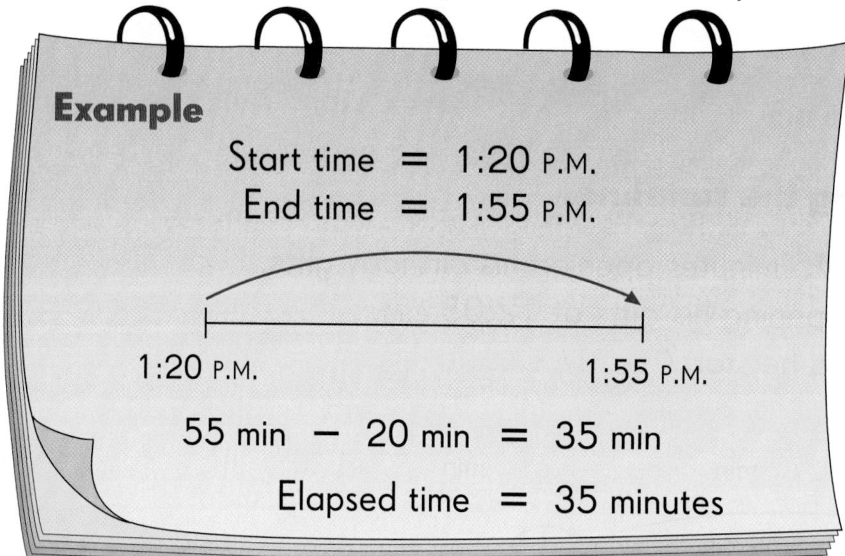

Example
Start time = 1:20 P.M.
End time = 1:55 P.M.
1:20 P.M.
1:55 P.M.
55 min − 20 min = 35 min
Elapsed time = 35 minutes

4. Solve.

   a. Who takes the longest time to read a story?

   b. Who takes the shortest time to have lunch?

   c. Who takes the shortest time to play a game?

Let's Practice

Tell what time it will be.

1. 2 hours after 7:00 P.M.
2. 3 hours after 2:45 A.M.
3. 35 minutes after 9:00 P.M.
4. 25 minutes after 8:50 A.M.

Find how much time has passed. Draw a timeline to help you.

5. 5:45 P.M. to 6:20 P.M.
6. 3:25 A.M. to 4:10 A.M.
7. noon to 4:55 P.M.
8. 11:20 A.M. to 2:35 P.M.

Solve.

9. A train leaves Town P at 7:30 A.M.
It arrives at Town Q at 11:45 A.M.
How long is the trip?

10. A movie starts at 7:15 P.M.
It lasts 2 hours 15 minutes.
What time does it end?

11. A chef starts work at 8:45 A.M.
He usually works for 8 hours.
Today, he leaves a half hour early.
What time does he leave the restaurant?

12. Mr. Williams takes 2 hours 40 minutes to drive from Town A to Town B.
He arrives at Town B at 2:25 P.M.
What time did he start from Town A?

13. Sally finished her hike at 4:35 P.M.
She hiked for 2 hours 20 minutes.
She took a 15-minute rest during her hike.
What time did she begin hiking?

14. A hospital nurse gave a patient medicine every 4 hours, 4 times a day.
The patient took his first tablet for the day at 9:30 A.M.
At what time should he take the last tablet for the day?

ON YOUR OWN

Go to Workbook B:
Practice 5, pages 155–158

Lesson 16.6 Measuring Temperature

Lesson Objectives

- Read a Fahrenheit thermometer.
- Choose the appropriate tool and unit to measure temperature.
- Use a referent to estimate temperature.

Vocabulary

temperature	thermometer
degrees	Fahrenheit (°F)
cold	cool
warm	hot

Learn Introduction to measuring temperature.

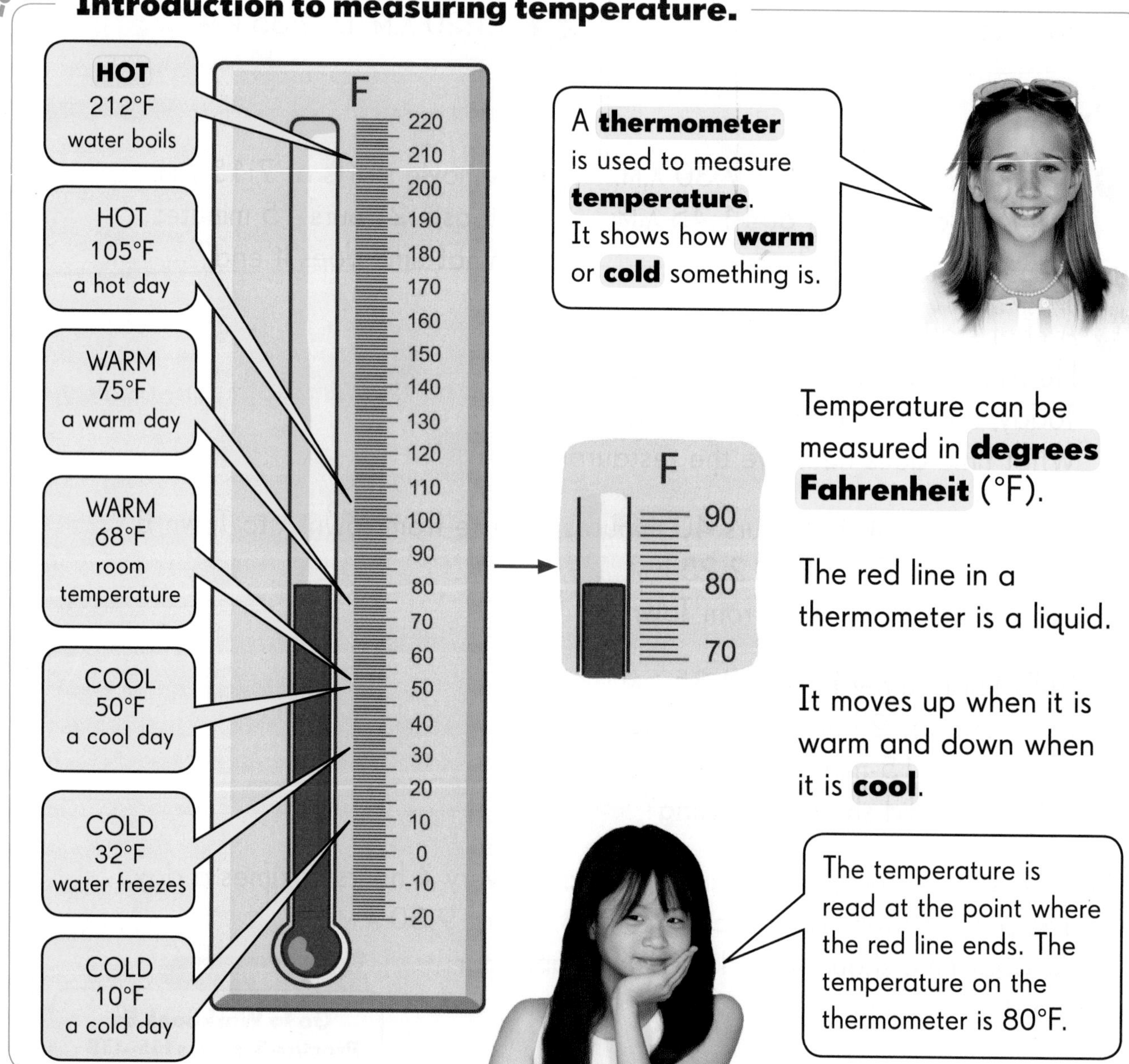

Temperature can be measured in **degrees Fahrenheit** (°F).

The red line in a thermometer is a liquid.

It moves up when it is warm and down when it is **cool**.

Guided Learning

Find each temperature, including its unit. Then describe the temperature as hot, warm, cool, or cold.

1. F: 10, 0, -10

2. F: 110, 100, 90

3. F: 80, 70, 60

4. F: 50, 40, 30

5. F: 200, 190, 180

6. F: 60, 50, 40

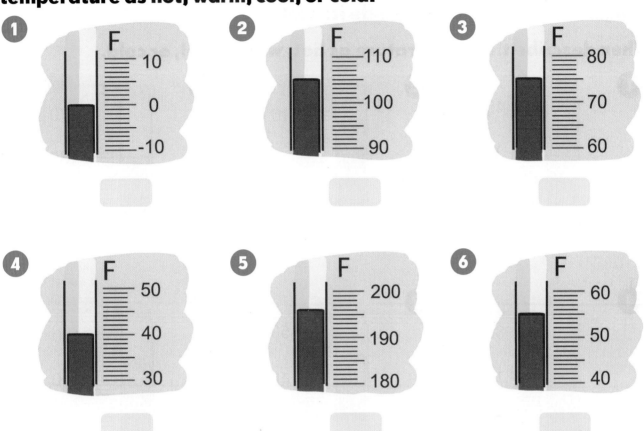

Decide which temperature matches the activity.

7. 8. 9.

Let's Practice

Find each temperature. Include its unit.

Then describe the temperature as hot, warm, cool, or cold.

1 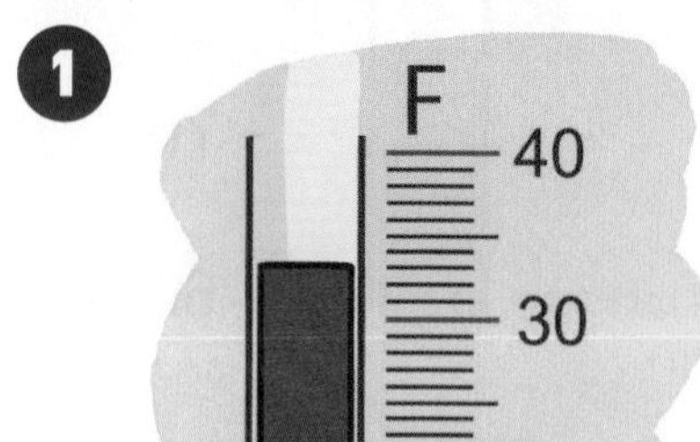

2 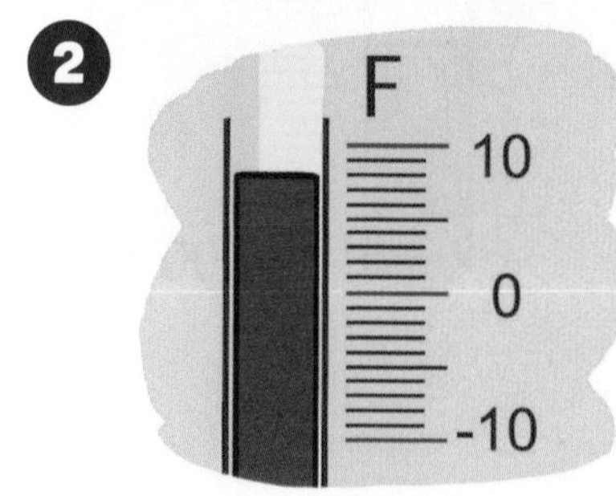

3 

4 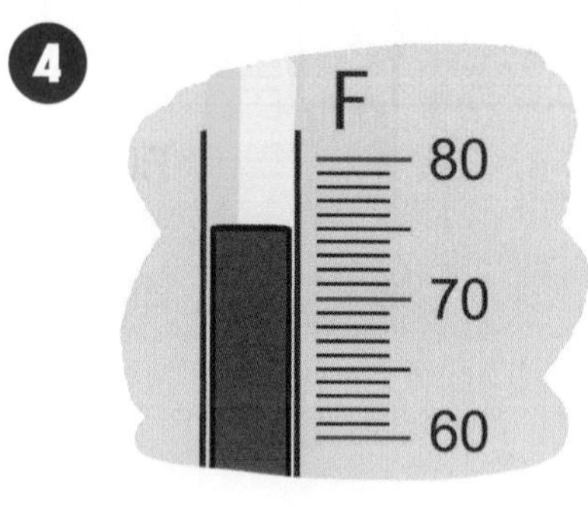

5 

6 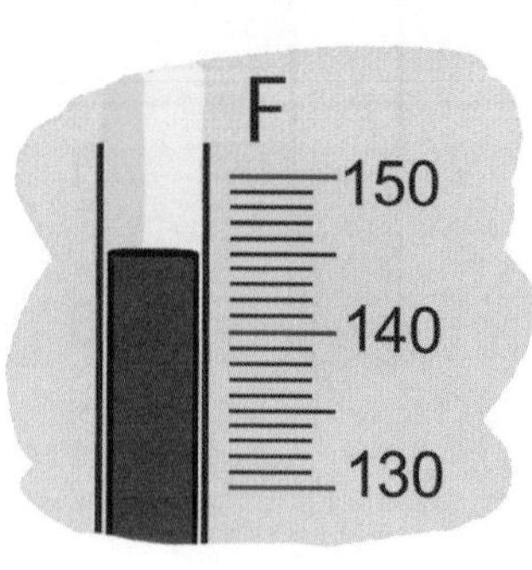

Decide which temperature matches the activity.

7 

ON YOUR OWN

Go to Workbook B:
Practice 6, pages 159–162

Lesson 16.7 Real-World Problems: Time and Temperature

Lesson Objectives

- Solve up to two-step word problems on time.
- Solve word problems involving temperature.

Learn: Solve one- or two-step real-world word problems involving time.

Rafael is a city tour guide.
He gives 45-minute tours.
He is paid \$30 an hour.
On Saturday, he gave 8 tours.

a. How many hours did Rafael spend giving the 8 tours on Saturday?

b. How much did Rafael earn by giving 8 tours?

a.
1 tour → 45 min
8 tours → 8 × 45 min
= 360 min
= 6 h

$$\begin{array}{r} \overset{4}{4}\,5 \\ \times \quad 8 \\ \hline 3\,6\,0 \end{array}$$

1 h = 60 min
6 h = 6 × 60 min
Think of the multiplication table of 6.
6 × 6 = 36
So, 6 × 60 = 360.

Rafael spends 6 hours on giving the 8 tours.

b.
1 hour → \$30
6 hours → 6 × \$30
= \$180

6 × 3 = 18
6 × 30 = 180

Rafael earned \$180 for giving 8 tours.

Guided Learning

Solve.

1. A train makes several 45-minute scenic tours three times a week. Each tour costs $13 for each child.

45-minute Scenic Train Tour

Day	Mon	Wed	Fri
Number of Tours	6	6	6
Length of each Tour	45 min		

a. How many hours and minutes does the train go on Wednesday?

b. How much does it cost for 1 child to go on tours for 90 minutes?

a. ___ ○ ___ = ___ min

= ___ h ___ min

The train runs for ___ hours ___ minutes on Wednesday.

b. 45 min → $ ___

90 min → ___ ○ $ ___

= $ ___

90 min = 45 min × ___

It costs $ ___ for a child to go on tours for 90 minutes.

2 Raul spends 1 hour 40 minutes doing his homework.
Then he spends another 45 minutes on his piano practice.
He finishes his homework and piano practice at 5:30 P.M.
What time did he begin doing his homework?

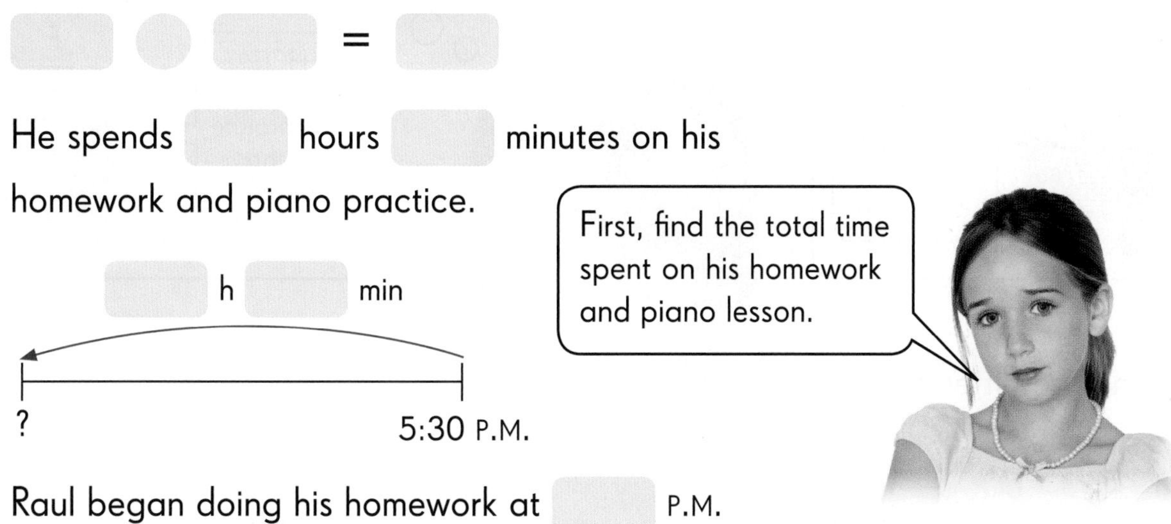

Raul began doing his homework at ____ P.M.

3 Melissa arrives at a train station.
Her watch shows the time as 6:45 A.M.
Her watch is 20 minutes slow.

a What is the actual time shown on the train station's clock?

b The train arrives 10 minutes later.
What time does the train arrive according to the train station's clock?

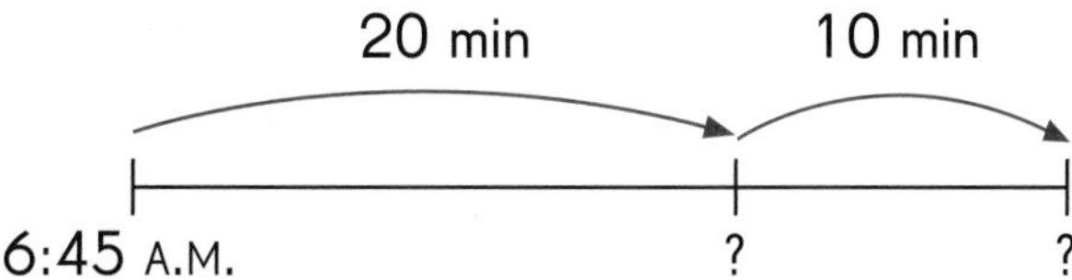

a 6:45 A.M. → + 20 min → ____

The actual time shown on the train station's clock is ____

b ____ A.M. → 10 min later → ____

According to the train station's clock, the train arrives at the train station at ____

Learn Solve real-world word problems involving temperature.

The temperature in the mountains today is 65°F.
The temperature in the desert today is 130°F.

Find the difference between the temperatures.

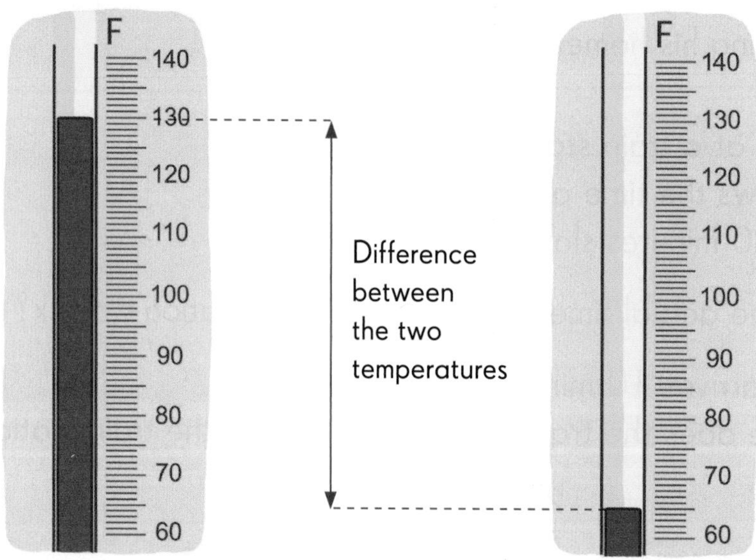

Count on.
The difference is 65°F.

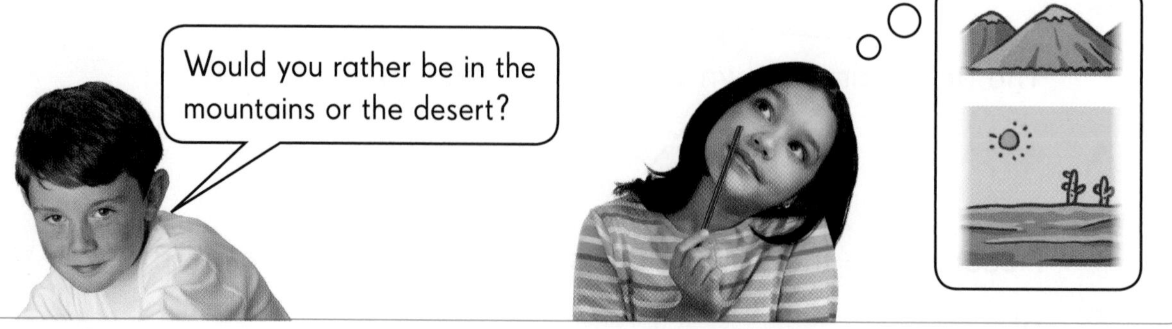

Guided Learning

Complete the story.
Use the numbers shown.

4

 9  38 

The high temperature recorded yesterday was ____ °F for a desert in Arizona and ____ °F for Florida. Arizona's temperature was the higher of the two.

At night, Arizona had a low temperature of ____ °F, while Florida's low temperature was ____ °F, ____ °F less than Arizona's.

Let's Practice

Solve.

1. Ken takes 45 minutes to paint a chair.
   How long would he take to paint 7 similar chairs? ____

2. A clock shows 11:40 A.M.
   It is 35 minutes slow.
   What is the actual time? ____

3. A clock shows 3:10 P.M.
   It is 25 minutes fast.
   What is the actual time? ____

4. Chris leaves his grandmother's house at 7:15 P.M.
He takes 1 hour 40 minutes to travel home.
What time does he reach home?

5. Florence takes 4 hours 55 minutes to drive from Town A to Town B.
She reaches Town B at 4:45 P.M.
What time does she leave Town A?

6. Ms. Ramirez prepares meals for senior citizens.
It takes her 15 minutes to prepare each meal.
She prepares 8 meals.

   a. How many hours does she spend preparing the 8 meals?

   b. How many meals could she prepare in 3 hours?

7. Darryl drove 1 hour 35 minutes from Town A to Town B.
After that, he drove 2 hours 45 minutes from Town B to Town C.
He reached Town C at 7:15 P.M.
What time did he leave Town A?

8. Tonya went to school for a band concert.
She arrived at school at 7:15 P.M. according to her watch.
Her watch was 30 minutes fast.

   a. What was the actual time?

   b. She arrived just in time for the concert.
   The concert ended at 9:00 P.M.
   How long did the concert last?

9 When Max went to camp in the morning, the temperature was 67°F.
When he got home after dinner, it was 48°F.
Is the temperature shown on each thermometer correct?

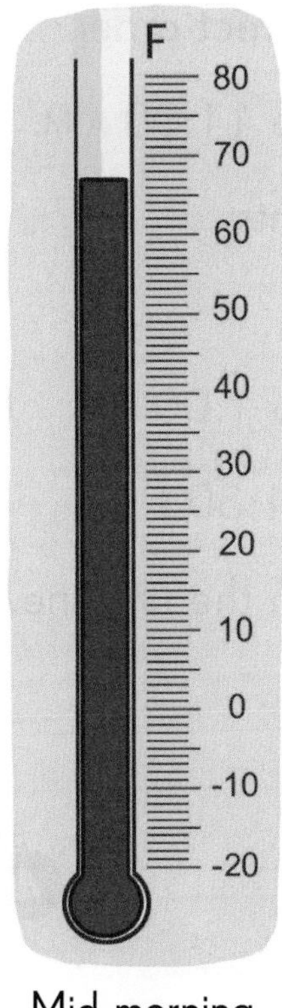

Mid-morning

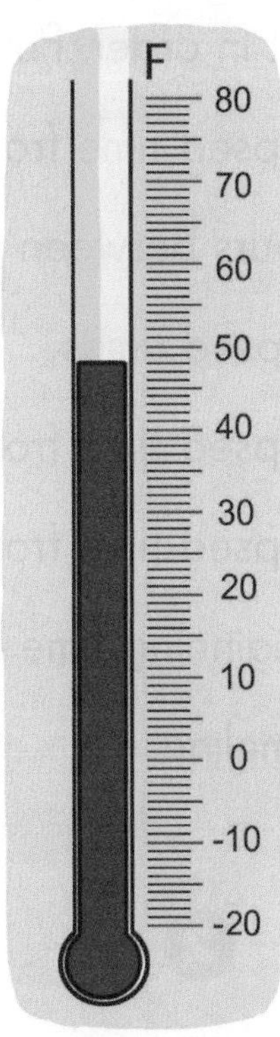

Night

Was it cooler in the morning or at night?
Explain your answer.

10 Rachel is going on a trip.
It is 72°F where she is going.
Describe what kind of clothes she should pack.
Explain your thinking.

ON YOUR OWN

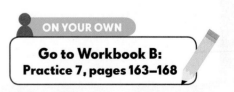

Go to Workbook B:
Practice 7, pages 163–168

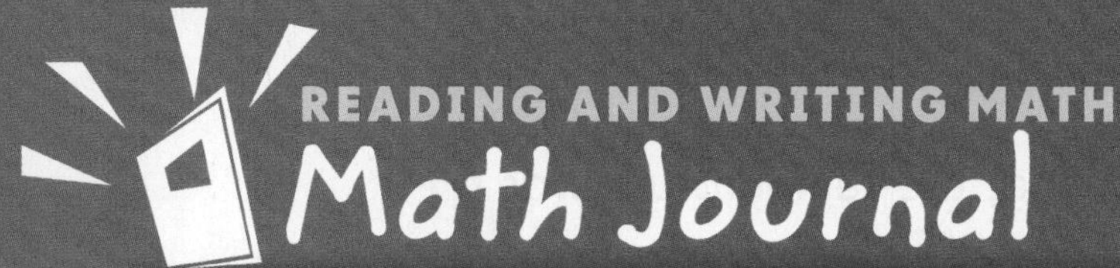

1. The steps for finding the elapsed time from 10:20 A.M. to 1:30 P.M. are not in order. Put them in the correct order.

   a. Find the elapsed time from 10:20 A.M. to 11:00 A.M.

   b. Mark the hours between the two endpoints.

   c. Add the elapsed times.

   d. Find the elapsed time from 11:00 A.M. to 1:00 P.M.

   e. Find the elapsed time from 1:00 P.M. to 1:30 P.M.

   f. Mark the beginning time and end time on the timeline.

   g. Draw the timeline.

2. Find the elapsed time from 1:15 P.M. to 11:20 P.M. Determine whether the steps are the same as 1 and rewrite the steps that are different.

CRITICAL THINKING SKILLS

Put On Your Thinking Cap!

PROBLEM SOLVING

1 Andrew takes a plane from Dallas to Chicago at 8:15 A.M.
The flight takes 3 hours 40 minutes.
There are flights from Chicago to Dallas every 3 hours from 8:15 A.M.
Andrew wants to return to Dallas on the same day.
What is the latest flight that he can take?

2 Complete the story. Use the numbers shown.

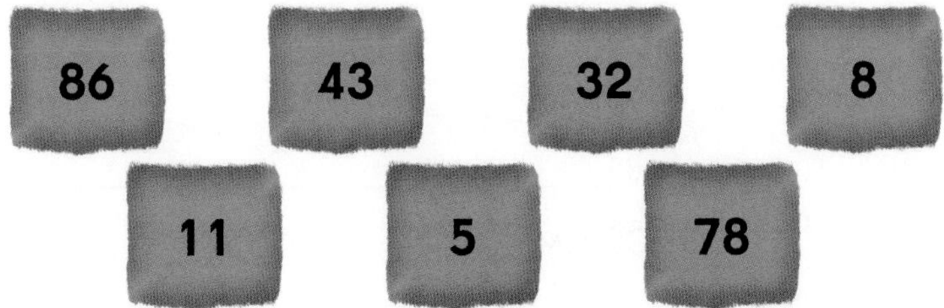

The high temperature yesterday was ______ degrees Fahrenheit. It is the highest it has been for the past ______ days. The low temperature was ______ degrees Fahrenheit, which was about half the high. It is only ______ degrees above freezing (which is ______ degrees Fahrenheit).

Tomorrow's temperature is predicted to be ______ degrees Fahrenheit, which is ______ degrees lower than yesterday's high.

ON YOUR OWN

Go to Workbook B: Put On Your Thinking Cap! pages 171–172

Chapter Wrap Up

Study Guide

You have learned...

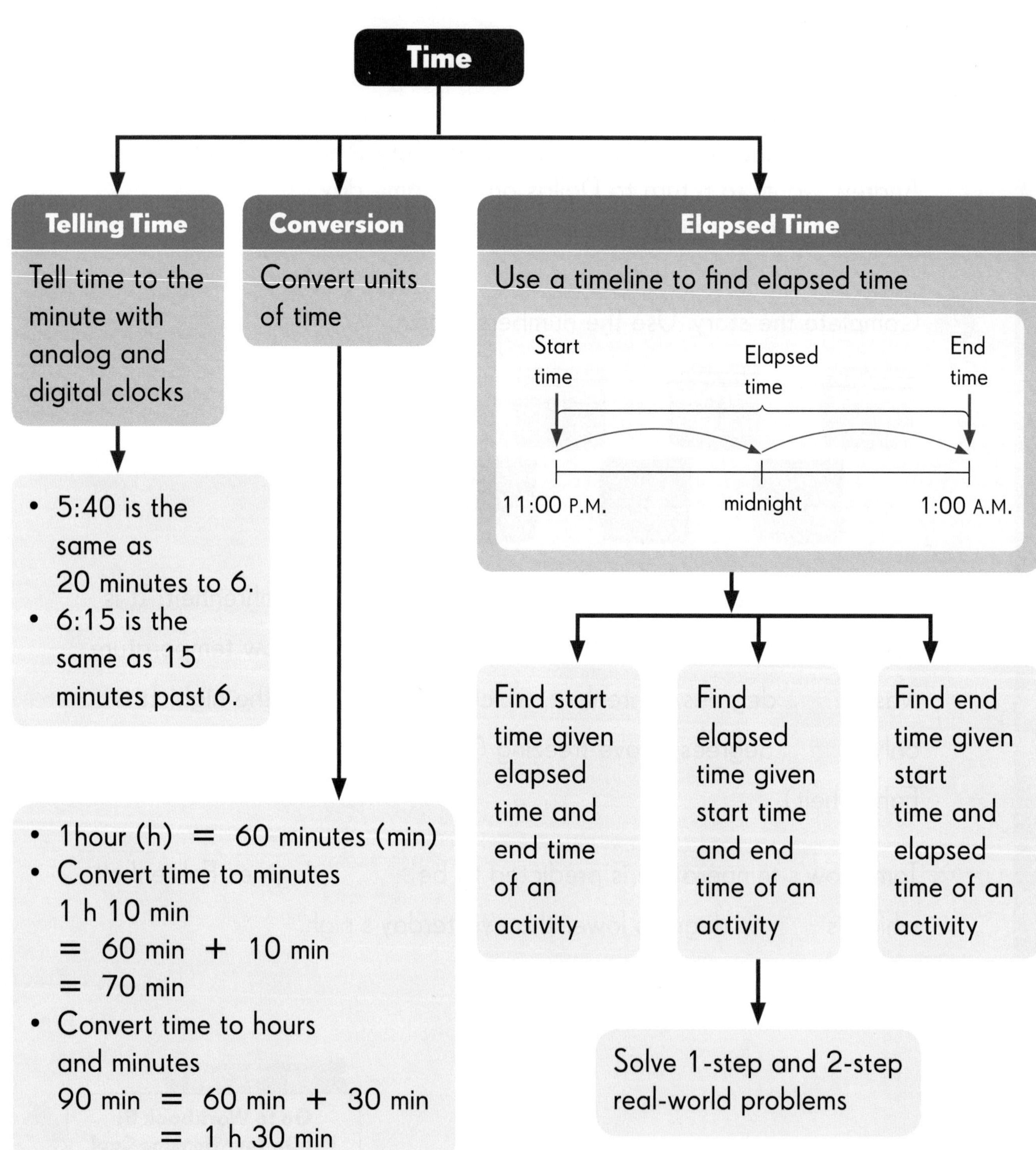

Time
Telling Time
Tell time to the minute with analog and digital clocks
• 5:40 is the same as 20 minutes to 6.
• 6:15 is the same as 15 minutes past 6.
Conversion
Convert units of time
• 1 hour (h) = 60 minutes (min)
• Convert time to minutes
1 h 10 min
= 60 min + 10 min
= 70 min
• Convert time to hours and minutes
90 min = 60 min + 30 min
= 1 h 30 min
Elapsed Time
Use a timeline to find elapsed time
Start time
Elapsed time
End time
11:00 P.M.
midnight
1:00 A.M.
Find start time given elapsed time and end time of an activity
Find elapsed time given start time and end time of an activity
Find end time given start time and elapsed time of an activity
Solve 1-step and 2-step real-world problems

- Time can be used to tell when activities start and end, or how long an activity will last.
- Temperature can be used to understand what the weather will be like.

Temperature

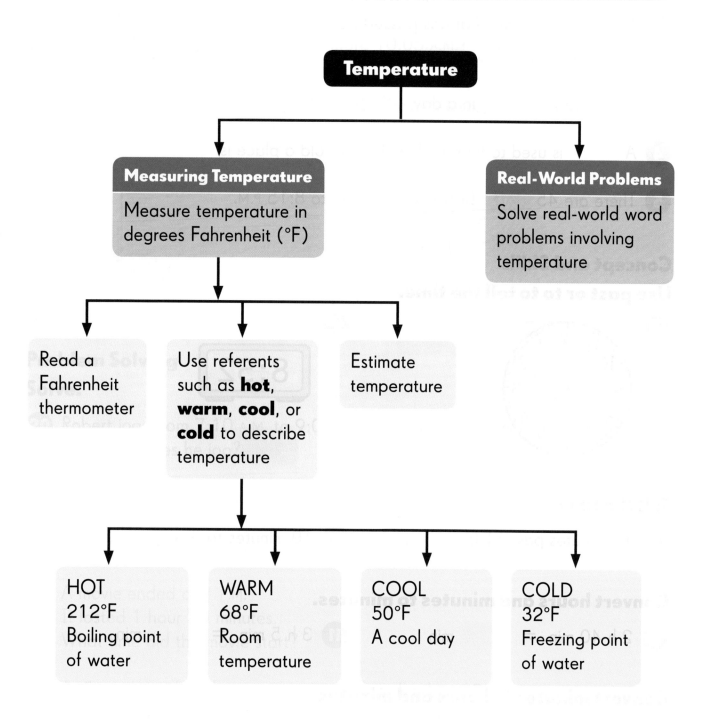

Measuring Temperature

Measure temperature in degrees Fahrenheit (°F)

- Read a Fahrenheit thermometer
- Use referents such as **hot**, **warm**, **cool**, or **cold** to describe temperature
  - HOT 212°F Boiling point of water
  - WARM 68°F Room temperature
  - COOL 50°F A cool day
  - COLD 32°F Freezing point of water
- Estimate temperature

Real-World Problems

Solve real-world word problems involving temperature

Make triangles using the geoboard.

Example

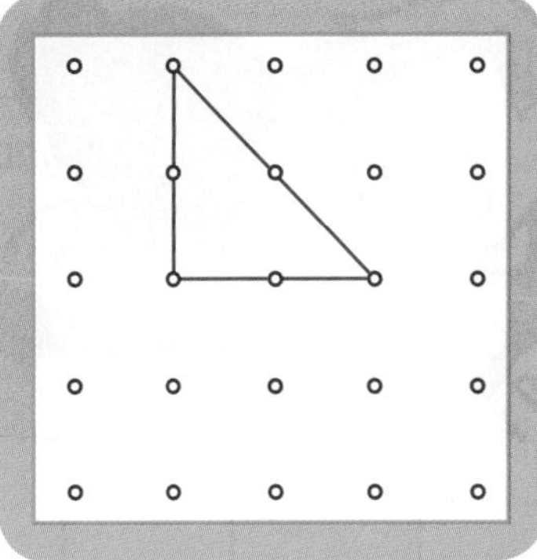

The triangles must look different from one another.

1. Make five different triangles. In what ways are they different?
2. How many sides and angles does each triangle have?
3. What can you say about the number of sides and angles in a triangle?

Make rectangles using the geoboard.

4. Make five different rectangles. In what ways are they different?
5. How many sides does each rectangle have?
6. What can you say about the number of sides and angles in a rectangle?

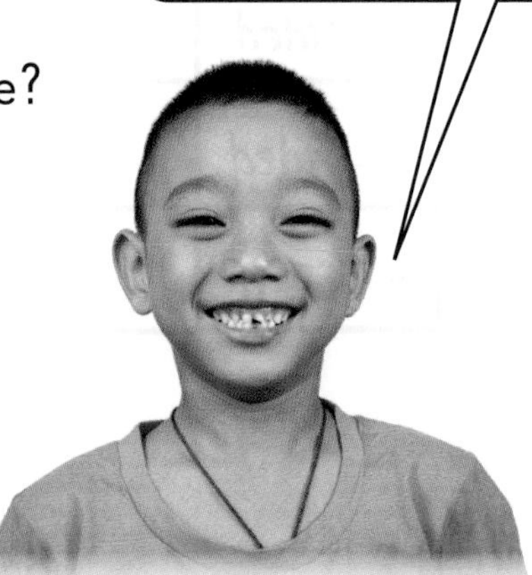

The rectangles must look different from one another.

Let's Practice

Name each figure as a point, line, or line segment.

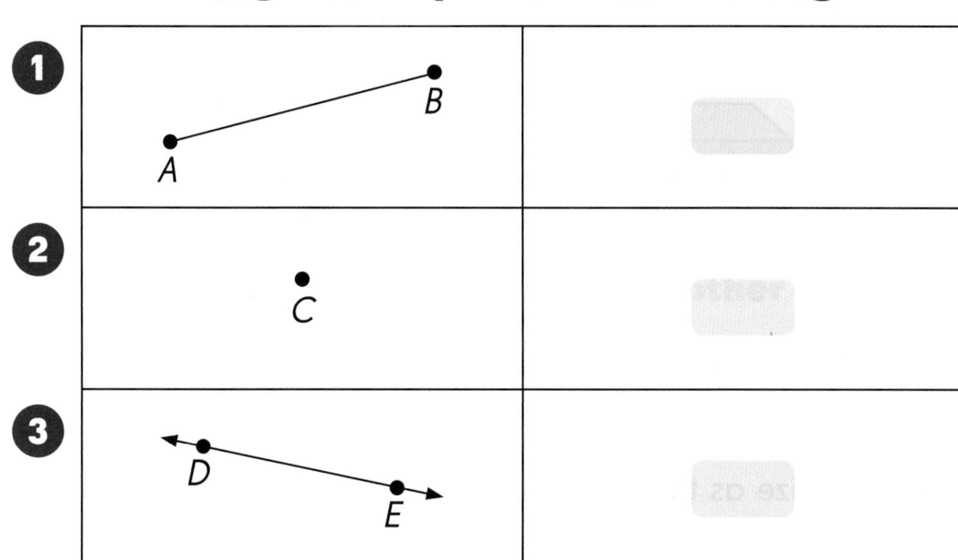

Decide whether each pair of craft sticks forms an angle.

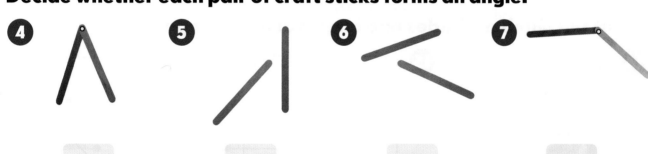

4 

5 

6 

7 

Find the number of angles on each object.

8 

9 

10 

Guided Learning

Compare the angles. Use  to help you.

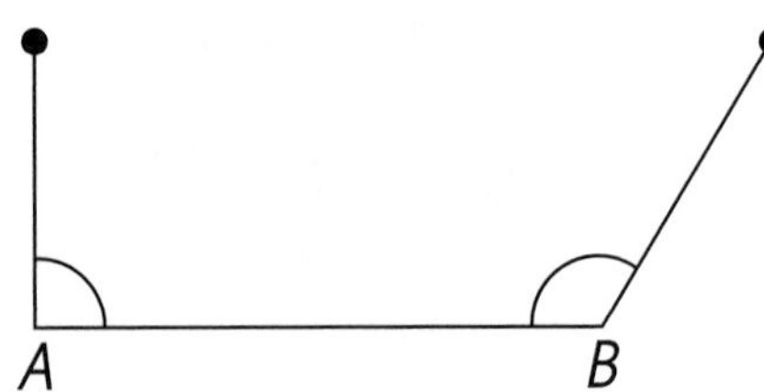

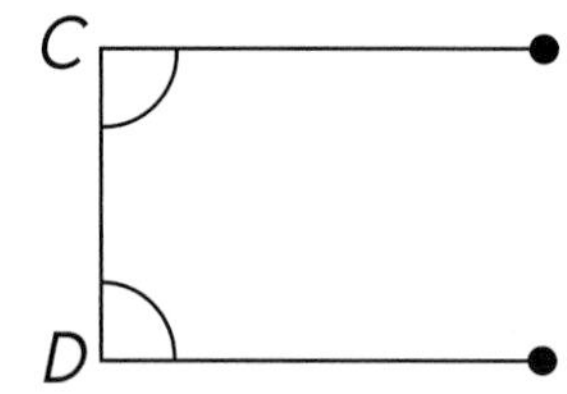

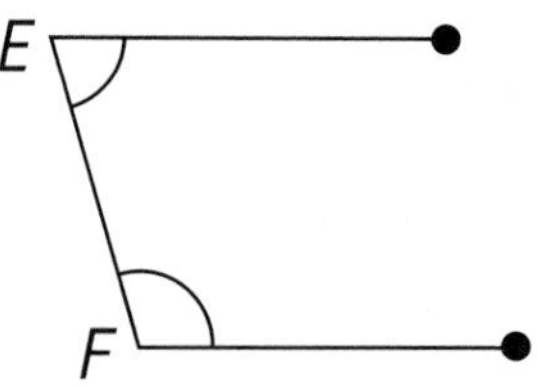

1. Which angles are the same size as right angles? Angles ______
2. Which angles are greater than right angles? Angles ______
3. Which angle is less than a right angle? Angle ______

Hands-On Activity

Materials:
- drawing paper
- fasteners
- paper strips labeled 1 and 2

STEP 1 Using one set of strips, paste Strip 2 on drawing paper.
Fasten Strip 1 onto Strip 2 so that only Strip 1 moves.

STEP 2 Turn Strip 1 to form an angle as shown below.

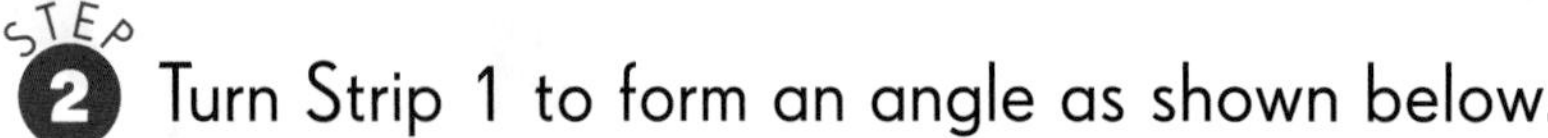

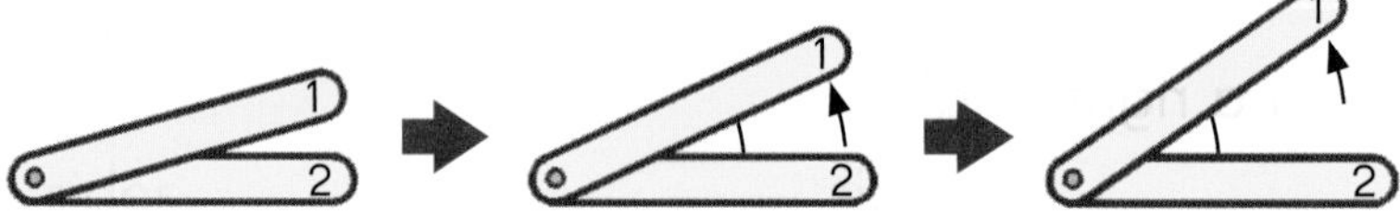

STEP 3 Use the strips to make
- a right angle
- an angle less than a right angle
- an angle greater than a right angle
- an angle which is about twice as large as a right angle

Learn

Find right angles in plane shapes.

This is a square. The sides of a square meet to form right angles.

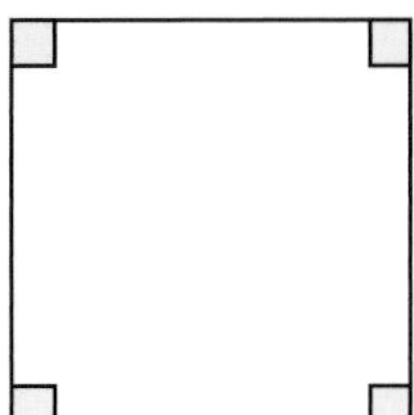

There are four right angles in a square.

Guided Learning

Find the number of right angles in each shape. Use  to help you.

4 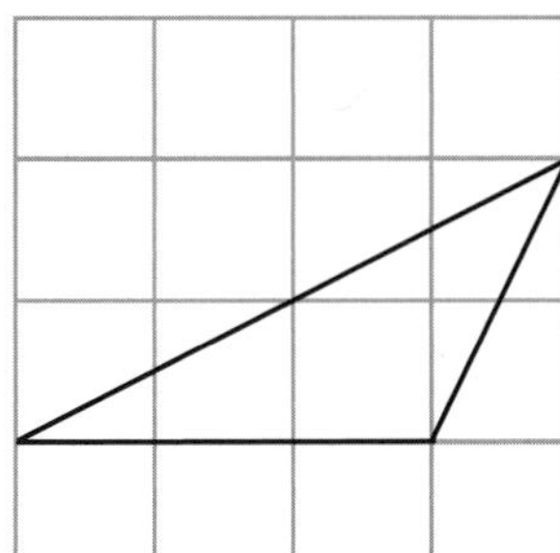

5 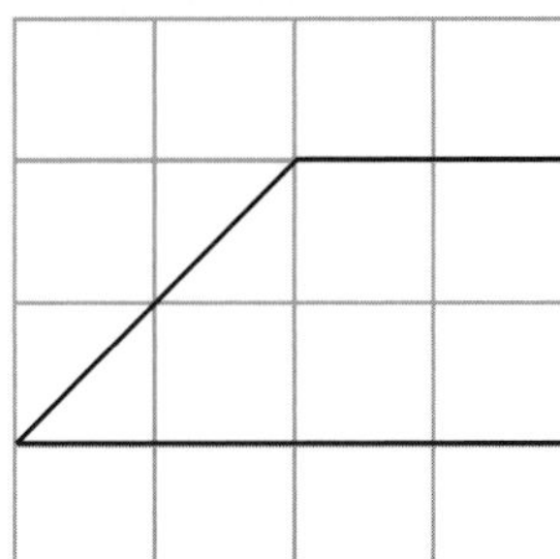

6 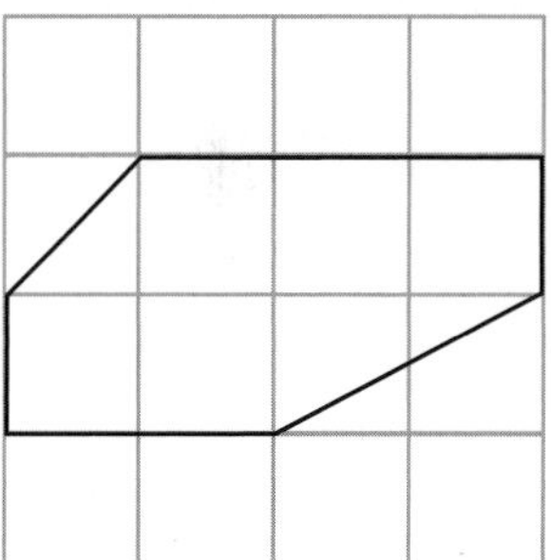

Hands-On Activity

Make shapes using the geoboard.
Then draw the shapes on grid paper.

Materials:
- a geoboard
- rubber bands
- grid paper

1. Make your own shape with seven sides and at least one right angle.
   How many angles are greater than a right angle?
   How many angles are less than a right angle?
   How many angles are the same size as right angles?
2. Make a shape that has a right angle, two angles less than a right angle, and one angle greater than a right angle.
3. Make a shape that has a right angle, two angles greater than a right angle, and one angle less than a right angle.

Let's Practice

Decide whether each angle is greater than, same as, or less than a right angle.

1 

2 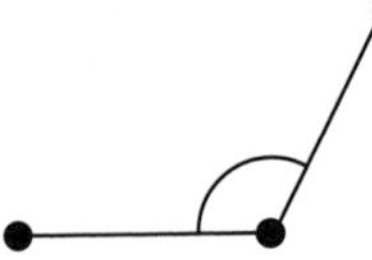

3 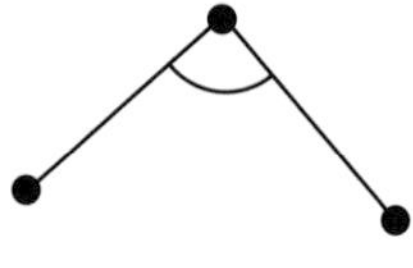

Find the number of right angles in each plane shape.

Use to help you.

4 

5 

6 

Find the number of angles less than a right angle.

Use  **to help you.**

7 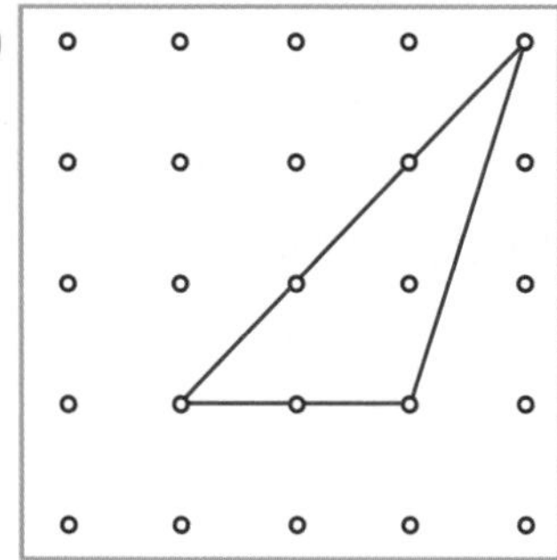

8 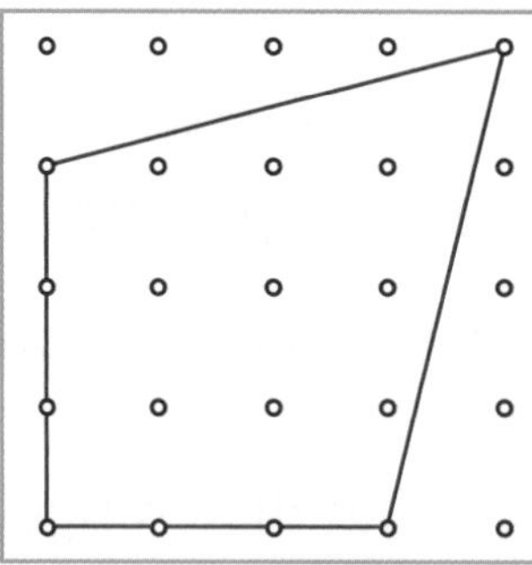

9 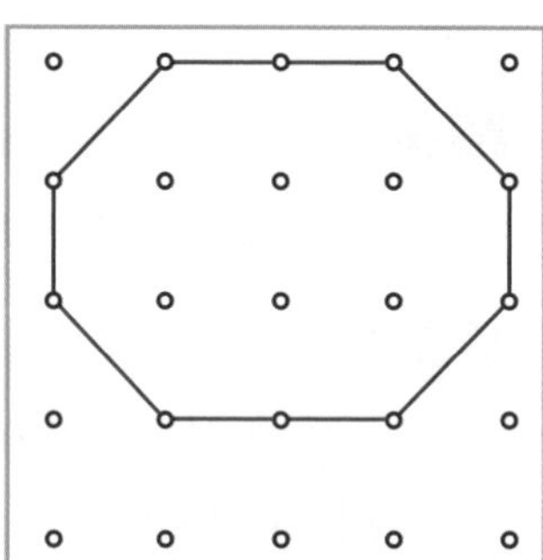

Draw the shape on grid paper.

10 Draw a four-sided shape with one angle greater than a right angle and one angle less than a right angle.

ON YOUR OWN

Go to Workbook B: Practice 2, pages 179–180

Lesson 17.3 Perpendicular Lines

Lesson Objective

- Define and identify perpendicular lines.

Vocabulary
perpendicular lines
is perpendicular to

Learn Identify perpendicular lines.

The lines shown are perpendicular line segments.

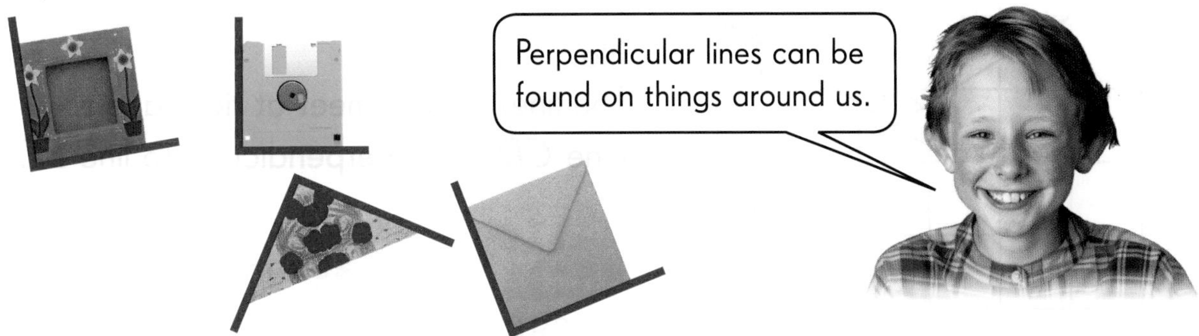

Perpendicular lines can be found on things around us.

What are perpendicular lines?

Perpendicular lines are two lines that meet at right angles.

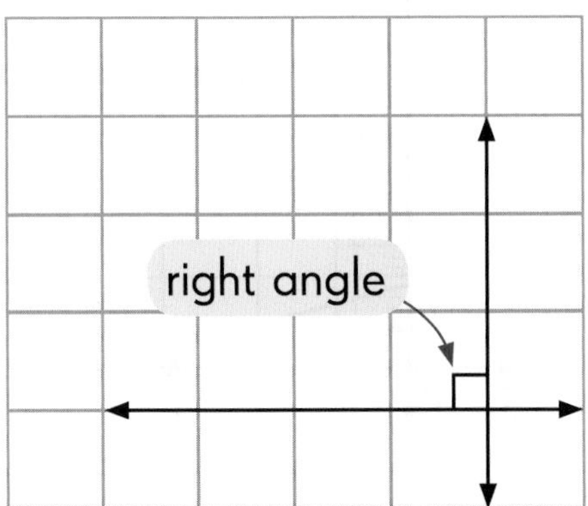

These two lines are perpendicular lines. They meet at right angles.

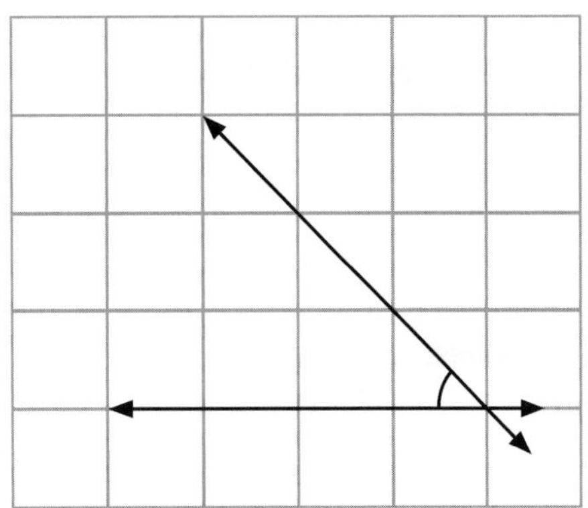

These two lines are not perpendicular lines. They do not meet at right angles.

Continued on next page

Let's Practice

Tell whether the lines are perpendicular.

1 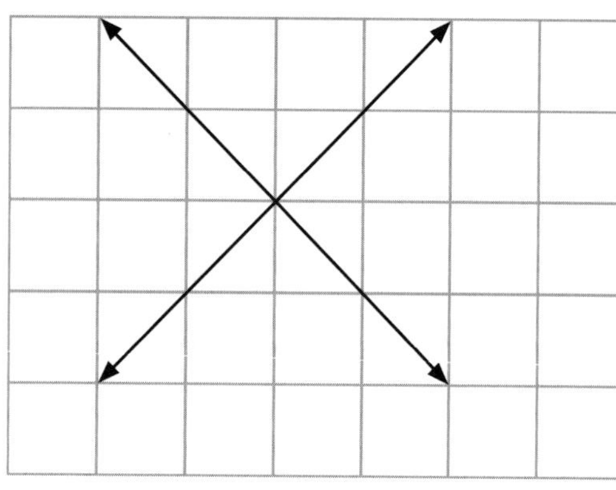

2 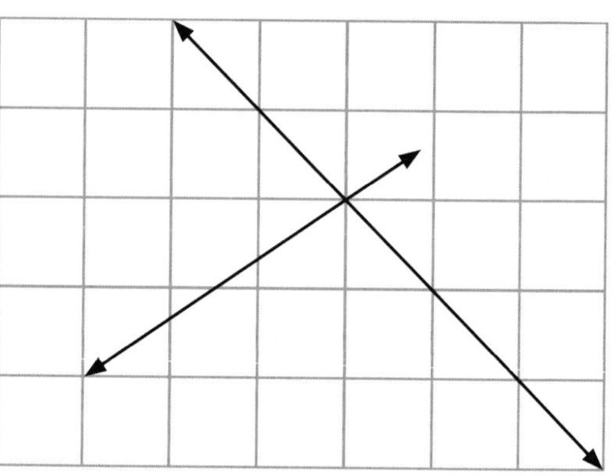

Identify the perpendicular line segments in each figure.

3 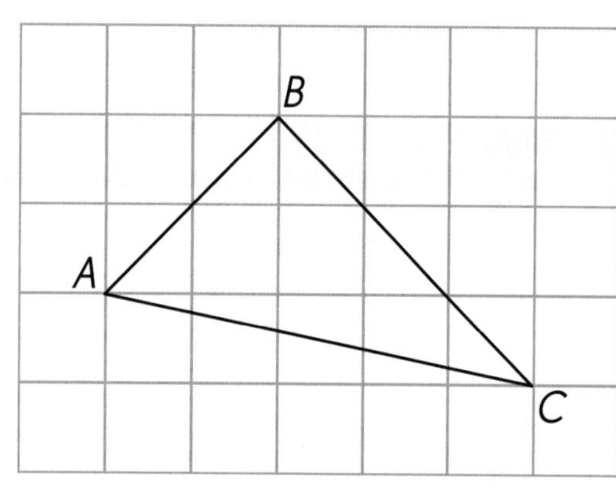

4 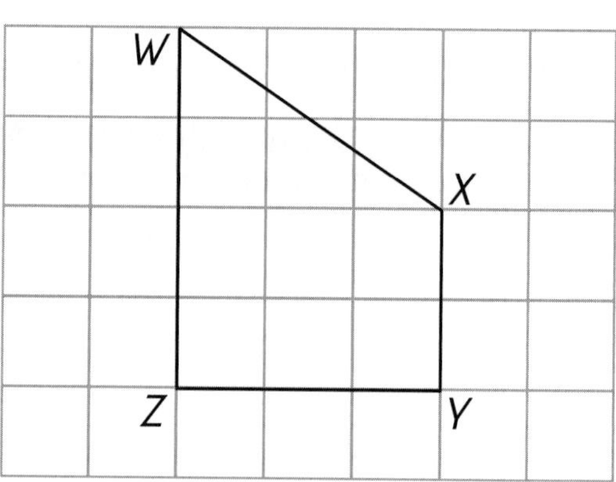

Find two pairs of perpendicular line segments on each object.

5 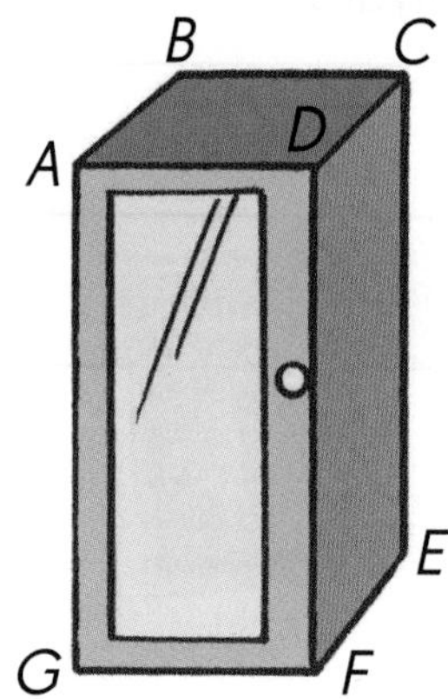

6 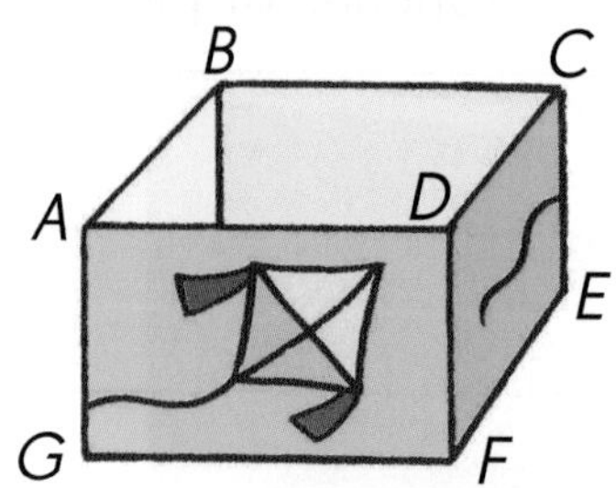

ON YOUR OWN

Go to Workbook B:
Practice 3, pages 181–184

Lesson 17.4 Parallel Lines

Lesson Objective

- Define and identify parallel lines.

Vocabulary
parallel lines
is parallel to

Learn: Identify parallel lines.

Parallel line segments can be found on objects around you.

Parallel lines are two lines that will not meet no matter how long you draw them.
The distance between them is always the same.

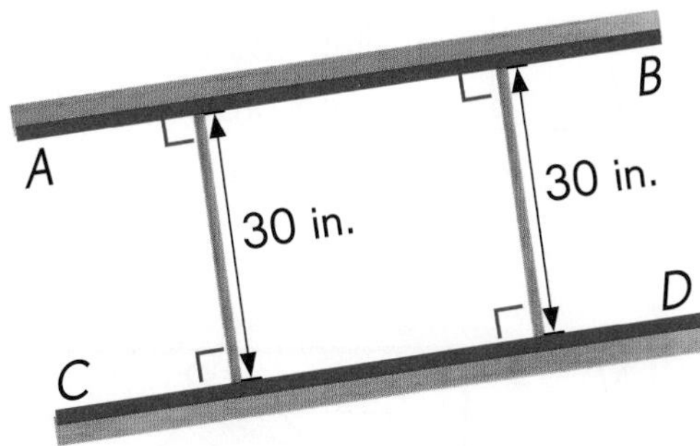

AB and *CD* are a pair of parallel line segments.

Continued on next page

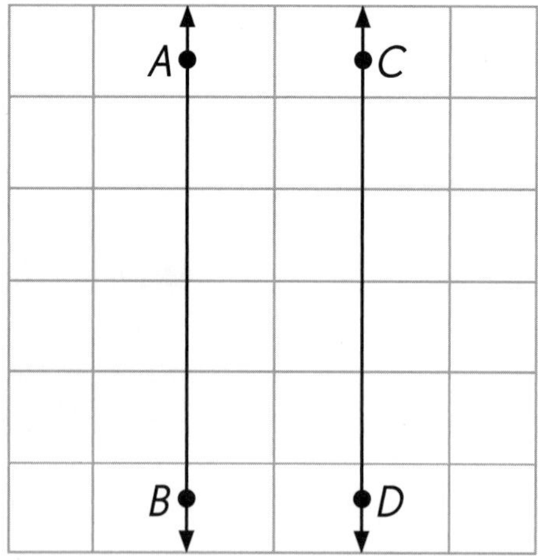

Line AB and line CD are parallel.
Line AB **is parallel to** line CD.

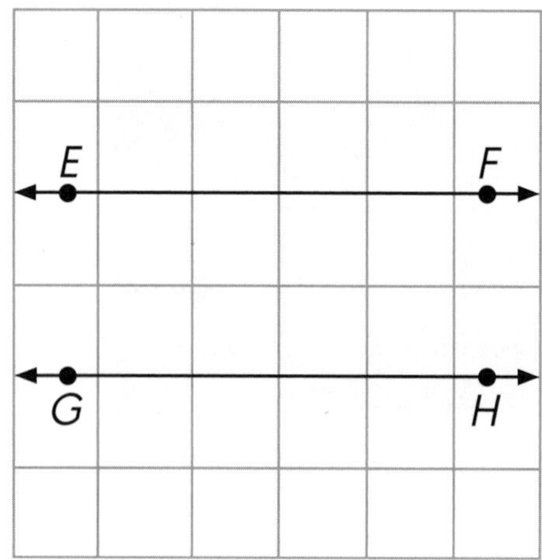

Line EF and line GH are parallel.
Line EF is parallel to line GH.

Look at the lines drawn on the grid.

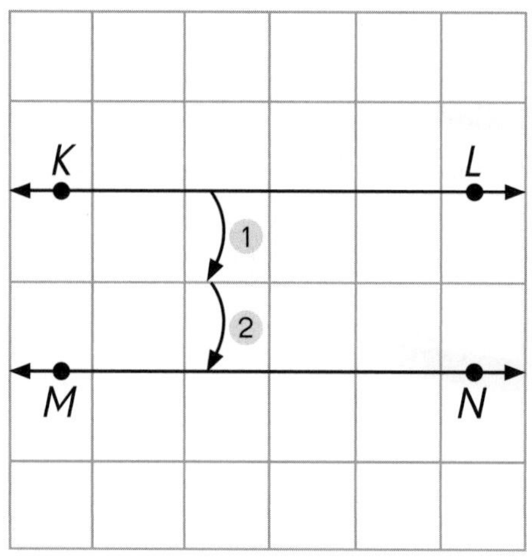

Line KL and line MN are parallel. You can use a ruler and draw them like this from left to right.

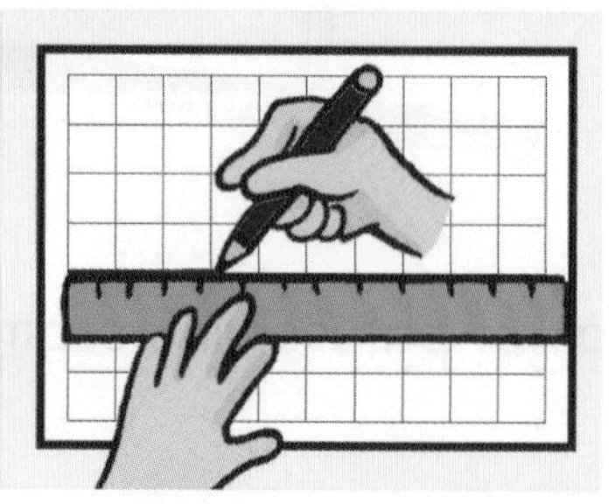

What is the distance between the lines?

Count the number of square units between the lines.

Line *KL* is always 2 square units from line *MN*.
So, line *KL* is parallel to line *MN*.

Line *OP* is always 2 square units from line *QR*.
So, line *OP* is parallel to line *QR*.

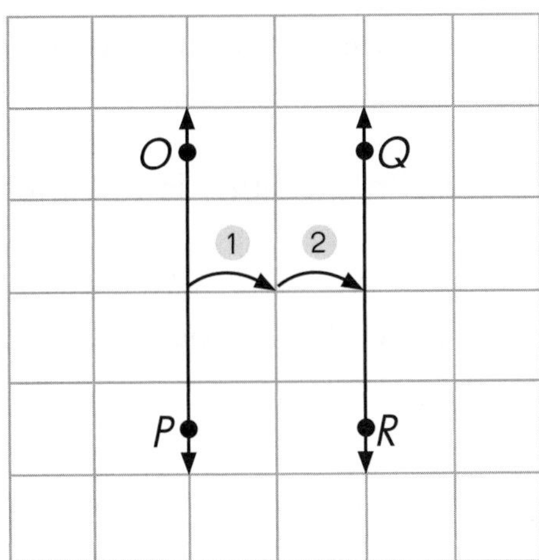

Line *OP* and line *QR* are parallel. You can use a ruler and draw them straight down like this.

Continued on next page

Are line *ST* and line *UV* always the same distance apart?

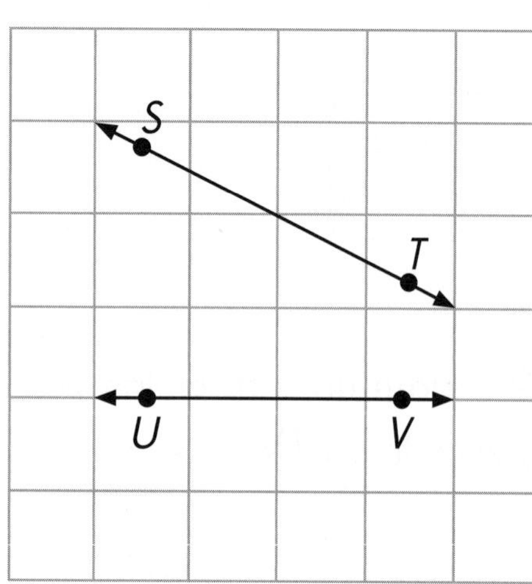

No.

Point *S* is 3 square units away from point *U*.

Point *T* is 1 square unit away from point *V*.

The distance between the lines is not the same.

Line *ST* and line *UV* are not parallel to each other.

Are line *PQ* and line *MN* parallel?

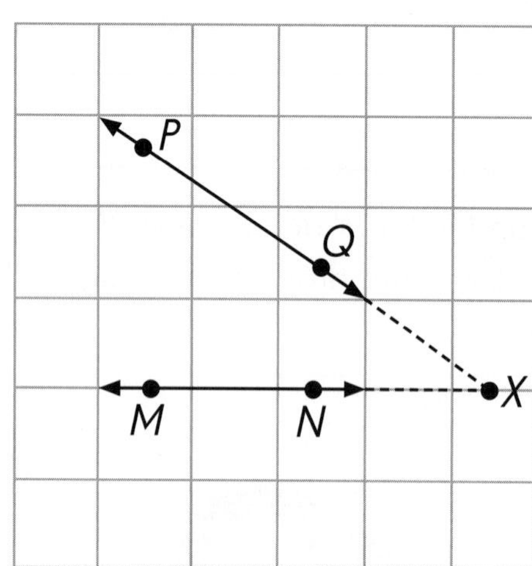

No.

If you make line *PQ* and line *MN* longer by drawing the dotted lines as shown, they will meet at point *X*.

The distance between the lines is not the same.

Line *PQ* and line *MN* are not parallel to each other.

Guided Learning

Find parallel lines.

Which pairs of lines are parallel?

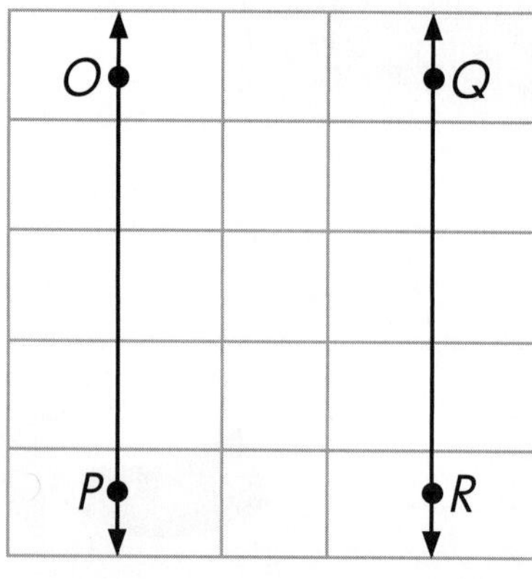

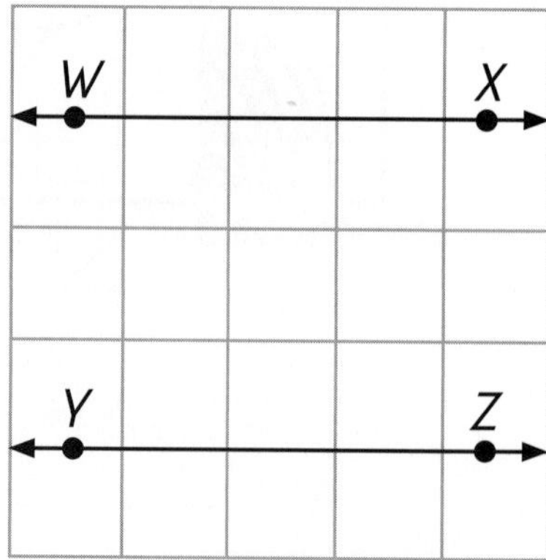

2 Name the pairs of parallel line segments in each figure.

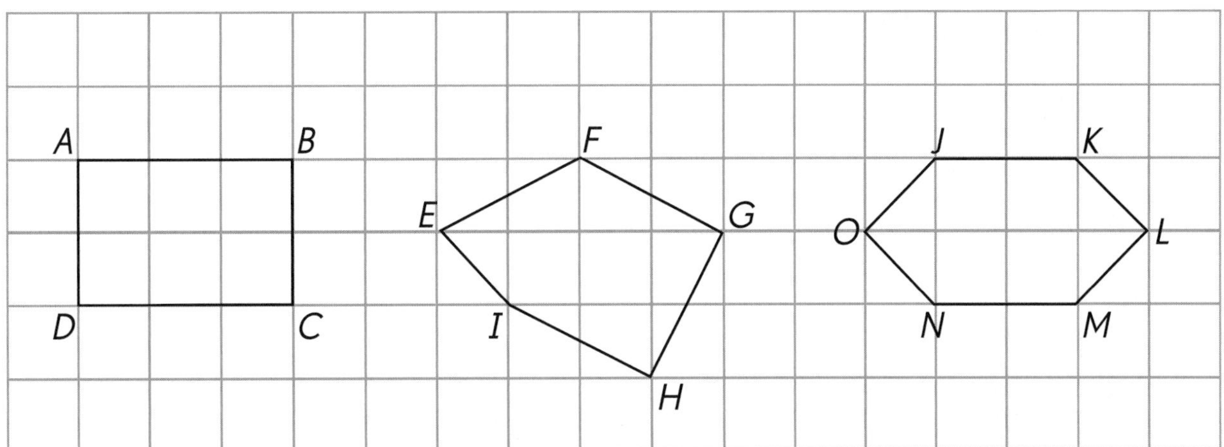

3 Find pairs of parallel line segments on each object.

Copy the parallel lines onto grid paper.

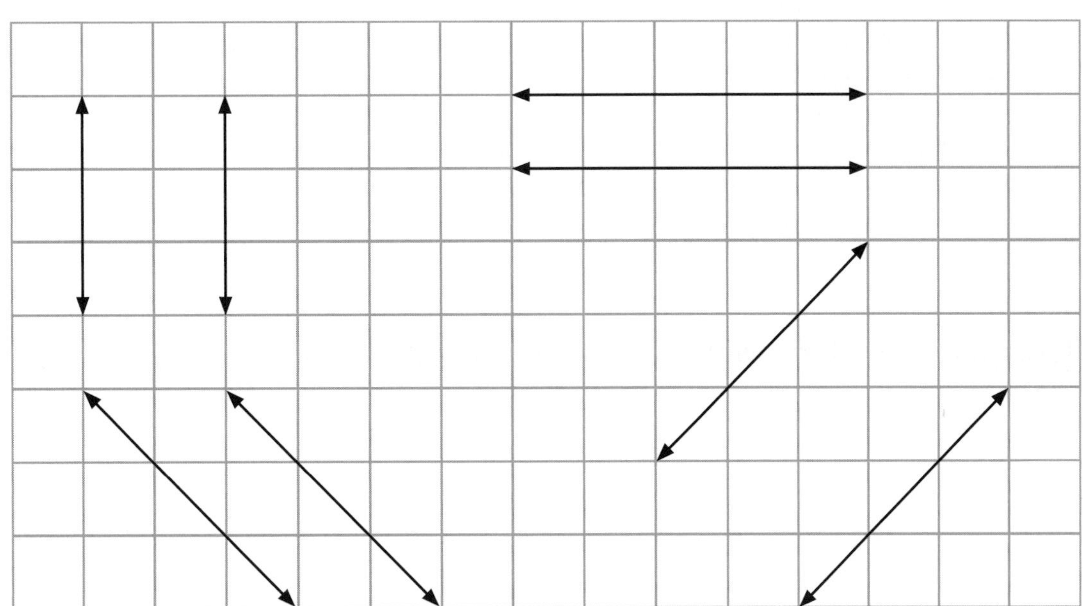

Hands-On Activity

STEP 1 Look around your classroom and school.

STEP 2 Find items with parallel line segments and items with no parallel line segments.

STEP 3 Record the items and places in charts.

With Parallel Line Segments	Places Where I Found the Items
benches	hallways

With No Parallel Line Segments	Places Where I Found the Items
branches of plants	schoolyard

STEP 4 Compare your items with those found by other groups.

Let's Practice

Tell whether the lines are parallel.

1

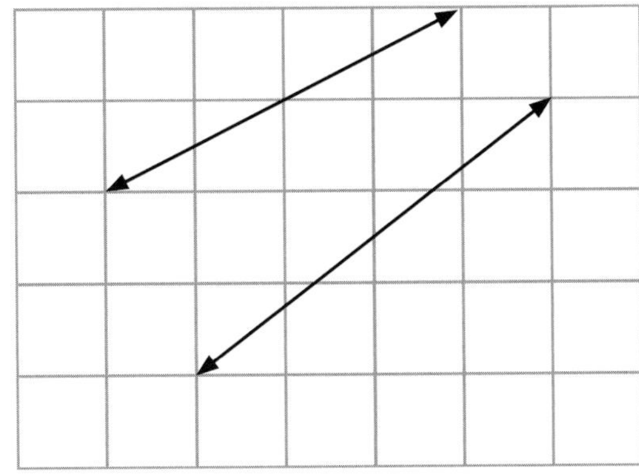

2

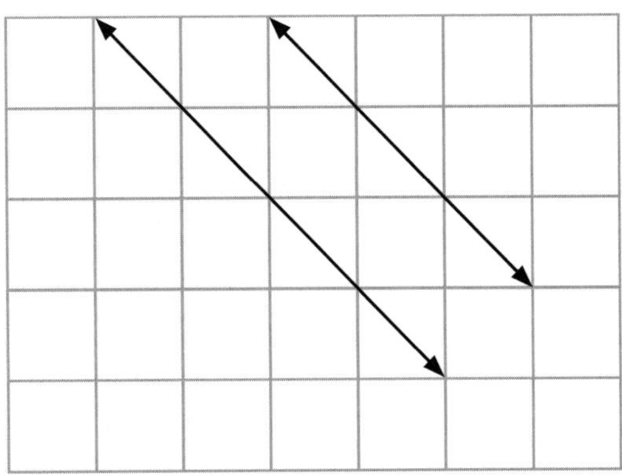

Identify the parallel line segments in each figure.

3

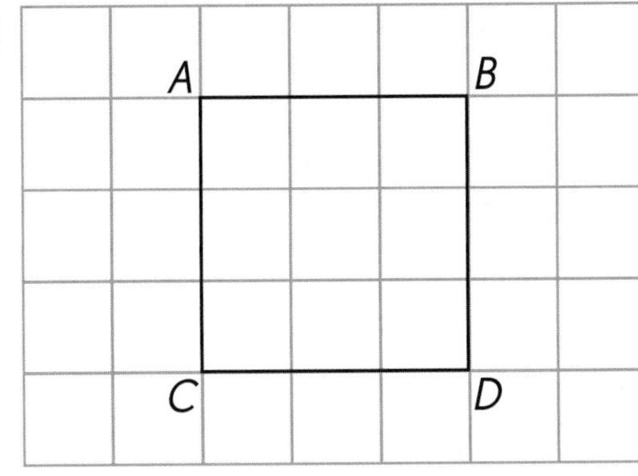

4

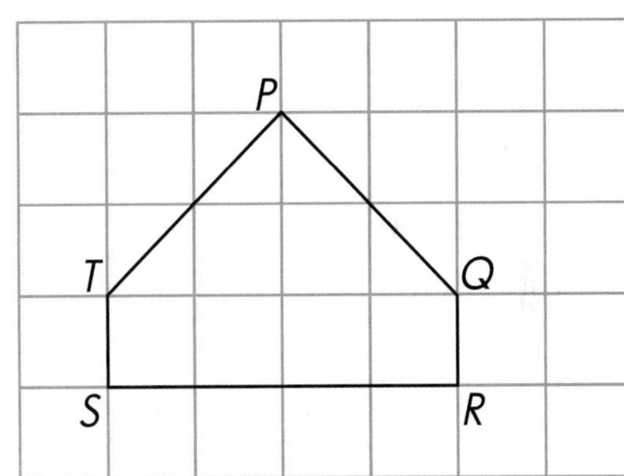

Find two pairs of parallel line segments on each object.

5

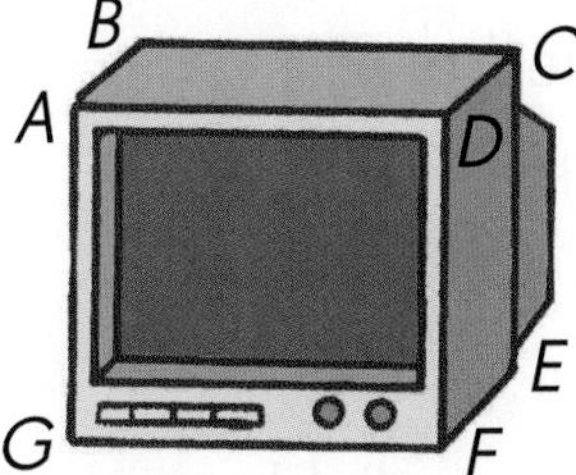

6

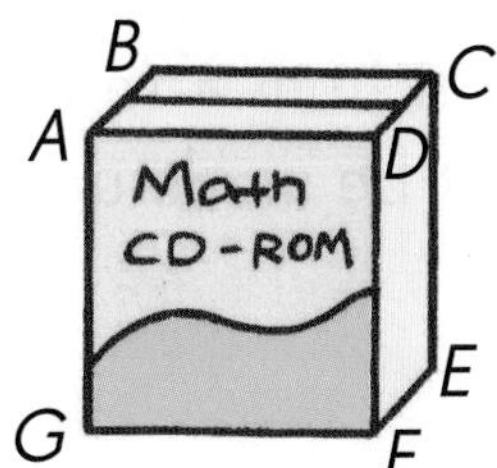

ON YOUR OWN

Go to Workbook B:
Practice 4, pages 185–188

CRITICAL THINKING SKILLS

Put On Your Thinking Cap!

PROBLEM SOLVING

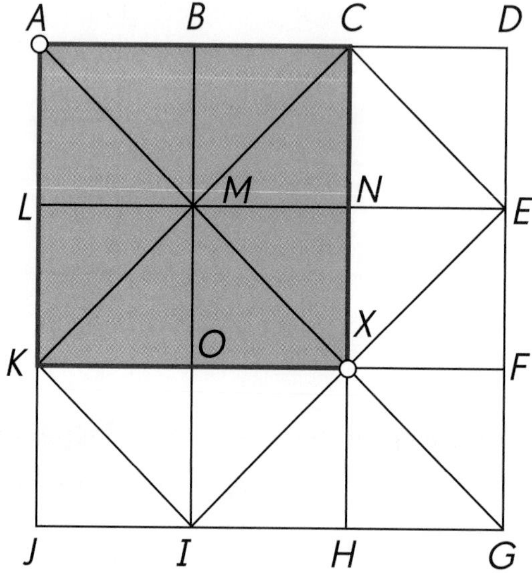

1. Name three pairs of perpendicular line segments in the diagram.

2. You are standing at *X*. You want to go to *A*. What is the shortest path to *A*?

3. Are there any line segments perpendicular to the shortest path? Name two.

4. Find three paths from *X* to *A* that are within the shaded area. Each path must be made up of one or more pairs of perpendicular line segments.

Use five craft sticks to make a figure that has four pairs of parallel line segments and four pairs of perpendicular line segments.

5. What shape do you get?

PROBLEM SOLVING

Cut out the seven pieces of a tangram.

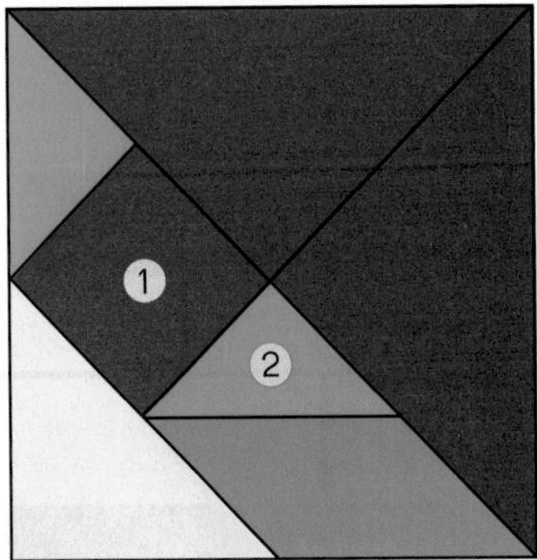

1
2

A tangram is a Chinese puzzle of seven pieces which can be pieced into a square.

6 The shape below is made up of two tangram pieces. It has two right angles, one angle smaller than a right angle, and one angle greater than a right angle.

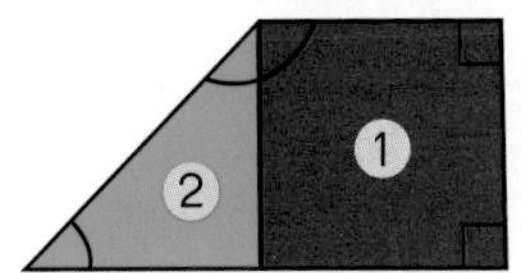

Now, form two more shapes which have two right angles, one angle smaller than a right angle, and one angle greater than a right angle each, using

a three tangram pieces

b four tangram pieces

7 Arrange six pieces of the tangram to form a shape which has three right angles and two angles greater than a right angle.

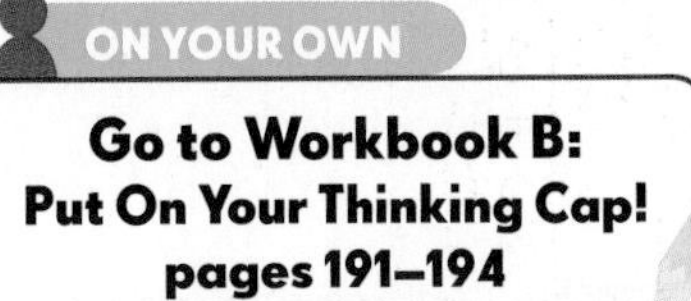

Chapter Wrap Up

Study Guide

You have learned...

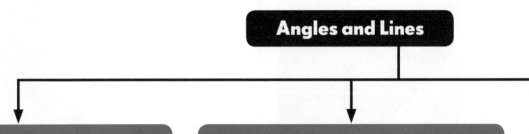

Angles and Lines

Point, Line, Line Segment

A point is an exact location in space.
Point A (A)

A

A line is a straight path that goes on without ends in both directions.
Line AB or line BA

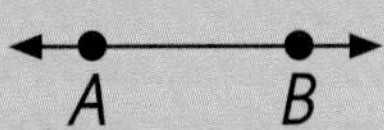

A line segment is part of a line. It has two endpoints.
Line segment AB or line segment BA

Angles

An angle is formed by two line segments with the same endpoint.

A folded piece of paper can be used to check for right angles.

It can also be used to check if other angles are greater than or less than a right angle.

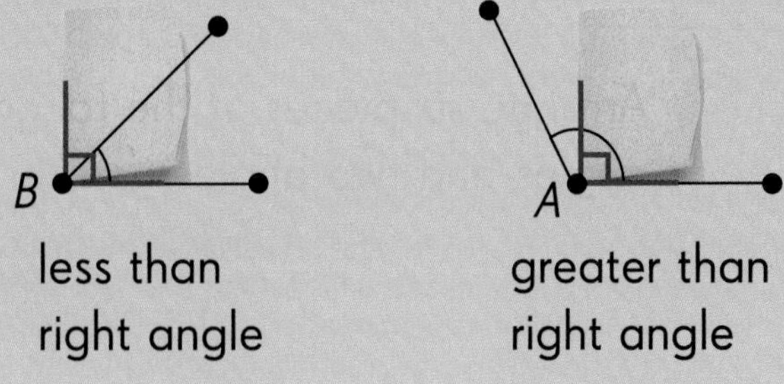

less than right angle

greater than right angle

▶ Angles and lines can be found all around us. These can be described with special names.

Perpendicular Lines and Segments

Perpendicular lines and line segments meet at right angles.

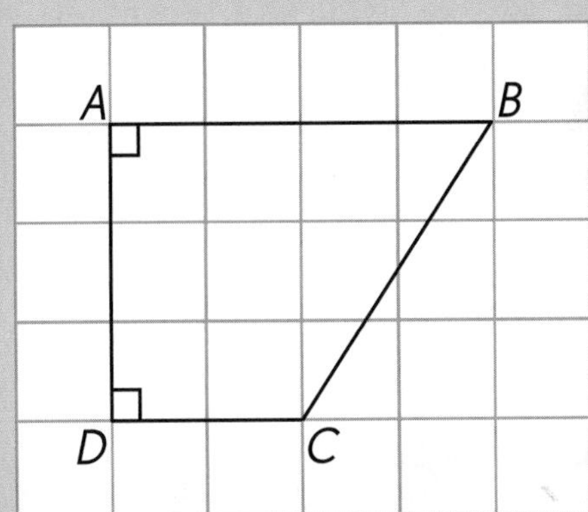

Perpendicular line segments:
Line segments *AB* and *AD*
Line segments *AD* and *DC*

Parallel Lines and Segments

Parallel lines and line segments will not meet no matter how long you draw them. The distance between them is always the same.

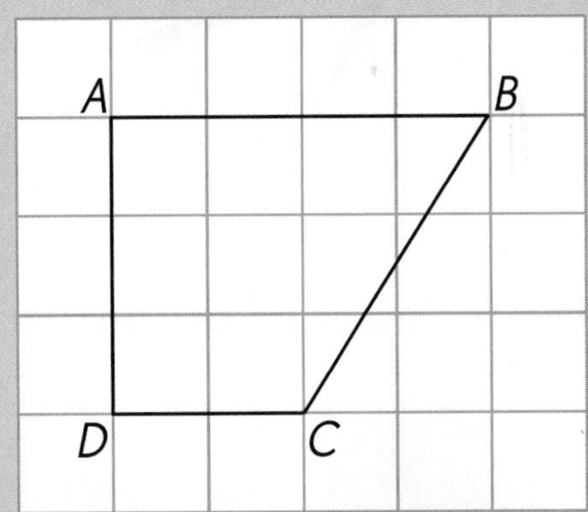

Parallel line segments:
Line segments *AB* and *DC*

Chapter Review/Test

Vocabulary

Choose the correct word.

line
line segment
right angle
perpendicular lines
parallel lines

1. A ______ has no endpoints.

2. ______ do not meet no matter how long you draw them.

3. A ______ is formed when two line segments meet at a point and are perpendicular to each other.

4. Two lines that meet at a right angle are called ______.

Concepts and Skills

5. Which of these form an angle? ______

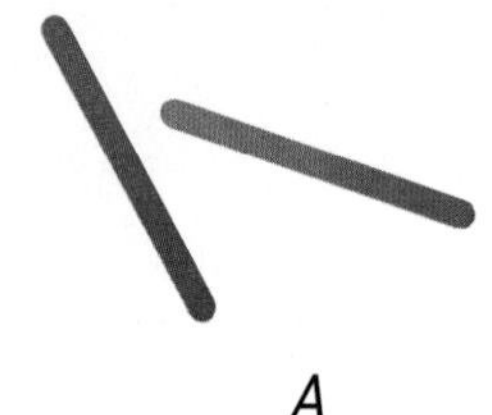

A

B

Find the number of angles in each object or shape.

6. 

______

7. 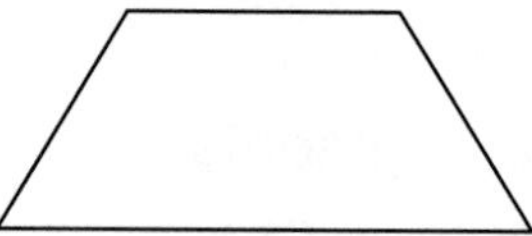

______

8. Which angles are the same size as right angles? Angles ______

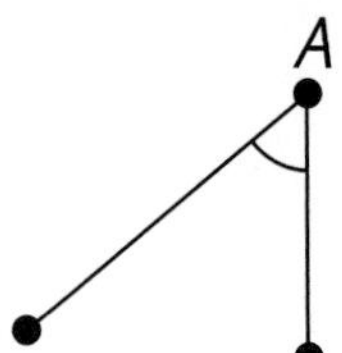

A

B

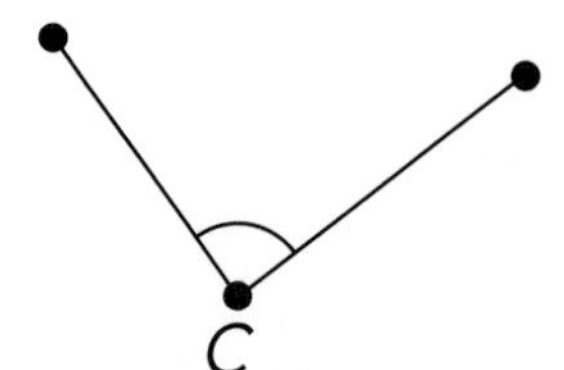

C

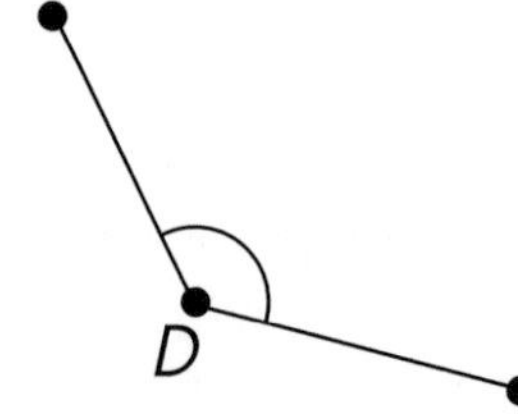

D

9 Find the number of sides and angles of the shape.

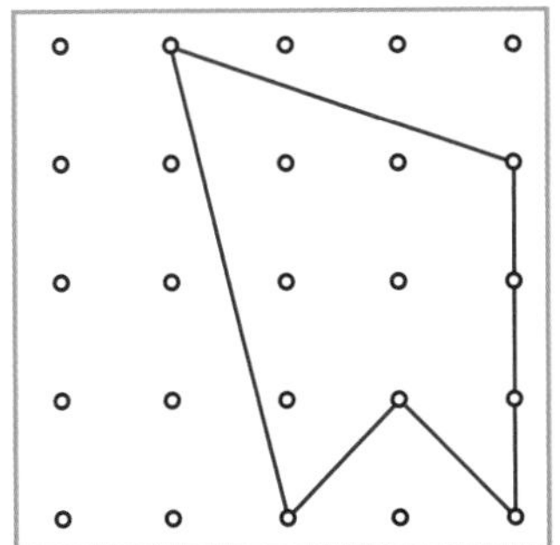

sides angles

10 Identify the perpendicular line segments.

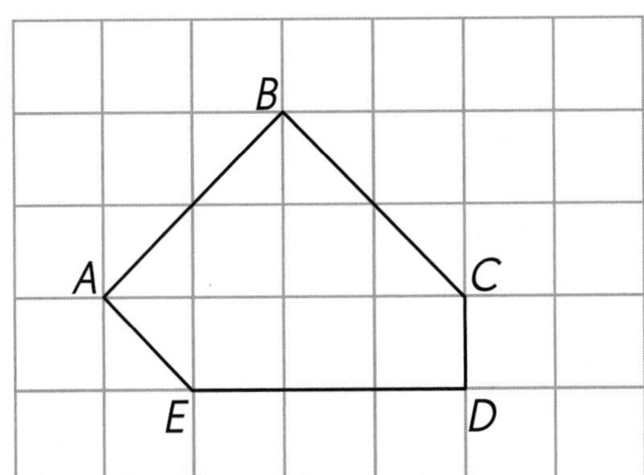

11 Identify the parallel line segments.

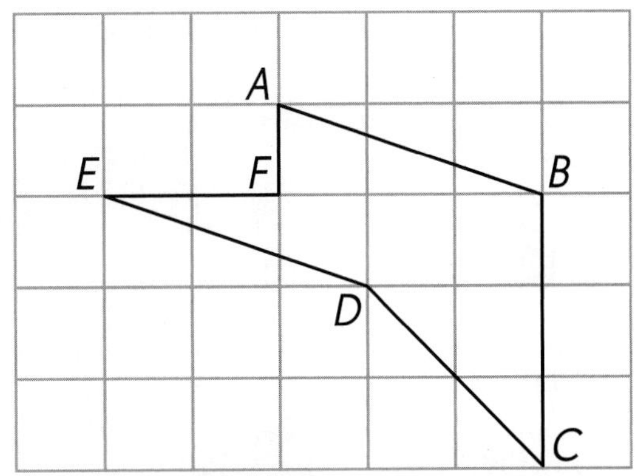

Problem Solving

12 You are walking parallel to Argos Road.
On which road are you walking?

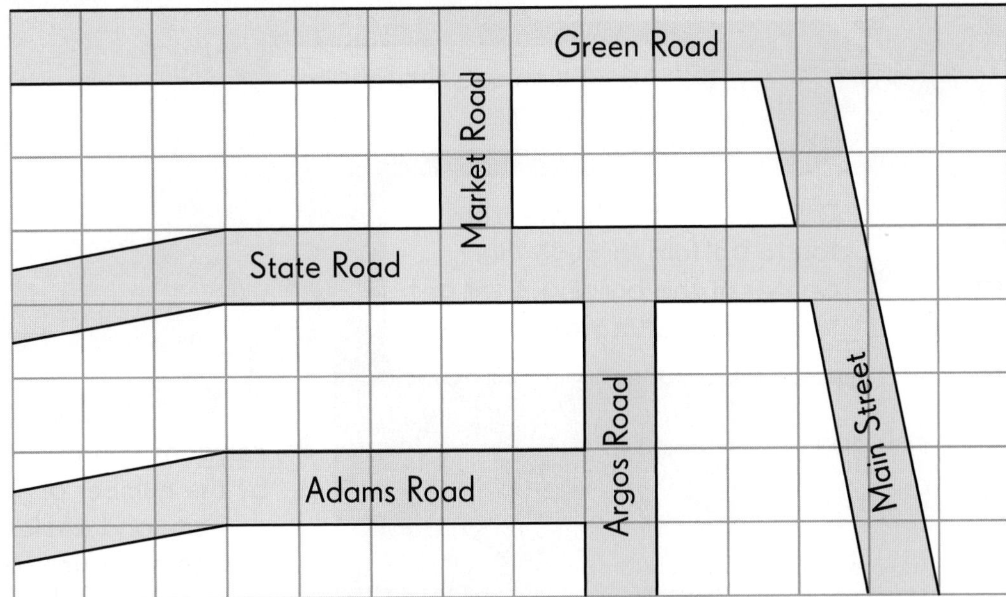

Two-Dimensional Shapes

This is the White House. There are many plane shapes in this building.

Yes, I can see rectangles and triangles.

If I draw a straight line from top to bottom through the center of the building, I will get two parts that match exactly.

Lessons

18.1 Classifying Polygons
18.2 Congruent Figures
18.3 Symmetry

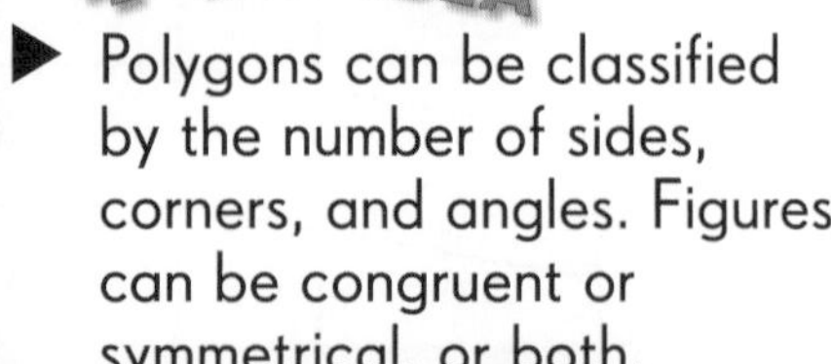

BIG IDEA

▶ Polygons can be classified by the number of sides, corners, and angles. Figures can be congruent or symmetrical, or both.

Recall Prior Knowledge

Counting the number of sides, corners, and angles of plane shapes

Plane Shape	Number of Sides	Number of Corners	Number of Angles
circle	0	0	0
triangle	3	3	3
square	4	4	4
rectangle	4	4	4
trapezoid	4	4	4
hexagon	6	6	6

Combining plane shapes to form other plane shapes

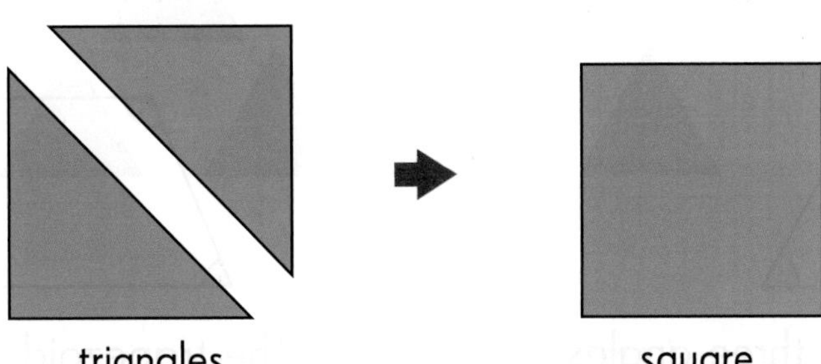

Two triangles can be combined to form a square.

Hands-On Activity

Materials:
- polygons

WORK IN PAIRS

1. Identify each polygon and find the number of sides, angles, and vertices.

Record the information in the table.

Polygons	Number of Sides	Number of Angles	Number of Vertices

What can you say about the number of sides, angles, and vertices of a polygon?

2. Walk around your school or classroom.
Look for objects that have the shapes listed in the table.

Polygons	Objects
Triangle	
Square	
Rectangle	
Pentagon	
Hexagon	
Octagon	

Learn Identify quadrilaterals.

These are **quadrilaterals**.

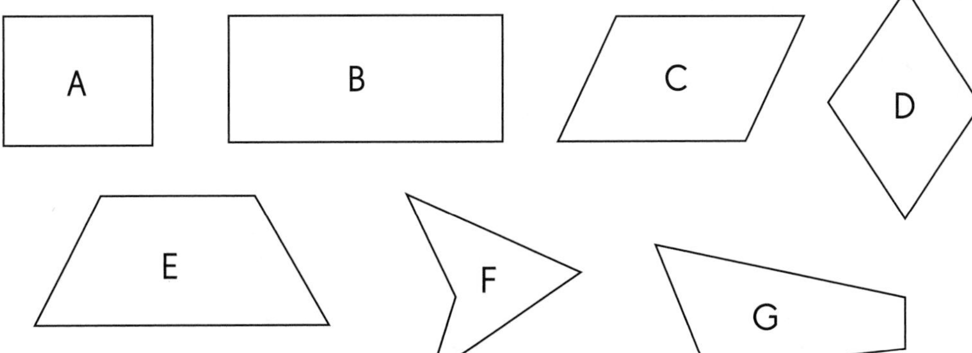

Quadrilaterals are polygons with 4 sides and 4 angles.

The outline of the door is a quadrilateral because it has 4 sides.

The outline of a notebook is a quadrilateral.

The outlines of a television, a kite, and a whiteboard are quadrilaterals too.

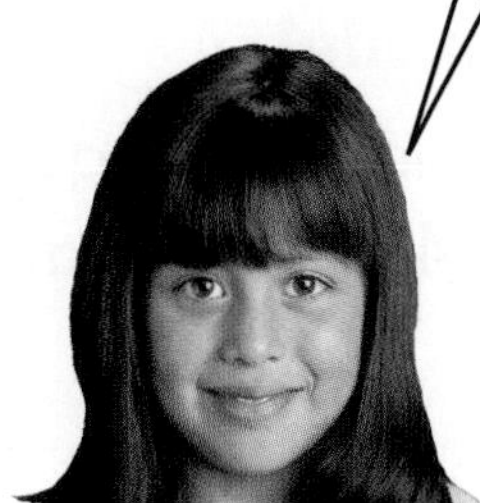

Guided Learning

Choose the quadrilaterals.

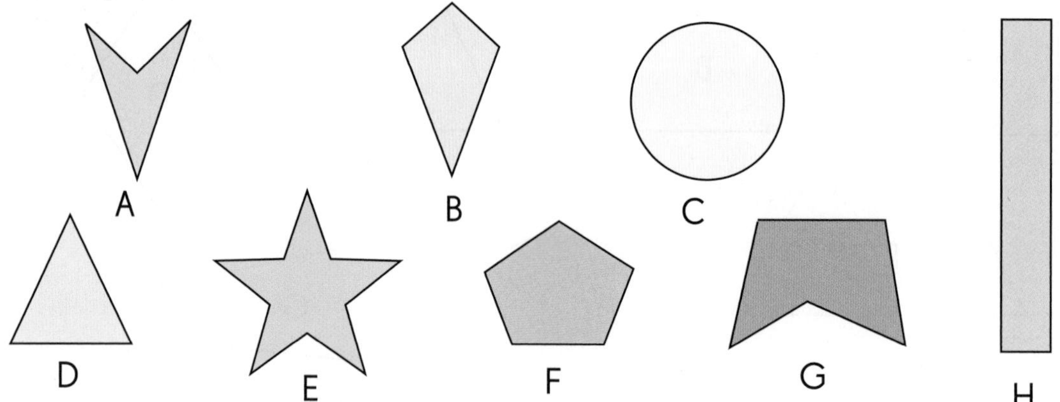

Choose true or false for each statement.

14 The outline of a ruler is a quadrilateral.

15 The outline of a bottle cap is a quadrilateral.

16 The outline of a postcard is a quadrilateral.

17 The outline of an envelope is a quadrilateral.

Learn **Identify quadrilaterals and their properties.**

Some quadrilaterals have special names.
They are classified by

a pairs of sides that are parallel.

b sides that are of equal length.

c angles that are right angles.

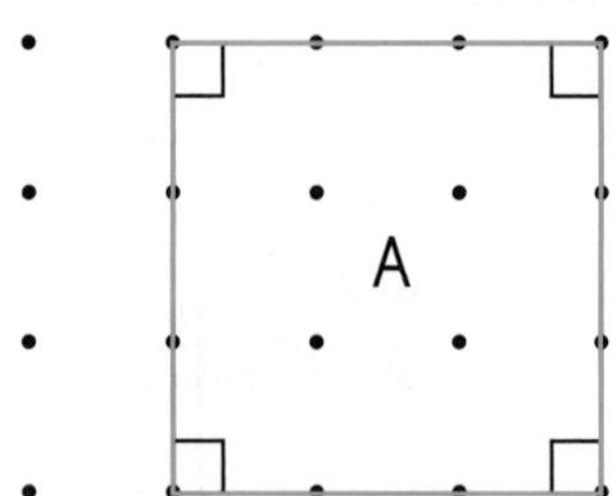

Figure A is a square.
Opposite sides of a square are **parallel**.
All sides of a square are of equal length.
All 4 angles of a square are right angles.

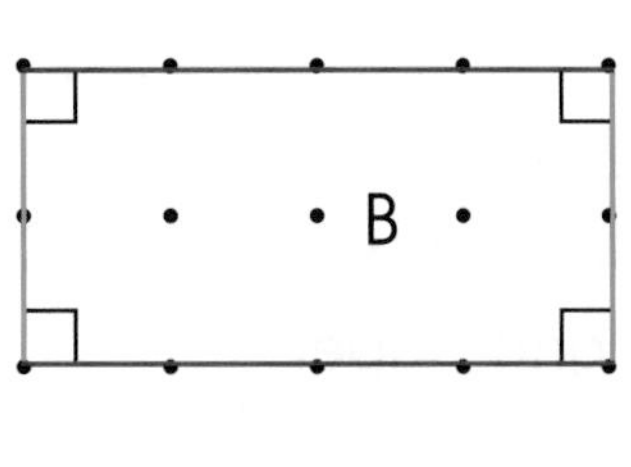

Figure B is a rectangle.
Opposite sides of a rectangle are parallel.
Only the opposite sides of a rectangle need to be of equal length.
All 4 angles of a rectangle are right angles.

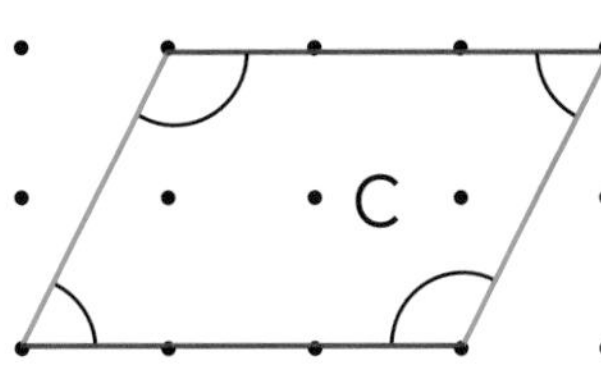

Figure C is a parallelogram.
Opposite sides of a parallelogram are parallel.
Only the opposite sides of a parallelogram need to be of equal length.
There are 4 angles in a parallelogram.

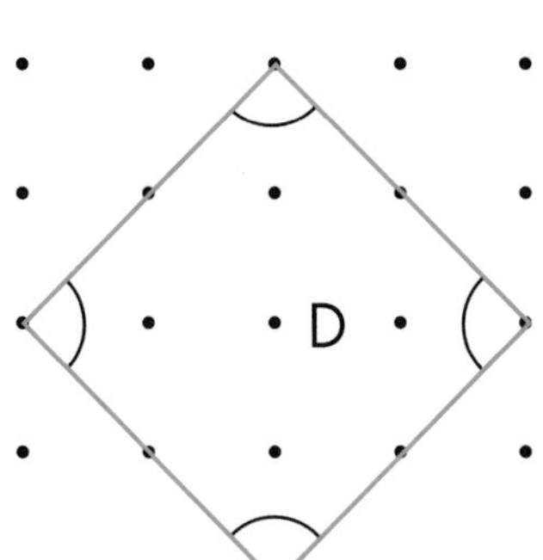

Figure D is a **rhombus**.
Opposite sides of a rhombus are parallel.
All sides of a rhombus are of equal length.
There are 4 angles in a rhombus.

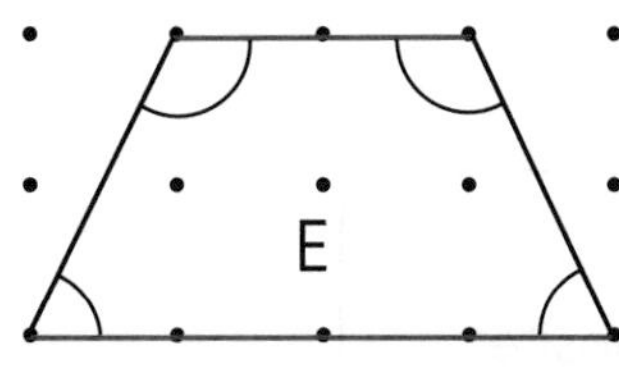

Both figures E and F are trapezoids.
Only one pair of opposite sides are parallel.
There are 4 angles in a trapezoid.
A trapezoid can have 2 right angles as in figure F.

Squares, rectangles, parallelograms, and rhombuses have two pairs of opposite sides that are parallel.

I can think of the rhombus as a parallelogram with four sides that are of equal length.

STEP 1 Cut along the dotted lines on a copy of this figure. You will get the 7 shapes.

STEP 2 Use 3 or 4 shapes to make other polygons. Identify each polygon.

STEP 3 Ask your partner to list the shapes used. Then classify the shapes used.

STEP 4 One partner then uses all 7 pieces to make a figure.

STEP 5 The other partner breaks the figure apart and uses the 7 shapes to make the original square.

Guided Learning

Trace and cut out the polygons to make other polygons. You may use more than one of each type of polygon.

31

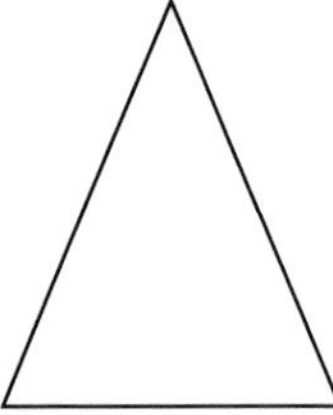

32 **Find how many polygons are in the figure. List them.**

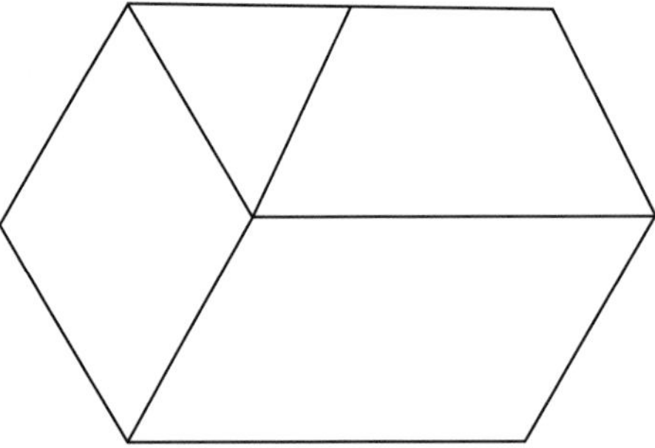

Let's Practice

Complete the table. Choose yes or no.

1

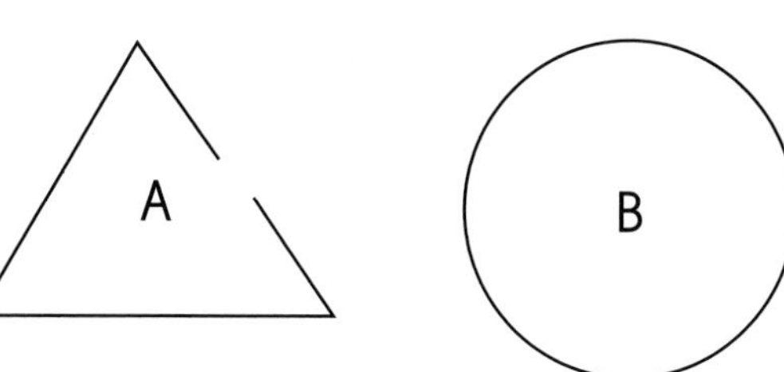

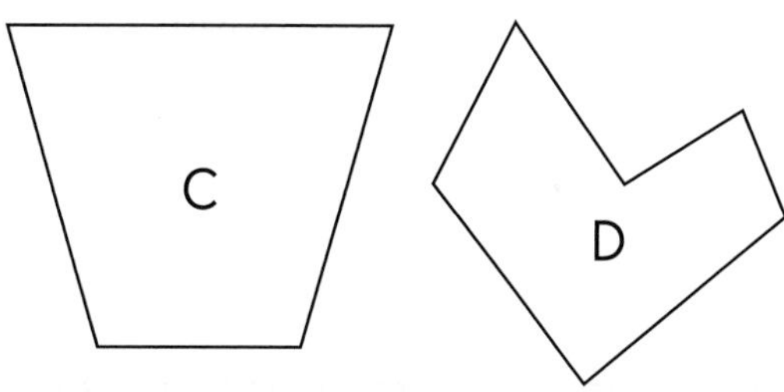

Property	Figure A	Figure B	Figure C	Figure D
It is a closed figure.				
There are 3 or more line segments.				

Fill in the blanks.

2 Figures ___ and ___ are polygons.

Complete the table.

3

Figures	Name	Number of Sides	Number of Angles	Number of Vertices
			3	3
		4		
	Pentagon		5	5
		6	6	
				8

Lesson 18.2 Congruent Figures

Vocabulary
slide
flip
turn
rotate
congruent

Lesson Objectives

- Identify a slide, flip, and turn.
- Slide, flip, and turn shapes to make congruent figures.
- Identify congruent figures.

Learn Plane figures can slide, flip, and turn.

You can move figures in different ways.

Imagine pushing this figure from here to there. You slide it along.

The figure of the dog has been slid along from left to right.

To **slide** a figure is to move it along in any direction.

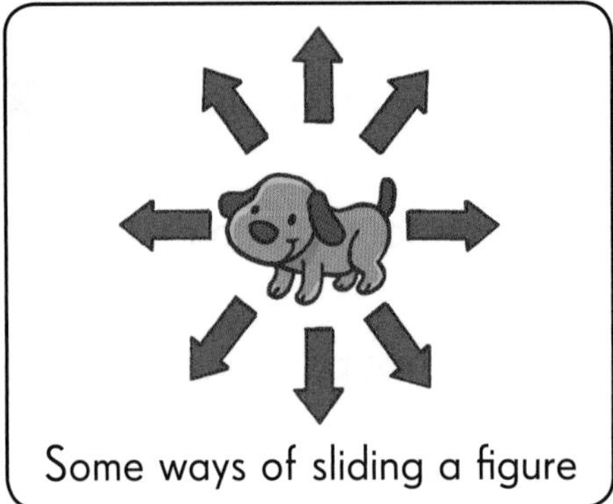

Some ways of sliding a figure

When I hold the letter D in front of a mirror, the image in the mirror is like the back side of the letter D.

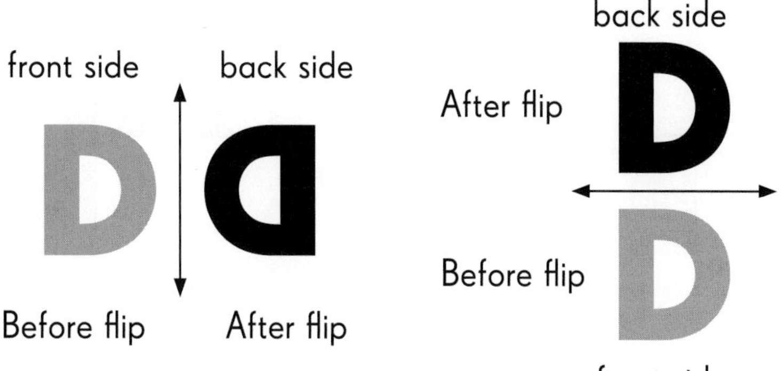

The letter D has been flipped over a line.
To **flip** a figure is to turn it front to back over a line.

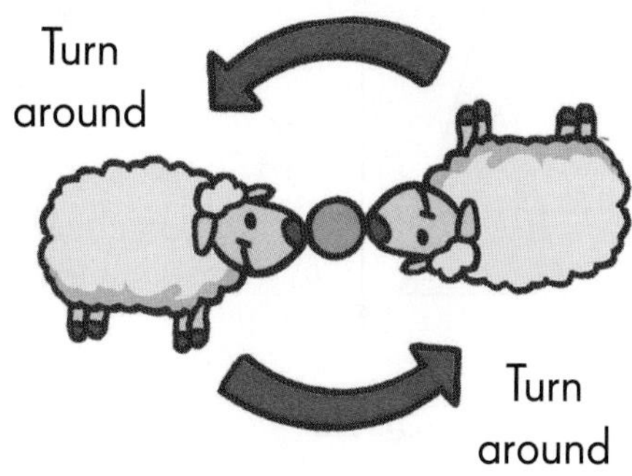

The figure of the sheep has been turned through a half turn.
To **turn** a figure is to **rotate** it about a point.

Flips, slides, and turns are movements that change the position of figures.

But the shape and size of the figures remain unchanged.

Two figures that have the same shape and size are **congruent**.

Guided Learning

Trace one of the two figures. Cut it out and place it on top of the other figure. Decide which sets of shapes have been slid along in any direction and are congruent.

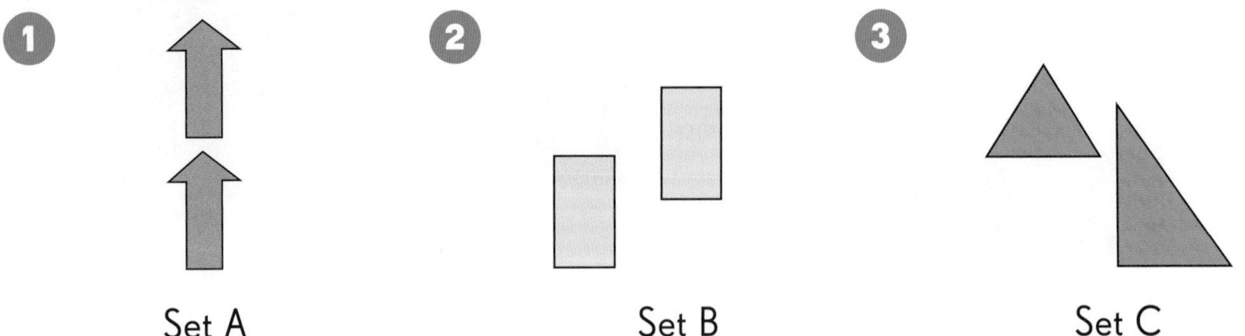

1 Set A

2 Set B

3 Set C

Trace one of the two figures. Cut it out and place it on top of the other figure. Decide which sets of shapes are flipped and congruent.

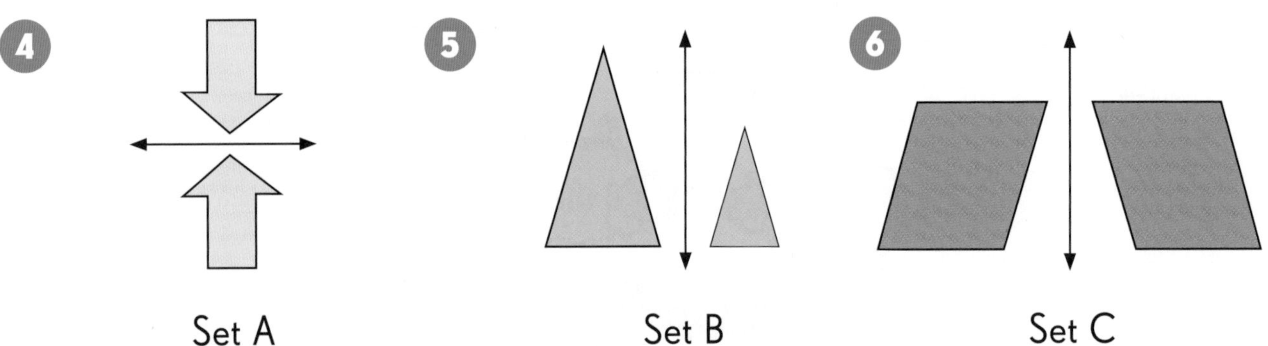

4 Set A

5 Set B

6 Set C

Trace one of the two figures. Cut it out and place it on top of the other figure. Decide which sets of shapes have been turned about a point and are congruent.

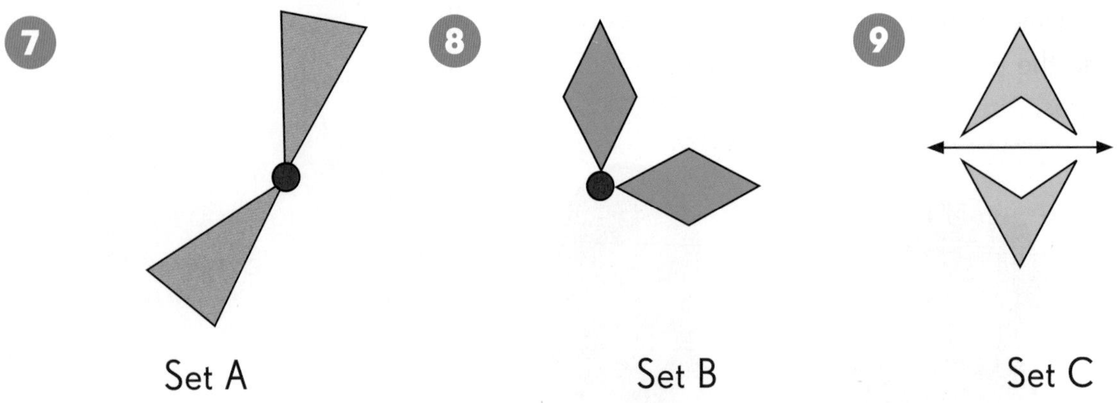

7 Set A

8 Set B

9 Set C

Learn

Identify pairs of congruent figures.

Congruent figures have the same shape and size.

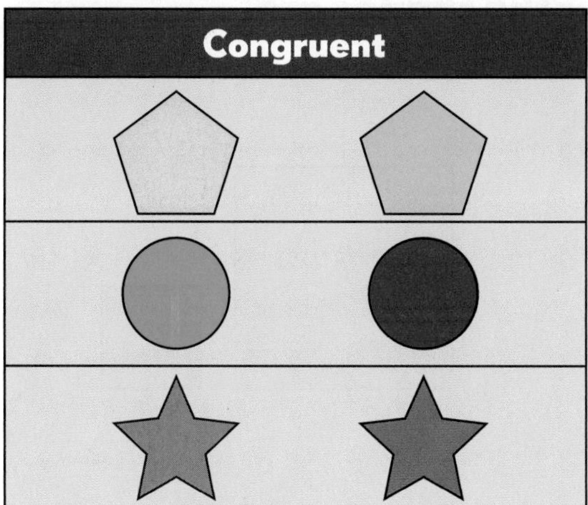

How can you be sure that these figures are congruent figures?

Put one on top of the other to see if they fit exactly.

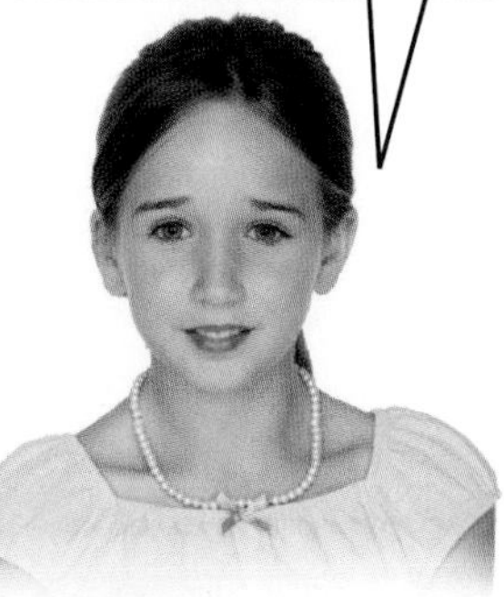

Can two figures appear in different positions and be congruent?

Yes, if they are the same shape and size. You could show it by placing one figure on top of the other figure.

Not Congruent			
Reason	• Same shape • Not the same size	• Not the same shape • Not the same size	• Not the same shape

Guided Learning

Trace one of the two figures. Cut it out and place it on top of the other figure. Decide whether the shapes are congruent. Choose yes or no.

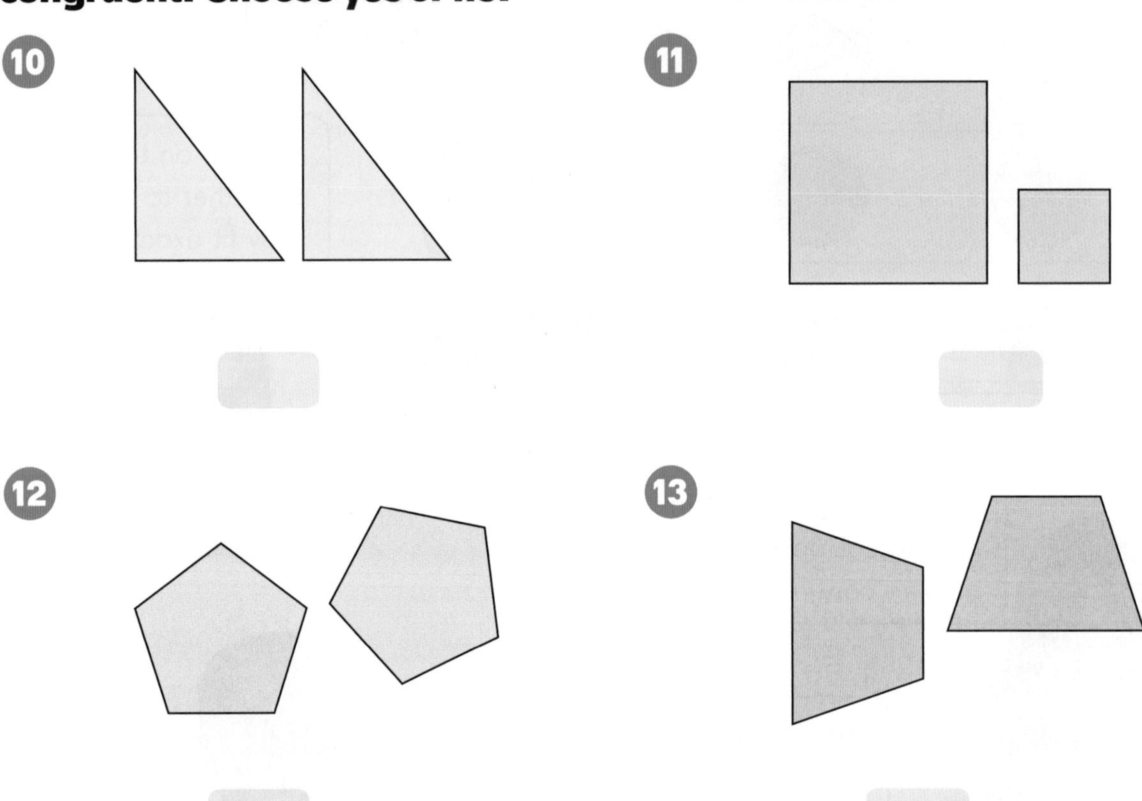

Complete. Use dot paper or grid paper to help you.

14 Draw two congruent hexagons. Draw a third hexagon that is not congruent.

A hexagon is a six-sided polygon.

15 Draw two congruent shapes. Then draw a third shape having the same shape but not congruent.

16 Draw two congruent parallelograms. Then draw a third parallelogram that is not congruent.

Look at the U.S. flag.

17 How many stars are there?

18 Are all the stars congruent?

19 Identify the stripes that are congruent.

Hands-On Activity

Materials:

- a geoboard
- rubber bands

Use a geoboard and some rubber bands.

1. Make two figures that are congruent.
   Explain to your partner why the figures are congruent.

2. Make two figures that are not congruent.
   Explain to your partner why the figures are not congruent.

Trace the first figure A. Cut it out and place it on top of figure B.

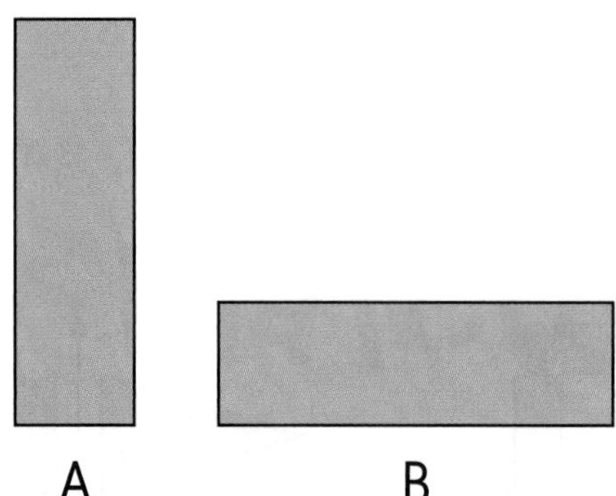

6 **Choose true or false. Use your figures to help you.**

Statements	True	False
The two rectangles are congruent.		
Rectangle A was flipped to make rectangle B.		
Rectangle A was slid to make rectangle B.		
Rectangle was turned to make rectangle B.		

Trace the first figure. Cut it out and place it on top of the other figures. Then choose a figure which is congruent.

5

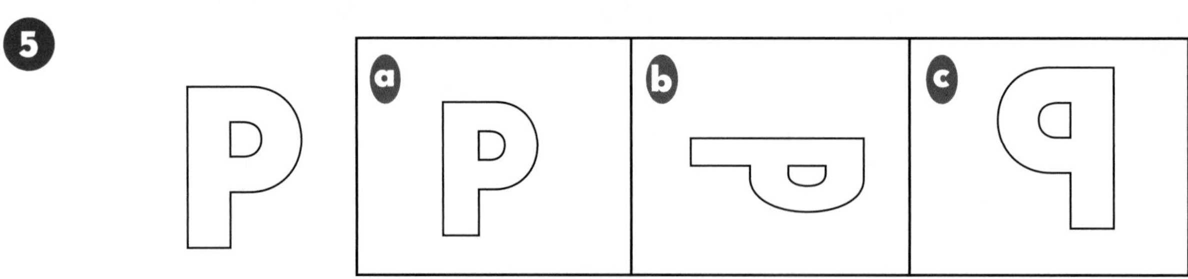

ON YOUR OWN

Go to Workbook B: Practice 2, pages 203–206

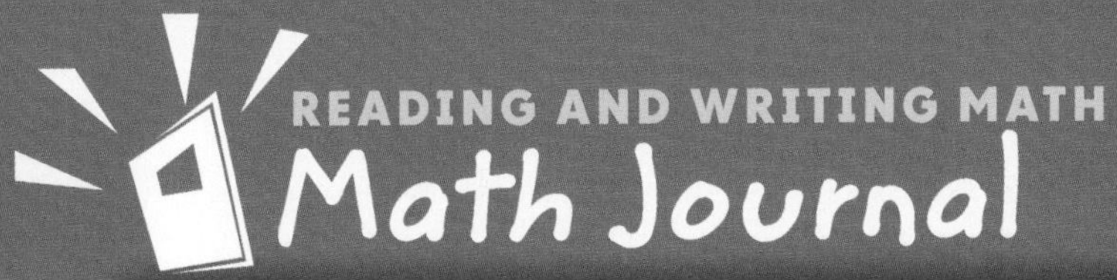

1. Rachel drew a pentagon with 5-inch sides. Tom drew an octagon with 5-inch sides. Tom says his figure is congruent to Rachel's.

   Is Tom correct? Explain why or why not.

Two figures are congruent when they have the same shape and size.

2. Kelly and Kelvin each drew a trapezoid. Kelly says that her figure is congruent to Kevin's. Explain how you will check whether the two figures are congruent.

Lesson 18.3 Symmetry

Vocabulary
symmetry
line of symmetry

Lesson Objectives

- Identify symmetric figures.
- Use folding to find a line of symmetry.

Learn Recognize symmetric figures.

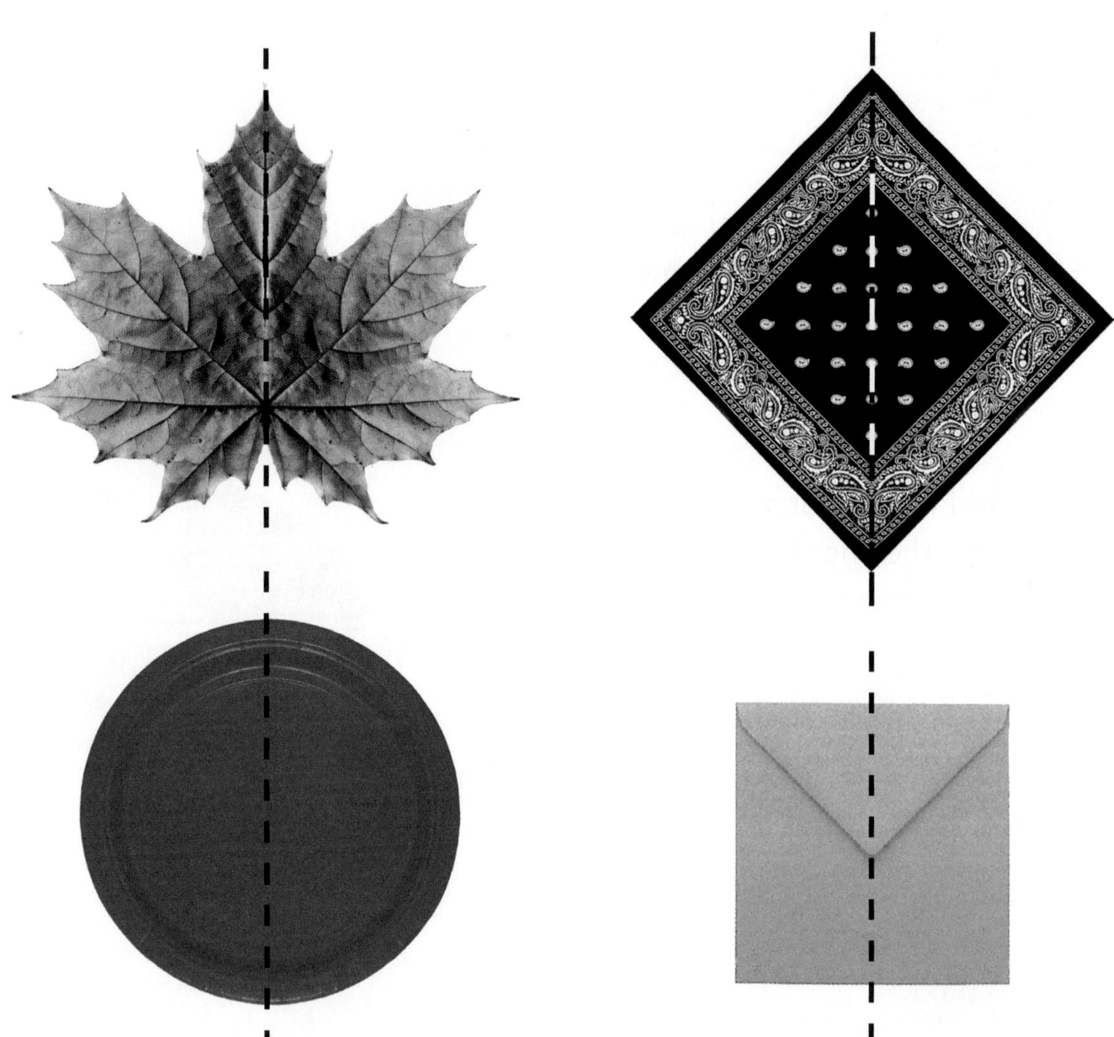

These figures have **symmetry**.
We say they are symmetric.
Each figure is divided into halves by a dotted line.
When the figure is folded along this line, the halves match exactly.

Learn

Use folding to find a line of symmetry to identify symmetric figures.

Fold Figure A along the dotted line.

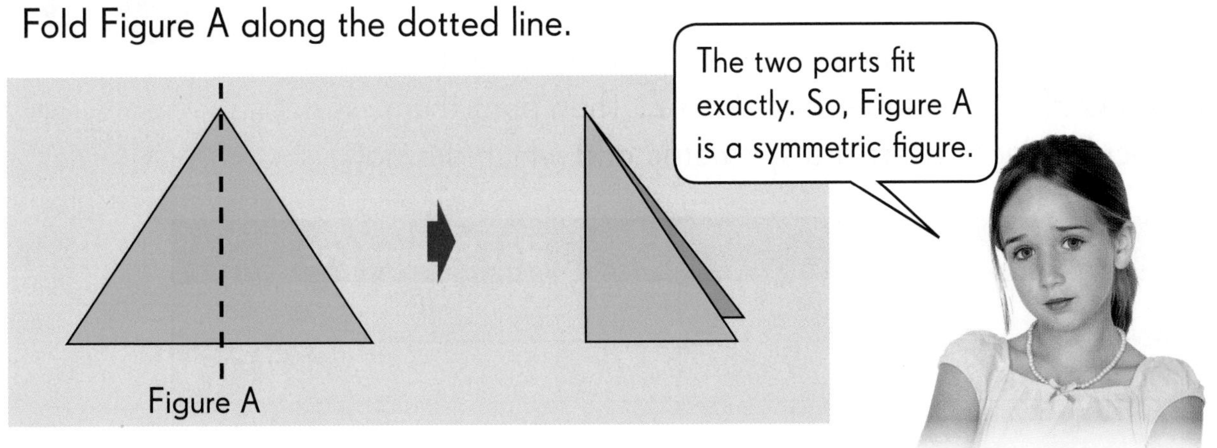

The two parts fit exactly. So, Figure A is a symmetric figure.

Figure A

The figure is divided into congruent halves by the dotted line. The congruent halves fit exactly when folded along the dotted line. The dotted line is called a **line of symmetry**.

Fold Figure B along the dotted line as shown.

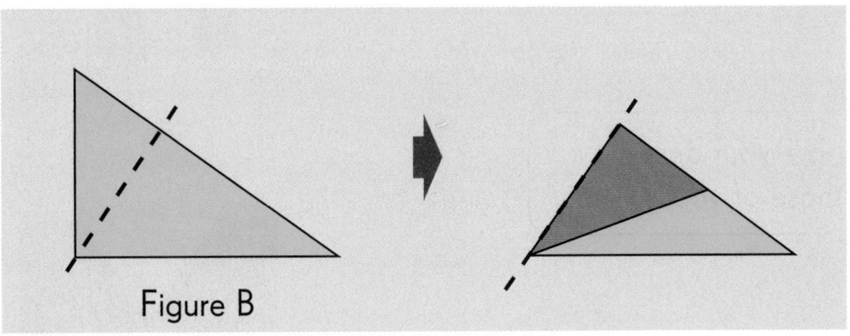

Figure B

The two parts do not fit exactly.

The dotted line is **not** a line of symmetry.

Trace Figure B and cut it out. Then fold it in different ways to find if it still has a line of symmetry.

You cannot find a line of symmetry on Figure B. So, Figure B is not a symmetric figure.

Hands-On Activity

Use the drawing tool in your computer to write the capital letters of the alphabet from A to Z. Then print them. Decide which letters are symmetric and which are not.

Symmetric	Not Symmetric
X	R

Compare your answers with those of your friends.

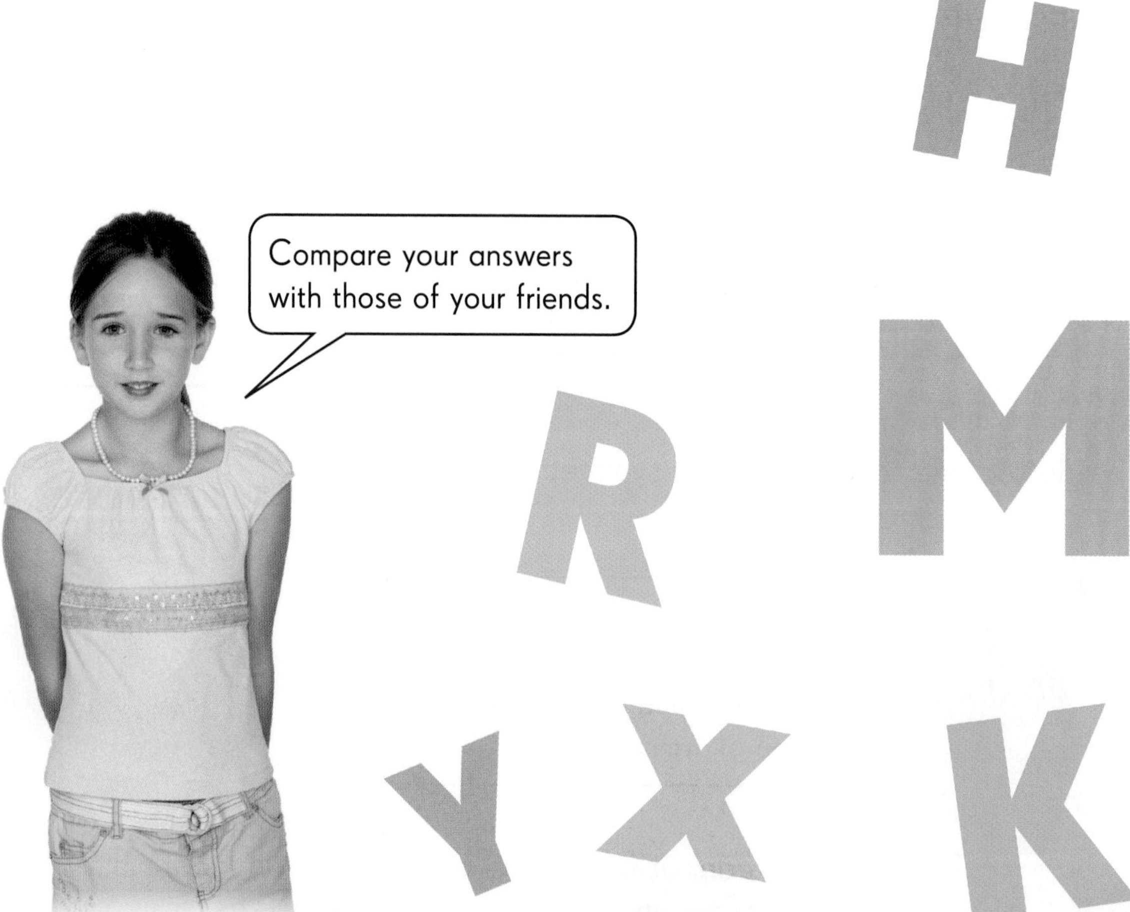

Guided Learning

Choose the symmetric figures. Figures ___

1

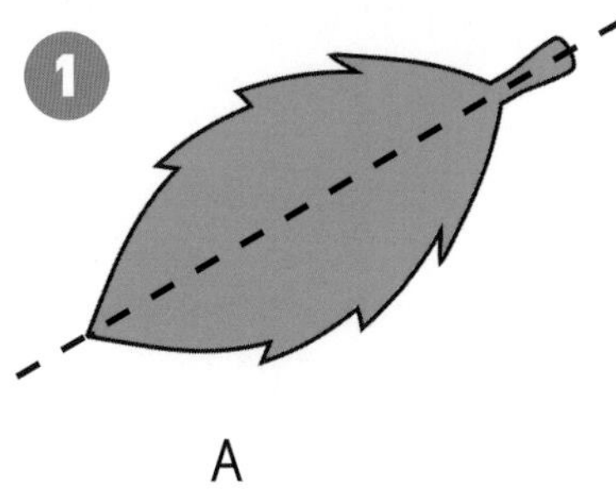

A

B

C

List the symmetric figures. Figures ___

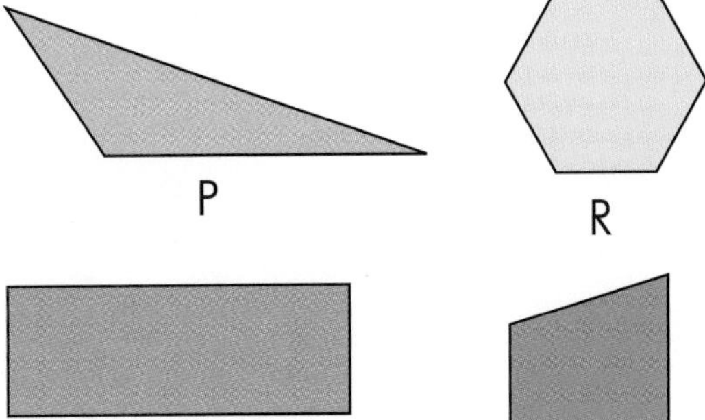

P R

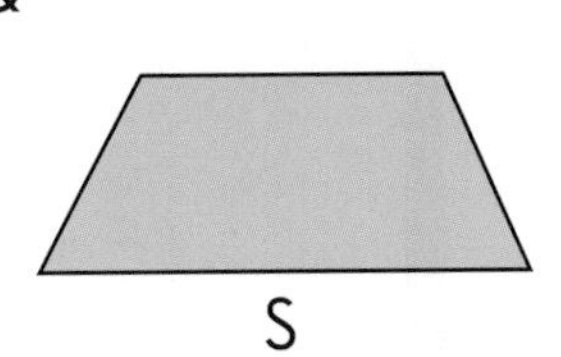

Q T

S

You can trace and cut out each figure. Then, fold it in various ways to find if it has a line of symmetry.

Decide which of the dotted lines are lines of symmetry. ___

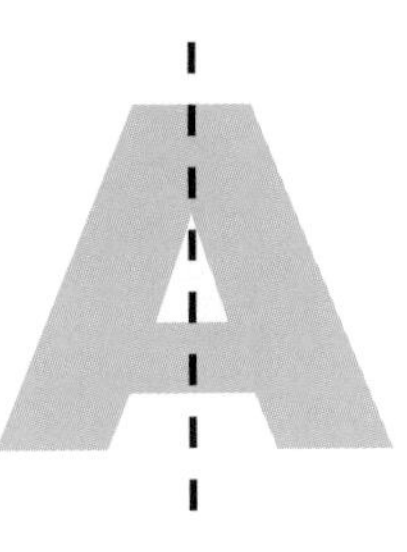

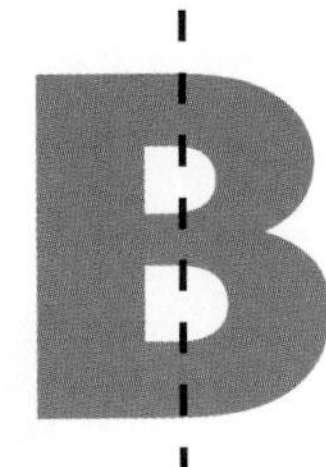

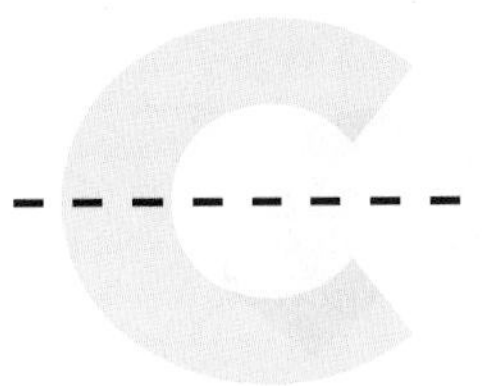

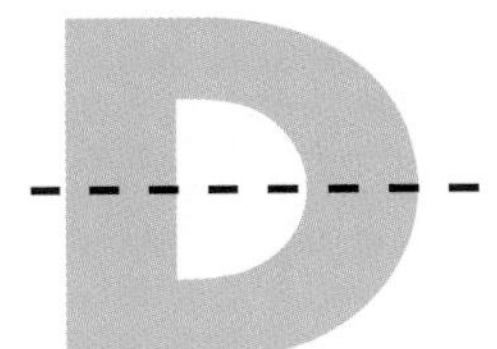

Let's Practice

Complete.

1. Find the symmetric figures. Figures ______

Figure A

Figure B

Figure C

Figure D

Figure E

Figure F

Rita drew this picture below using the drawing tools in her computer.

Name the symmetric figures.

2

3 Draw a picture showing at least 5 symmetric figures.

4 Make a list of objects around you that are symmetric.

A leaf, a kite, a scarf, and an envelope are some objects that might be symmetric.

ON YOUR OWN
Go to Workbook B: Practice 3, pages 207–208

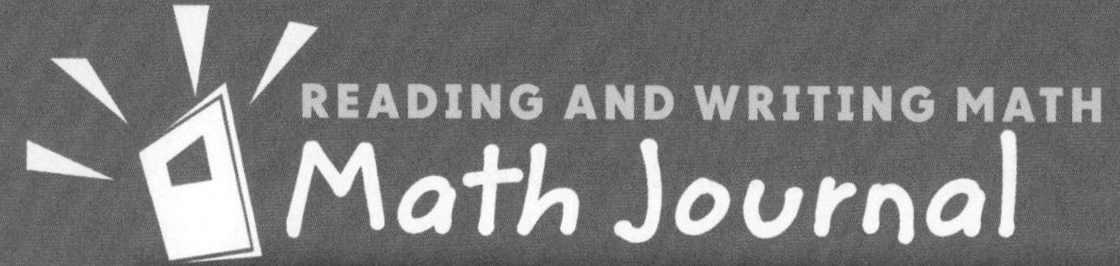

The letters P and Q are not symmetric figures.

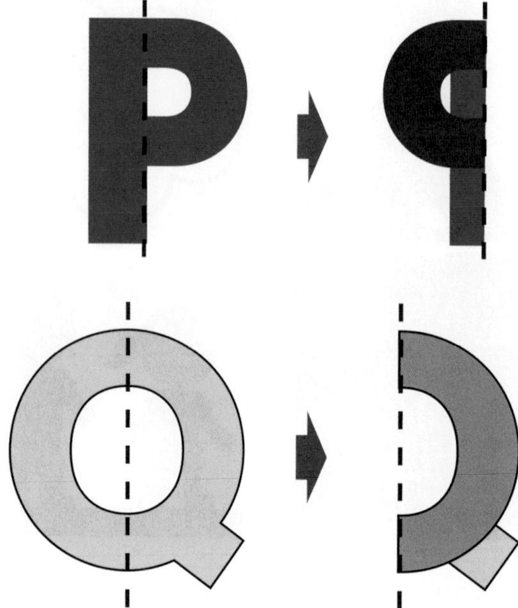

1. Explain why are these not symmetric figures.

First, recall what makes a symmetric figure. Then check for symmetry in a figure by identifying a line of symmetry.

2. How would you check for symmetry in a figure?

CRITICAL THINKING SKILLS

Put On Your Thinking Cap!

PROBLEM SOLVING

How many kinds of triangles can you find?

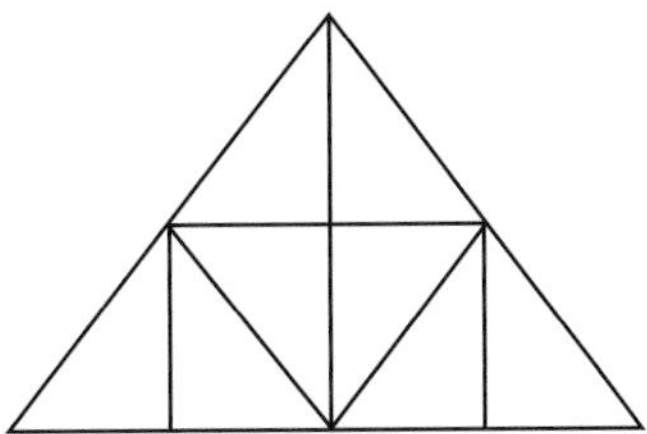

Use square grid paper to draw each triangle you find.
Then find the total number of triangles.
Are there any congruent triangles?
If yes, how many sets of congruent triangles are there?

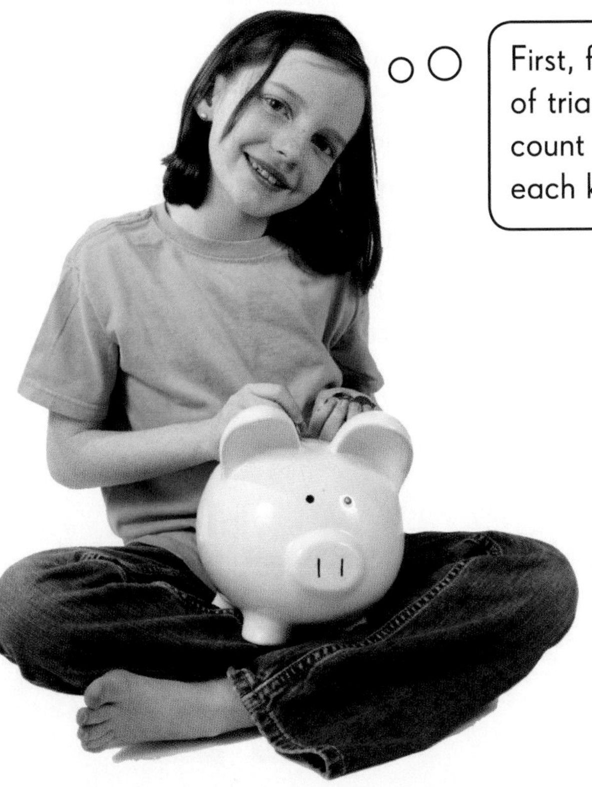

First, find how many kinds of triangles there are. Then, count the total number of each kind of triangle.

ON YOUR OWN

Go to Workbook B: Put On Your Thinking Cap! pages 209–210

Chapter Wrap Up

Study Guide

You have learned...

Two-Dimensional Shapes

Classifying Polygons

A polygon is a closed plane figure formed by three or more line segments. Polygons have vertices, sides, and angles.

Examples of special polygons:

1. Triangle
2. Quadrilateral
3. Pentagon
4. Hexagon
5. Octagon

Special Quadrilaterals:

1. Square
2. Rectangle
3. Parallelogram
4. Rhombus
5. Trapezoid

Combine and separate polygons.

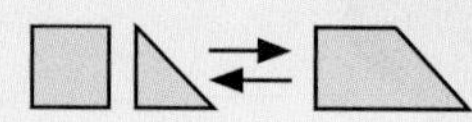

Congruent Figures

Figures with the same shape and size are congruent.

Example

To make congruent figures, slide, flip, and turn figures. These movements change the position of the figures but their own shape and size remain unchanged.

slide

flip

turn

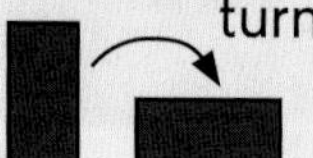

▶ Polygons can be classified by the number of sides, corners, and angles. Figures can be congruent or symmetrical, or both.

Symmetry

A symmetric figure has a line of symmetry. This line divides the figure into congruent halves. When folded along the line of symmetry, the halves fit exactly.

This is a line of symmetry.

This is not a line of symmetry.

Recall Prior Knowledge

Multiplication as repeated addition

$7 + 7 + 7 + 7 + 7 = 35$
$5 \times 7 = 35$

Using an area model to multiply

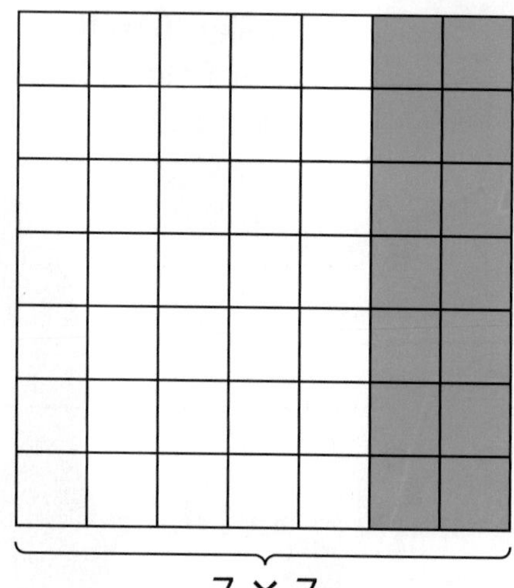

$$\begin{aligned} 7 \times 7 &= 5 \text{ groups of } 7 + 2 \text{ groups of } 7 \\ &= 5 \times 7 + 2 \times 7 \\ &= 35 + 14 \\ &= 49 \end{aligned}$$

Showing a shape on dot paper and on square grid paper

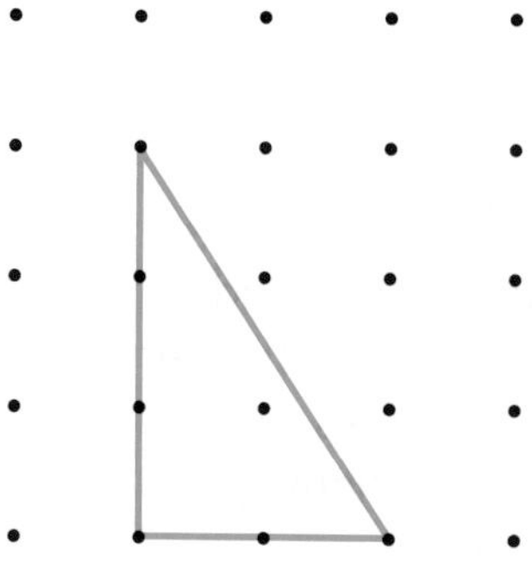

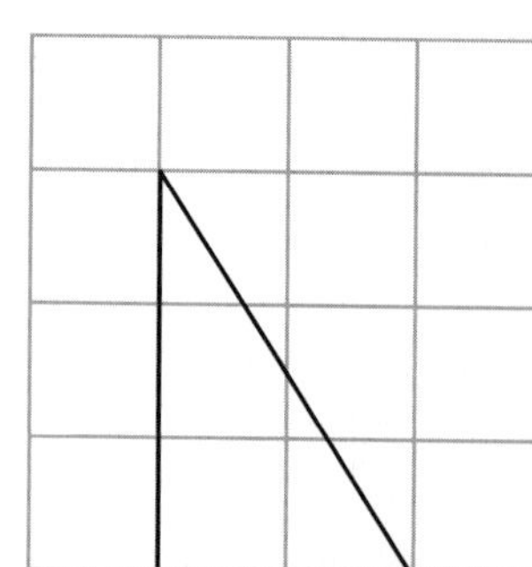

Measuring length with a ruler

Measure the lengths of the line segments and curves.

Line segment A

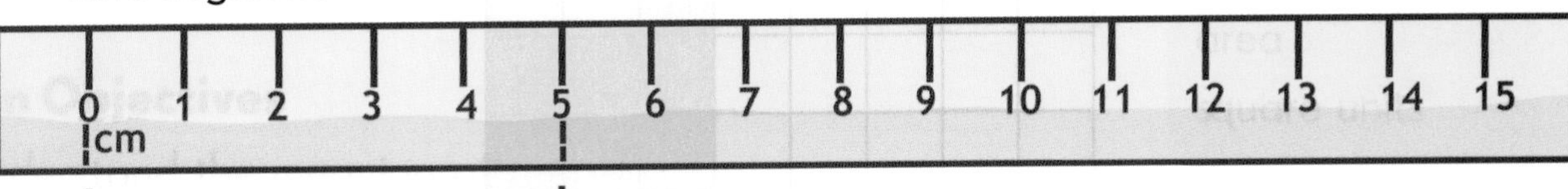

Curve B

Line segment C

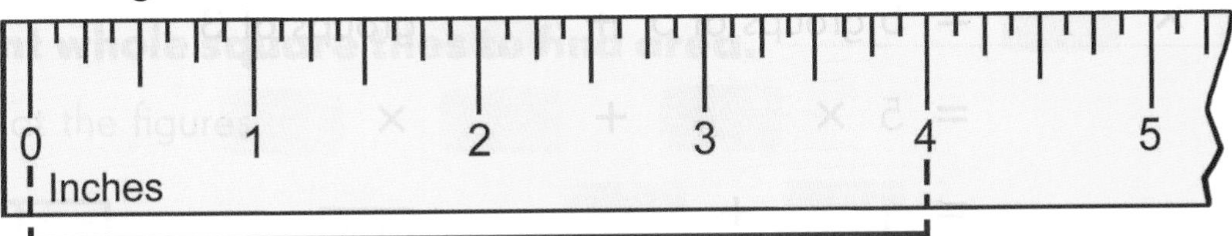

Curve D

Use a string and a ruler to measure the curves.

Line segment A is 5 centimeters long.
Curve B is 6 centimeters long.
Line segment C is 4 inches long.
Curve D is 5 inches long.

✔ Quick Check

Express each multiplication fact as an addition fact. Then find the product.

1. 4 × 4 = ___ = ___
2. 4 × 6 = ___ = ___
3. 4 × 7 = ___ = ___
4. 4 × 8 = ___ = ___

Guided Learning

Look at the figures and answer the questions.

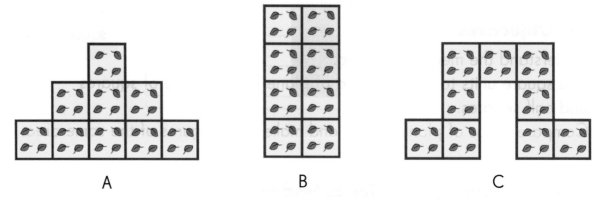

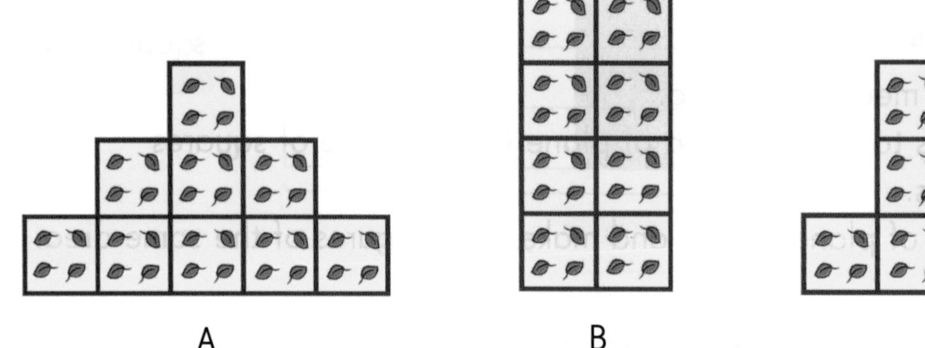

1. How many square tiles make each figure?
2. Each tile is one square unit. What is the area of each figure?
3. Which figure has the smallest area?
4. Which two figures have the same area?

Learn **Using square units and half-square units to measure area.**

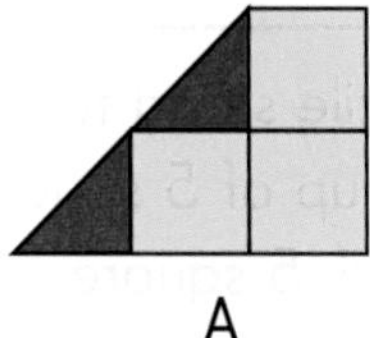

Figure A is made up of squares and half-squares.

is 1 square unit.

is $\frac{1}{2}$ square unit.

is equal to .

make 1 square unit.

Figure A is made up of 4 squares of the same size. Its area is 4 square units.

Guided Learning

The figure is made up of square and half-square tiles. Express the area in square units.

5 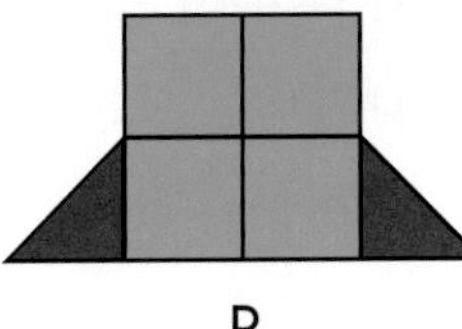

B

Each square is one square unit.

Figure B is made up of ___ squares of the same size.

The area of Figure B is ___ square units.

Hands-On Activity

Materials:
- 10 square tiles
- 10 half-square tiles

Work in groups of four.

1. Make four different figures. Use 4 squares and 2 half-squares for each figure. Find the area of each figure in square units.
2. Make four different figures, each with an area of 6 square units. How many squares and half-squares did you use for each figure?
3. Make your own figure. Then work with your group to complete the description.

   The figure is made up of ___ squares and ___ half-squares.

   The area of the figure is ___ square units.

Materials:
- red paper
- blue paper

4 Work with a partner.
Use a few pieces of red and blue paper.
Trace the red shape and blue shape and cut them out.
Make forty pieces of the red shape and twenty pieces of the blue shape.

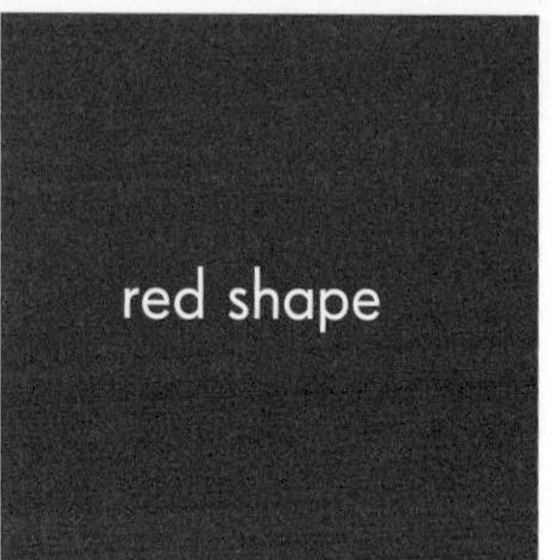

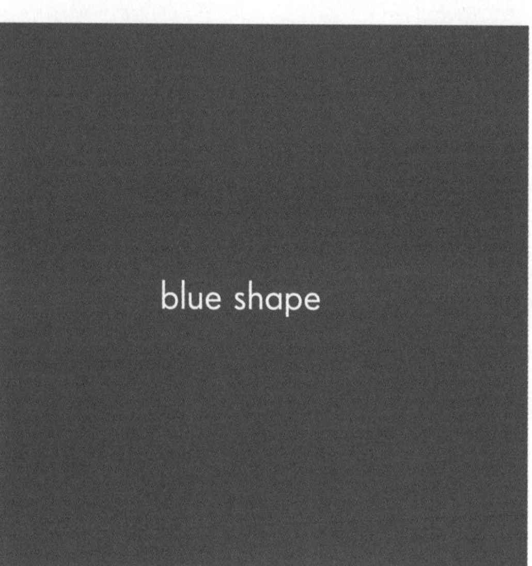

Follow the directions and complete.

STEP 1 Place red shapes over the cover of your Mathematics book.
How many did you use?
The area of the cover of the book is about ______ red shapes.

STEP 2 Place blue shapes over the cover of your Mathematics book.
How many did you use?
The area of the cover of the book is about ______ blue shapes.

STEP 3 Discuss your findings.

Let's Practice

Solve. The figures are made up of square and half-square tiles.

Find the area of each figure.
Give your answer in square units.

1. 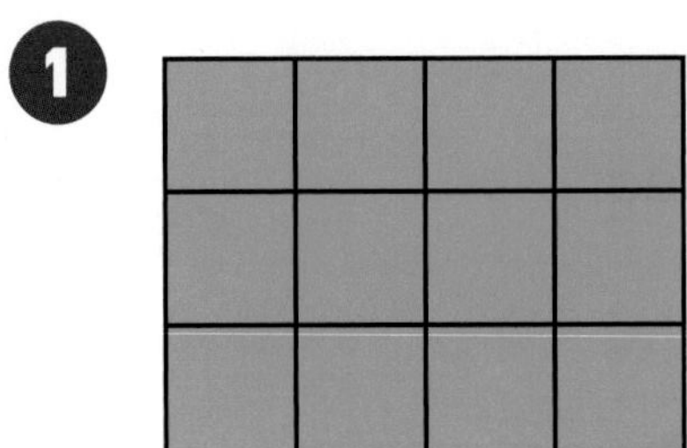

A

_____ square units

2. 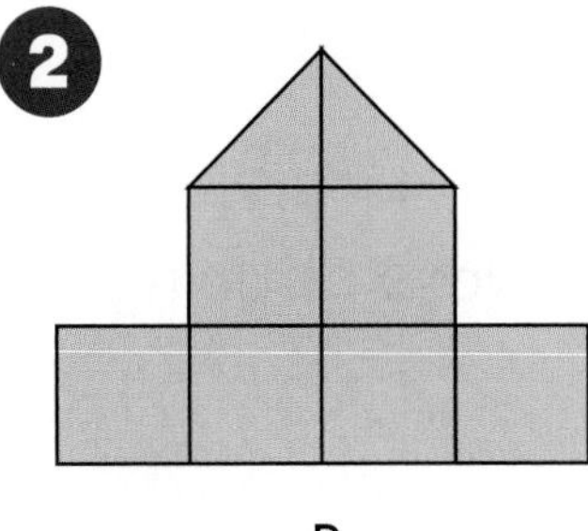

B

_____ square units

3. Which figure has the smaller area? Figure _____
4. Which figure has the larger area? Figure _____

Find the area of each figure.
Give your answer in square units.

5. 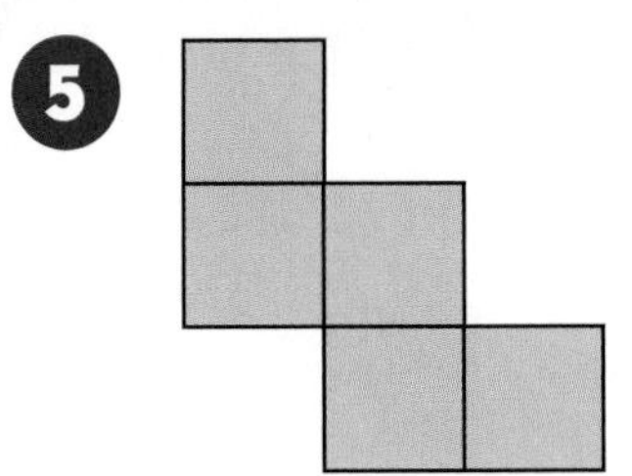

A

_____ square units

6. 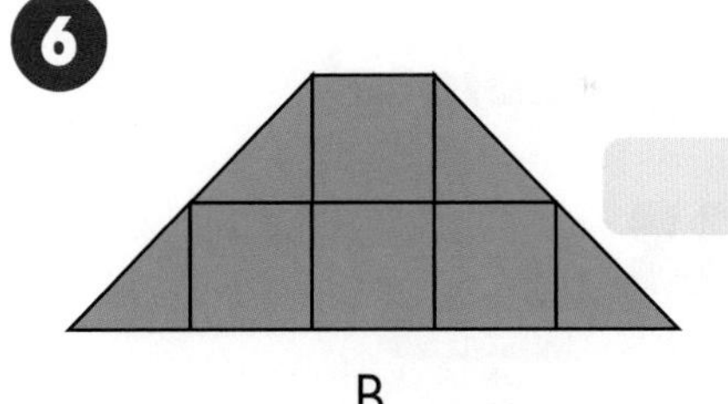

B

_____ square units

7. C

_____ square units

8. 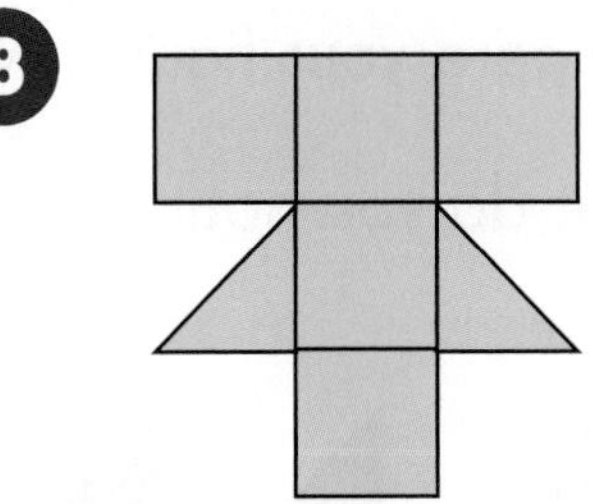

D

_____ square units

9. Which figure has the smallest area? Figure _____
10. Which figure has the largest area? Figure _____
11. Which figures have the same area? Figure _____ and _____

12 Which two figures have the same area? Figures ___ and ___

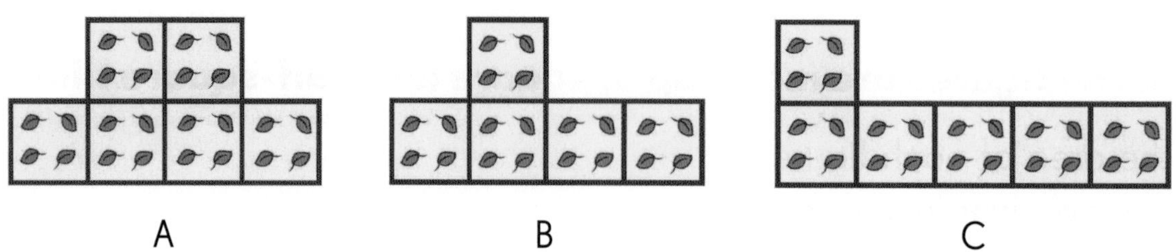

13 You want Figures A, B, and C to have the same area. Explain two ways of doing this.

ON YOUR OWN
Go to Workbook B: Practice 1, pages 211–214

WORK IN PAIRS

1 You have nine half-square tiles. Use all the tiles to make three figures. Compare your figures with those made by your classmates.

What do you notice about the areas of the figures?

2 Complete.

Rectangle	Number of rows	Number of squares in each row	Multiplication sentence	Area (Count how many)
	2	3	2 × 3 = 6	6

I can find the area of a rectangle by counting the number of squares.

I can find the area by using multiplication.

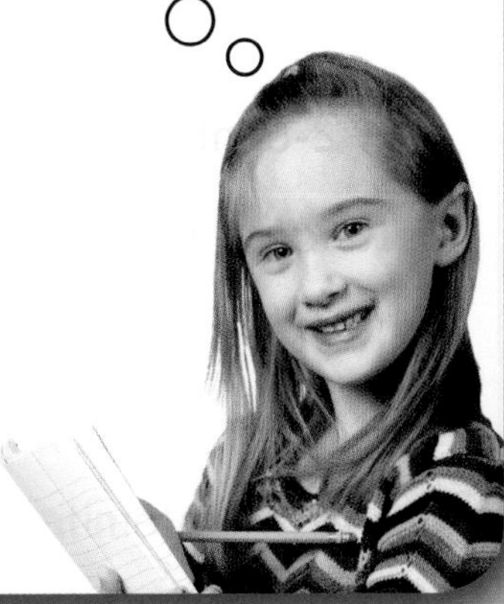

Both methods give the same answer.

Guided Learning

Complete.

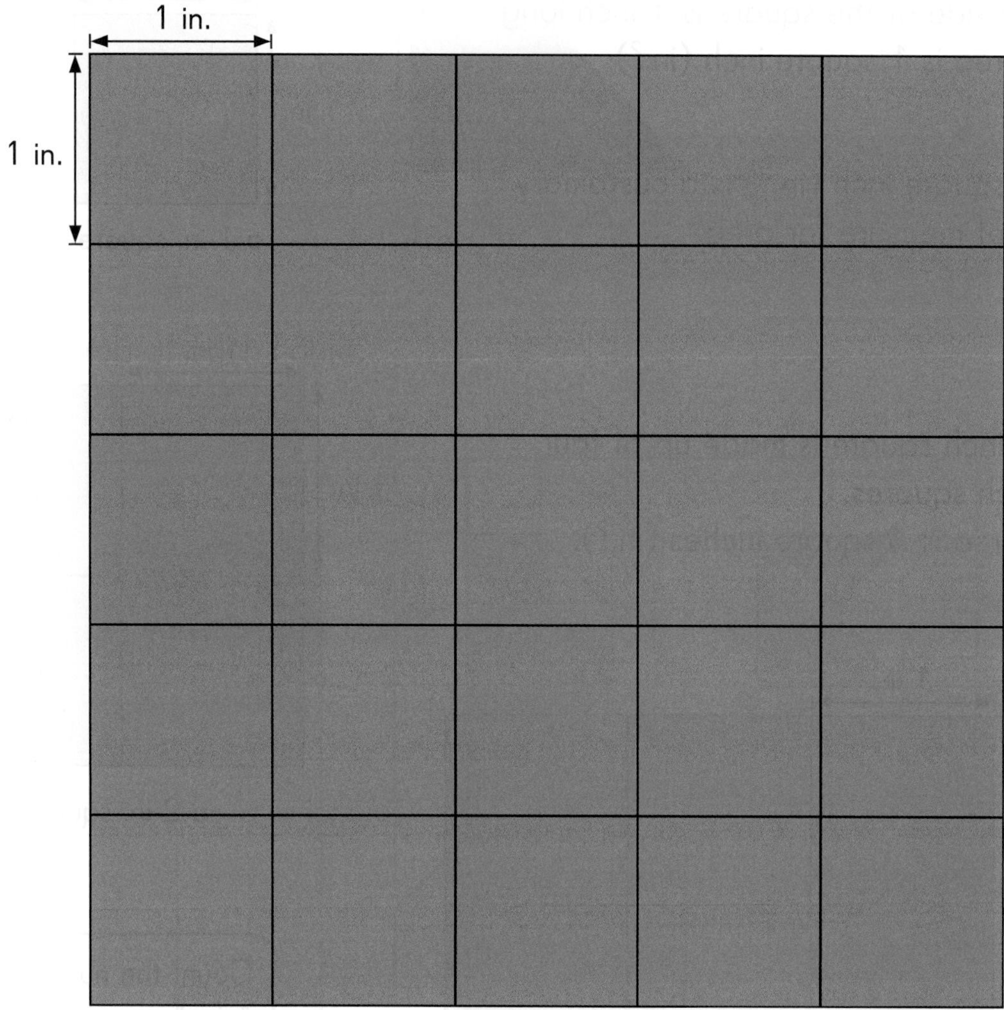

a 5-in. square

9. A 5-inch square is made up of ____ 1-inch squares.

10. The area of each 1-inch square is ____ square inch.

11. So, the area of the 5-inch square is ____ square inches.

The figures are made up of square and half-square tiles.

12 Find the area of this figure.

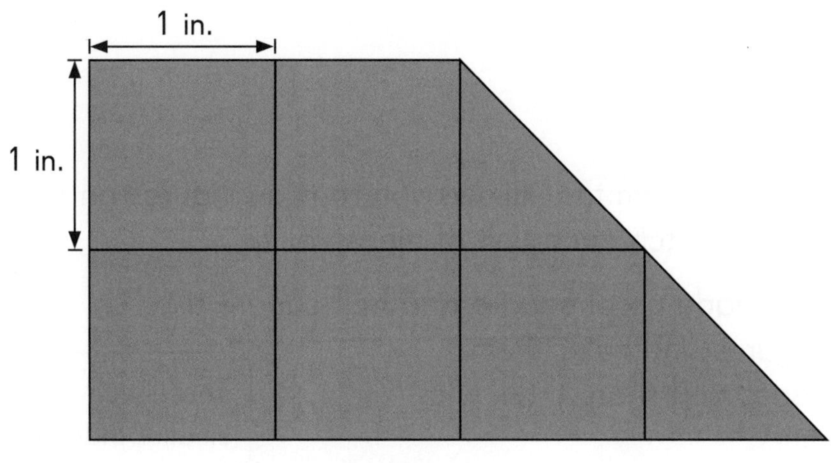

Area = ▭ in.²

What is the area of each figure?

13

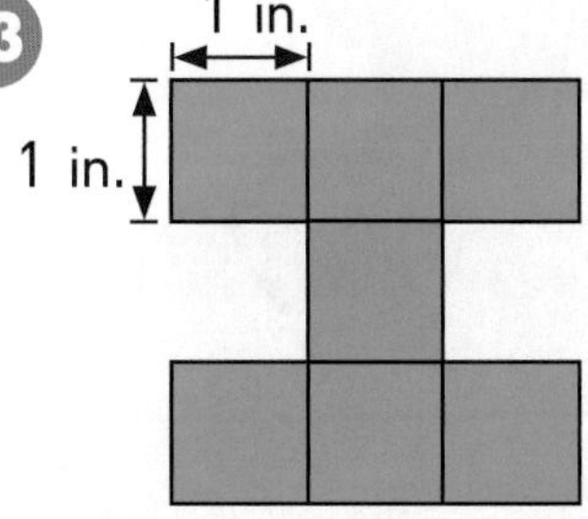

A

Area = ▭ in.²

14

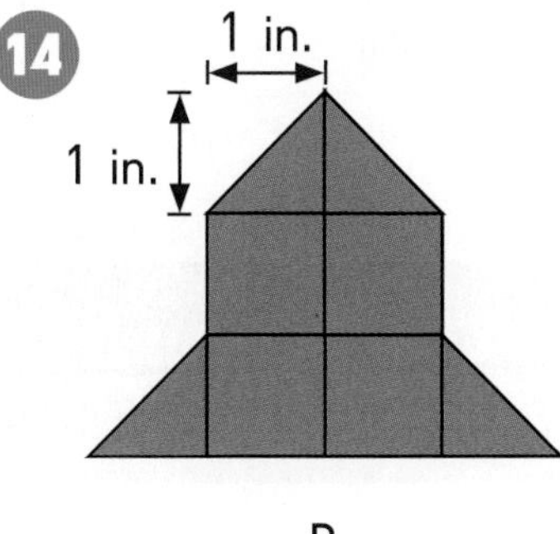

B

Area = ▭ in.²

15

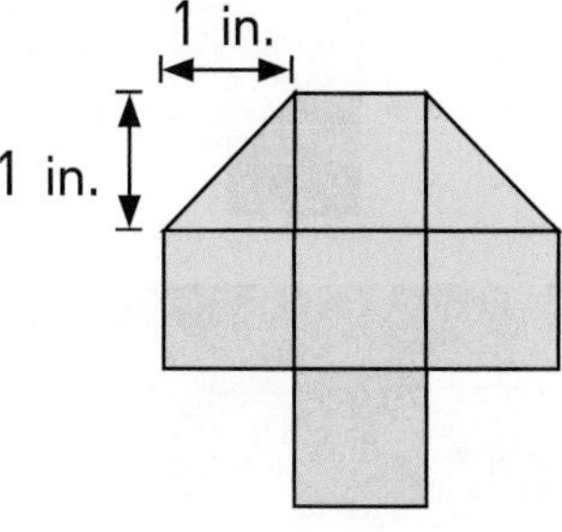

C

Area = ▭ in.²

These inch squares are smaller than in real life.

16 Which figure has a smaller area, figure A or B? Figure ▭

17 Which two figures have the same area? Figures ▭  and ▭

18 You want Figure A and Figure B to have the same area.

Explain two ways of doing this. ▭

Use a computer program that allows you to draw figures on a grid.
Resize the grid to match each unit of measure.

The figures are made up of square and half-square tiles.
Draw these figures and color them.
Print your shapes and share them with your classmates.

These inch squares are smaller than in real life.

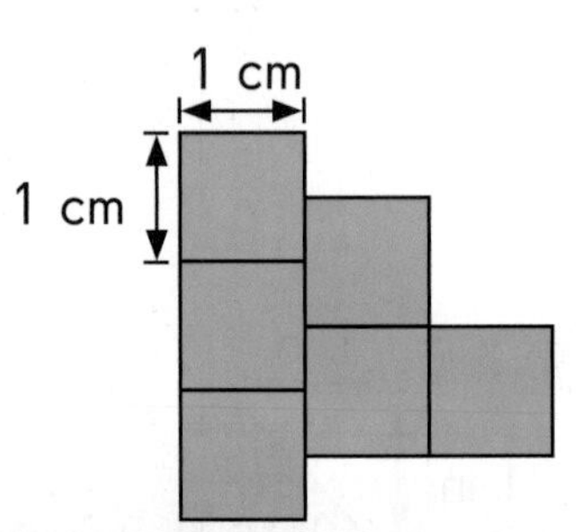

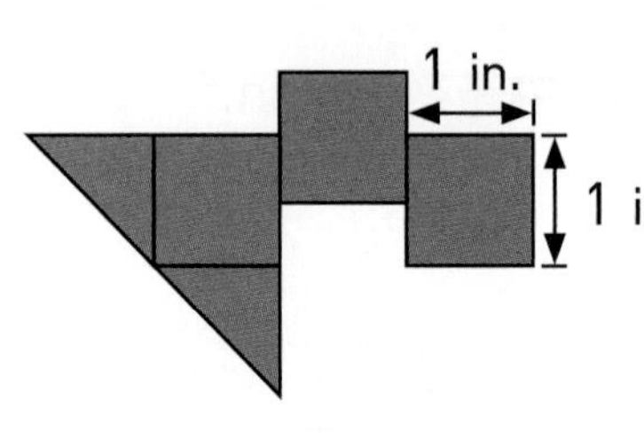

Let's Practice

Solve. The figures are made up of square and half-square tiles. Find the area of each figure.

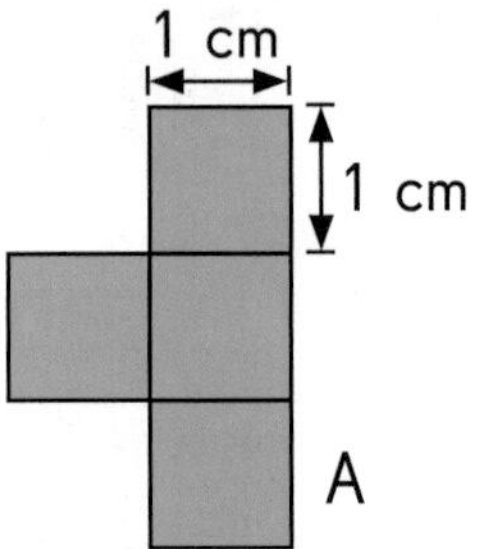

Area = ___ cm^2

2

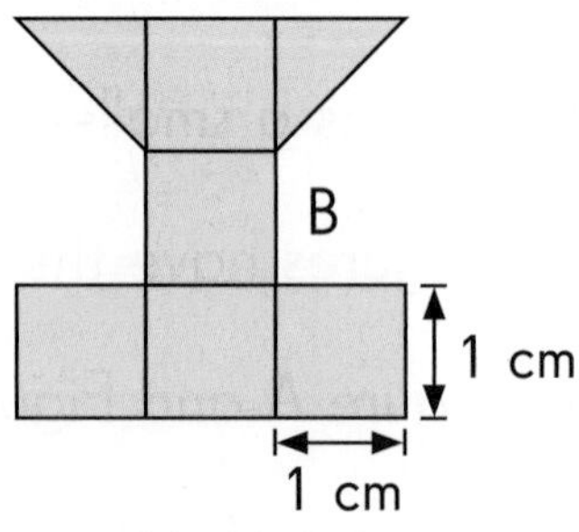

Area = ___ cm^2

3. Which figure has a larger area? Figure ______

4. You want both figures to have the same area.
Explain two ways of doing this. ______

Find the area of each figure.

5.

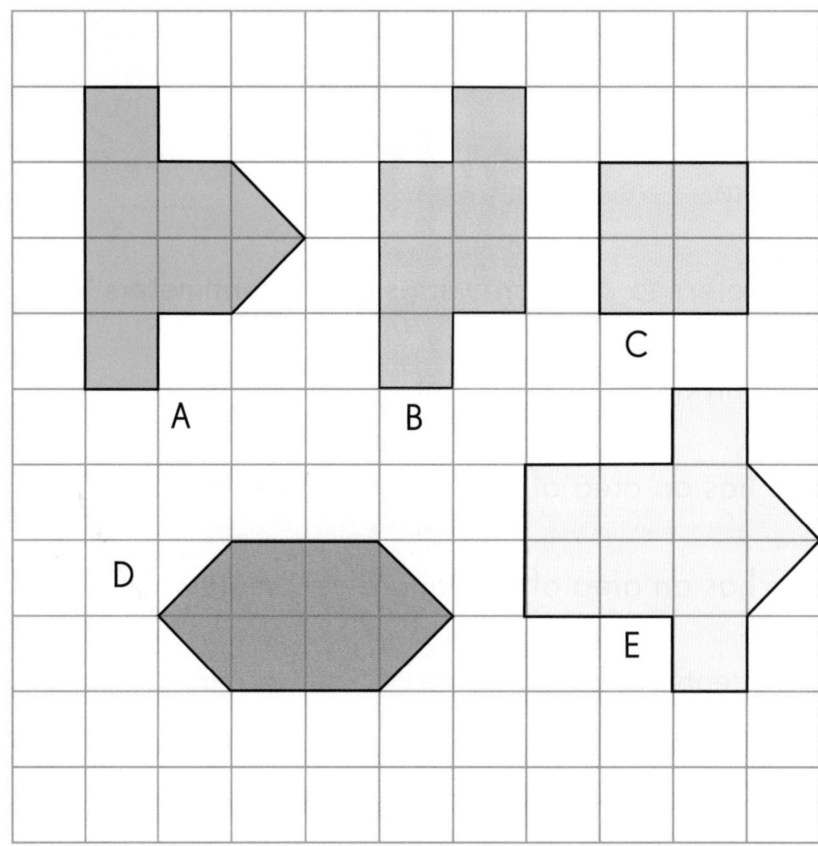

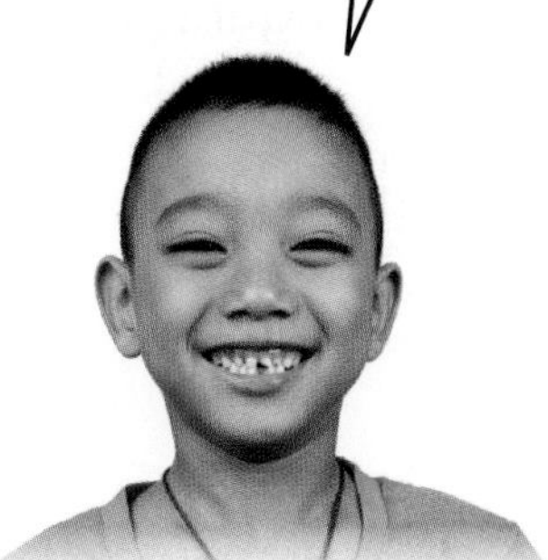

6. Which figure has the smallest area? Figure ______

7. Which figure has the largest area? Figure ______

8. Which figures have the same area? Figures ______ and ______

ON YOUR OWN

Go to Workbook B:
Practice 2, pages 215–218

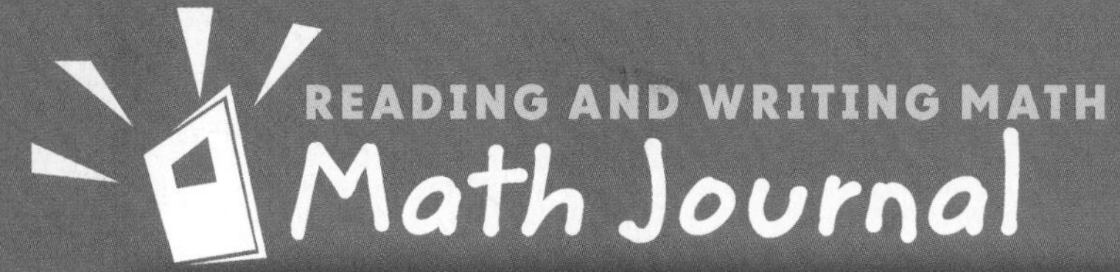

Is 4-centimeter square the same as 4 square centimeters?

Choose the statements that explain the answer to the girl's question.

1. 4 square centimeters is another way of saying 4-centimeter square.

2. A 4-centimeter square refers to a square with sides 4 centimeters long.

3. 4 square centimeters is an area measurement.

4. A 2-centimeter square has an area of 4 square centimeters.

5. A 4-centimeter square has an area of 16 square centimeters.

Draw figure(s) to show a 4-centimeter square and 4 square centimeters.

Lesson

19.3 Square Units (m^2 and ft^2)

Lesson Objectives

- Use square meters and square feet to find and compare the area of plane figures.
- Estimate the area of small and large surfaces.

Vocabulary
square meter (m^2)
square foot (ft^2)

Learn

Find the number of square meters that cover a surface.

Each side of this table top is 1 meter long.
Its area is 1 **square meter** (m^2).

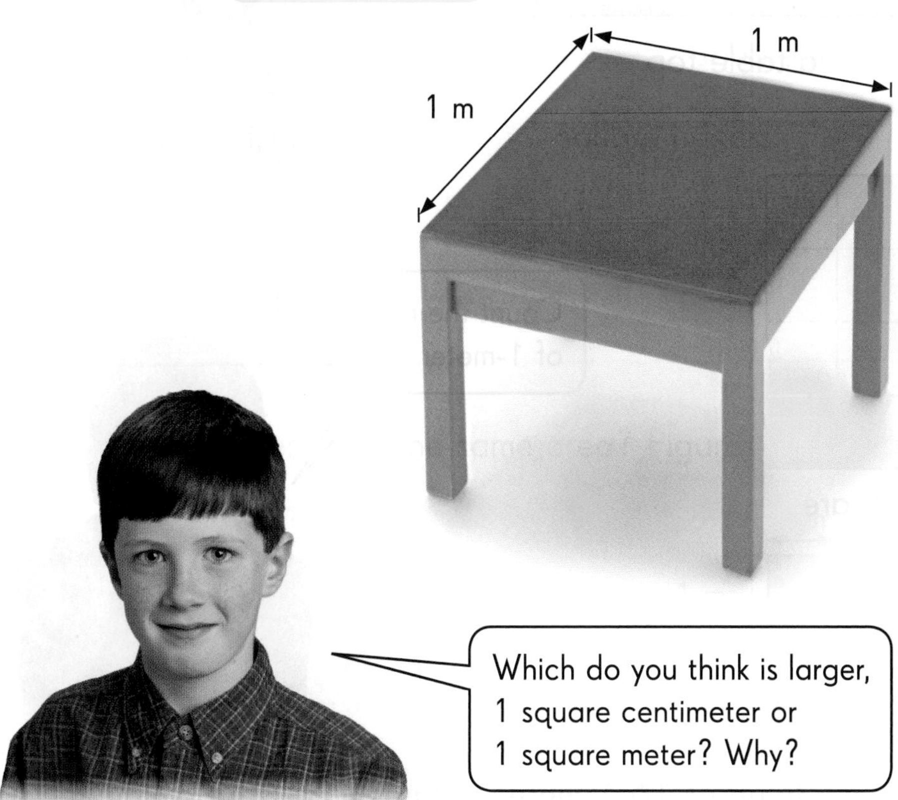

1 m
1 m
Which do you think is larger,
1 square centimeter or
1 square meter? Why?

The square meter (m^2) is also a metric unit of measure for area.
1 square meter (m^2) is larger than 1 square centimeter (cm^2).

Continued on next page

Learn Find the number of square feet that cover a plane surface.

Each side of this floor tile is 1 foot long.
Its area is 1 **square foot** (ft^2).

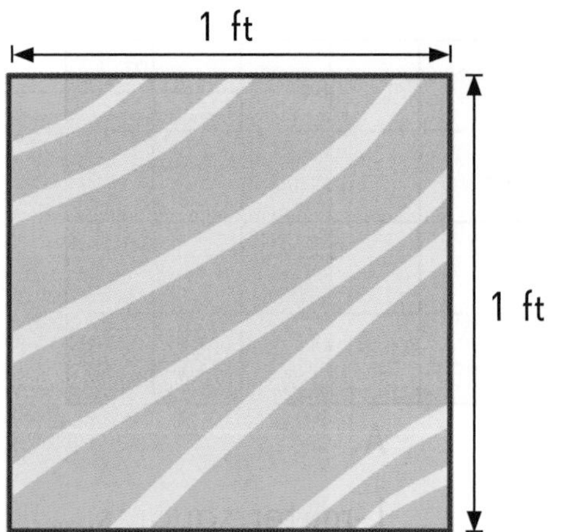

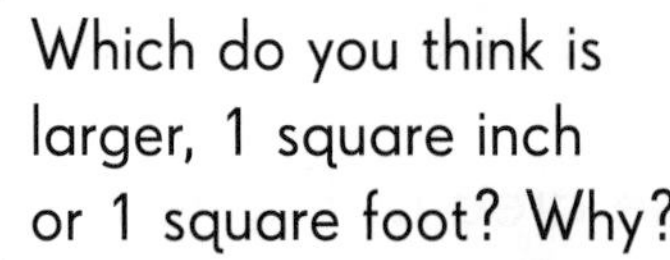

Which do you think is larger, 1 square inch or 1 square foot? Why?

The square foot (ft^2) is also a customary unit of measure for area.
1 square foot is larger than 1 square inch.

The floor tile is 1 square foot.
The stamp has an area of 1 square inch.

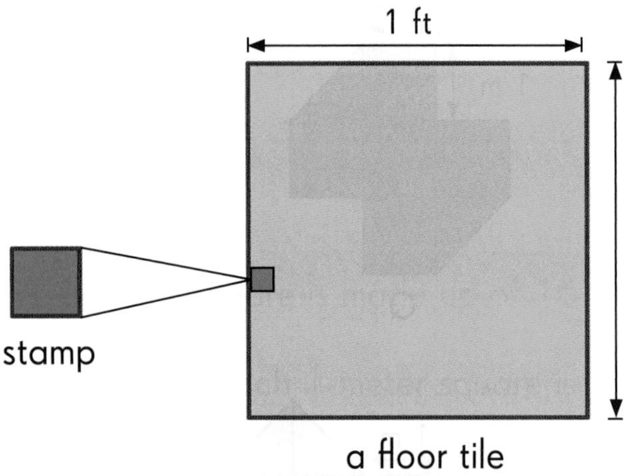

The picture compares the sizes of the stamp and the floor tile. It shows how small 1 square inch is compared to 1 square foot.

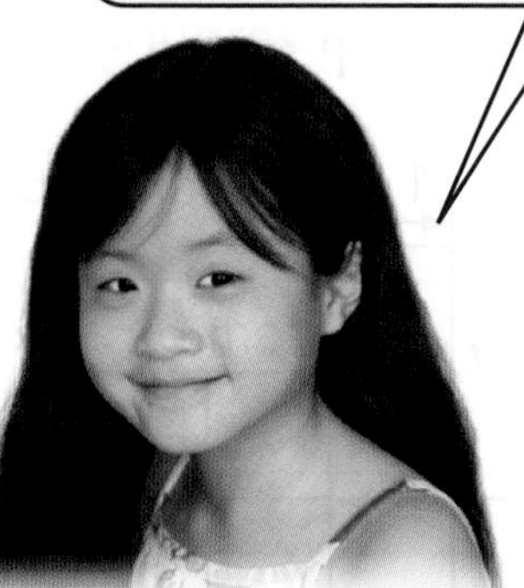

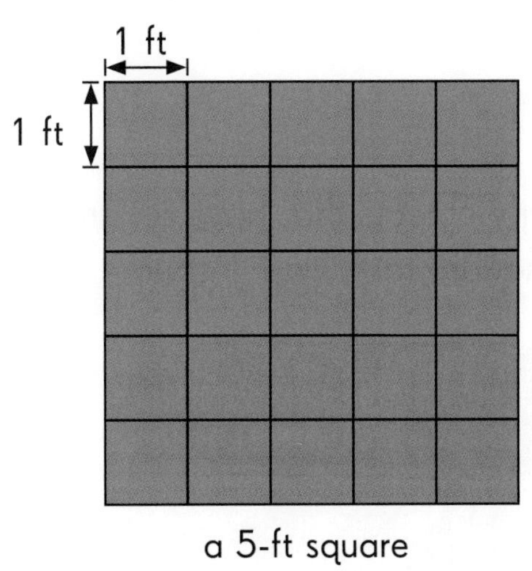

a 5-ft square

A 5-feet square is made up of twenty-five 1-foot squares.
The area of each 1-foot square is 1 square foot.
So, the area of the 5-feet square is 25 square feet.

Guided Learning

Complete. The figures are made up of square and half-square tiles.

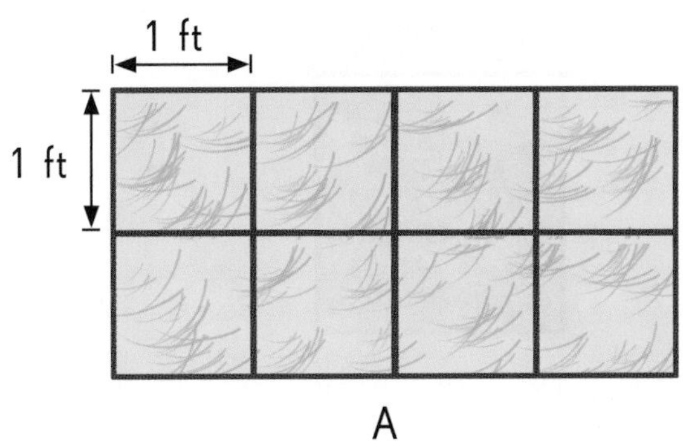

A

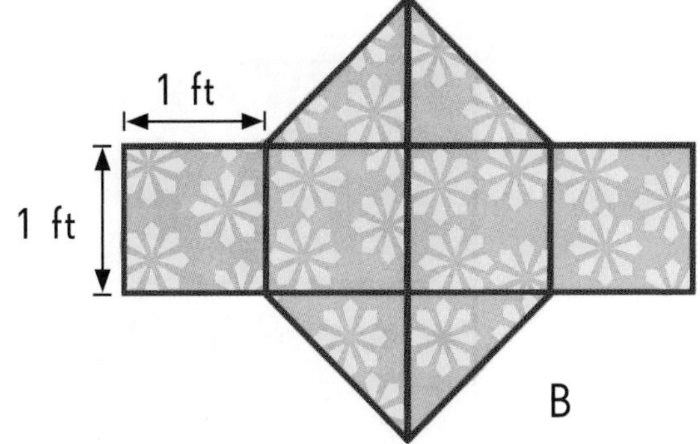

B

7 Figure A is made up of ______ 1-foot tiles.

8 The area of each 1-foot tile is ______ square foot.

9 So, the area of Figure A is ______ square feet.

10 The area of Figure B is ______ square feet.

11 Which figure has a smaller area, Figure A or Figure B? Figure ______

Hands-On Activity

Look around your classroom and home. Identify objects that have an area of about 1 square centimeter, 1 square inch, 1 square foot, and 1 square meter.

Area	Objects I found in school	Objects I found at home
About 1 cm^2		
About 1 m^2		
About 1 $in.^2$		
About 1 ft^2		

Use gift wrap and tape to make a square piece of paper with an area of 1 square meter and 1 square foot.

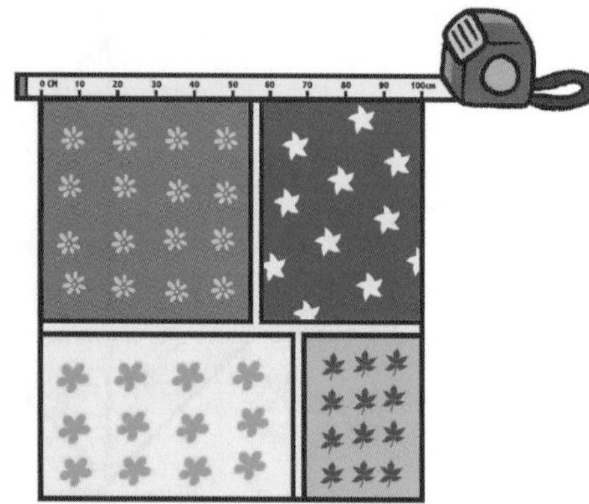

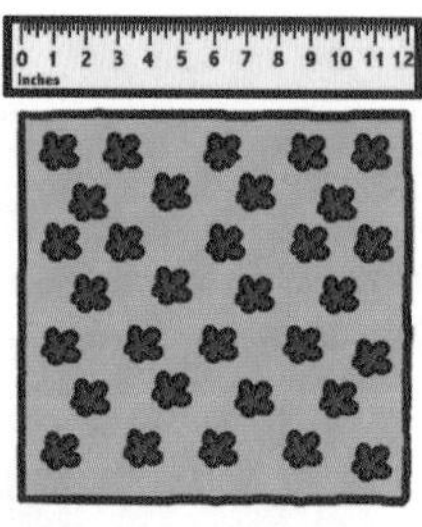

Use both pieces of papers to estimate the area of these objects in your classroom.

Object	Estimated Area	
	Square meter (m^2)	Square foot (ft^2)
Door		
Your Table		

Let's Practice

Solve. The figures are made up of square and half-square tiles.

Find the area of each figure.

1

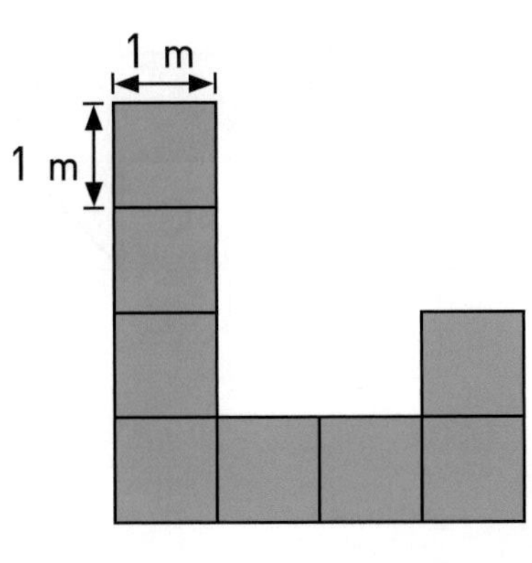

Area = ☐ m^2

2

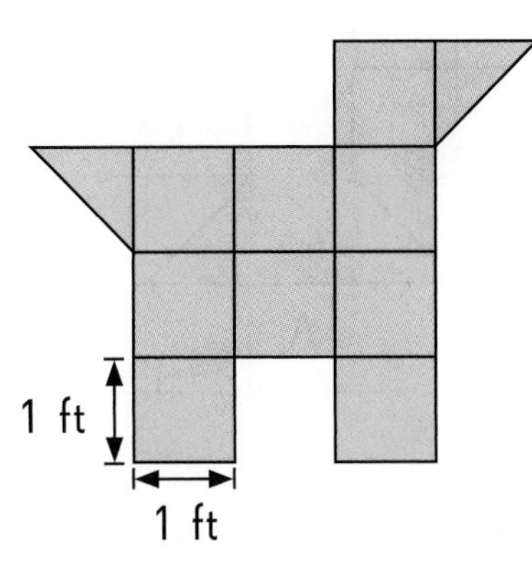

Area = ☐ ft^2

Find the area of each figure.

3

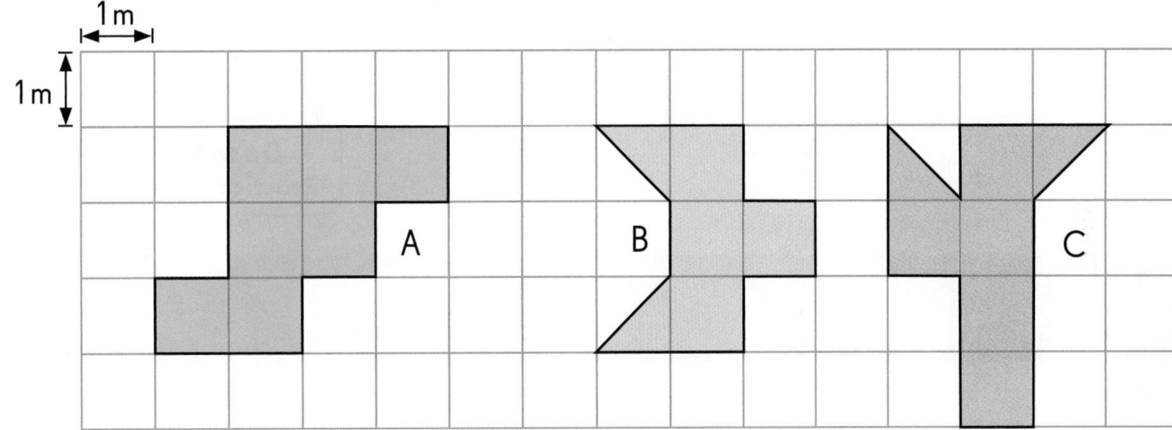

4 Which figure has the smallest area? Figure ☐

5 Which figure has the largest area? Figure ☐

6 Which figure has an area 1 m^2 less than Figure A? Figure ☐

Find the area of each figure.

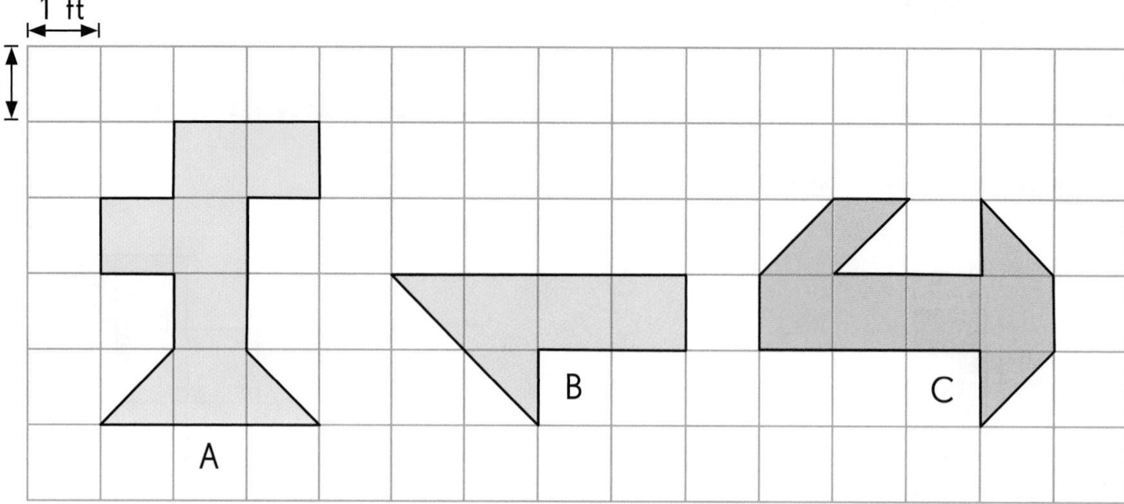

8. Which figure has the smallest area? Figure ______

9. Which figure has the largest area? Figure ______

10. Which figure has an area 2 ft^2 larger than Figure B? Figure ______

ON YOUR OWN

Go to Workbook B: Practice 3, pages 219–222

Let's Explore!

Use a square grid paper.
Label a small square in the grid as 1 m^2.
Draw as many different figures as possible of area 3 square meters. Color each figure.
Do not use half-squares.
Do not draw similar figures you can get by turning.

Example

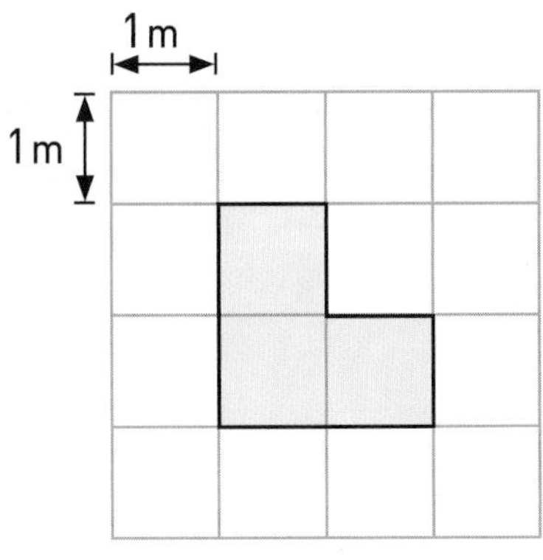

I can only draw a figure once and the squares can be joined either along an edge or a vertex.
I cannot draw similar figures which I can get by turning.

I can get figures A, B, and C by turning the figure in the example.

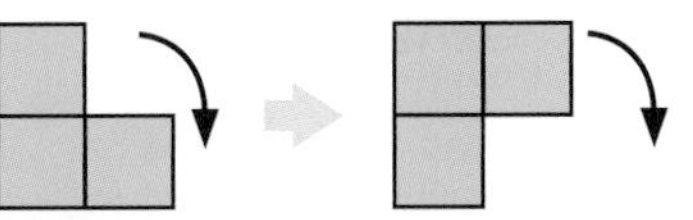

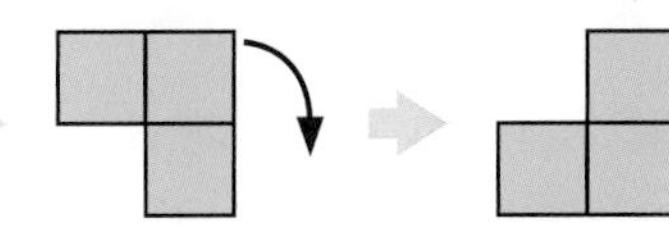

Example Figure A Figure B Figure C

So, I cannot draw figures A, B, and C because they are similar to the example.

How many other figures can you draw?

Lesson 19.4 Perimeter and Area

Lesson Objectives
- Understand the meaning of perimeter.
- Compare the area and perimeter of two figures.
- Find the area of figures to solve real-world problems.

Vocabulary
perimeter

Learn Find the perimeter and area of a figure.

Look at the rectangle on the geoboard.

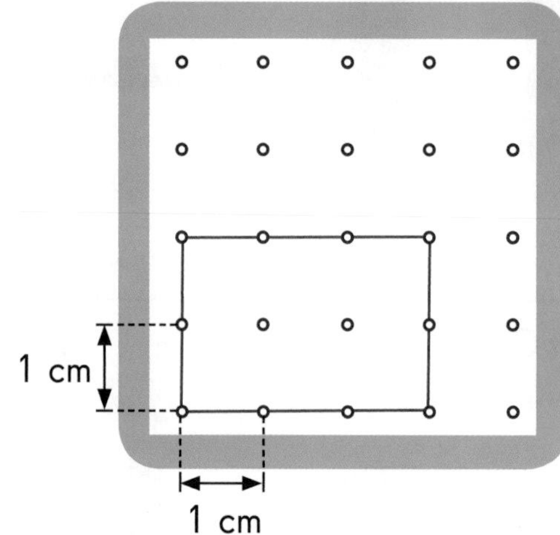

The **perimeter** of the rectangle is the distance around it. To find the perimeter, you find the length of each side of the rectangle in centimeters and add them.

$3 + 2 + 3 + 2 = 10$

So, the perimeter of the rectangle is 10 centimeters.

The area of the rectangle is 6 square centimeters.

Look at the figure.

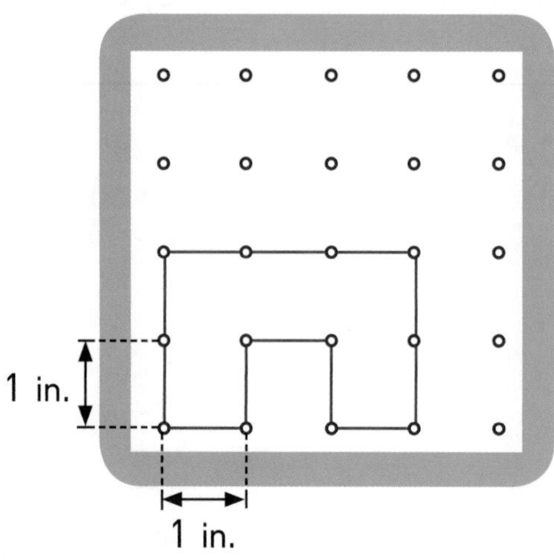

You can also measure perimeter in meters and feet.

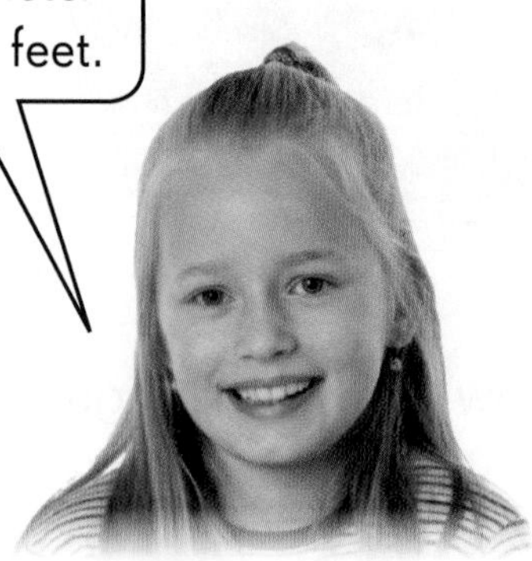

The perimeter of this figure is 12 inches.
Its area is 5 square inches.

Perimeter can be measured in centimeters (cm), inches (in.), meters (m), and feet (ft).
Area can be measured in square centimeters (cm^2), square inches ($in.^2$), square meters (m^2), and square feet (ft^2).

Guided Learning

Complete.

Look at the two figures on the geoboard.

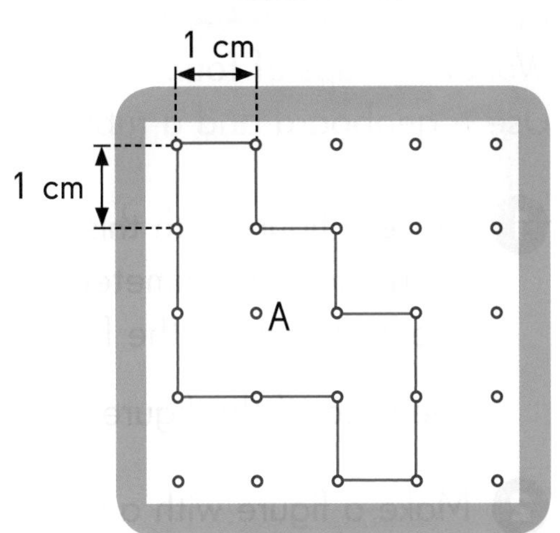

They have the same perimeter.

1. The perimeter of each figure is ___ centimeters.

They do not have the same area.

2. The area of Figure A is ___ square centimeters.

3. The area of Figure B is ___ square centimeters.

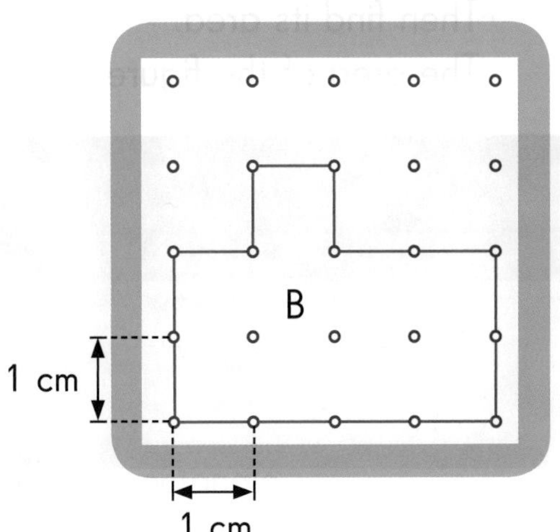

Find the perimeter and area of each figure.

4. 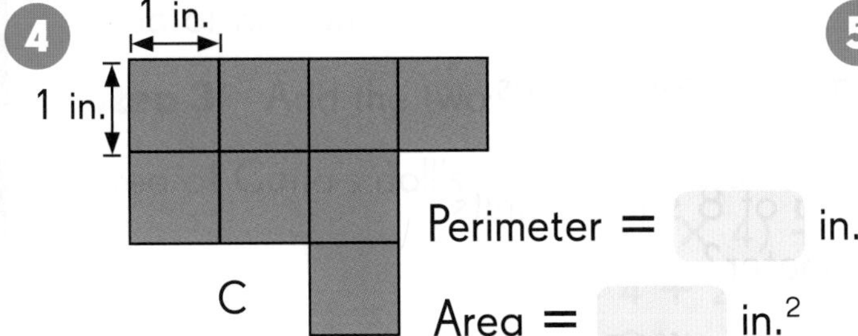

Perimeter = ___ in.

Area = ___ $in.^2$

5. 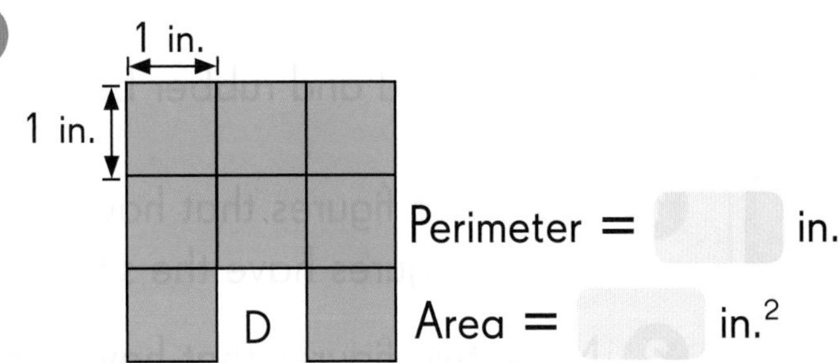

Perimeter = ___ in.

Area = ___ $in.^2$

6. Do Figures C and D have the same area? Explain your answer.

7. Do they have the same perimeter? Explain your answer.

Guided Learning

Solve.

8 The fish pond at the park has a length of 8 meters and a width of 6 meters. What is the area of the fish pond?

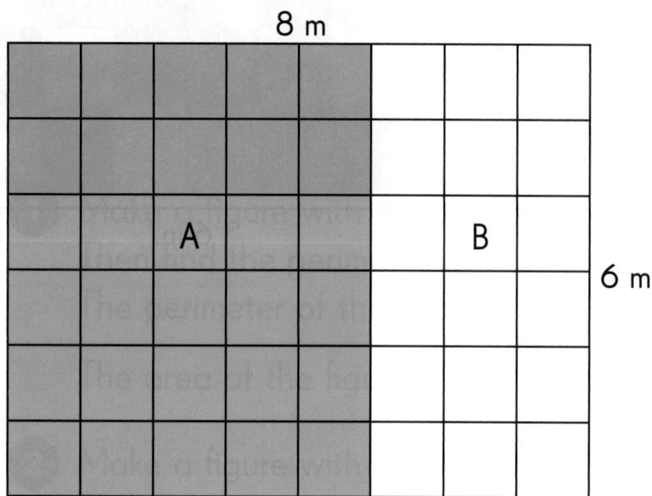

Method 1

____ m × ____ m = ____ m^2

The area of the fish pond is ____ square meters.

Method 2

Area of Rectange A = ____ × ____

Area of Rectange B = ____ × ____

Area of the fish pond = ____ × (____ + ____)

= (____ × ____) + (____ × ____)

= ____ + ____

= ____ m^2

The area of the fish pond is ____ square meters.

Let's Explore!

Use a geoboard and rubber bands to make these figures.

1. Make as many different rectangles as you can with an area of 12 square units, and record their lengths and widths in the table.

2. Write their area as a multplication fact.

Area (square units)	Length	Width	Multiplication fact
12			
12			
12			

Draw area models to represent these rectangles.
Then, write their areas as multiplication facts.

3. 8 square units

4. 10 square units

5. 14 square units

Learn **Find the area of a figure by separating it into two rectangles, then add the area of both rectangles to solve real-world problems.**

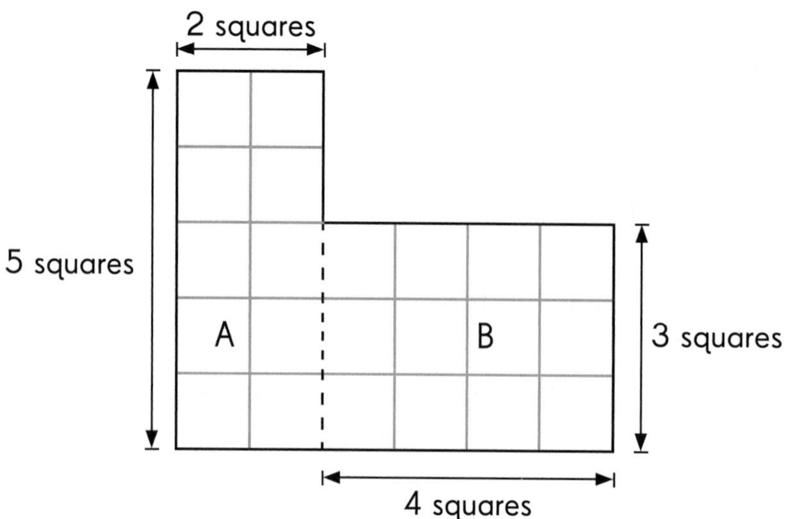

To find the area of the figure, first you separate the figure into two rectangles.
Then, use multiplication to find the area of each rectangle.
Now, add the two areas together.

Area of Rectangle A = 5 × 2 = 10 square units

Area of Rectangle B = 4 × 3 = 12 square units

Area of the figure = 10 + 12 = 22 square units

The area of the figure is 22 square units.

Guided Learning

Solve.

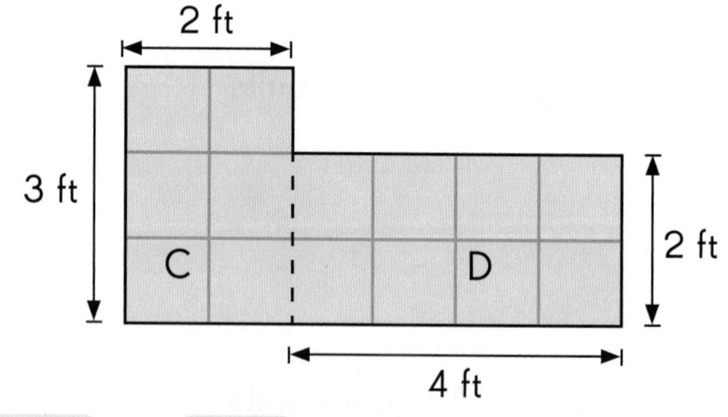

9 Jermain buys square-foot tiles for his driveway.
What is the area of his driveway?

Area of Rectangle C = ___ × ___ = ___ square feet

Area of Rectangle D = ___ × ___ = ___ square feet

Area of the driveway = ___ + ___ = ___ square feet

The area of the driveway is ___ square feet.

Let's Practice

Complete.

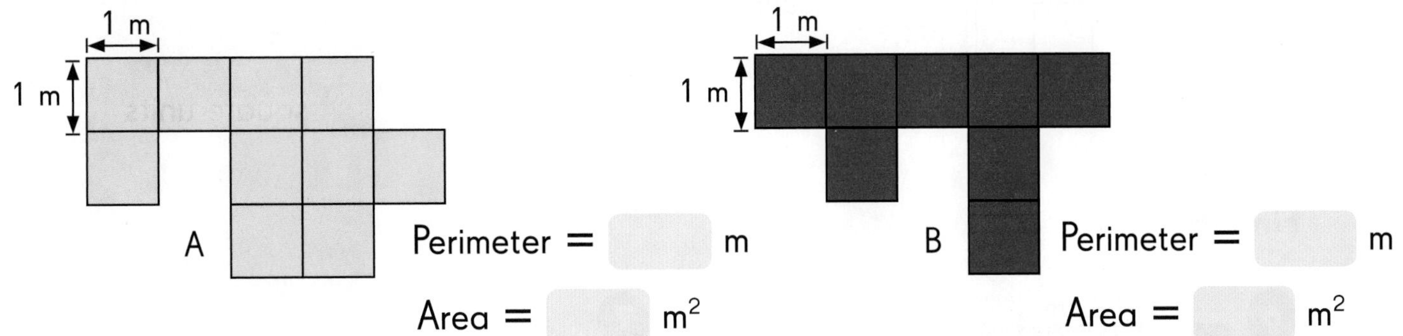

Figure A: Perimeter = ___ m
Area = ___ m^2

Figure B: Perimeter = ___ m
Area = ___ m^2

1. Do Figures A and B have the same area? Explain your answer. ___

2. Do they have the same perimeter? Explain your answer. ___

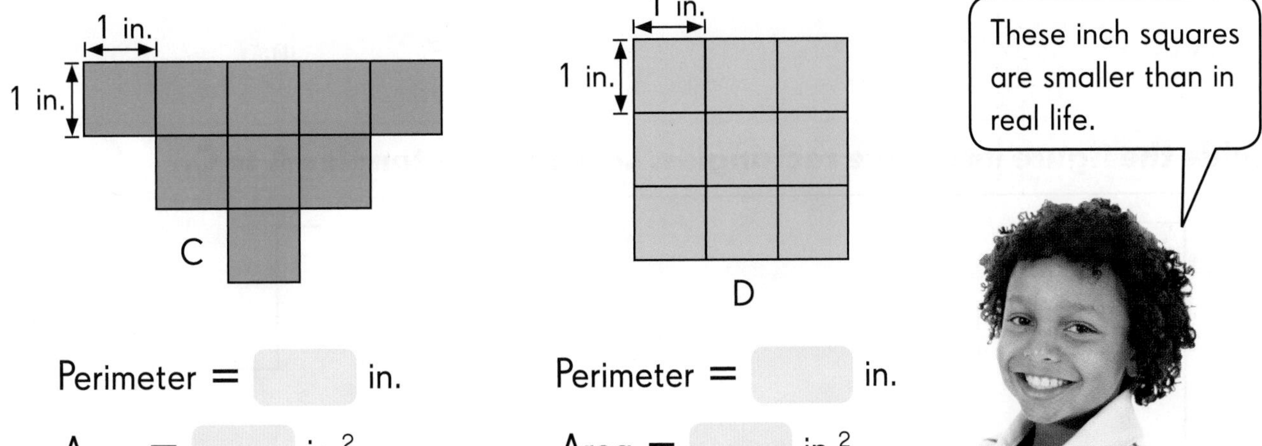

Figure C: Perimeter = ___ in.
Area = ___ $in.^2$

Figure D: Perimeter = ___ in.
Area = ___ $in.^2$

3. Do Figures C and D have the same area? Explain your answer. ___

4. Do they have the same perimeter? Explain your answer. ___

Complete the following.

5 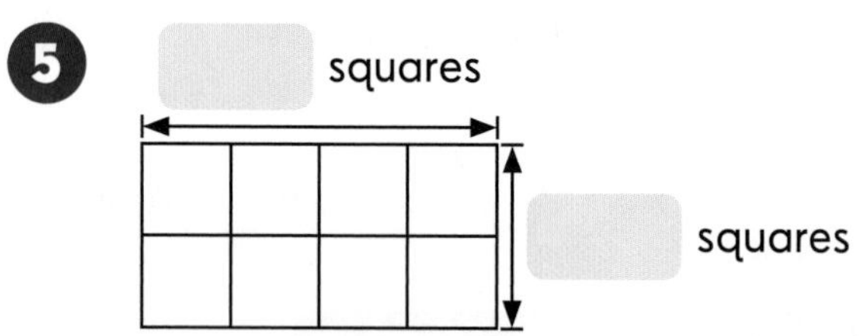

Length = ___ squares

Width = ___ squares

Area = ___ × ___

= ___ square units

Find the area.

6 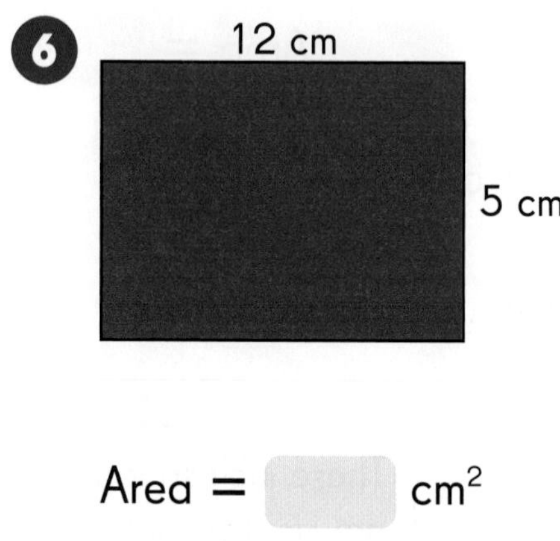

Area = ___ cm^2

7 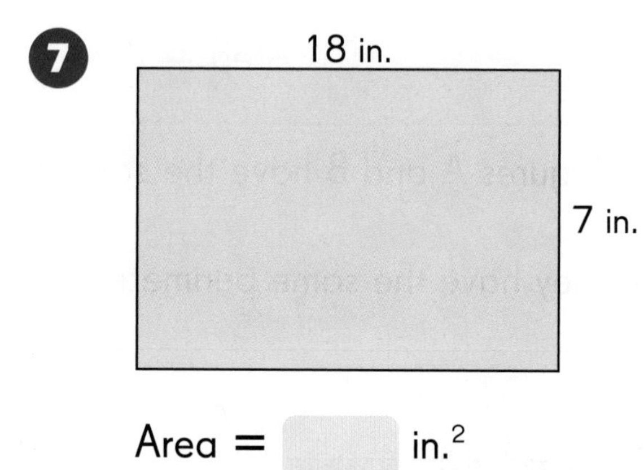

Area = ___ $in.^2$

Divide the figure into three rectangles. Label the rectangles A to C.

8 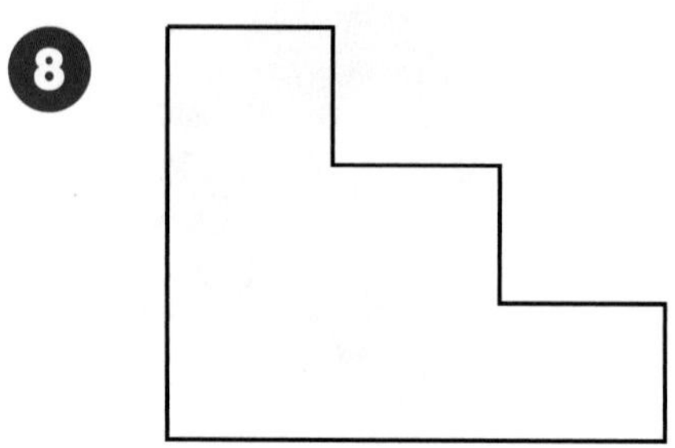

9 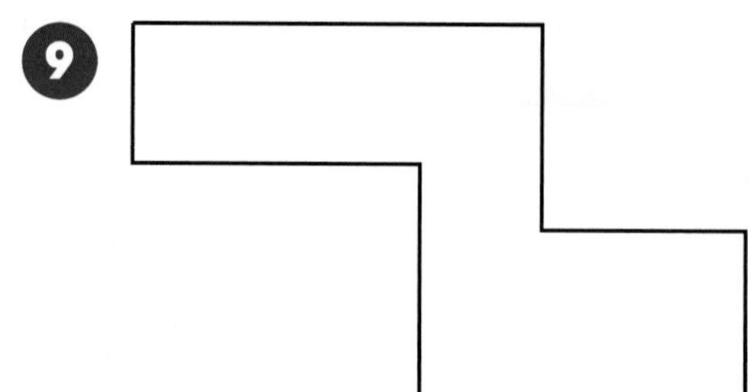

Draw a line to separate the figure. Then solve.

10 The Campo family has a "L" shaped swimming pool in their backyard. What is the total area of the swimming pool? ______ m^2

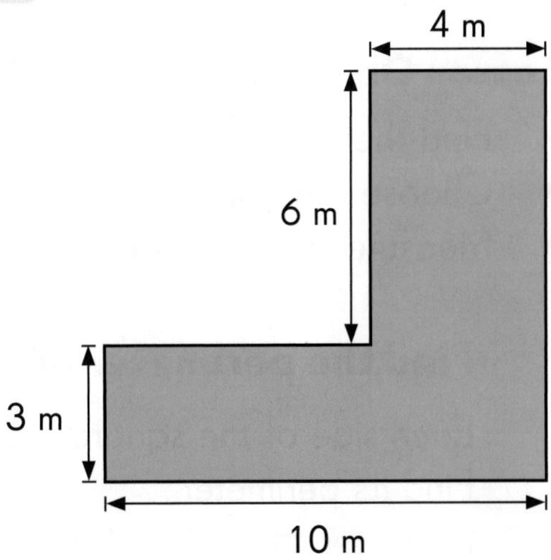

11 Two neighbors Kim and Mario, share a vegetable garden at a community farm. The farm's rule is that no garden can occupy more than 50 square meters. What is the total area of their vegetable garden? ______ m^2

Did they follow the rule? ______

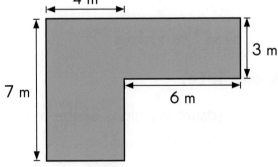

4 m
3 m
7 m
6 m

ON YOUR OWN

Go to Workbook B: Practice 4, pages 223–228

Lesson 19.5 More Perimeter

Lesson Objectives

- Find the perimeter of a figure by adding up all its sides.
- Choose the appropriate tool and units of length to measure perimeter.
- Measure the perimeter of surfaces of objects and places.

Learn: Find the perimeter of figures.

Each side of the square is 6 centimeters long.
Find its perimeter.

Perimeter = 6 + 6 + 6 + 6
= 24 cm

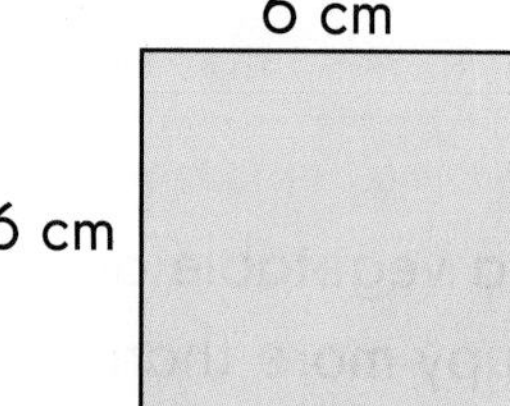

The perimeter is 24 centimeters.

Guided Learning

Complete.

1. Measure the sides of the rectangle in centimeters. Find its perimeter.

Perimeter = ___ + ___ + ___ + ___
=  cm

Use a centimeter ruler to measure the length of the sides.

The perimeter is  centimeters.

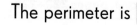

2. Find the perimeter of the figure.

Perimeter = ☐ + ☐ + ☐ + ☐ + ☐

= ☐ in.

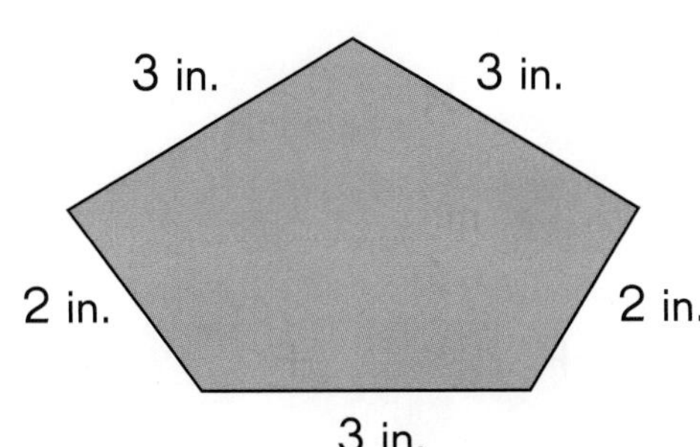

3. The width of a rug is 14 feet. Its length is twice its width. What is the perimeter of the rug?

Length = ☐ × ☐

= ☐ ft

Perimeter = ☐ + ☐ + ☐ + ☐

= ☐ ft

The perimeter of the rug is ☐ feet.

4. Four square tiles with 12-centimeter sides were used to cover the surface of a large square tile. What is the perimeter of the large square tile?

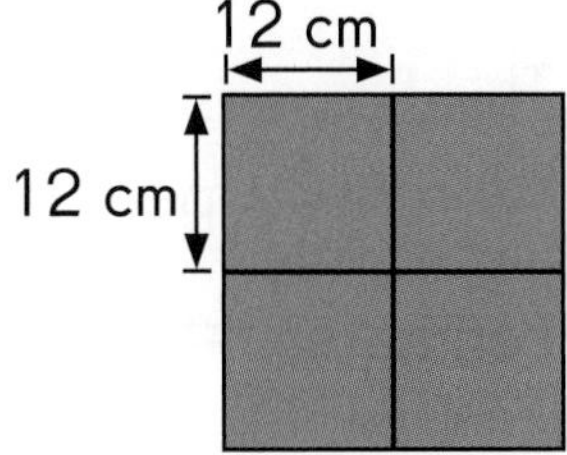

Length of one side of the large square tile

= ☐ × ☐

= ☐ cm

Perimeter of the large square tile

= ☐ + ☐ + ☐ + ☐

= ☐ cm

The perimeter of the large square tile is ☐ centimeters.

5 The width of a rectangular field is 35 meters long. Its length is three times as long as its width. Ian ran around the field once. How far did he run?

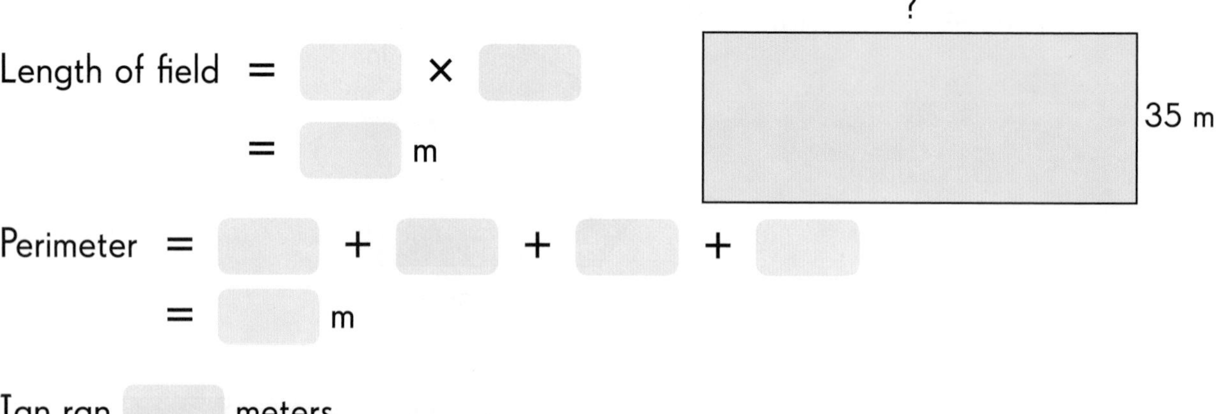

Length of field = ___ × ___

= ___ m

Perimeter = ___ + ___ + ___ + ___

= ___ m

Ian ran ___ meters.

Hands-On Activity

These are some sticks with different lengths.

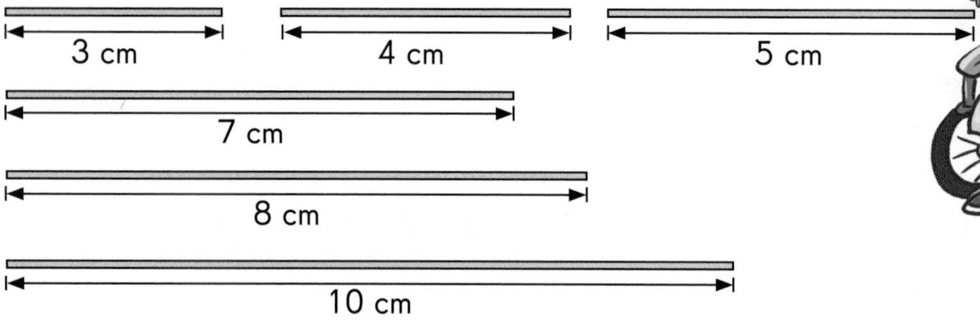

3 cm

4 cm

5 cm

7 cm

8 cm

10 cm

1 This figure is made with some of the sticks. What is its perimeter?

Perimeter = ___ cm

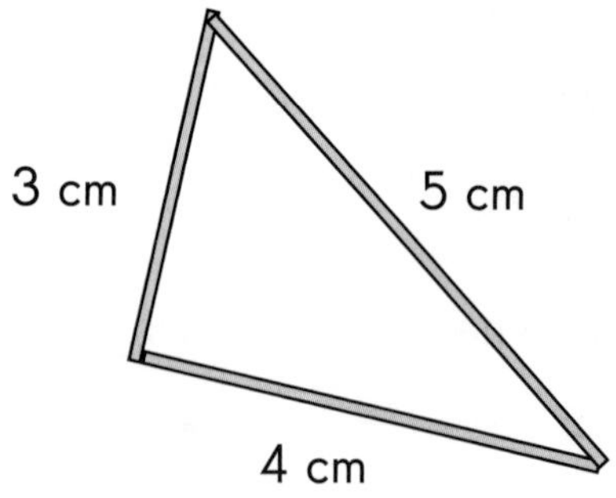

3 cm

5 cm

4 cm

2 Make two different figures using the sticks. Find the perimeter of each.

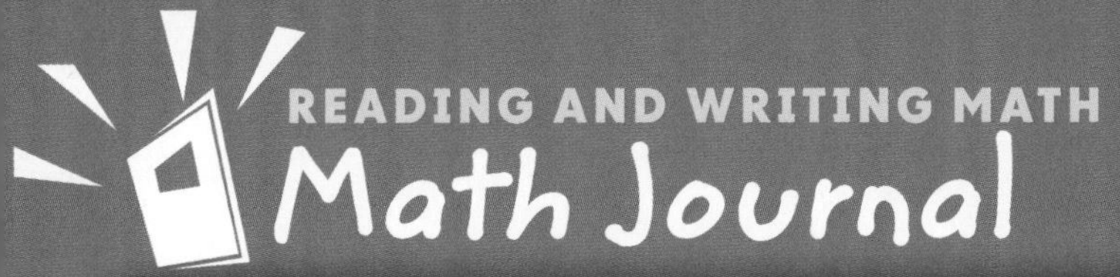

1. Write how you would find the perimeter of your classroom. Include each step.

What lengths do I have to measure?
What tools do I use to measure?
How do I find the perimeter from my measurements?

2. Your best friend was absent from class and missed the lesson on perimeter. Write a letter to him explaining the term. Use diagrams to help you.

First, think of an example to illustrate the term. Then think of a unit of measure to be used in the example.

Let's Practice

Solve.
Measure the sides of the figure with a centimeter ruler.
Then find the perimeter.

1. 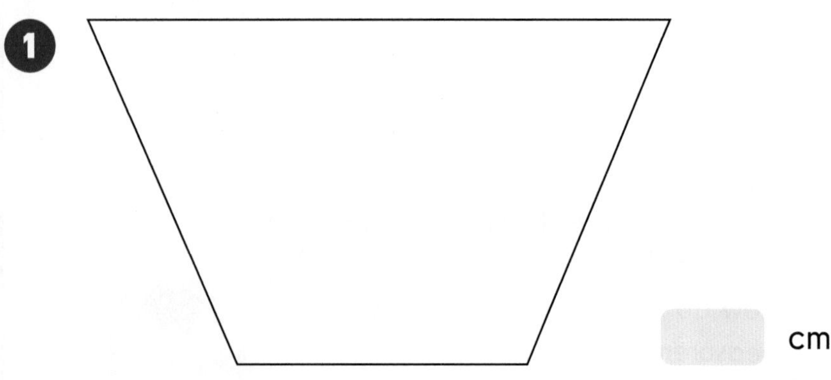

 cm

2. 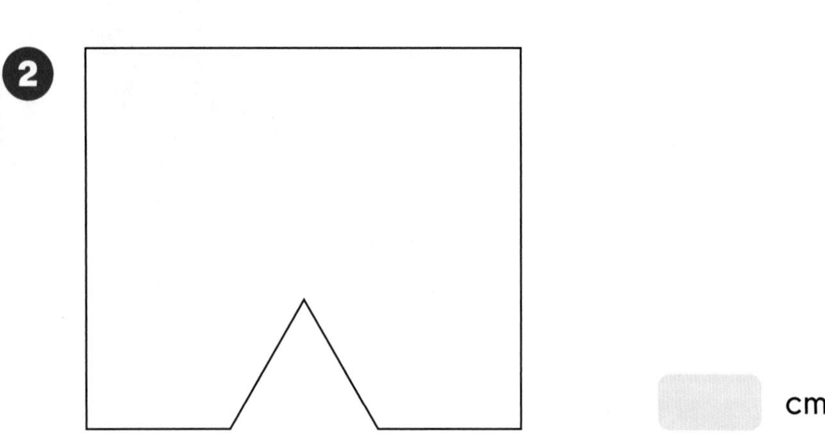

 cm

Find the perimeter of each square.

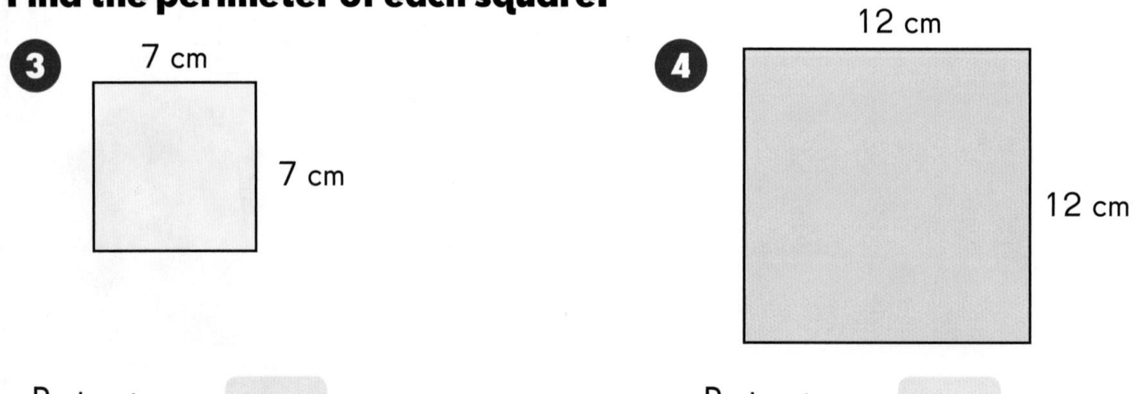

3. Perimeter = cm

4. Perimeter = cm

5. Each side of a square is 8 meters.
Find the perimeter of the square. ____ m

Find the perimeter of each rectangle.

6. 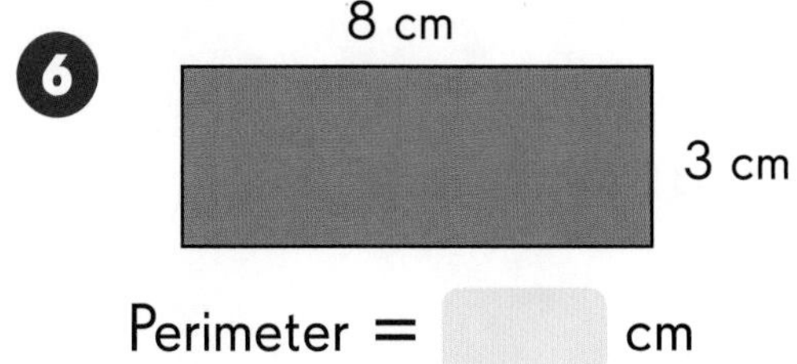

Perimeter = ____ cm

7. 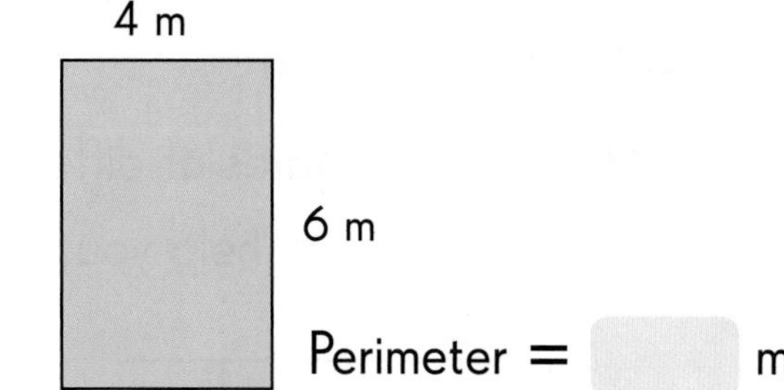

Perimeter = ____ m

Find the perimeter of each figure.

8. 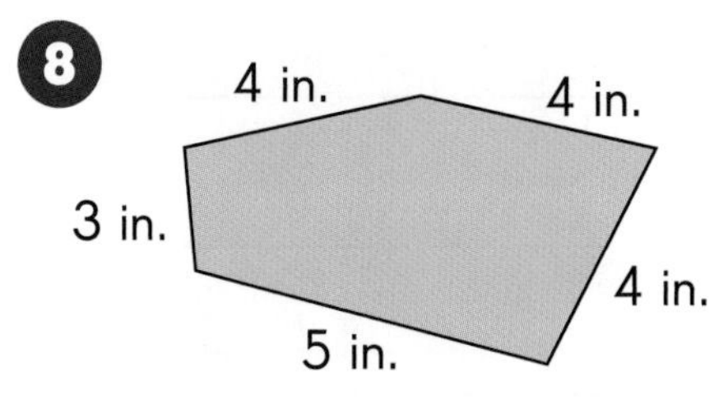

Perimeter = ____ in.

9. 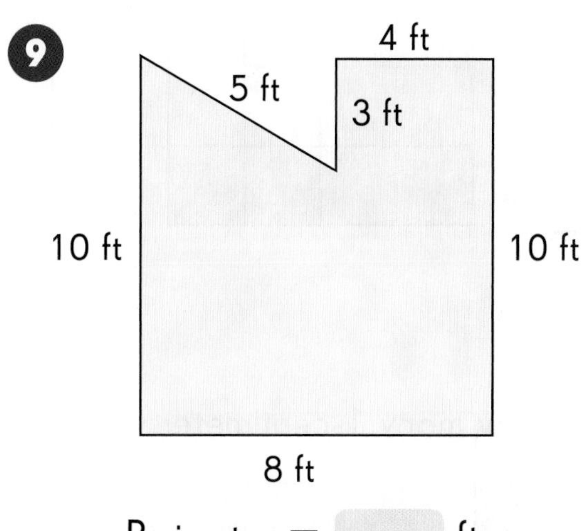

Perimeter = ____ ft

10. Mr. Carlson has a garden with these sides. He wants to put a fence around his garden. Find the length of fencing he needs. ____ m

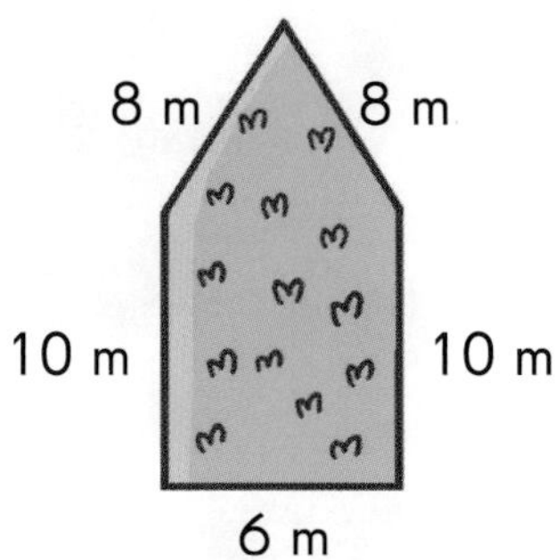

ON YOUR OWN

Go to Workbook B: Practice 5, pages 229–235

CRITICAL THINKING SKILLS

Put On Your Thinking Cap!

PROBLEM SOLVING

1. How many squares of different sizes can you find in this figure?
Use the chart to help you find the answer.

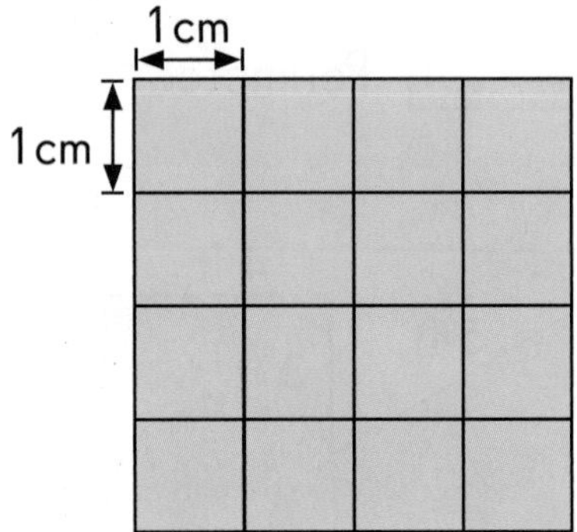

Size of Square	Number of Squares
1-cm	
2-cm	
3-cm	
4-cm	

2. How many 1-centimeter squares are in each figure?

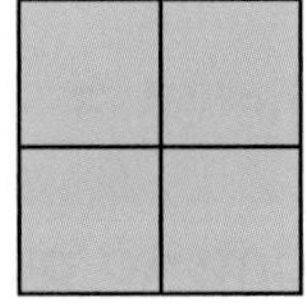

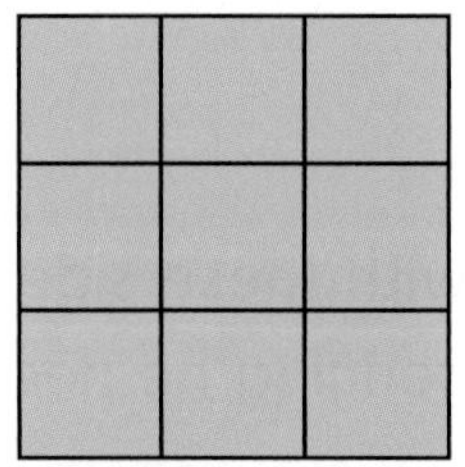

Figure	Number of Squares
1	1
2	1 + ___ = ___
3	1 + ___ + ___ = ___

3. What pattern do you see? Describe it.

4. How many squares would there be in Figure 10?

ON YOUR OWN

Go to Workbook B: Put On Your Thinking Cap! pages 237–240

Chapter Wrap Up

Study Guide

You have learned...

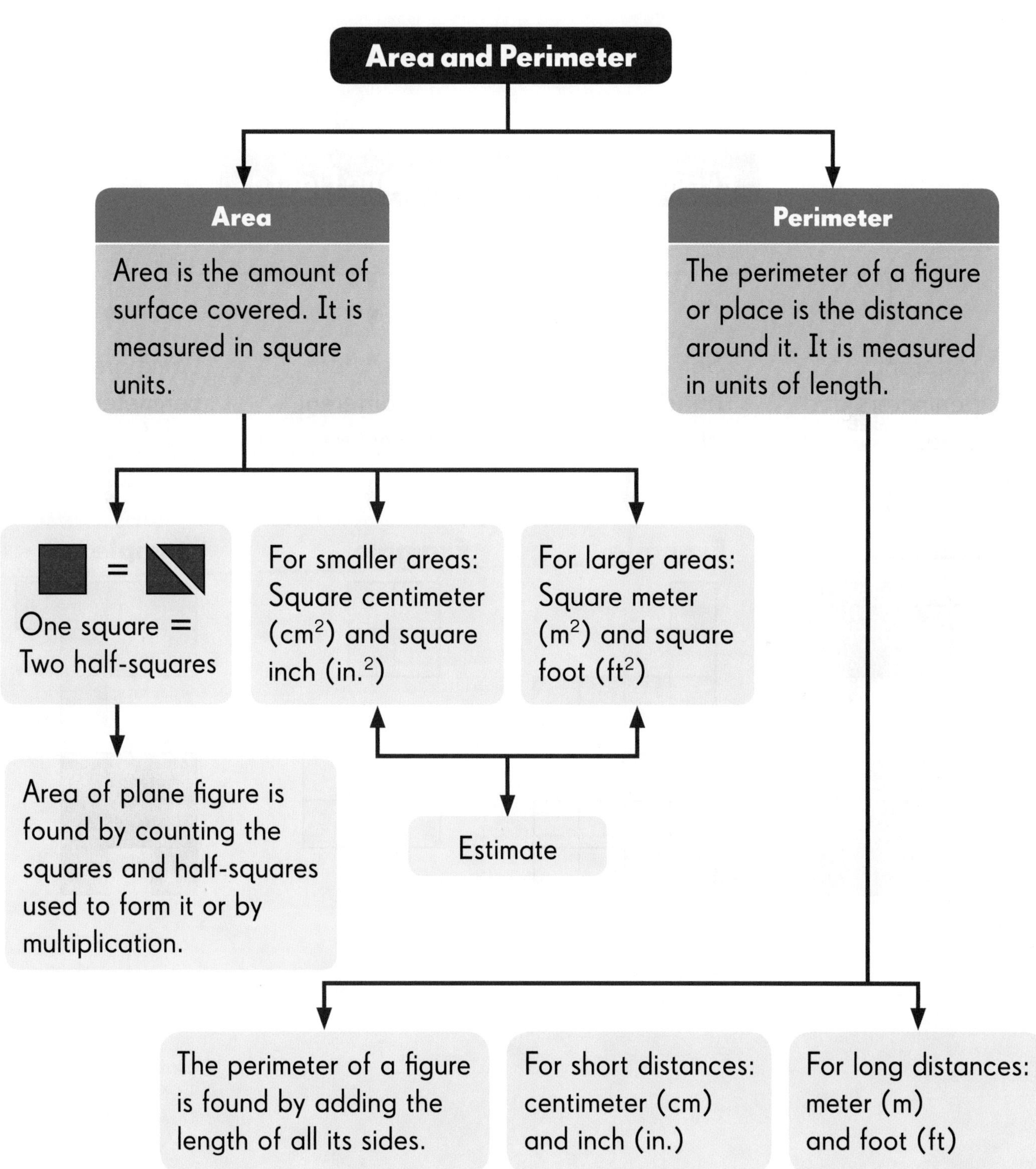

Area and Perimeter
Area
Area is the amount of surface covered. It is measured in square units.
Perimeter
The perimeter of a figure or place is the distance around it. It is measured in units of length.
=
One square = Two half-squares
For smaller areas: Square centimeter (cm²) and square inch (in.²)
For larger areas: Square meter (m²) and square foot (ft²)
Area of plane figure is found by counting the squares and half-squares used to form it or by multiplication.
Estimate
The perimeter of a figure is found by adding the length of all its sides.
For short distances: centimeter (cm) and inch (in.)
For long distances: meter (m) and foot (ft)

▶ Explore and understand units used to find perimeter and area of figures and analyze the relationship between them.

Perimeter and Area of Plane Figures

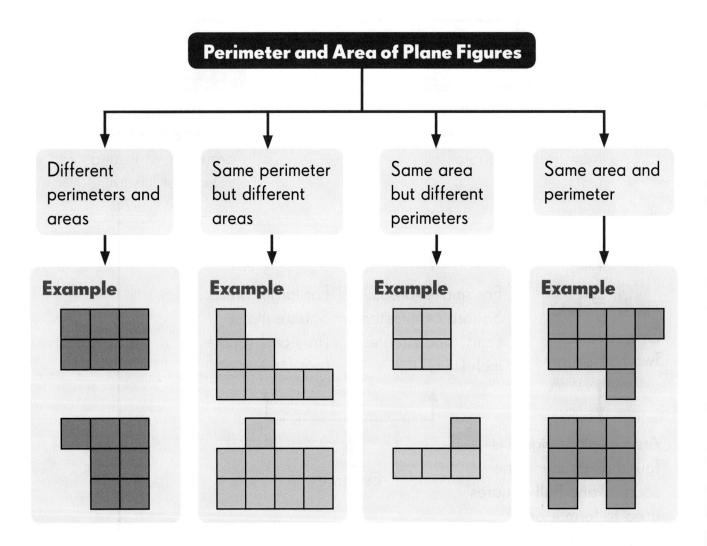

Different perimeters and areas

Example

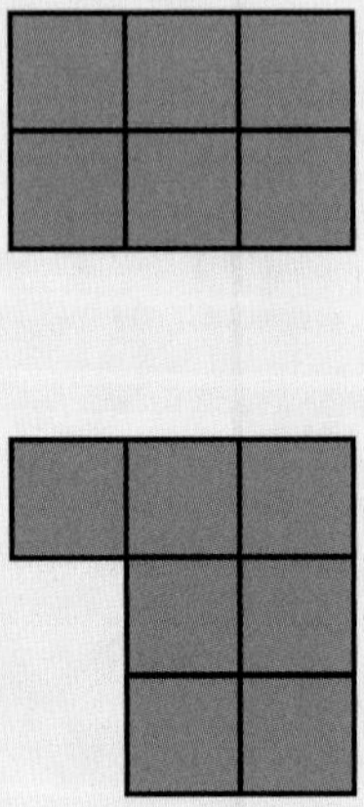

Same perimeter but different areas

Example

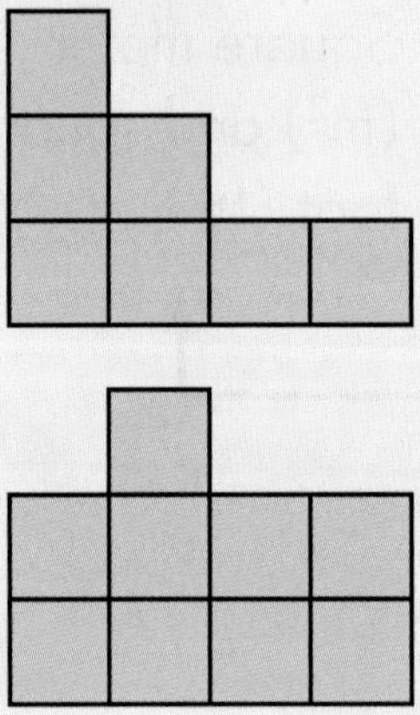

Same area but different perimeters

Example

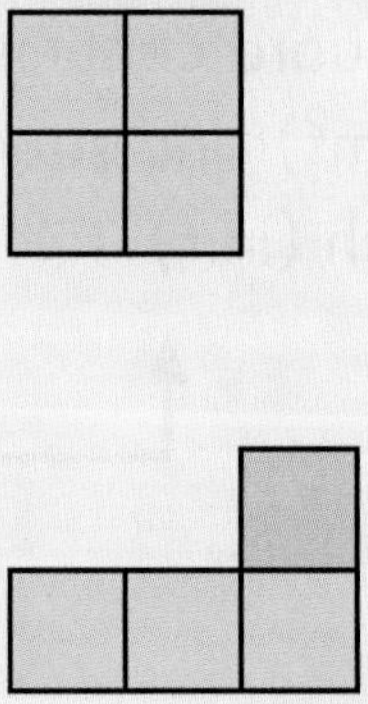

Same area and perimeter

Example

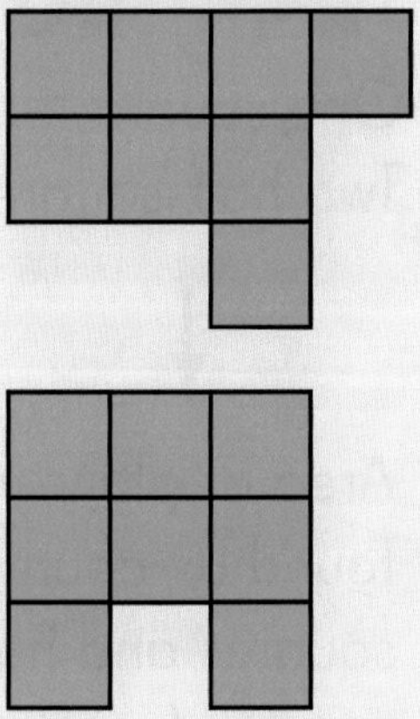

Chapter Review/Test

Vocabulary

Complete the sentences.

area
perimeter
centimeters
meter
inches
feet

1. The amount of surface covered is the ____.
2. The distance around a figure or place is its ____.
3. The perimeter of a stamp is about 8 ____ or 4 ____.
4. The area of a teacher's table is about 9 square ____ or 1 square ____.

Concept and Skills

Complete. The figures are made up of square and half-square tiles. Find the area of each figure.

5. 6. 7. 8.

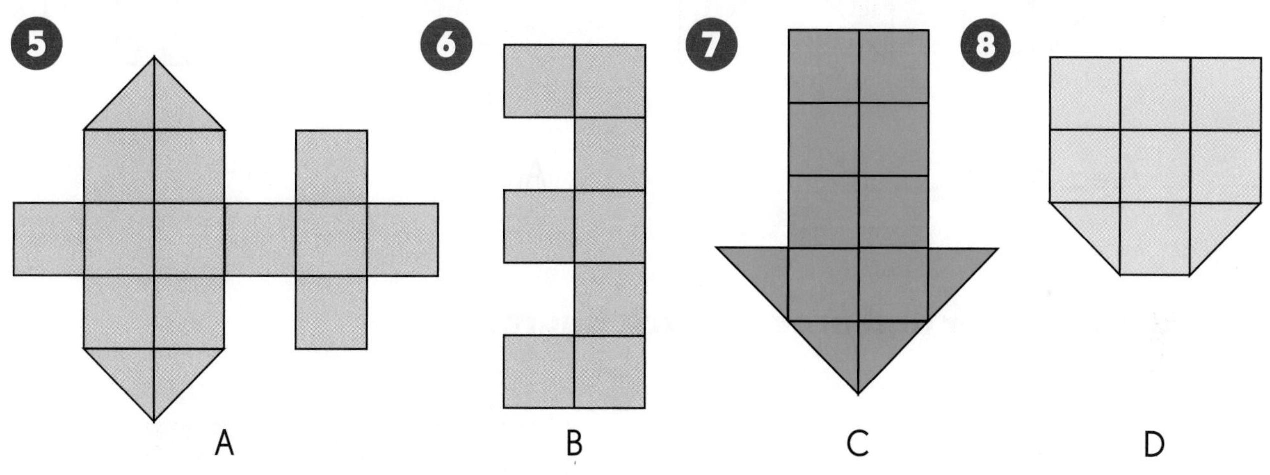

____ square units ____ square units ____ square units ____ square units

9. Which figure has the largest area? Figure ____
10. Which figures have the smallest area? Figures ____ and ____
11. Which two figures have the same area? Figures ____ and ____
12. You want Figure A and Figure C to have the same area. Explain two ways of doing this. ____

The figures are made up of square and half-square tiles. Find the area of each figure.

13

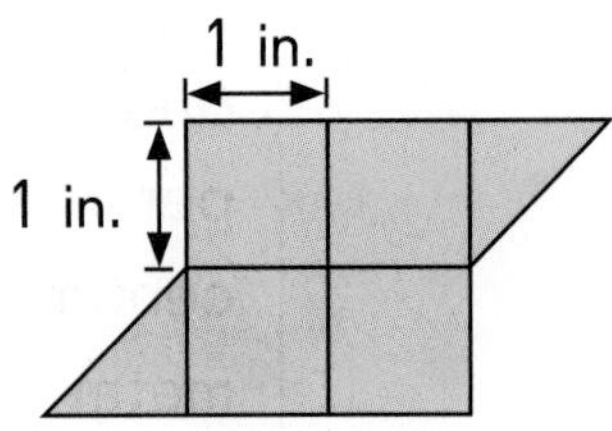

Area = ☐ in.^{2}

14

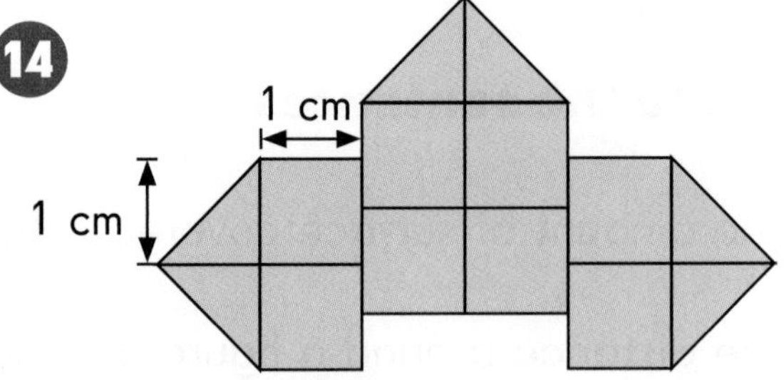

Area = ☐ cm^2

15

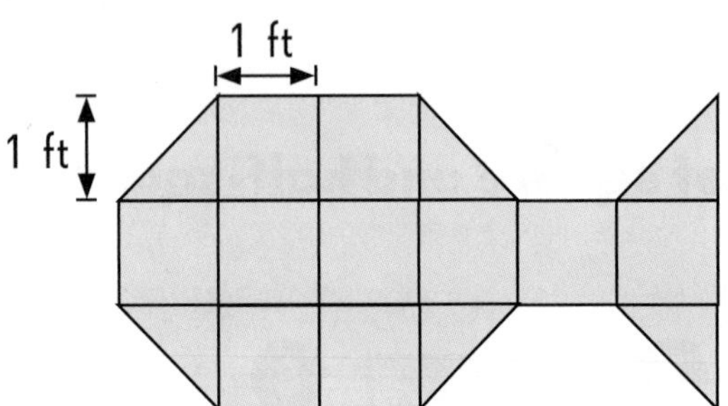

Area = ☐ ft^2

16

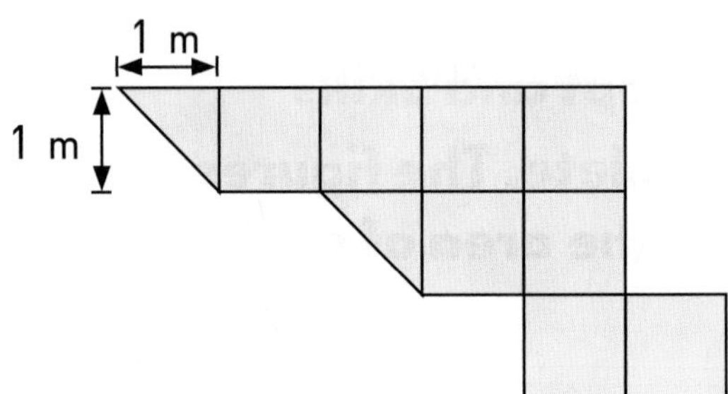

Area = ☐ m^2

Find the perimeter and area of each figure.

17

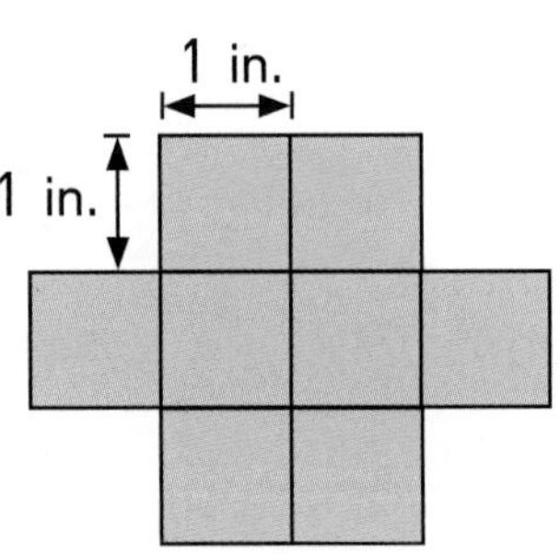

Perimeter =  in.

Area = ☐ in.^{2}

18

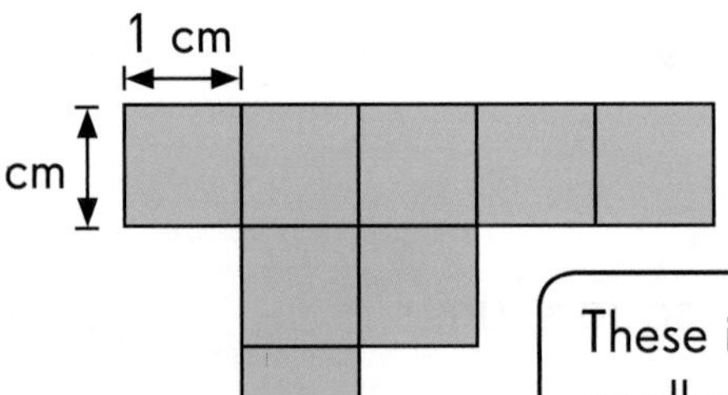

Perimeter =  cm

Area =   cm^2

These inch squares ar
smaller than in real lif

Find the perimeter and area of each figure. Then answer the questions.

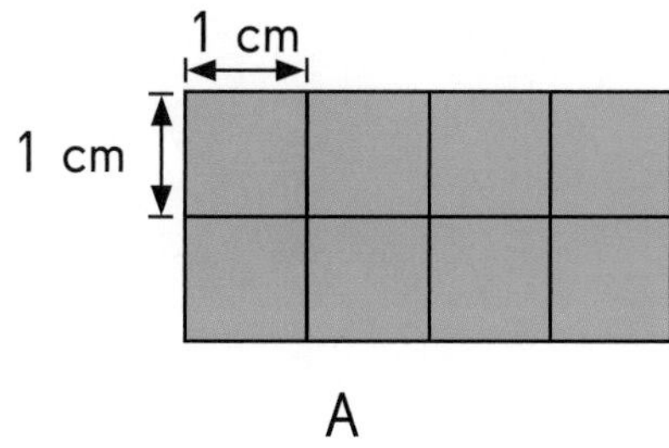

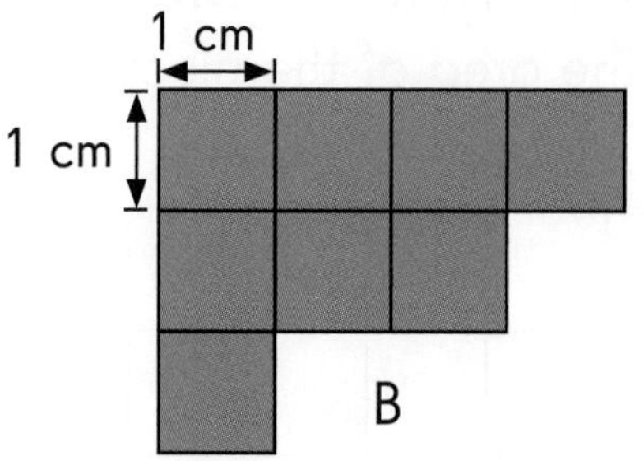

19 Do Figures A and B have the same area?

20 Do they have the same perimeter?

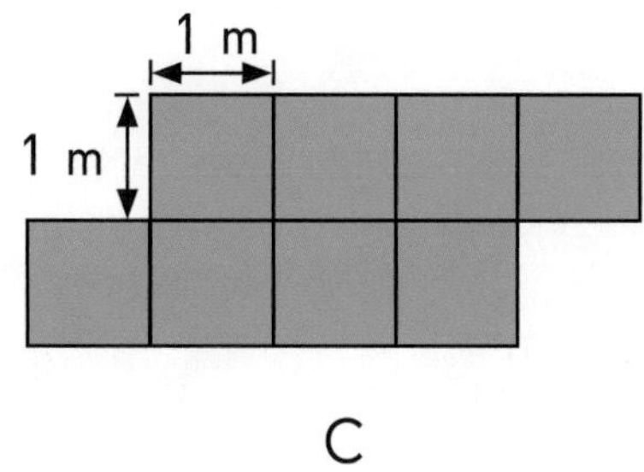

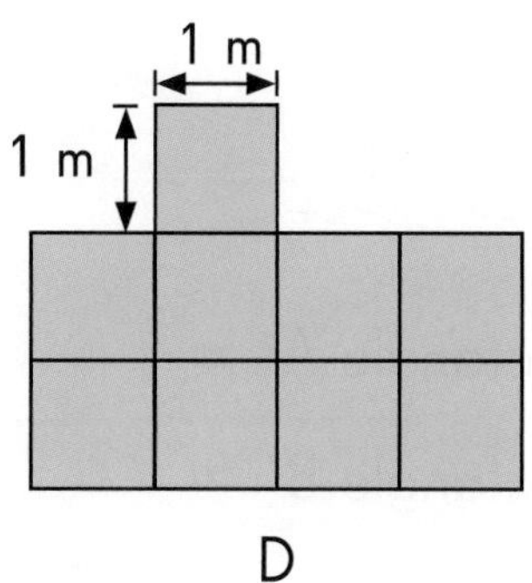

21 Do Figures C and D have the same area?

22 Do they have the same perimeter?

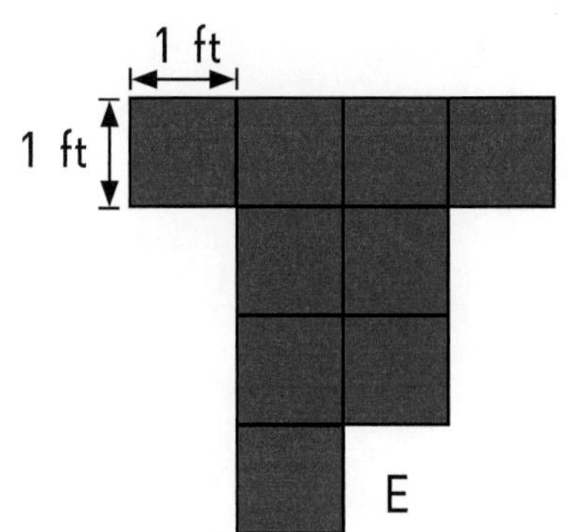

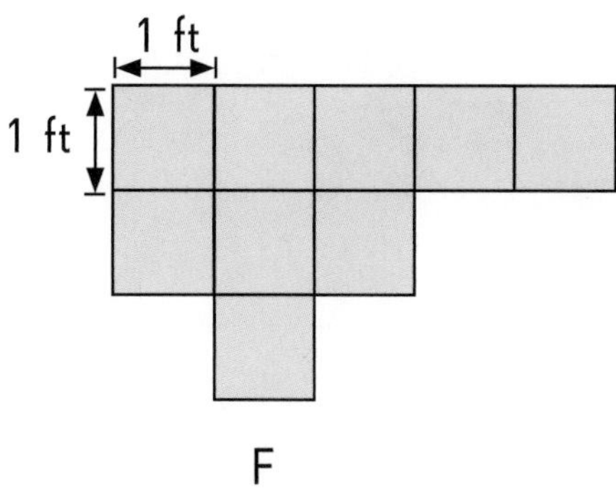

23 Do Figures E and F have the same area?

24 Do they have the same perimeter?

Find the areas.

25 Matt needs a piece of cloth with a length of 6 meters and a width of 5 meters to sew an apron for his Grandmother.
What is the area of the piece of cloth?

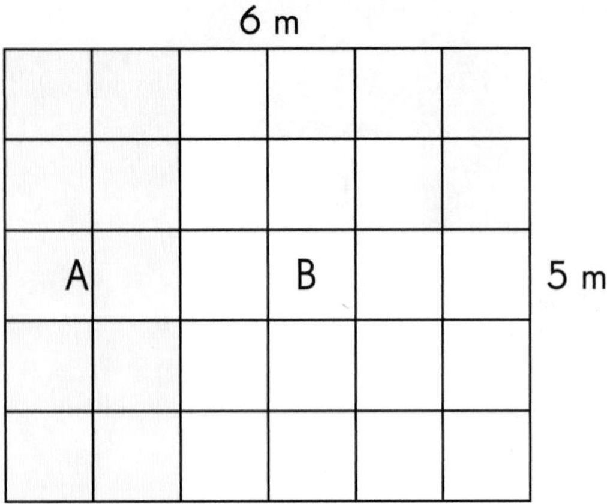

Method 1

☐ × ☐ = ☐ m^2

Method 2

Area of Rectangle A = ☐ × ☐ m^2

Area of Rectangle B = ☐ × ☐ m^2

Area of the cloth = ☐ × (☐ + ☐)

= (☐ × ☐) + (☐ × ☐)

= ☐ + ☐

= ☐ m^2

26 A plot of land has a length of 10 meters and a width of 8 meters.
What is the area of the plot of land?

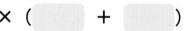

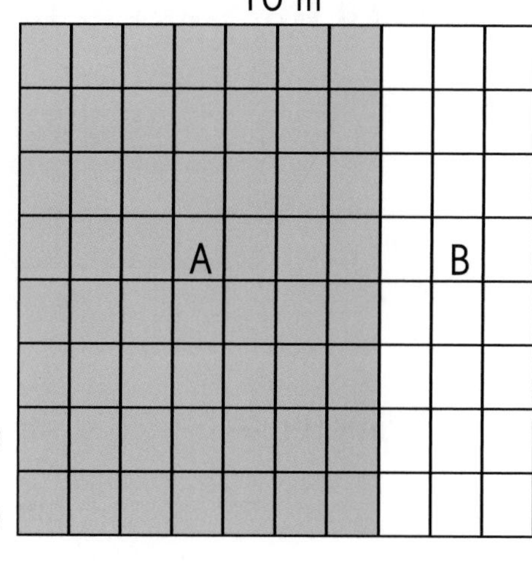

Method 1

___ × ___ = ___ m^2

Method 2

Area of Rectangle A = ___ × ___ m^2

Area of Rectangle B = ___ × ___ m^2

Area of the plot of land = ___ × (___ + ___)

= (___ × ___) + (___ × ___)

= ___ + ___

= ___ m^2

27 The diagram shows Tim's garden.
What is the total area of his garden? ___ m^2

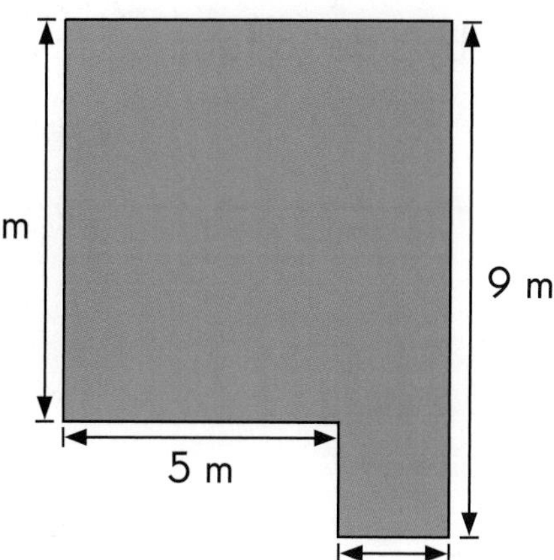

28 The diagram shows Jasmine's desk.
She wants to cover the top of her desk with glass.
What is the total area of the glass she needs? ___ ft^2

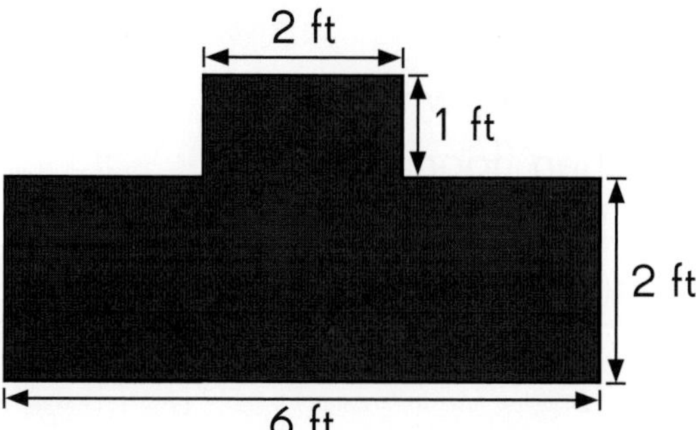

Measure the sides of the parallelogram. Find its perimeter.

29

Perimeter = ☐ + ☐ + ☐ + ☐

= ☐ cm

Problem Solving

30 A rectangular field is 10 meters by 5 meters. A fence is put around it. How long must the fence be? ☐ m

31 Two square tiles each with a side length of 6 centimeters are placed side by side to form a rectangle. What is the perimeter of the rectangle? ☐ cm

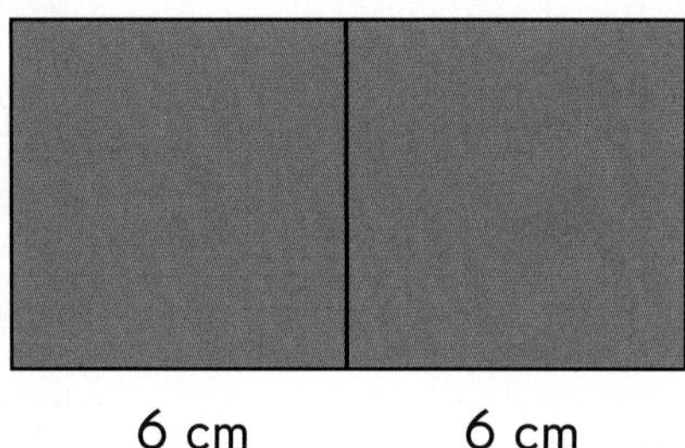

32 The diagram below shows a kitchen floor.

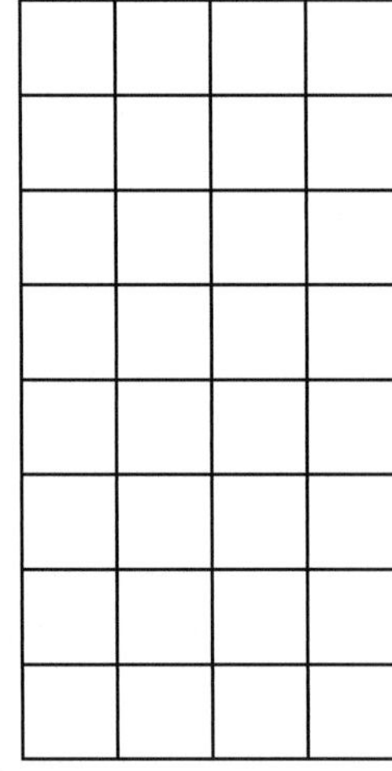

Mr. Thompson needs alternating white and blue tiles to cover the kitchen floor. How many tiles of each color should he buy? ☐

Glossary

A

- **angle**

  When two line segments share the same endpoint, they form an angle.

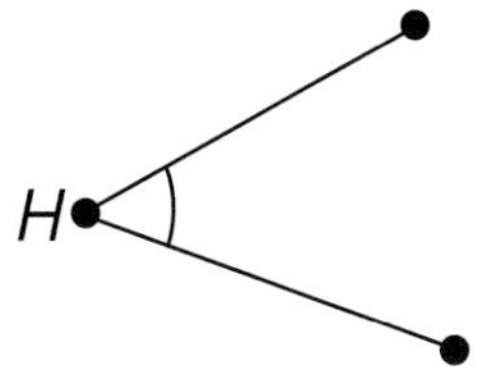

This is angle H.

- **area**

  Area is the number of square units needed to cover the surface of each figure.

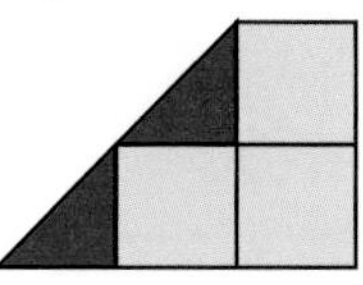

The area of this figure is 4 square units.

- **axis**

  An axis is a grid line that can be either vertical or horizontal.
  See **horizontal axis** and **vertical axis**.

B

- **bar graph**

A bar garph is a chart with rectangular bars of lengths proportional to the values that they represent

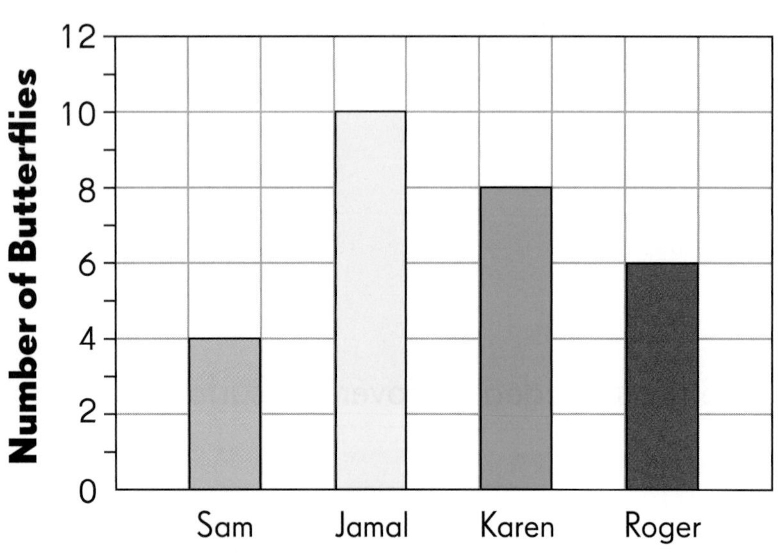

- **benchmark**

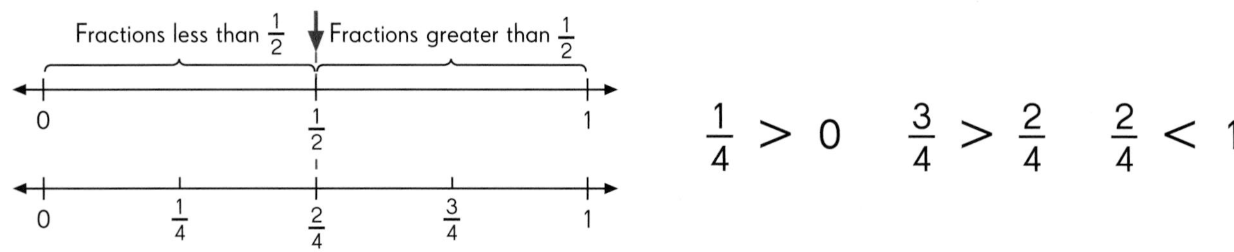

$\frac{1}{4} > 0 \quad \frac{3}{4} > \frac{2}{4} \quad \frac{2}{4} < 1$

The common benchmarks for comparing fractions are 0, $\frac{1}{2}$, and 1.

- **break apart polygon**

  This is an example of how to break a polygon apart.

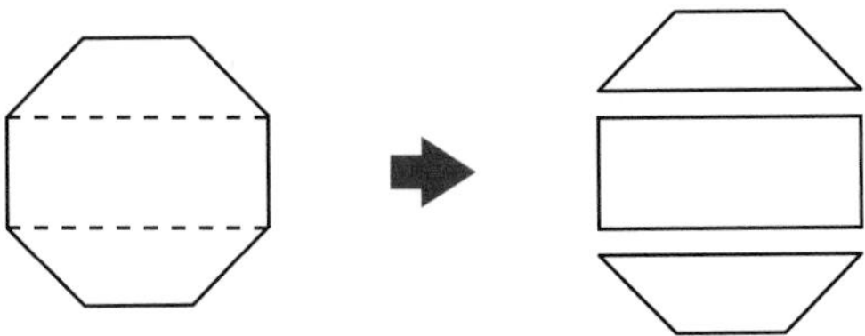

  An octagon can be broken apart into one rectangle and two trapezoids.
  See **polygon**.

C

- **capacity**

  Capacity is the amount of liquid that a container can hold.

- **centimeter (cm)**

  Centimeter is a metric unit of length.
  It is used to measure shorter lengths.
  Write cm for centimeter.
  100 cm = 1 m

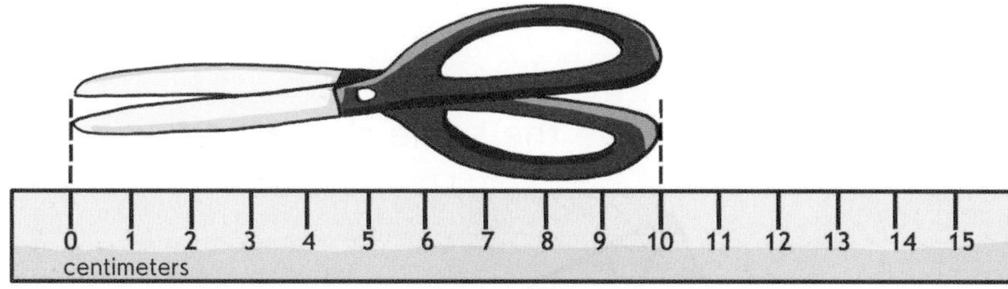

  The pair of scissors is 10 centimeters long.

- **closed plane figure**

  A closed plane figure is a plane figure that starts and ends at the same point.

  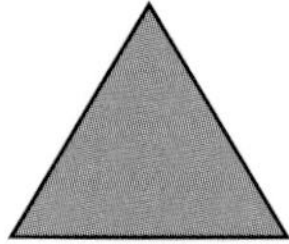 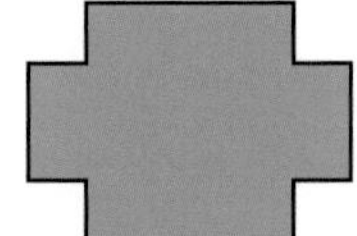 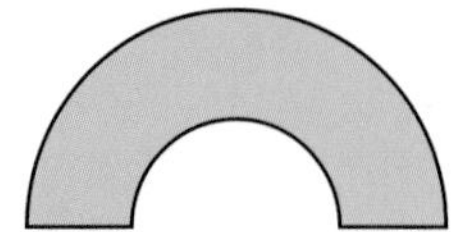

  These are examples of closed plane figures.

- **cold**

  Use cold, cool, warm, and hot as referents to estimate temperature.
  When the temperature outside is 32°F, it is cold.

- **combine polygons**

  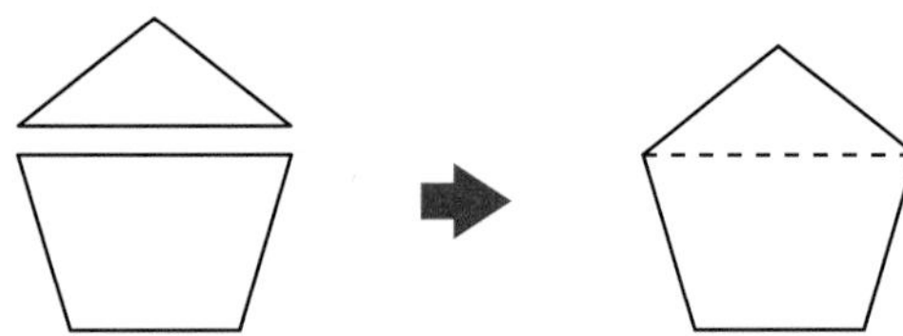

  A triangle and a trapezoid can be joined to form a pentagon.
  This is an example of how polygons can be combined.
  See **polygon**.

- **congruent**

  Identical figures are congruent. They have the same shape and size.

  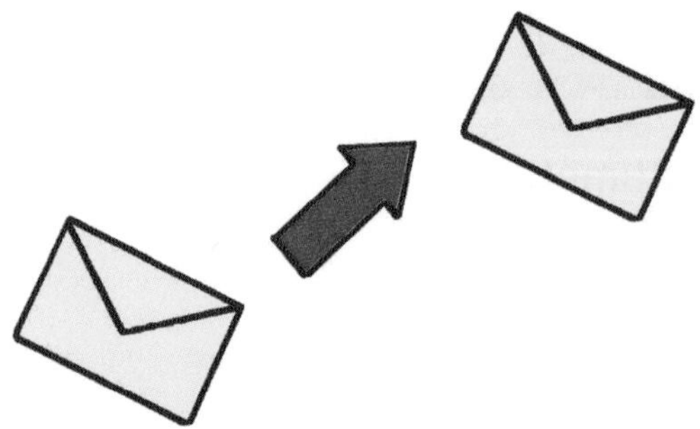

- **convert**

  You can convert units of measurement.

  For example, these conversions express time in minutes or hours and minutes.

  $$\begin{aligned} 1 \text{ h } 10 \text{ min} &= 60 \text{ min} + 10 \text{ min} \\ &= 70 \text{ min} \end{aligned}$$

  $$\begin{aligned} 135 \text{ min} &= 120 \text{ min} + 15 \text{ min} \\ &= 2 \text{ h } 15 \text{ min} \end{aligned}$$

- **cool**

  When the temperature outside is 50°F, it is cool.

  See **cold**.

- **cup (c)**

  Cup is a customary unit of capacity. Write c for cup.

- **degrees Fahrenheit (°F)**

  This is the customary unit of measurement for temperature.

- **denominator**

  A denominator is the number below the line in a fraction. It shows the number of equal parts into which the whole is divided.

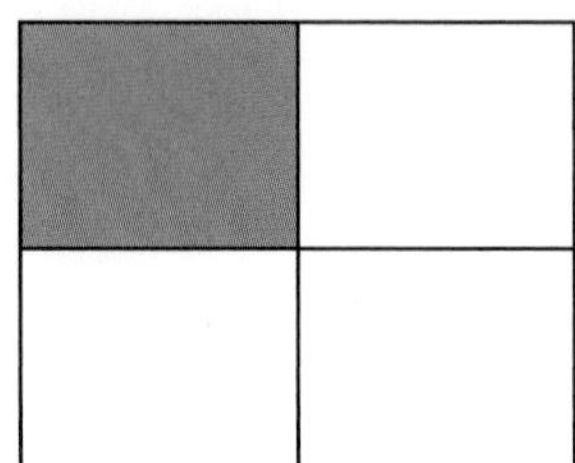

$\frac{1}{4}$ of the rectangle is shaded.

In the fraction $\frac{1}{4}$, 4 is the denominator.

- **distance**

  Distance is the length between one place and another.

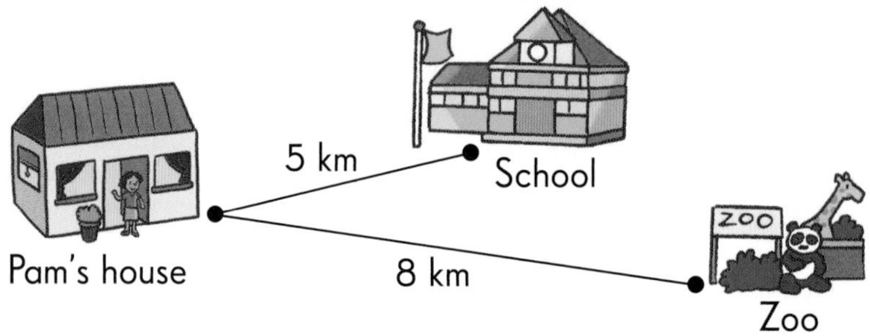

The distance between Pam's house and the zoo is 8 kilometers.

- **dollar**

  A dollar is the basic currency of countries such as the United States and Canada. It is written using a $.

- **elapsed time**

Elapsed time is the amount of time that has passed between the start and the end of an activity.

Start:

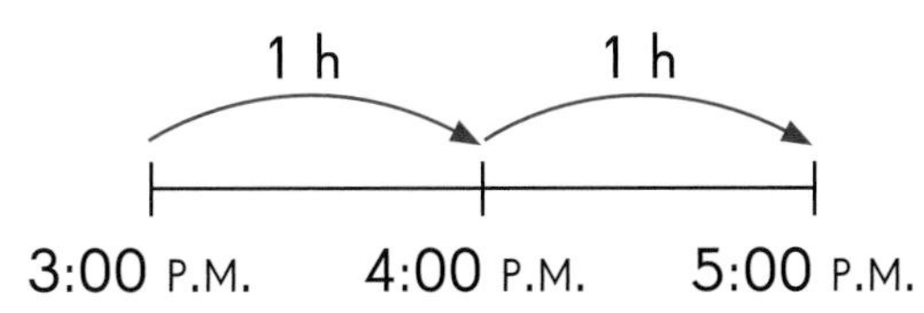

End:

Tom's soccer practice lasted 2 hours.
2 hours is the elapsed time between 3:00 P.M. and 5:00 P.M.

- **endpoint**

Endpoint is the end of a line segment.

See **line segment**.

- **equal parts**

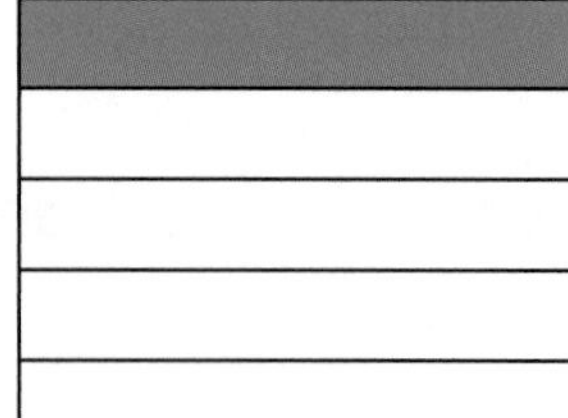

This whole is made up of 5 equal parts.

$\frac{1}{5}$ is 1 out of the 5 equal parts.

- **equivalent fractions**

Equivalent fractions are two or more fractions that name the same parts of a whole.

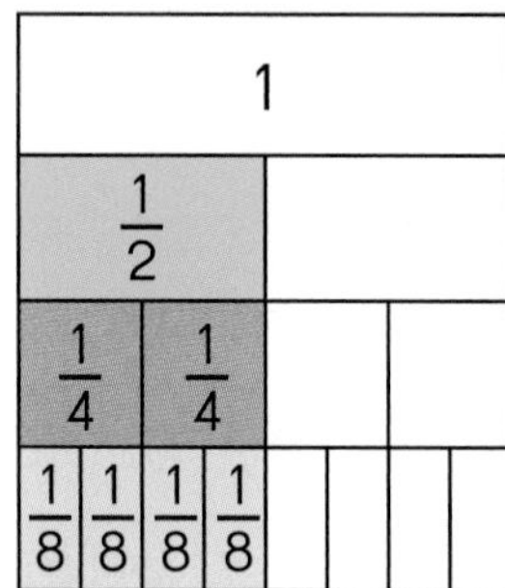

$\frac{1}{2}$, $\frac{2}{4}$, and $\frac{4}{8}$ name the same parts of a whole.

F

- **Fahrenheit (°F)**

  See **degrees Fahrenheit**.

- **flip**

  Turn a shape front to back over a line.

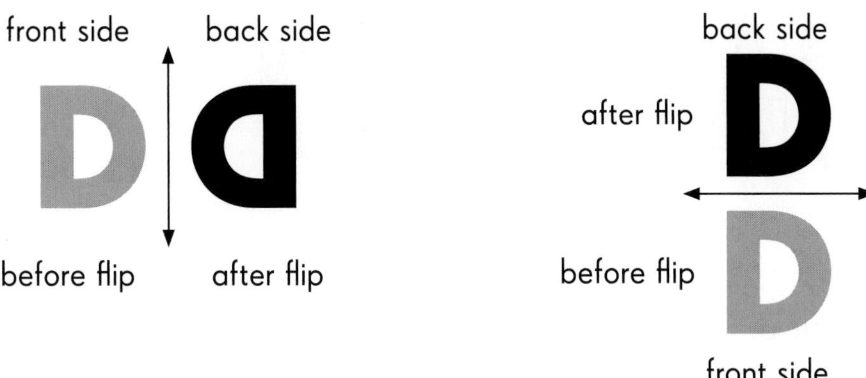

- **foot (ft)**

  Foot is a customary unit of length.
  Write ft for foot.
  1 ft = 12 in.

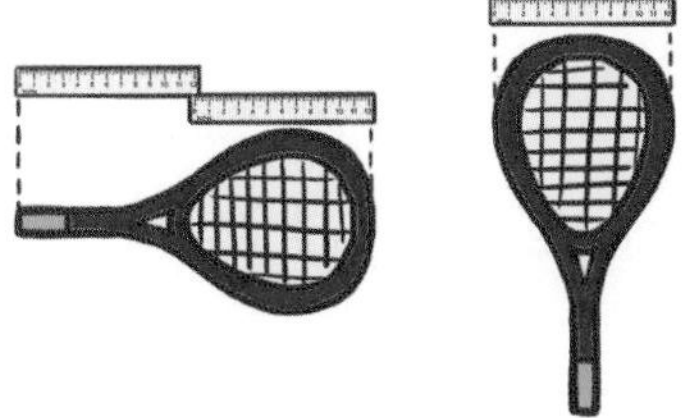

The length of the tennis racket is 2 feet.
The width of the tennis racket is 1 foot.

G

- **gallon (gal)**

Gallon is a customary unit of capacity.
Write gal for gallon.
1 gal = 4 qt

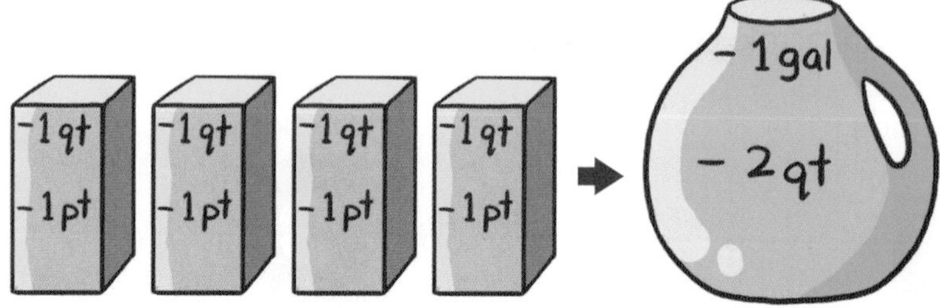

- **gram (g)**

Gram is the metric unit of mass.
It is used to measure the mass of lighter objects.
Write g for gram.
1,000 g = 1 kg

The mass of the pencil case is 500 grams.

- **greater than (>)**

$\frac{3}{5}$ is greater than $\frac{3}{6}$.

- **greatest**

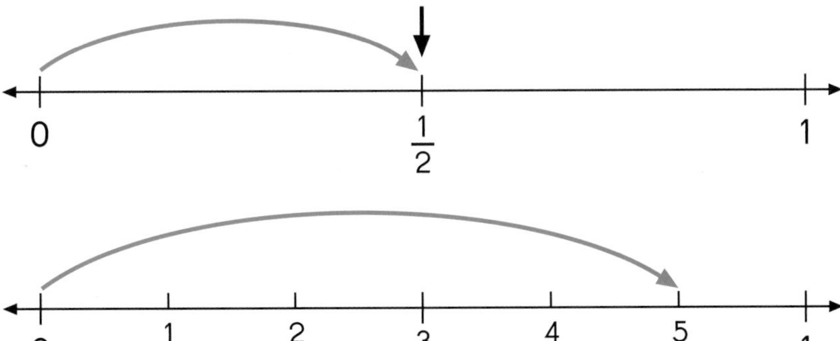

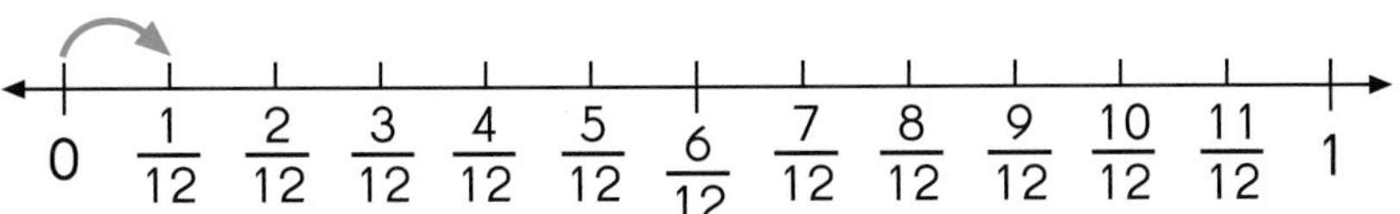

$\frac{5}{6}$ is the greatest fraction.

H

- **half inch**

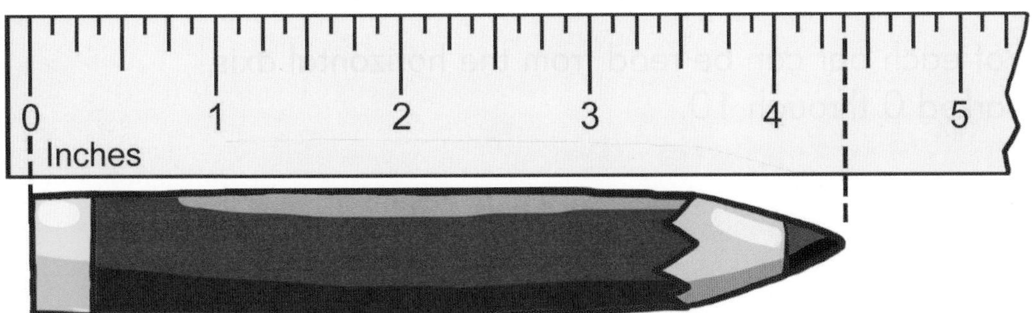

The length of the pencil is $4\frac{1}{2}$ inches, measured to the nearest half-inch.

See **inch**.

- **hexagon**

  A hexagon is a polygon that has six sides.

  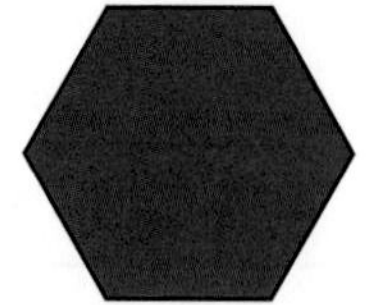

  See **polygon**.

- **horizontal axis**

  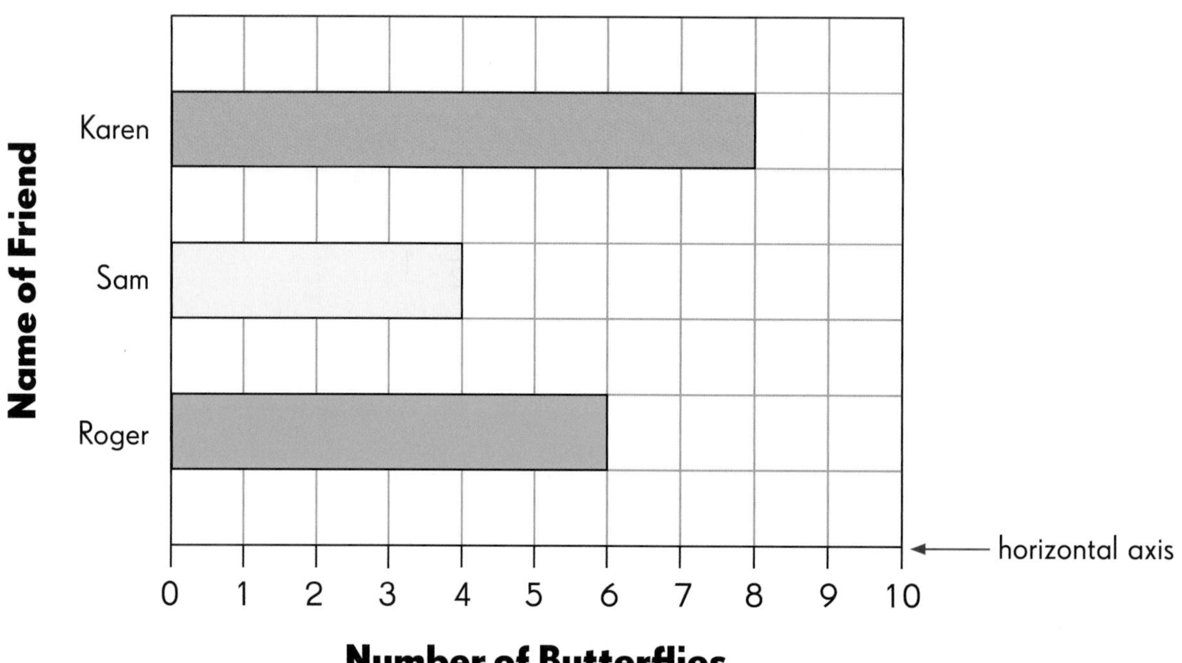

  The value of each bar can be read from the horizontal axis, which is marked 0 through 10.

  See **axis**.

- **hot**

  When the temperature outside is 105°F, it is hot.

  See **cold**.

- **hour (h)**

  It is a unit of measurement of time.
  There are 60 minutes in 1 hour.
  Write h for hour.
  60 min = 1 h

  See **minute**.

I

- **inch (in.)**

  Inch is a customary unit of length.
  Write in. for inch.
  12 in. = 1 ft

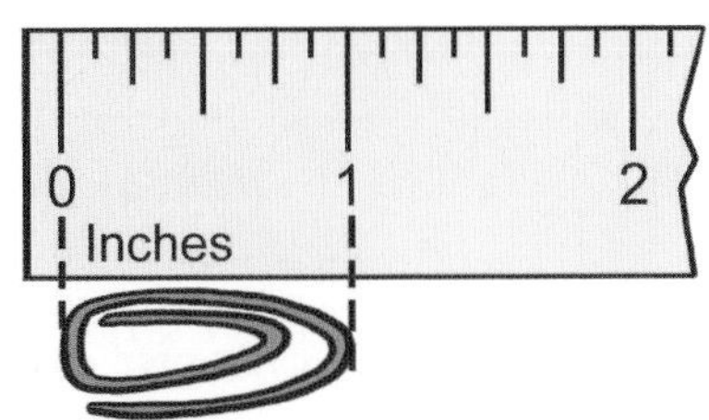

The paper clip is 1 inch long.

  See **foot**.

- **is parallel to**

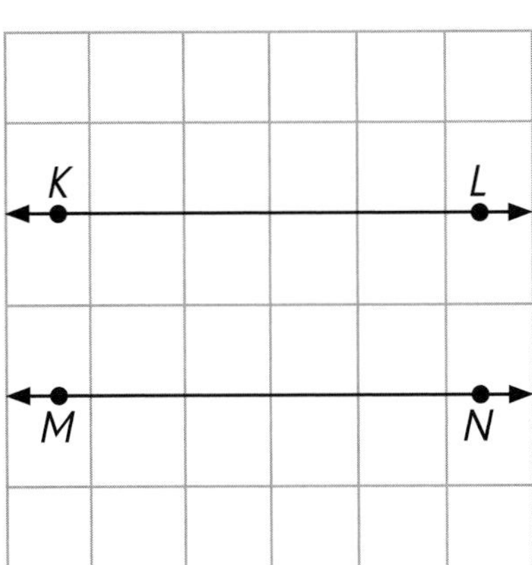

Line *KL* is parallel to line *MN*.

- **is perpendicular to**

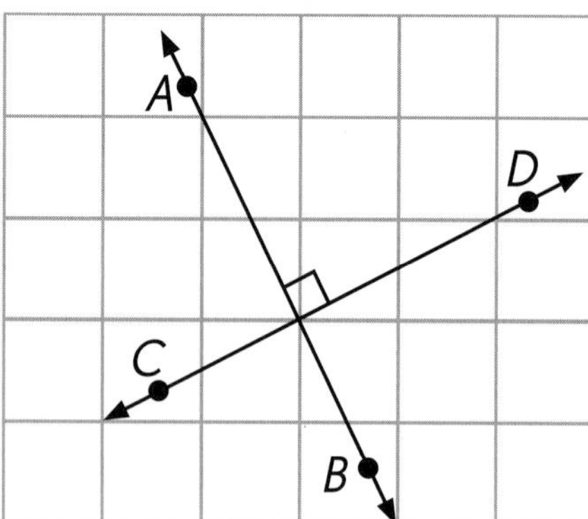

Line AB is perpendicular to line CD.

K

- **kilogram (kg)**

Kilogram is a metric unit of mass.
It is used to measure the mass of heavier objects.
Write kg for kilogram.
1 kg = 1,000 g

The mass of the bananas is 1 kilogram.

See **gram**.

- **kilometer (km)**

  Kilometer is a metric unit of length.
  It is used to measure length and distance.
  Write km for kilometer.
  1 km = 1,000 m

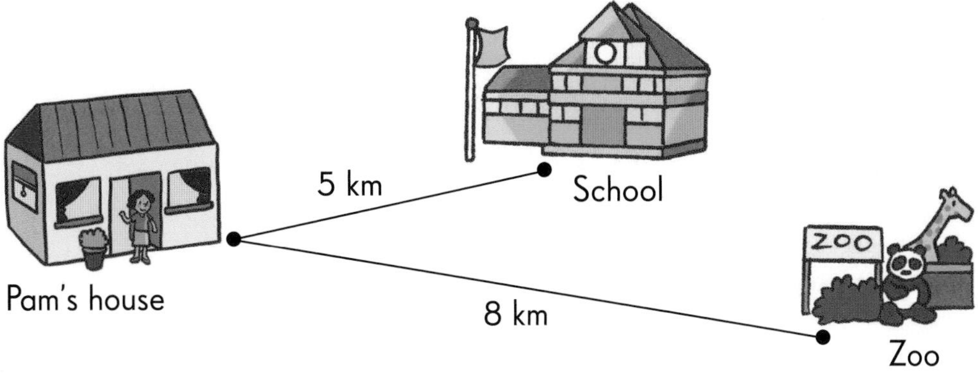

  The distance between Pam's house and the school is 5 kilometers.

L

- **least**

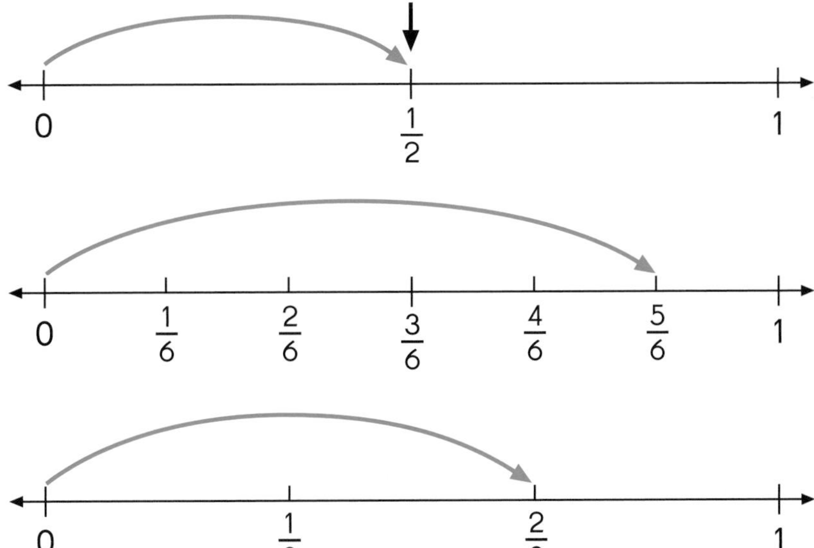

  $\frac{1}{2}$ is the least fraction.

- **less than (<)**

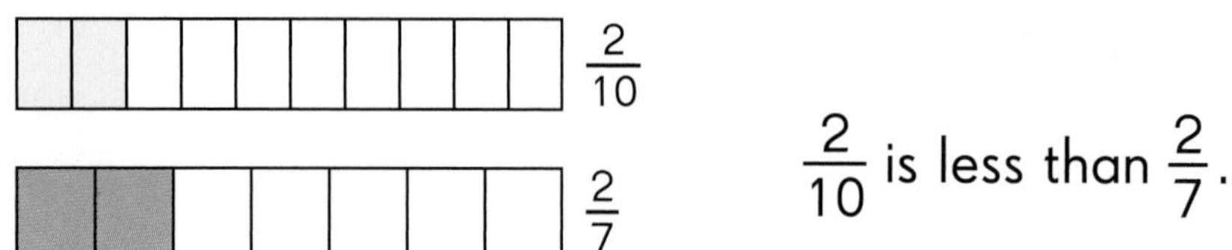

$\frac{2}{10}$ is less than $\frac{2}{7}$.

- **like fractions**

  Like fractions are fractions with the same denominators.
  $\frac{1}{4}$ and $\frac{3}{4}$ are like fractions.

  See **unlike fractions**.

- **line**

  A line is a straight path. It goes on without end in both directions as shown by the arrowheads.

  This line passes through points *A* and *B*. This is line *AB* or *BA*.

- **line of symmetry**

  A line that divides a figure into congruent halves. The halves fit exactly over each other when folded along this line.

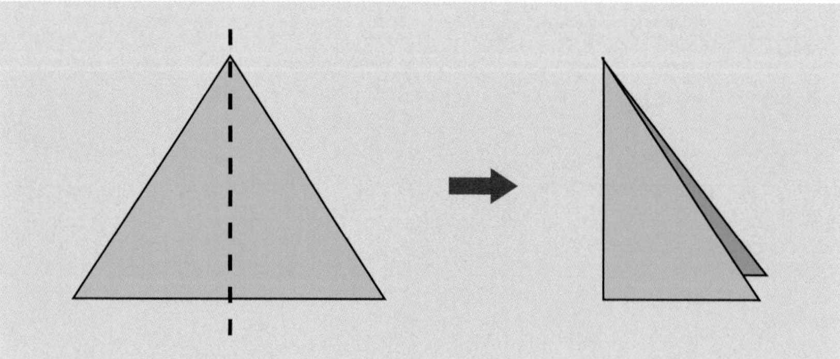

- **line plot**

  A line plot is a diagram that uses a number line to show how often an event happens.

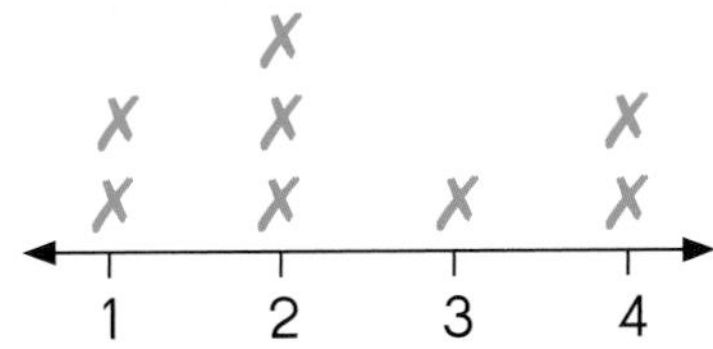

Number of Birthday Cards Received

- **line segment**

  A line segment is part of a line. It has two endpoints.

This is line segment *CD*.

- **liter (L)**

  Liter is a metric unit of volume and capacity.
  Write L for liter.
  1 L = 1,000 mL

The measuring cup holds 1 liter of water.

M

- **meter (m)**

  Meter is a metric unit of length.
  Write m for meter.
  1 m = 100 cm

  See **centimeter**.
  See **kilometer**.

- **mile (mi)**

  Mile is a customary unit of length.
  Write mi for mile.

  A 1-mile brisk walk will usually take about 20 minutes.

- **milliliter (mL)**

  Milliliter is a metric unit of volume and capacity.
  Write mL for milliliter.
  1,000 mL = 1 L

The measuring cup holds 250 milliliters of water.

- **minute (min)**

  It is a unit of measurement of time.
  Write min for minute.
  60 min = 1 h

  Each small marking stands for 1 minute.
  The minute hand shows 5 minutes.

N

- **number line**

This is a number line. Use a number line to help you find equivalent fractions and compare fractions.

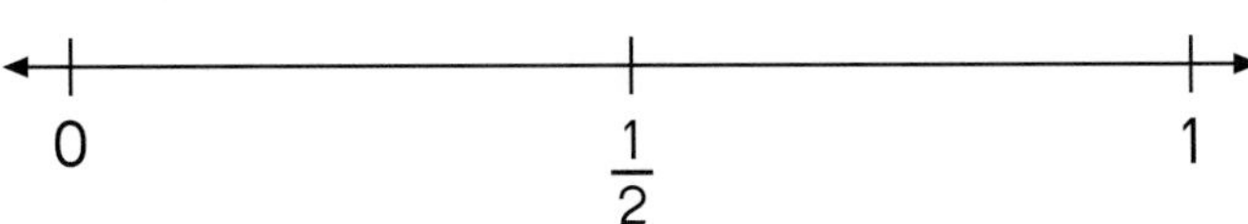

- **numerator**

A numerator is the number above the line in a fraction. It shows the number of shaded parts in a whole.

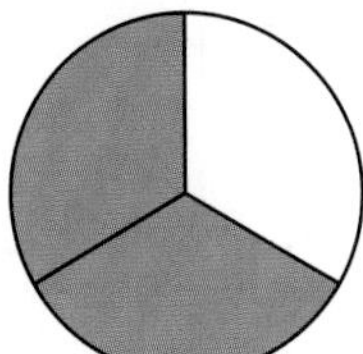

$\frac{2}{3}$ of the circle is shaded.

In the fraction $\frac{2}{3}$, 2 is the numerator.

O

- **octagon**

An octagon is a polygon that has eight sides. This is an example of an octagon.

See **polygon**.

- **open plane figure**

An open plane figure is a plane figure that does not start and end at the same point.

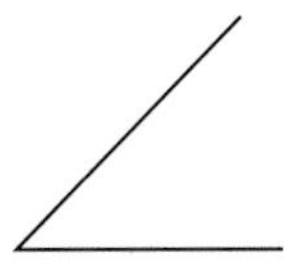
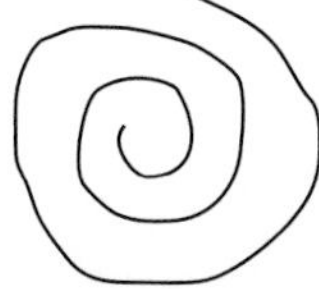
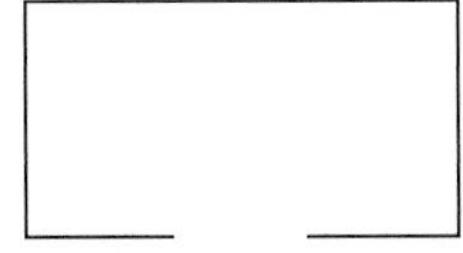

These are examples of open plane figures.

- **ounce (oz)**

Ounce is a customary unit of weight.
Write oz for ounce.
16 oz = 1 lb

The weight of one slice of bread is about 1 ounce.

P

- **parallel lines**

Parallel lines are two lines that will not meet no matter how long they are drawn.

See **is parallel to**.

- **parallelogram**

A parallelogram is a quadrilateral with two opposite sides that are parallel. Only the opposite sides of a parallelogram need to be equal.

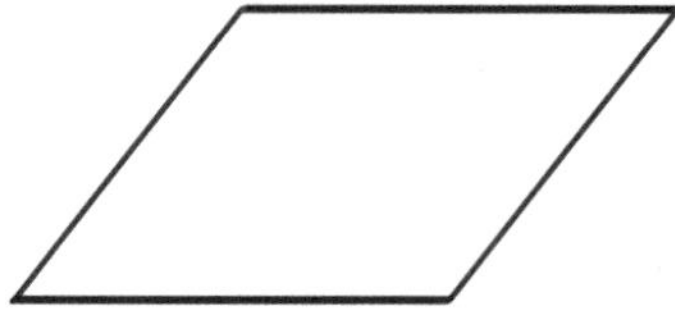

These are examples of parallelograms.

See **quadrilateral** and **parallel lines**.

- **past**

9:20 A.M. is 20 minutes past 9 A.M.

- **pentagon**

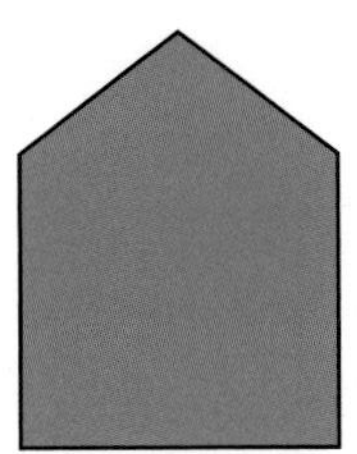

A pentagon is a polygon that has five sides.
This is an example of a pentagon.

See **polygon**.

- **perimeter**

Perimeter is the distance around a figure. Perimeter can be measured in linear units such as centimeters, inches, meters, and feet.

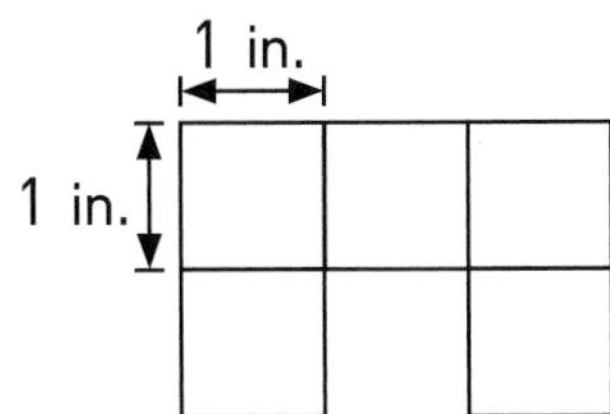

The perimeter of this figure is 12 inches.

- **perpendicular lines**

  Perpendicular lines are two lines that meet at right angles.

  See **is perpendicular to**.

- **picture graph**

  A picture graphs is a kind of graph that shows relationships in statistics using pictures.

Butterflies Seen

Sam		4
Jamal		10
Karen		8
Roger		6
Key: Each stands for 1 butterfly.		

- **pint (pt)**

  Pint is a customary unit of capacity.
  Write pt for pint.
  1 pt = 2 c

- **plane figure**

  A plane figure is a flat figure. It can be open or closed.

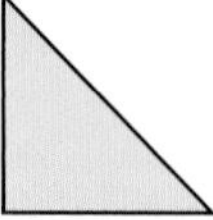
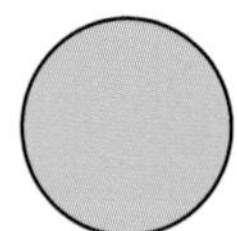
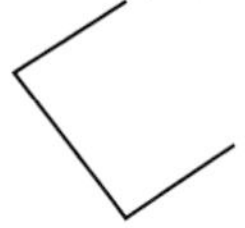

These are examples of plane figures.

- **point**

  A point is an exact location in space.

  •
  A This is point *A* or *A*.

- **polygon**

  A polygon is a closed plane figure formed by three or more line segments.

  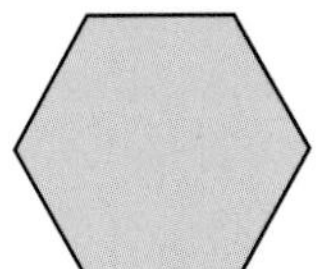  These are examples of polygons.

  See **closed plane figures.**

- **pound (lb)**

  Pound is a customary unit of weight.
  Write lb for pound.
  1 lb = 16 oz

  The weight of the loaf of bread is about 1 pound.

Q

- **quadrilateral**

  A quadrilateral is a polygon that has four sides and four angles.

 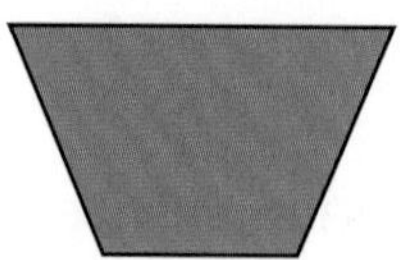 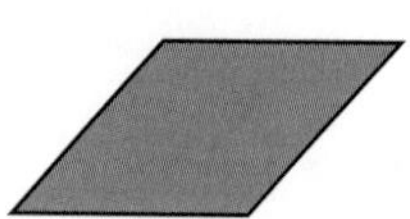

These are examples of quadrilaterals.

See **polygon**.

- **quart (qt)**

  Quart is a customary unit of capacity.
  Write qt for quart.
  1 qt = 2 pt

R

- **rhombus**

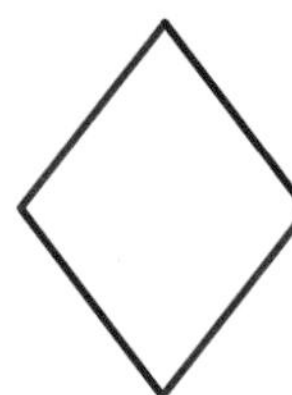

A rhombus is a parallelogram with sides that are equal in length.

See **parallelogram**.

- **right angle**

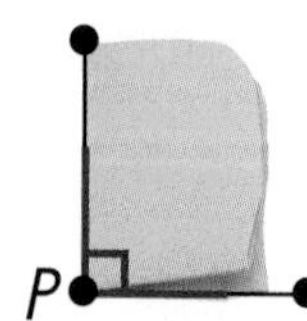

Angle *P* is a right angle. Use the corner of a folded paper to check for a right angle.

- **rotate**

  To change the position of a shape by turning about a point.

  See **turn**.

S

- **scale**

  A scale is the numbers that run along the vertical or horizontal axis of a graph.

  See **horizontal axis** and **vertical axis**.

- **simplest form**

  $$\frac{2}{4} = \frac{1}{2}$$

  (numerator and denominator each $\div 2$)

  $\frac{1}{2}$ is a fraction in its simplest form.

- **slide**

  Move a figure in any direction to a new position.

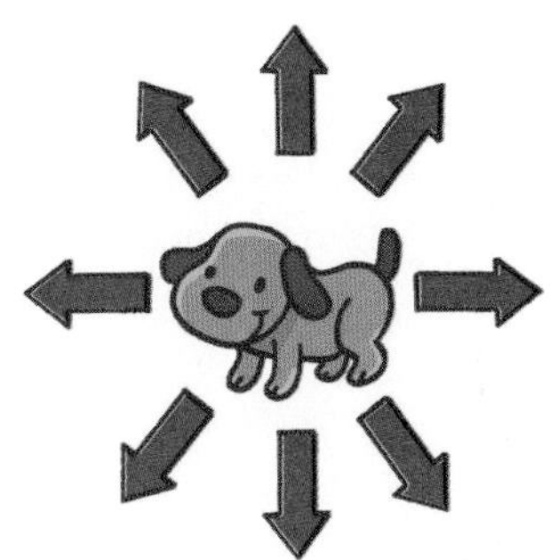

- **square centimeter (cm^2)**

  Square centimeter is a metric unit of measure for area.
  Write cm^2 for square centimeter.

  1 cm
  1 cm

  This is a 1-centimeter square.
  Its area is 1 square centimeter (cm^2).

- **square foot (ft^2)**

  Square foot is a customary unit of measure for area.
  Write ft^2 for square foot.

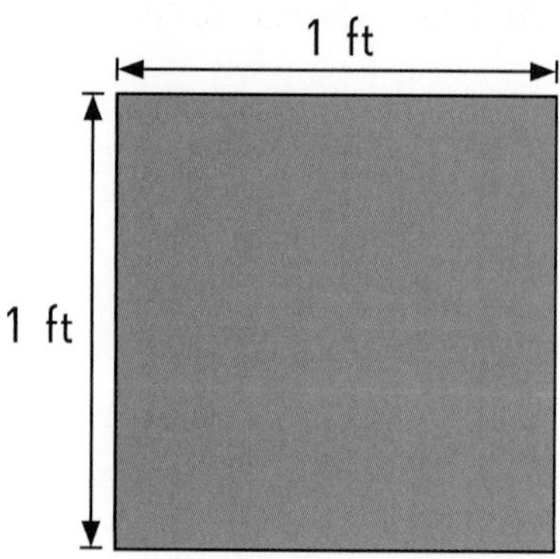

A 1-foot square has an area of 1 square foot (ft^2).

- **square inch ($in.^2$)**

  Square inch is a customary unit of measure for area.
  Write $in.^2$ for square inch.

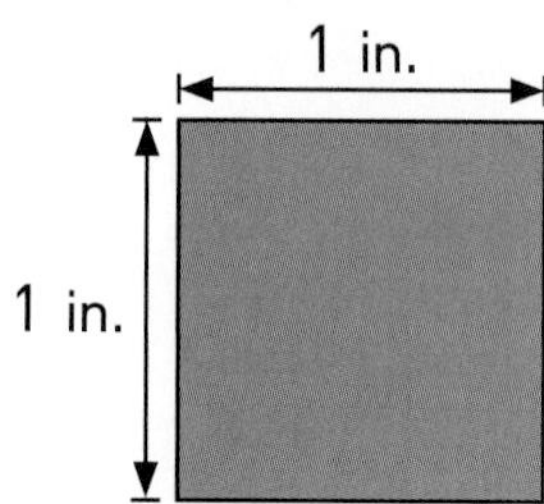

This is a 1-inch square.
Its area is 1 square inch ($in.^2$).

- **square meter (m^2)**

  Square meter is a metric unit of measure for area.
  Write m^2 for square meter.

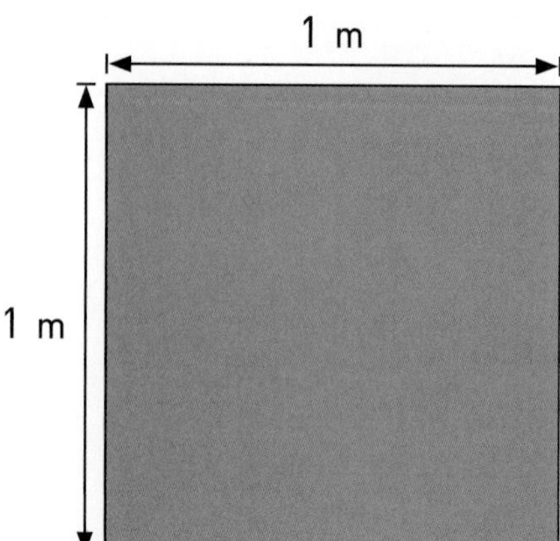

A 1-meter square has an area of 1 square meter (m^2).

- **square units**

  Square units are units such as square centimeter, square inch, square foot, and square meter that are used to measure area.

- **survey**

  A survey is a method of collecting information or data.

- **symmetry**

  Occurs when two halves of a figure fit each other exactly when folded along a line.

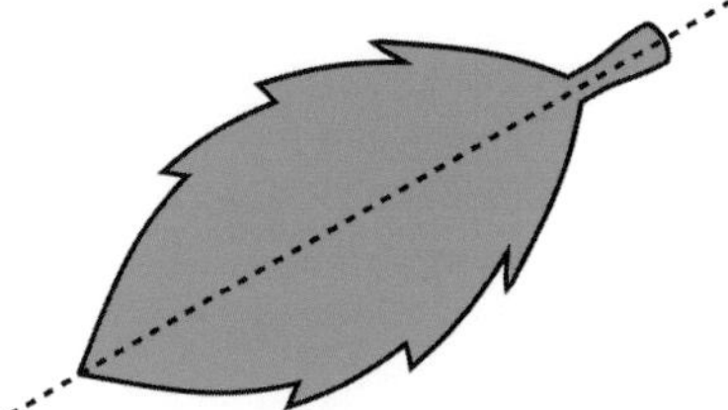

T

- **tangram**

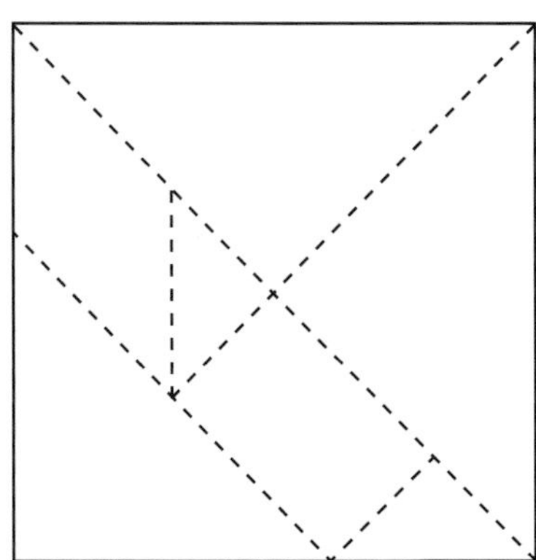

A tangram is made up of seven polygons that can be put together to make a square.

- **temperature**

  Temperature is a measure of how hot or cold something is.

- **thermometer**

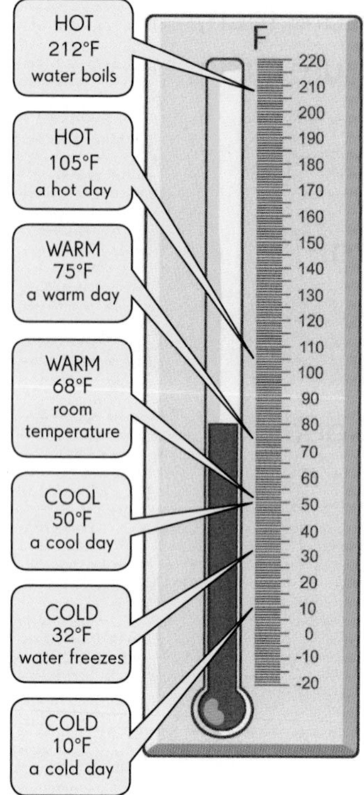

Thermometers are used to measure temperature.

- **timeline**

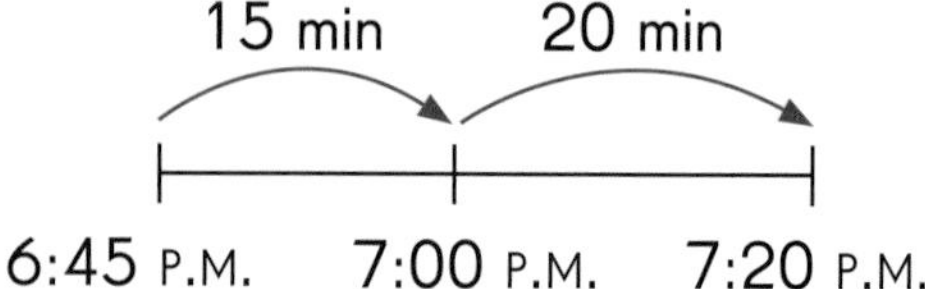

Use a timeline to help you find elapsed time.

See **elapsed time**.

- **to**

9:20 A.M. is 40 minutes to 10 A.M.

- **ton (T)**

Ton is a customary unit of weight
Write T for ton.

The weight of a car is 1 ton.

- **trapezoid**

A trapezoid is a quadrilateral that has one pair of parallel sides.

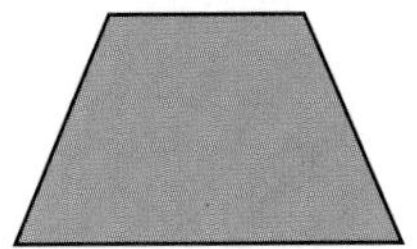

This is an example of a trapezoid.

- **turn**

Rotate a figure about a point.

See **rotate**.

U

- **unit fraction**

A unit fraction is a fraction whose numerator is 1.

$\frac{1}{2}$, $\frac{1}{5}$, and $\frac{1}{100}$ are unit fractions.

- **unlike fractions**

  Unlike fractions are fractions with different denominators.

  $\frac{2}{10}$ and $\frac{2}{7}$ are unlike fractions.

  See **like fractions**.

V

- **vertex**

  A vertex is a point where two sides of a polygon meet.

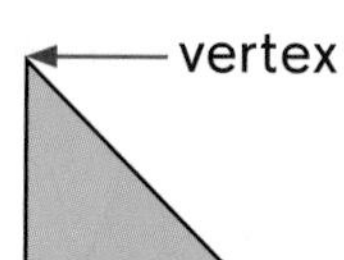

- **vertical axis**

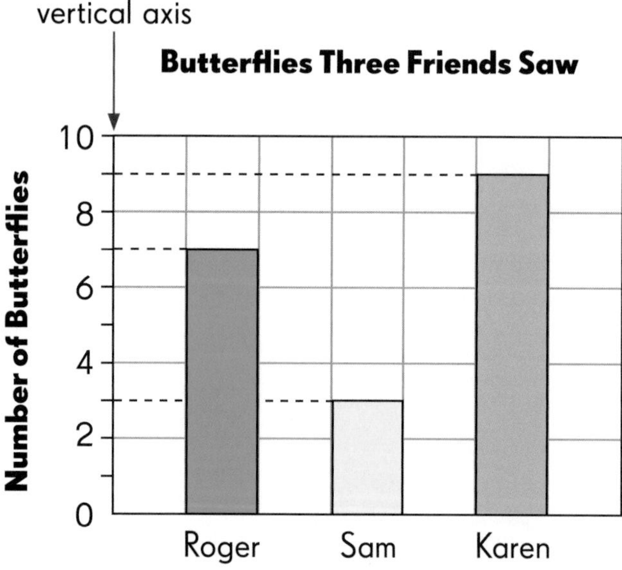

  The value of the bars can be read from the vertical axis, which is marked 0, 2, 4, 6, 8, and 10.

  See **axis**.

- **volume**

  Volume is the amount of liquid in a container.

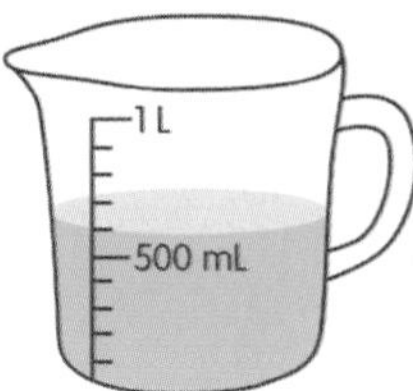

W

- **warm**

  When the temperature outside is 75°F, it is warm.

  See **cold**.

- **whole**

  A fraction is part of a whole.
  Divide a rectangular cake into 5 equal parts.

$\frac{5}{5}$ is a whole.

Y

- **yard (yd)**

  Yard is a customary unit of length.
  Write yd for yard.

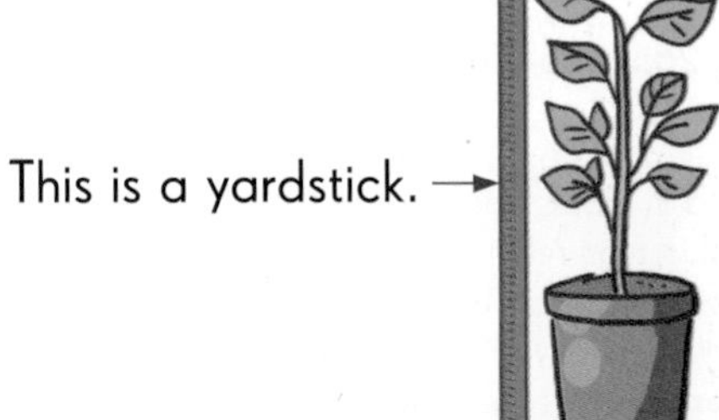

The height of the plant is 1 yard.

Index

Pages listed in black type refer to Pupil Book A.
Pages in blue type refer to Pupil Book B.
Pages in *black italic* type refer to Workbook (WB) A pages.
Pages in *blue italic* type refer to Workbook (WB) B pages.
Pages in **boldface** type show where a term is introduced.

D

Pages listed in black type refer to Pupil Book A.
Pages in blue type refer to Pupil Book B.
Pages in *black italic* type refer to Workbook (WB) A pages.
Pages in *blue italic* type refer to Workbook (WB) B pages.
Pages in **boldface** type show where a term is introduced.

E

F

Pages listed in black type refer to Pupil Book A.
Pages in blue type refer to Pupil Book B.
Pages in *black italic* type refer to Workbook (WB) A pages.
Pages in *blue italic* type refer to Workbook (WB) B pages.
Pages in **boldface** type show where a term is introduced.

M

Pages listed in black type refer to Pupil Book A.
Pages in blue type refer to Pupil Book B.
Pages in *black italic* type refer to Workbook (WB) A pages.
Pages in *blue italic* type refer to Workbook (WB) B pages.
Pages in **boldface** type show where a term is introduced.

Pages listed in black type refer to Pupil Book A.
Pages in blue type refer to Pupil Book B.
Pages in *black italic* type refer to Workbook (WB) A pages.
Pages in *blue italic* type refer to Workbook (WB) B pages.
Pages in **boldface** type show where a term is introduced.

O

P

Pages listed in black type refer to Pupil Book A.
Pages in blue type refer to Pupil Book B.
Pages in *black italic* type refer to Workbook (WB) A pages.
Pages in *blue italic* type refer to Workbook (WB) B pages.
Pages in **boldface** type show where a term is introduced.

S

Pages listed in black type refer to Pupil Book A.
Pages in blue type refer to Pupil Book B.
Pages in *black italic* type refer to Workbook (WB) A pages.
Pages in *blue italic* type refer to Workbook (WB) B pages.
Pages in **boldface** type show where a term is introduced.

Photo Credits

cover: Butterfly ©Don Hammond/Design Pics/Corbis, cover: Sunflower ©Dave Thompson/Life File/ Photodisc/Getty Images. Images provided by Houghton Mifflin Harcourt, xvitl: ©MCE, xvitm: ©MCE, xvibr: ©MCE, xvitr: ©MCE, xvibl: ©Digital Stock (Four Seasons) Photo CD, 2tr: ©iStock/digitalhallway, 2bl: ©iStock/jaroon, 4tr: ©MCE, 4br: ©MCE, 5tl: ©MCE, 5tr: ©MCE, 6r: ©MCE, 6l: ©MCE, 7l: ©MCE, 7r: ©MCE, 8l: ©MCE, 8r: © iStock/klikk, 11t: ©Stockbyte Photo CD, 11b: ©iStock/sextoacto, 12b: ©Image Source Photo CD, 12t: ©Stockbyte Photo CD, 14: ©quavondo/iStock, 15t: ©MCE, 16t: ©MCE, 17l: ©MCE, 17r: ©MCE, 18l: ©MCE, 18r: ©Comstock Klips Photo CD, 20b: ©quavondo/iStock, 20t: ©Stockbyte Photo CD, 21t: ©Image Source Photo CD, 21b: ©Sean Locke/iStock, 23: ©Image Source Limited, 25: ©iStock/sextoacto, 27: ©Image Source Limited, 36t: ©Image Source Photo CD, 36b: ©Houghton Mifflin Harcourt, 39: ©iStock/ LindaYolanda, 40: ©iStock/paulaphoto, 42b: ©Image Source Limited, 42t: ©iStock/AnnettVauteck, 43: ©Stockbyte Photo CD, 44: ©Image Source Limited, 45tl: ©MCE, 45tr: ©MCE, 45br: ©MCE, 45bl: ©MCE, 46: ©iStock/digitalhallway, 48: ©Stockbyte/Getty Images, 49b: ©iStock/jaroon, 49t: ©iStock/paulaphoto, 51tl: ©Stockbyte/Getty Images, 51mr: ©Image Source Limited, 51br: ©iStock/digitalhallway, 51ml: ©Image Source Limited, 51bl: ©iStockphoto.com/Ogphoto, 51tr: ©Image Source Limited, 52: ©MCE, 54: ©iStock/ JBryson, 63: ©iStock/AnnettVauteck, 64: ©Stockbyte Photo CD, 68: ©mconnors/morgueFile.com, 70: ©Stockbyte Photo CD, 72: ©Image Source Limited, 77: ©quavondo/iStock, 84: ©Stockbyte Photo CD, 85: ©Stockbyte Photo CD, 87: ©Sean Locke/iStock, 92: ©iStock/digitalhallway, 98: ©iStock/paulaphoto, 100: ©Sean Locke/iStock, 102l: ©Stockbyte/Getty Images, 102r: ©Stockbyte Photo CD, 112: ©iStock/ digitalhallway, 117t: ©Stockbyte Photo CD, 117b: ©iStockphoto.com/Ogphoto, 118b: ©Image Source Photo CD, 118t: ©Stockbyte Photo CD, 121: ©Image Source Limited, 123: ©Stockbyte/Getty Images, 126b: ©iStock/sextoacto, 126t: ©iStock/sampsyseeds, 126m: ©Image Source Limited, 127b: ©Stockbyte Photo CD, 127t: ©quavondo/iStock, 128: ©iStock/ paulaphoto, 131t: ©Sean Locke/iStock, 131m: ©iStock/JBryson, 131b: ©iStock/princessdlaf, 134br: ©Comstock/Getty Images, 134t: ©iStock/ drewmeredith, 134bl: ©iStock/AnnettVauteck, 137: ©Stockbyte Photo CD, 138b: ©iStock/digitalhallway, 138t: ©Image Source Limited,140b: ©Comstock/Getty Images, 140t: ©iStockphoto.com/Ogphoto, 141: ©iStock/paulaphoto, 142t: ©Stockbyte/Getty Images, 142b: ©iStockphoto.com/Ogphoto, 143t: ©Stockbyte Photo CD, 143b: ©iStock/sextoacto, 144: ©iStock/ daaronj, 148: ©Stockbyte/Getty Images, 149l: ©Comstock Klips Photo CD, 149m: ©Comstock Klips Photo CD, 149r: ©Image Source Limited,150tl: ©Comstock Klips Photo CD, 150tr: ©Comstock Klips Photo CD, 150bl: ©MCE, 150br: ©MCE, 152: ©Stockbyte Photo CD, 153: ©Stockbyte Photo CD, 156b: ©iStock/JBryson, 156t: ©iStock/paulaphoto, 158: ©iStock/daaronj, 164: ©iStock/sextoacto, 165bl: ©iStock/gbh007, 165br: ©iStock/sampsyseeds, 165t: ©Stockbyte Photo CD, 168b: ©Stockbyte/Getty Images, 168t: ©iStock/isitsharp, 169t: ©Image Source Limited, 169b: ©iStock/paulaphoto, 170t: ©Image Source Limited, 170b: ©iStock/daaronj, 171t: ©iStock/ JBryson, 171b: ©iStock/digitalhallway, 172tr: ©Stockbyte/Getty Images, 172tl: ©Image Source Limited, 172tm: ©Image Source Limited, 172bl: ©iStock/drewmeredith, 172br: ©Image Source Limited, 174b: ©Sean Locke/iStock, 174m: ©quavondo/iStock, 174t: ©iStock/JBryson, 175: ©Stockbyte Photo CD, 176: ©iStock/digitalhallway, 180t: ©Image Source Photo CD, 180b: ©Image Source Limited, 180m: ©Stockbyte Photo CD, 183tl: ©iStockphoto.com/ Ogphoto, 183tr: ©iStock/sampsyseeds, 183b: ©iStock/ paulaphoto, 185: ©Image Source Limited, 186br: ©iStock/drewmeredith, 186bl: ©Image Source Limited, 186tr: ©Stockbyte Photo CD, 186tl: ©iStock/ LindaYolanda, 187t: ©Image Source Limited, 187b: ©Stockbyte Photo CD, 188: ©iStock/isitsharp, 191: ©iStock/isitsharp, 192t: ©Image Source Limited, 192b: ©iStock/sampsyseeds, 197t: ©Stockbyte Photo CD, 199: ©iStock/paulaphoto, 201m: ©iStock/isitsharp, 201r: ©Stockbyte Photo CD, 201l: ©Image Source Limited, 205: ©Image Source Limited, 206: ©iStock/ jaroon, 207t: ©Sean Locke/iStock, 207b: ©Image Source Limited, 208bl: ©Stockbyte Photo CD, 208t: ©iStockphoto.com/Ogphoto, 208br: ©Image Source Limited, 209l: ©Stockbyte/Getty Images, 209r: ©Stockbyte Photo CD, 213: ©iStock/JBryson, 217: ©iStock/digitalhallway, 224: ©iStock/daaronj, 226b: ©quavondo/iStock, 226m: ©iStock/jaroon, 226t: ©iStock/daaronj, 227t: ©Image Source Limited, 227b: ©Image Source Limited, 231br: ©iStock/isitsharp, 231bl: ©iStockphoto.com/Ogphoto, 231t: ©iStock/ paulaphoto, 232: ©Image Source Limited, 234b: ©Comstock/Getty Images, 234t: ©Image Source Limited, 235: ©iStock/isitsharp, 236: ©Image Source Limited, 238: ©iStock/gbh007, 239: ©iStock/ drewmeredith, 240: ©quavondo/iStock, 242: ©Image Source Limited, 245: ©iStock/AnnettVauteck, 246t: ©iStock/digitalhallway, 246m: ©iStock/ skywaytoheaven, 246b: ©Image Source Limited, 247t: ©iStock/sampsyseeds, 247b: ©Stockbyte Photo CD,

250b: ©Image Source Limited, 250t: ©Image Source Limited, 253t: ©Image Source Limited, 253b: ©iStock/sampsyseeds, 254: ©iStock/digitalhallway, 255: ©Image Source Photo CD, 256br: ©iStock/sextoacto, 256t: ©Image Source Limited, 256bl: ©Stockbyte Photo CD, 269b: ©Stockbyte Photo CD, 269t: ©iStock/drewmeredith, 271bl: ©Jamalludin Bin Abu Seman Din/Dreamstime.com, 271t: ©Image Source Limited, 271mr: ©Stockbyte Photo CD, 271ml: ©MCE, 271l: ©MCE, 271l: ©Igorr/Dreamstime.com, 271mr: ©iStock/diane39, 271br: ©dorne/morgueFile.com, 272: ©iStock/sampsyseeds, 274t: ©iStock/jaroon, 274b: ©iStock/paulaphoto, 277ml: ©iStock/JBryson, 277tl: ©MCE, 277tr: ©MCE, 277b: ©MCE, 278: ©MCE, 279t: ©Stockbyte Photo CD, 279b: ©MCE, 280: ©MCE, 281r: ©Stockbyte Photo CD, 281tm: ©MCE, 281bl: ©MCE, 281br: ©MCE, 281tl: ©MCE, 282: ©MCE, 284r: ©iStock/klikk, 287tr: ©MCE, 287b: ©MCE, 287tl: ©bosela/morgueFile.com, 288: ©iStockphoto.com/Ogphoto, 289b: ©iStock/sextoacto, 289t: ©iStock/drewmeredith, 291r: ©iStock/klikk, 295: ©Sean Locke/iStock, 296: ©MCE, 298b: ©Brokensphere/Wikimedia Commons/CC BY-SA 3.0 (http://creativecommons.org/licenses/by-sa/3.0/deed.en), 298t: ©MCE, 300r: ©Comstock/Getty Images, 300l: ©Image Source Limited, 306: ©iStock/sextoacto, 307: ©iStock/drewmeredith, 308tl: ©Stockbyte Photo CD, 308b: ©iStock/JBryson, 308tr: ©iStock/paulaphoto, 311bl: ©Stockbyte/Getty Images, 311br: ©Image Source Limited, 311tl: ©Igorr/Dreamstime.com, 311mr: ©iStock/diane39, 311mr: ©Jamalludin Bin Abu Seman Din/Dreamstime.com, 311ml: ©iStock/carlosalvarez, 311tm: ©iStockphoto.com/Simfo, 311bm: ©Stockbyte Photo CD, 313l: ©quavondo/iStock, 313r: ©iStock/JBryson, 314l: ©Stockbyte Photo CD, 314r: ©Image Source Limited, 316t: ©Stockbyte/Getty Images, 316br: ©iStock/paulaphoto, 316bl: ©Stockbyte Photo CD, 321: ©iStock/sampsyseeds, 322t: ©Sean Locke/iStock, 322b: ©iStock/JBryson, 323t: ©Image Source Limited, 323b: ©iStock/gbh007, 325mr: ©iStock/isitsharp, 325t: ©iStock/drewmeredith, 325tr: ©Image Source Limited, 325l: ©Image Source Limited, 326: ©iStock/JBryson, 331: ©Comstock/Getty Images, 332br: ©MCE, 332tl: ©Digital Stock (Four Seasons) Photo CD, 332tr: ©iStock/jcphoto, 332bl: ©iStockphoto.com/Jane Norton, 333t: ©Image Source Photo CD, 333bl: ©Stockbyte Photo CD, 333br: ©iStockphoto.com/Ogphoto, 334: ©Image Source Limited, 335: ©iStock/drewmeredith, 337: ©Stockbyte Photo CD, 338: ©iStock/daaronj, 339: ©iStock/princessdlaf, 345l: ©Image Source Limited, 345r: ©Stockbyte Photo CD, 346: ©Comstock/Getty Images, 347: ©Image Source Limited, 349r: ©Sean Locke/iStock, 349l: ©Image Source Limited, 350: ©iStock/sextoacto, 355l: ©iStock/isitsharp, 355m: ©Image Source Limited, 355r: ©iStock/sampsyseeds, 357: ©Stockbyte Photo CD, 359: ©Image Source Limited, 361: ©iStock/JBryson, 362: ©Stockbyte Photo CD, 363: ©iStock/paulaphoto, 364: ©Sean Locke/iStock, 365b: ©Stockbyte Photo CD, 365t: ©MCE, 366t: ©Comstock/Getty Images, 366b: ©iStock/drewmeredith, 368t: ©iStock/JBryson, 368b: ©Image Source Limited, 369: ©Stockbyte Photo CD, 373t: ©Image Source Limited, 373b: ©iStock/daaronj, 374: ©iStock/jaroon, 381: ©iStock/digitalhallway, 384b: ©Stockbyte/Getty Images, 384t: ©Image Source Limited, 385: ©Jonsafari/Wikimedia Commons/CC BY-SA 3.0 (http://creativecommons.org/licenses/by-sa/3.0/deed.en), 387b: ©iStock/digitalhallway, 387t: ©iStock/AnnettVauteck, 390: ©Stockbyte Photo CD, 394: ©iStock/digitalhallway

Acknowledgements

The publisher wishes to thank the following organization for sponsoring the various objects used in this book:

Noble International Pte Ltd
Unit cubes p. 120

The publisher also wishes to thank the individuals who have contributed in one way or another and all those who have kindly loaned the publisher items for the photographs featured.